THE ENCYCLOPEDIA
OF
DRESSMAKING

THE ENCYCLOPEDIA
·OF·
DRESSMAKING

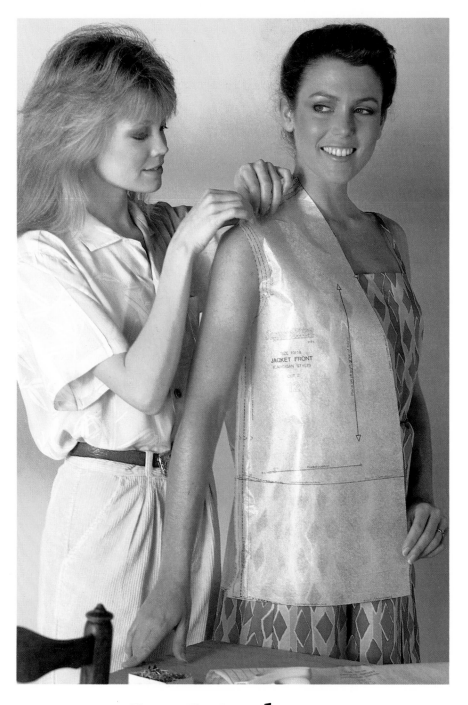

Joy Mayhew

ORBIS·LONDON

Acknowledgments
The artwork was drawn by the following
artists: Lindsay Blow, Bill le Fever, Eugene
Fleury, Chris Hurst, Susie Lacone, Colin
Salmon, Sue Sharples, Sheila Tizzard,
Catherine Ward and Charmian Watkins.
The photographs on the following pages are
by courtesy of: Burda 15, 141, 160; Butterick 16;
Camera Press 231; Maudella 184; McCalls 33, 162,
233; Simplicity 177; Style 160, 177; and Vogue
15. The remainder of the photographs were
taken by the following photographers: Jan
Baldwin, Tom Belshaw, Brian Boyle, Steve
Campbell, Allan Grainger, Chris Harvey,
Hank Kemme, Liz McAulay, Tino Tedaldi and
Nick Wright.
The graph patterns on pages 74, 75, 88, 98, 120,
148-50, 171 and 198 are copyright Maudella
Patterns Co. Ltd., 39-41 Chapel Street,
Bradford, West Yorkshire BD1 5BZ; the graph
patterns on pages 41, 74, 155, 207, 221 and 224
are copyright Eaglemoss Publications Ltd.

Cover: Jan Baldwin, Tom Belshaw, Brian Boyle,
Steve Campbell, Allan Grainger, Chris Harvey,
McCalls and Tino Tedaldi
Half title page: Burda
Title page: Tino Tedaldi

© Eaglemoss Publications Limited 1983, 1984

First published in Great Britain
by Orbis Publishing Limited, London 1985

This material previously appeared in the
partwork *SuperStitch*

Printed in Spain

ISBN 0-85613-687-5

Contents

Introduction

Finding the exact outfit you want, ready made in the shops, can be a frustrating experience. The chances are you'll end up with a compromise. The colour, the style or the fabric type may not really be what you wanted, and the fit and finish can leave a lot to be desired. If you want complete freedom of choice, you must make your own clothes. This way, you can choose just the colour, fabric and style you have visualised, use better-quality trim and, of course, your garments will be well made and fit perfectly!

There's a great deal of satisfaction to be gained from making and actually wearing your first successful garment, but, as with any other worthwhile home craft, things don't always go smoothly the first time. For instance, there are quite a few techniques, such as buttonholing, making pockets and inserting zips, that are not fully covered in the brief instructions that come with paper patterns. That's where this encyclopedia is invaluable. As well as explaining all the basic points you need to consider before cutting out and starting to sew, it shows exactly how to work some of those processes you may have skipped before, or avoided when selecting a pattern.

Follow the simple instructions throughout this book and you will gain confidence with each item completed. Everything is explained simply, the step-by-step diagrams are clear, and the guidance on the finishing touches – including the importance of perfect pressing – helps to ensure that professional look.

As well as being an excellent guide to good dressmaking, there's the bonus of *free* patterns throughout this book. Yes, you do have to draw them up yourself, but, although the photographed clothes look so elegant, they are basically simple, classic shapes that won't date. Another advantage of these patterns is that there is a choice of fittings to suit individual proportions. All you do is enlarge them from the graph, choosing the appropriate size lines. If you have never before made anything to wear, start with a simple skirt – either the gathered or soft-pleated dirndl (it's just a rectangle of fabric) or a smoother A-line style. As you gain confidence, add an easy blouse, a dress, even a collarless jacket. Make them in co-ordinating colours and you'll have produced a whole new outfit to be proud of. With such a tempting array of fabrics now in the shops there has never been a better time to start to sew . . . a glance through these pages will convince you that it's worthwhile to take up, or develop, the hobby of dressmaking.

Joy Mayhew, 1985

PART 1

Getting ready to sew

The Encyclopedia of Dressmaking is designed to teach the home dressmaker all the essential skills necessary for making up a basic classic wardrobe. The introductory chapters in this section contain vital information for the beginner and are also a useful reference for the more experienced home sewer. As well as a glossary of basic stitches and an A-Z of fabrics, there is a checklist of equipment, threads and machine attachments, all of which are invaluable to refer to as a quick reminder.

Graph patterns are given for all the garments described in this book and it is a simple matter to enlarge these multi-size patterns on to dressmaker's graph paper using a flexicurve. Alternatively, the detailed making-up instructions can be applied to any similar commercial patterns – enlarging on their instructions with detailed diagrams explaining the more difficult points and suggesting short cuts or professional touches to use.

As ready-made clothes are designed to fit the average figure, the great advantage of home dressmaking, apart from being able to choose exactly the style you wish to make, is that you can adjust the pattern and make sure it fits perfectly. This section explains how to chart your own measurements for a permanent record.

Finally, why not make up some useful pressing aids and follow the helpful rules on pressing at all stages of making up to achieve a really professional finish to your garments?

Choosing and using fabrics

The successful dressmaker develops an eye for colour and pattern and cleverly combines fabrics and styles that complement each other. It's not just a matter of instinct – once you know what a fabric is made of and how to handle it, you'll be able to see the potential it offers.

The best way of envisaging how a fabric will look made up is to see it draped on a model. Then you can appreciate its colour, texture, pattern and weight, just as if it were a completed garment. But this is not always possible, so if a roll of fabric appeals to you, remove it from the rack, stand in front of a full-length mirror and unroll a couple of metres. Hold it up against yourself – will it suit you?

Colour is the first clue. However lovely on the roll some fabrics, when held near the face, seem to drain it of its natural colour. Some fine fabrics may look a suitable colour but lose their density when unrolled. When you find a fabric that flatters your complexion, then you've found one that suits you. Always ask to take the roll to the daylight. If the shop has strip lights, ask to see it under an ordinary tungsten bulb, too.

Feel the texture of the fabric: is it soft, crisp, rough or smooth? Smooth, matt-textured fabrics are more flattering to a larger figure than bulky, loosely woven ones, which are fine for slimmer types. Rough-textured fabrics may need lining, as they can snag lingerie and may irritate the skin. Silky fabrics emphasize curves; matt ones disguise them.

Think about the fabric weight. Will it hang well? Fold the edge under to see how it will hem; try to imagine your finished skirt or dress. Does the fabric have a pronounced pattern? Will it be possible to match it on the seams? Will it mean buying extra fabric? If in doubt, ask the sales staff, who should be able to advise you.

Pattern or fabric first?

Successful dressmaking depends a great deal on how well the fabric works with the style of the garment. There are no rules about buying either the fabric or the paper pattern first, but the advantage of having a pattern first is that it provides valuable guidelines for suitable types of fabric and gives exact quantities for different sizes.

Estimating fabric needs

Beautiful fabrics are the inspiration for lovely clothes. If you choose the fabric first, then search for a suitable style to make it up in, you will need to have some idea of how much to buy. Without a pattern it is impossible to get it exactly right, but there are several ways of making an estimate. The easiest way is to look at a pattern catalogue for the kind of garment you want to make. All fairly straight styles – whether skirts, dresses, trousers, or coats – need roughly the same amount of fabric. Similarly, full-skirted garments take more or

When choosing a fabric, drape it around you and you will get a better idea of what it will look like when made up.

less the same as each other.

If there is no pattern book to hand, hold the fabric against you – from waist to hem for a skirt; from neck to hem for a dress. Add extra for hem and seam allowances. If fabric is narrow (90cm/36in, 115cm/45in) double the measurement (one length for the back and one for the front). If it is wide (140cm/54in, 150cm/60in) only one length is necessary. In either case extra will be needed for sleeves, collars, etc. This is when a paper pattern is invaluable as these extras can take varying amounts of fabric, depending on their shape and pattern layout.

Buying napped fabrics

Some fabrics have a special texture that means they have a right and a wrong way up – this is called the nap. On fabrics with a nap, such as velvet which has a pile that runs in one direction, or mohair, or fake fur, all the pattern pieces must be laid in the same direction.

This will take more fabric – a rough guide is that you will need an extra 20cm/8in per metre/yard. This will also allow you to match pattern repeats if necessary. If you have a commercial pattern, the exact length to buy for a napped fabric should be printed on the envelope. If not, lay the pattern out with all the pieces in the same direction on another length of the same width fabric. This will tell you how much to buy.

Fabrics with one-way designs

If a fabric has a design that must be the right way up, you will also need to lay your pattern pieces in the same direction. To calculate how much extra fabric to buy, measure a complete pattern repeat (from the top of a motif to where the next one starts beneath it) and add this amount to every metre quoted for non-napped fabrics. This will also allow you to match pattern repeats at the seams.

What to look for

Labels The label attached to the fabric roll should state the composition of the fabric and the percentages of the fibres in it. If it does not, ask the assistant to look it up in the order book. For the best results, treat your fabric according to its highest fibre content. For instance, to make a garment in a cotton/polyester blend, treat it as cotton. However, the polyester indicates that a poly/cotton sewing thread should be used. You can expect the garment to handle, wear and wash like cotton, but it will need little ironing.

Colour Check that the fabric has been evenly dyed. Ideally, examine it in daylight.

Check too for colour fastness. Dye should not come off on a dampened finger.

Print Check that the design printed on the fabric meets the selvedges at a right angle. If it does not your garment will look crooked and patterns will not match at the seams.

Weave In all woven fabrics, the weave should be even, and the weft (crosswise) threads should meet the selvedge at right angles. The closer the weave, the stronger the fabric. If you are using a loose weave for a skirt or coat, line it to prevent 'seating'.

A-Z guide to fabrics

Characteristics and uses	Fibre content	Characteristics and uses	Fibre content
ACETATE Silky finish, drapes well. Blended with other fabrics, it adds to their strength and beauty. Makes up into fabrics like taffeta, satin, brocade, jerseys and linings.	Man-made, cellulose based	**BROCADE** All-over raised design with contrasting colours and surfaces, often incorporating metallic threads. Comes in many weights for different garments.	Silk and man-made
ACRILAN Wool-like, bulky and soft. Comfort without weight, good pleat retention, recovers quickly from creasing. Wovens and knitteds. Used for dresses, suits and jumpers.	Acrylic fibre (from oil)	**CALICO** Hard-wearing plain weave, usually printed, in various weights. Shirts and interfacings.	Cotton
BARATHEA Closely woven, pebbly effect. Dresses, suits and coats.	Silk, wool, rayon and blends	**CAMBRIC** Plain weave, medium weight. Summer dresses.	Cotton and linen
BATISTE Plain weave, lightweight, almost sheer. Dresses, lingerie, handkerchiefs.	Cotton, silk, wool, rayon and man-made	**CHALLIS** (ch as in chapter) Soft, lightweight fabric, usually printed in delicate patterns. Dresses and blouses.	Wool, cotton, rayon and blends

wool challis

cambric

brocade

chiffon

cotton

Flaws Check the fabric for flaws. These are often indicated by a tag placed on the selvedge by the manufacturer. If you find a flaw, you may be offered additional fabric to compensate for it, but if you think you may not be able to avoid the flaw when cutting out, you should insist on a fresh length of fabric.

Size Some fabrics are sized – given a finish for extra stiffness. If a powdery dust appears when you rub the fabric lightly between your fingers, too much size has been added. It will wash away, leaving the fabric limp.

Creasing Crumple some of the fabric in one hand. Unless it gradually recovers it will crease constantly in wear.

Price-tag Never buy a fabric just because it is a bargain.

Remnants Chosen with care, a remnant can prove a real bargain. But ask for details if you buy a remnant with no label.

Preparing for cutting out

Press your fabric if it has been folded and creased. Decide on the right side and wrong side of the fabric. The difference is often hardly discernible, but it will show on the garment. Most fabrics are preshrunk during manufacture, but in pure wool and wool blends, up to 2% shrinkage can still take place. This tends to happen when darts and seams are damp pressed, leaving the remaining fabric looking baggy'. To prevent this, damp press before making up.

To straighten the grain of a woven fabric before pinning on the pattern, pull or mark a thread across the width. Next pin the selvedges together. If the fold does not lie flat, give it a firm tug in the opposite direction to smooth it out.

Ten tips from buyers

Some top fabric buyers were asked to give their ten most helpful hints for choosing fabrics.

1 Is the fabric suitable for the garment you want to make – will it drape or hang correctly?

2 Will the pattern and/or colour suit you? If possible, hold the fabric up against you and look in a full length mirror.

3 Test for creasing. Crumple the fabric in one hand. How quickly does it return to normal?

4 Does the fabric fray? Will you need to spend a lot of time neatening seams?

5 If the fabric is fine, will it need lining?

6 Is it washable, or dry clean only?

7 Check for flaws – not always shown by a marker.

8 Is there a nap or one-way design? Remember to allow extra to compensate.

9 Check fabric width. Some patterns cannot be cut from narrow widths without unsightly joins.

10 Never be rushed into buying. If you can't decide, ask to take away a small snipping and think about it.

Characteristics and uses	Fibre content	Characteristics and uses	Fibre content
CHAMBRAY (ch as in shop) Coloured warp threads and a white filler thread create attractive variations of striped effects in plain cotton fabric. Children's clothes, shirts, pyjamas.	Cotton	COTTON Woven and knitted in many weights. (Most cotton fabrics listed under generic names.) All kinds of garments.	100% pure cotton
CHEESECLOTH Loose weave, uneven texture created by twisted yarns. Blouses and fully gathered skirts.	Cotton	CRÊPE Woven fabric with crinkled surface; frays easily; various widths. Blouses, dresses, evening wear.	Silk, cotton, wool, man-made
CHIFFON Plain weave sheer fabric with either a soft or a stiff finish. Blouses, scarves, evening dresses.	Silk and man-made	CRÊPE DE CHINE Sheer, soft, lustrous, silky fabric. Blouses, lingerie.	Silk and man-made
CORDUROY Ribbed pile fabric, hard-wearing; various weights. Skirts, trousers, jackets.	Cotton and man-made. Stretch cord: cotton/nylon	DENIM Strong, twill-weave fabric; hard-wearing. Various weights and colours. Jeans, skirts and jackets.	Cotton. Stretch denim: cotton/nylon

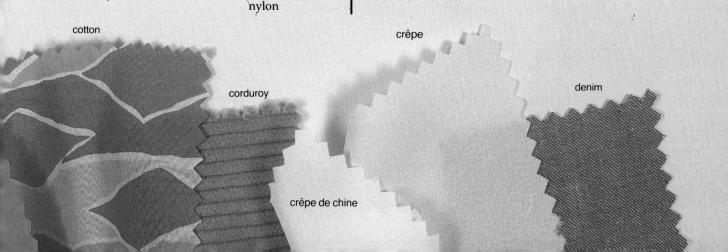

cotton

crêpe

corduroy

denim

crêpe de chine

A-Z guide to fabrics

Characteristics and uses	Fibre content	Characteristics and uses	Fibre content
DIMITY Sheer cotton featuring a fine, corded striped effect (also checks). Blouses, baby dresses.	Cotton	**LACE** Delicate, open-structured fabric, woven or knitted. Evening blouses, dresses, trimmings.	Silk, cotton and man-made
DUETTE Double jersey. Suits, coats, trousers, skirts.	Acrylic and polyester. (Trade names: Courtelle and Lirelle)	**LAMÈ** (Pronounced larmay.) Woven or knitted base covered with metallic threads, drapes well. Evening and stage wear.	Wool and man-made fabric into which plastic-coated and dyed metallic threads are woven
FAILLE Fine, horizontally ribbed fabric. Dresses, full skirts, evening wear.	Silk and man-made	**LAWN** Sheer, lightweight, smooth woven fabric. Blouses, handkerchiefs, summer dresses, baby dresses.	Cotton, fine linen, man-made and blends
FLANNEL Woven fabric, soft surface. Dresses, full skirts, evening wear.	Wool and blends		
FLANNELETTE Fine woven cotton fabric with surface brushed to provide warmth. Nightwear, blouses, skirts.	Cotton and man-made	**LEATHER FABRIC** Fabrics treated by special finishes to simulate leather. Skirts, jackets, coats, bags.	Cotton, wool with plastic or PVC coating
FOULARD Plain or twill weave, soft, lightweight. Scarves, blouses, flowing dresses.	Silk, cotton, rayon	**LINEN** Plain weave natural fabric with uneven surface texture. Strong, cool, absorbent. Skirts, trousers, suits.	Linen and blends
GABERDINE Twill weave, hardwearing fabric which can be shower-proofed. Suits, coats, rainwear.	Wool, cotton, blends. Stretch gaberdines=62% cotton/38% nylon	**MADRAS** Fine Indian cotton with interesting stripes and checks in weave. Blouses, skirts, dresses.	Cotton
GEORGETTE Fine, dull textured, chiffon-like (but heavier) with a crêpey finish. Blouses, scarves, evening wear.	Silk, wool and man-made	**MOHAIR** Knitted and woven fabrics including natural animal hair; soft and warm. Coats, jackets, shawls.	Hair from angora goat plus base of wool
GINGHAM Firm, washable, hard-wearing, light-weight cotton and cotton-like fabric. Blouses, dresses, overalls.	Cotton and blends	**MOIRÉ** (Pronounced mwaray.) Watermarked pattern giving a waved effect. Fairly stiff shiny fabric. Evening skirts, dresses and blouses.	Silks, rayons and man-made
JACQUARD Woven and knitted fabrics of complex structure and colour combinations. Dresses and suits.	Wool and man-made	**NEEDLECORD** Finely ribbed plain or printed corduroy. Skirts and dresses.	Cotton and man-made
JERSEY Knitted fabric (single and double knit) in various weights. Soft; good draping qualities; tends to stretch. Dresses, suits. (Double jersey with less stretch is suitable for trousers.)	Wool, cotton, silk and man-made and blends	**NET** Small, open mesh. Veils, trimmings and dance skirts.	Silk, cotton, rayon and nylon
		NYLON Fine woven or knitted fabric. Strong, non-absorbent, best blended with other fibres; useful blended for all garments. Skirts, overalls.	Synthetic: petrochemical fibre

crêpe georgette ——————— net   poplin   organdie   moiré

pongee silk   jacquard

Characteristics and uses	Fibre content	Characteristics and uses	Fibre content
ORGʌNDIE Sheer, woven fabric; can be very soft or crisp according to finish. Blouses, party dresses, collars and cuffs. The crisp one makes an excellent interfacing.	Cotton and man-made	**SILK Many varieties:** Pongee (pronounced ponjee): slight slub effect. Surah: twill weave, shiny, often printed, for scarves, blouses, dresses. Thai: takes dyes well in vivid colours. Tussore: wild silk, uneven texture, left in natural colour.	Silk
OTTOMAN Heavy, ribbed fabric, similar in appearance to faille, but with wider, more pronounced ribs.	Wool, silk and man-made	**SUEDE CLOTH** Woven or knitted fabric finished to resemble suede. Skirts, jackets, trousers, bags.	Synthetic blends
PEAU DE SOIE (Pronounced poderswa.) Soft silk with satin sheen. Dresses and blouses.	Silk, rayon	**TAFFETA** Interesting crisp fabric, plain or ribbed (faille), moiré (watermarked pattern), paper (lightweight). Evening wear.	Silk, rayon, nylon
PIQUÉ (Pronounced peekay.) Firm, medium weight, raised surface. Blouses, dresses and sportswear.	Cotton	**TOWELLING** Looped fabric for absorbency. Originally pure cotton. Robes and beachwear, stretch baby and children's wear, sports outfits.	Cottons and blends. Stretch towelling=65% cotton/35% nylon
POPLIN Smooth, soft-sheened, hardwearing, lightweight woven fabric. Shirts, blouses, summer dresses, children's clothes.	Cotton and blends	**TREVIRA** (Trade name) woven or knitted fabric. Skirts, jackets.	Polyester blended with natural fibre
P.V.C. Special, non-porous finish applied to woven or knitted base fabric. Aprons, rainwear, coats, capes, jackets, hats and trousers.	Polyvinylchloride	**TULLE** Very fine net. Evening and party dresses, veils.	Silk and nylon
RAYON Fabric made from regenerated cellulose – originally it resembled silk. Now best blended with other fibres.	Regenerated cellulose	**TWEED** Mostly woven but sometimes knitted. Usually checked patterns in particular colours according to place of origin, e.g. Harris tweed. Suits and coats.	Wool and wool blends
SAILCLOTH Strong, plain or basket weave fabric, originally stiff, for sails, now softer. Skirts, jackets, trousers.	Cotton and man-made	**VELVET** Warp pile fabric, woven. Various types: cut velvet (façonné) panne velvet: (silky pile smoothed one way). Various weights for day and evening wear. Capes, coats, suits, skirts, dresses.	Silk, cotton, man-made and blends
SATIN Special weave where threads 'float' over the base threads, giving a sheen. Evening wear, trimmings.	Silk, rayon, man-made	**VIYELLA** (Trade name) twill weave lightweight fabric. Soft style dresses and blouses. Baby and children's wear.	55% wool, 45% cotton
SEERSUCKER Puckered finish on cotton and cotton blends. Summer dresses, beachwear.	Cotton and cotton blends	**WOOL** Woven and knitted as pure wool and in blends with natural and man-made fibres to form many fabrics. Dresses, coats, suits, skirts.	Pure wool and blends
SHANTUNG Originally wild spun silk with a naturally occurring slub effect (as found in linen). Now a plain weave with an uneven surface from any fibre. Blouses, linings.	Silk and man-made	**WORSTED** Best quality wool, tightly woven, smooth, strong, wears well. Fine worsteds for winter dresses; suit and coat weights.	Pure wool and pure wool blended with man-made fibres

Note: 100% natural fibres = wool, cotton, linen and silk.
'Man-made' = synthetic fibres produced chemically.

tweed

taffeta

linen look

jersey

gaberdine

suede-look jersey

gingham

Choosing and using commercial paper patterns

Whether you want to make designer outfits or a collection of mix and match wardrobe basics, the paper pattern catalogues offer an abundance of ideas, specially designed to suit the various figure types. Decide which type best applies to you, and you are ready to start.

When you can't find the outfit you are looking for in a shop, don't despair. It is very likely that you will find it in the pages of a pattern book – ready to be made up at a fraction of the shop price.

Though the cost of paper patterns has increased over the years, they still represent good value for money, given the amount of hard work that goes into each design. And if you choose a designer pattern from the wide range that many pattern companies produce – and make it up in a complementary fabric – you will have a designer name outfit you could never otherwise afford. Even making up basic patterns has advantages over shop-bought clothes; you have total control over the fit and the finish, and you can use particularly successful patterns again and again in a variety of fabrics and colourways.

Read on for advice on choosing the patterns that are right for your figure type and will fit without the need for extensive alterations.

Recognising your figure type

Figure types – junior petite, misses, womens etc – are used in pattern books to help you find patterns that are right for you. They are necessary because the female form comes in many shapes and sizes, and one pattern range could not possibly be suitable for them all.

Pattern sizes, however, are based on standard body measurements (see page 20). Ask a friend to help you to take all your measurements over your usual undergarments, with the tape held neither too loose nor too tight. Pay particular attention to your bust measurement and nape of neck to back waist measurement, and check your height, too.

Assess your figure. If you are under 18 years old, you are probably still developing. If not, are you a little short in stature with proportionately small measurements, or well-proportioned and developed, or are you perhaps a little older, becoming fully mature and slightly larger in proportion? All these factors will determine your figure type and the pattern size that is best for you.

The chart on page 17 can be used as a guideline, but do make a final check in the back of a pattern book when buying a pattern. All the sizes are given there in more detailed charts and there are small differences in the way individual pattern companies categorise the figure types.

Do not try to choose a paper pattern size according to the size of garment you usually buy in a shop. Ready-to-wear sizes differ widely – one manufacturer's size 8 can be another's size 10 or even 12 – so be accurate and take your measurements properly.

Pattern books and patterns

The main source of commercial paper patterns is the counter catalogue produced by each pattern company, and displayed in fabric shops and department stores. They contain hundreds of designs, each with several variations, and are updated on a monthly or seasonal basis when some new patterns are introduced, indicating the latest fashion trends.

The key to using a pattern book efficiently is to know your figure type and size. Each catalogue has an information section, usually found at the back. This contains instructions for taking body measurements, explanations and diagrams of figure types, and size charts. The sizes are standard in all catalogues, but some offer a more comprehensive range of figure types to choose from. The best offer a wide range of sizes within each figure type, and cater for the whole family; some produce a separate catalogue for children.

Within the catalogue the designs are grouped together in sections such as Dresses or Sportswear, or in specific figure types, such as Misses or Junior. Between the sections are thick paper dividers, each clearly labelled and visible from the front of the catalogue, to enable you to turn quickly to the section you need.

Right: A selection of outfits from the major pattern companies. Some are special designer outfits – all illustrate how easy it is for today's home dressmaker to make herself a complete range of clothes from commercial paper patterns.

Points to remember when choosing a pattern

Dresses, blouses, coats and jackets Choose a pattern for your figure type in the size corresponding most nearly to your *bust* measurement. If your waist and hip measurements differ from those given, the pattern can be adjusted. Do not choose a size larger for coats and jackets to allow for wearing them over other clothes; this

has already been taken into consideration by the pattern makers.
Skirts and trousers Choose the pattern size by *hip* measurement. If your measurements differ from the pattern, it is easier to make alterations at the waist than at the hip.
When skirts or trousers are part of a multiple choice pattern which

also includes blouses or jackets choose by *bust* size.
Multi-size patterns These patterns eliminate the need for making extensive pattern adjustments if you do not conform to any one size. For example, you can make a jacket in size 10 and a skirt in size 12 from the same pattern.

Left: A wedding dress is complicated to make, but a satisfying achievement.

logue are grouped according to whether the garments are dresses, separates, evening wear and so on, rather than by figure types, check that the chosen style does come in your figure type and is available in your size. Where sizes at either extreme of the size range are not included, or a fabric width is not stated, it means that the style is suitable only for the sizes offered, or that it is impossible or uneconomic to cut from the fabric widths omitted.

Only when you have considered and checked all of these factors is it safe to go ahead and buy, or order the pattern. Large stores usually carry a comprehensive range of patterns in all sizes, but smaller outlets may have to order the pattern for you. If you jot all the details of the pattern down for reference while you are making your choice, you will still be able to go ahead and choose the fabric, threads etc, and put in an order for the pattern – arranging for it to be posted to your home, or to be collected from the store.

The pattern package

The pattern envelope repeats the information given on the catalogue page, with colour sketches or a photograph on the front and all fabric requirements and suggestions, sizes and measurements on the back. The envelope contains the pattern pieces printed on sheets of tissue paper, layouts showing how to position the pieces on different widths of fabric, and step-by-step instructions for making up the styles illustrated.

Pattern pieces for a simple design may be printed on a single sheet of tissue; more complicated designs may cover several sheets. Each pattern piece is numbered for easy reference, and corresponding numbers are used on the layout. Separate the pattern pieces, choose the numbers that are required for the style you are making up and place them on the fabric according to the appropriate layout.

Some pattern companies produce a pattern sheet for beginners with the pattern pieces already in the correct position on the tissue sheet. This is simply pinned directly to the fabric and the pieces cut out.

Look before you buy Patterns are not usually exchangeable, so read the information on the catalogue page with great care before buying, to make sure the pattern is suitable for you. If you are still in doubt, ask the shop assistant for advice; some of the main department stores have staff specially trained to give this guidance.

Each page in the catalogue tells you everything you need to know about the style illustrated, including fabric suggestions and requirements and written descriptions of the style of the garment.

Study the paragraph of detailed description, which tells you what is involved in making up the garment – for example, whether it is lined or cut on the cross. Some pattern companies illustrate all the pattern pieces used as well, which can be a useful guide as to the garment's complexity. Front and back views and any alternative features such as variations of neckline, sleeve or hem length are also shown. A photograph in the catalogue can give you a good idea of the garment, but the artist's impression, combined with the thumbnail sketches of the back views, is most important. It provides style detail such as the position of darts or seams, which do not show up clearly in a photograph. All this information should help you to decide whether you have the dressmaking skills to manage the techniques involved.

Finally, if the patterns in the cata-

Differences to look out for

The cutting line is clearly marked on all patterns so there is never any doubt about which line to follow when cutting out. The seamline is the line along which final stitching takes place, and between these two lines lies the 1.5cm/⅝in seam allowance.

Single size patterns have only one cutting line and a seamline marked 1.5cm/⅝in within it.

Multi-size patterns may have six cutting lines and although the seam allowance is normally included, for the sake of clarity, the actual seamline is not marked.

Continental multi-size patterns may not include the seam allowance at all, in which case first cut out all the pattern pieces following the cutting line for the appropriate size. Then pin them to the fabric and mark the seam allowances all the way round using tailor's chalk or a tracing wheel and dressmaker's carbon paper. The instructions may suggest the amounts to be added on, giving different allowances for different seams.

Study all the information printed on each pattern piece and on the instruction sheet *before* cutting out the fabric. Mark a ring around the fabric layout and view number to be followed. Make all the adjustments necessary to length, sleeves etc before pinning the pattern in place, and make sure you know whether or not seam allowances are included on your pattern. And do make a final check that appropriate pattern pieces are positioned on the fold. Mistakes made when cutting out could prove costly.

Figure types and pattern sizes

Misses

Height (without shoes)	Body description	Nape to waist	6	8	10	12	14	16	18	20	22	24
1.65–1.68m 5ft 5in–5ft 6in	Well proportioned and developed	Between 39.5–44.5cm	78	80	83	87	92	97	102	107	112	117cm
		15½–17½in	30½	31½	32½	34	36	38	40	42	44	46in

Miss Petite (mp)

Height (without shoes)	Body description	Nape to waist	6mp	8mp	10mp	12mp	14mp	16mp
1.57–1.63m 5ft 2in–5ft 4in	As above, but shorter overall	Between 37–40cm	78	80	83	87	92	97cm
		14½–15¾in	30½	31½	32½	34	36	38in

Junior

Height (without shoes)	Body description	Nape to waist	5	7	9	11	13	15
1.63–1.65m 5ft 4in–5ft 5in	Well proportioned, but short-waisted. Taller than Miss Petite	Between 38–41.5cm	76	79	81	85	89	94cm
		15–16¼in	30	31	32	33½	35	37in

Junior Petite (jp)

Height (without shoes)	Body description	Nape to waist	3jp	5jp	7jp	9jp	11jp	13jp
1.52–1.55m 5ft–5ft 1in	Well proportioned but petite	Between 35.5–39cm	76	79	81	84	87	89cm
		14–15¼in	30	31	32	33	34	35in

Women

Height (without shoes)	Body description	Nape to waist	38	40	42	44	46	48	50
1.65–1.68m 5ft 5in–5ft 6in	Larger, more mature figure	Between 44–46cm	107	112	117	122	127	132	137cm
		17¼–18in	42	44	46	48	50	52	54in

Half-size

Height (without shoes)	Body description	Nape to waist	10½	12½	14½	16½	18½	20½	22½	24½
1.57–1.60m 5ft 2in–5ft 3in	Fully developed figure with short back waist length	Between 38–41.5cm	84	89	94	99	104	109	114	119cm
		15–16¼in	33	35	37	39	41	43	45	47in

Working with graph and multi-size patterns

These comprehensive instructions on using paper patterns and preparing and cutting out fabric are as valuable to the experienced dressmaker as the beginner. Use them either for the versatile patterns in this book, or for any commercial pattern you choose.

A multi-size pattern is one of the most economical patterns, as it includes several sizes on each pattern piece. Many magazine patterns are prepared this way, and so are a few commercial paper patterns. From the dressmaker's point of view they have an advantage over one-size patterns in that you can make up the same garment in a variety of sizes for family and friends. If the pattern is printed on a graph, find the appropriate cutting line for your size and follow this when drawing up the graph pattern.

Similarly, if the pattern is printed full size, find the appropriate symbol for the cutting line for your size (clearly marked on the pattern) and follow this throughout.

Cutting out multi-size patterns

The full-size pattern pieces are usually printed on sheets of paper (often tissue) and numbered so that you can group together the pieces for each garment. Cut the pieces from the large tissue sheets as they are needed. Alternatively, if you want to make up a garment in more than one size you can trace off the pattern pieces from the original pattern.

If the pieces are creased, run a warm iron over them to smooth them out taking care not to tear them.

This makes it easier to position them on the fabric, and pin them accurately.

Making a pattern from a graph

Enlarging a pattern from a graph is a useful technique which gives you access to graph designs like the ones in this book, rather than always having to buy a pattern. If you use dressmaker's squared paper it is not as time-consuming as you may think or, if you prefer, you can rule up your own squared paper.

Understanding how these miniature patterns work also helps you develop an ability to design and make up your own patterns.

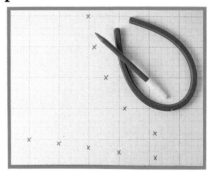

Marking crosses on large-scale paper.

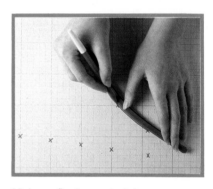

Using a flexicurve to join up crosses.

You will need
Dressmaker's pattern paper
  marked in centimetres
Pencil, rubber, scissors
Ruler (the longer the better)
A flexicurve or dressmaker's curved
  ruler for drawing curved areas
The graph is a scaled-down plan of a pattern which has to be enlarged. You can work with plain paper and rule a grid for yourself, but the quickest, easiest and most accurate way is to use pattern paper which is already marked out in 1cm and 5cm squares, and numbered down one side and along the lower edge. Check that the size of the squares on the graph corresponds with your pattern paper. (Some graphs are based on 2cm squares: for these you simply use two squares of 1cm graph pattern paper.)
Work on a firm surface – a piece of

hardboard or the kitchen table is suitable. Start by counting the number of squares across and down the graph and mark the same number of squares on the large-scale paper. Draw a rectangle on the paper to correspond with the outer limits of the graph. (This helps you to check later that you have transferred the graph correctly.)
1 Starting with any long straight lines, make a cross on the paper wherever the pattern outline intersects with a gridline on the graph. (Make sure you are transferring the right outline for your size if the graph is multi-sized.)

2 Join up the crosses. You can do this freehand, but a flexicurve, available from good stationers, makes the job very easy. A dressmaker's curved ruler or even a plate are useful alternatives. After completing all the outside lines, indicate other details such as the straight-grain line (use one of the vertical lines on the pattern paper) or the seamlines (usually 1.5cm/⅝in in from the edge). Label each pattern piece and add the size and any other important points such as foldlines and notches. (Notches on patterns are there to help you match two pattern pieces exactly.)
Cut out the pattern pieces with paper-cutting scissors. Where notches are shown on seam edges, cut round them so that they are not forgotten when cutting out the fabric.

Making pattern adjustments

Most commercial patterns and those printed on graphs are designed to fit an average figure. Therefore, to obtain a perfect fit you will probably have to adjust the pattern to make it conform to your figure.

It is worth taking the time and trouble to check the fit of the pattern before cutting out, either by cross-checking your measurements with those of the pattern, or by actually trying on the paper pattern. If the pattern is checked properly at this stage, only minor fitting adjustments should be necessary during making up. If you are still in doubt about the fit of a pattern even after checking, add 1.5cm/⅝in to side and sleeve seams only (*not* the armhole) before cutting out to allow plenty of extra fabric for any alterations.

At whatever stage you make alterations, do remember that the adjustments must be made to all corresponding pattern pieces. For example, if sleeve seams are adjusted, then the side seams must be adjusted in the same way. Always make a record of any alterations carried out on the pattern or at a later fitting stage. This saves time when using the pattern again, or using a similar one.

Finally, to preserve your pattern for future use and to retain an accurate record of the alterations, it helps if you reinforce the pattern with fusible interfacing. See below left for other ideas to preserve your pattern.

Below: Check your measurements against the pattern – trying on the bodice may help. Ask a friend to help you mark any alterations. If they are extensive, make a revised copy pattern (see below left).

Care of paper patterns

Tissue paper tears easily so use these tips to help you preserve your patterns.
- Fold and unfold tissue very carefully, and find the original folds when replacing pieces in the pattern envelope.
- Cut out, mark and remove pattern pieces in one sewing session, as moving the fabric with the pattern still pinned in position will tear the tissue.
- Remove pins carefully, and use the same pinholes when using the pattern again.
- If you have a paper punch use it to perforate the pattern on the appropriate markings and mark fabric with tacks or chalk through the holes to avoid tearing tissue.
- To repair a pattern, iron carefully and mend tears with sticky tape on each side.

Strengthening a new pattern
- Reinforce patterns that are to be used frequently by pressing lightweight, iron-on Vilene on to the printed side of the complete pattern. (On the reverse side it will cling to the fabric.) Perforate pattern to indicate position of markings. Keep pattern rolled, not folded.
- Take copies of your pattern on dressmaker's graph paper, by tracing round the pattern or using a tracing wheel and dressmaker's carbon paper. This is useful if pattern alterations are to be made.

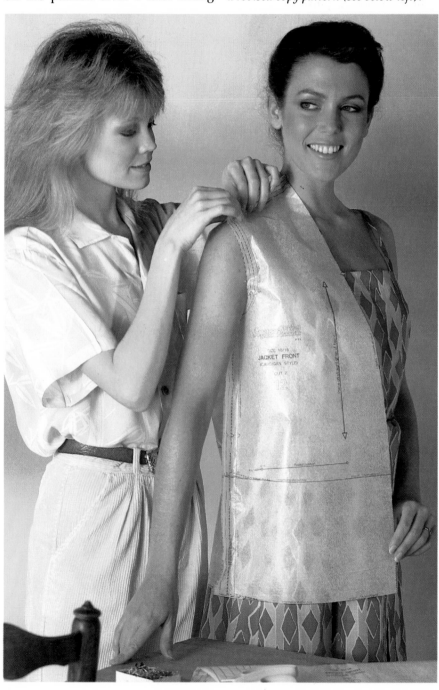

Chart your own measurements

Familiarize yourself with your measurements so that you always know how much you vary from any standard commercial pattern or from the graphs in this book. You can then make accurate adjustments to the pattern before cutting out. In this way you will only need to make minor alterations when you have cut out and tacked the garment.

Measure yourself at the points indicated on the diagram below and keep a note here or in a notebook – and don't forget to recheck your measurements if your weight changes. These measurements are enough for most sewing purposes. Where a style requires other vital statistics – for example the thigh measurement when making trousers – this will be mentioned in the appropriate chapter.

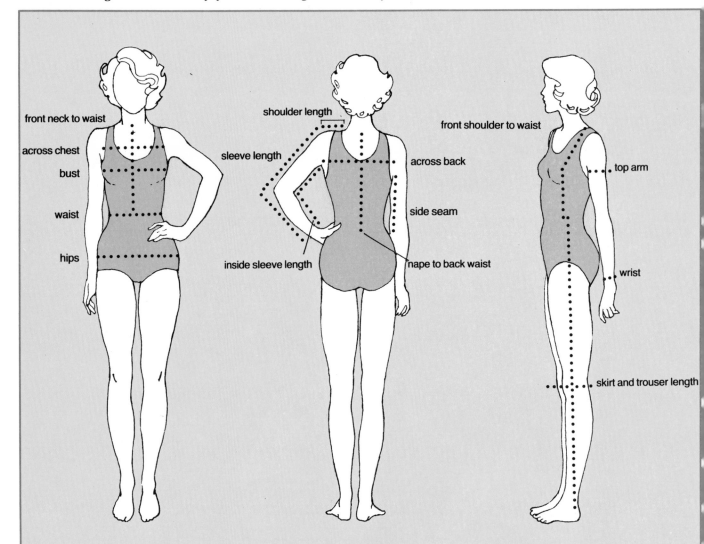

Fifteen vital statistics

Bust Over the fullest part at the front and at the same level straight across the back ....
Waist At your natural waistline, snugly, but not tight....................
Hips 18cm/7in down from your waist if you are a small size, 24cm/9½in for a large size ....
Across back About 14cm/5½in from nape of neck, over shoulder blades and between armhole seam ....

....
Across chest 7cm/3in from front neck base, straight across between

armhole seams ....
Shoulder length From the side of your neck to the end of your shoulder ....
Nape to back waist From your nape down the spine to your natural waist level ....
Front neck to waist From base of neck to front waist ....
Front shoulder to waist From centre front shoulder, over bust to waist ...

....
Side seam From underarm to side waist ....

Sleeve length With arm bent, from end of shoulder, over elbow, to outside wrist bone ....
Inside sleeve length From under arm out to elbow, and down to inside wrist ....
Top arm Round the fullest part, between the shoulder and the elbow ....
Wrist Over wrist bone ....
Skirt and trouser length From side of waist, over hip to knee, floor, or required lengths in between ....

....

Recognising pattern markings

Each pattern piece contains valuable information to help you make up your garment. These signs and symbols are common to all commercial paper patterns, both multi-size and one-size, so it is worth learning to recognise the important symbols.

Cutting line Marked by a variety of symbols in multi-size patterns, depending on size. Try to leave it on your pattern by cutting out 1mm/¹⁄₁₆in from the outside edge of the line, to preserve the pattern for future use.

Notches are diamond shapes, found on the cutting line. There may be one or more, numbered to match a notch or pair of notches on a corresponding seam – waist edge to waistband for example.

Cut outwards, not into the seamline.

Seamline Sometimes shown as a broken line on a pattern. If omitted, the seam allowance is 1.5cm/⁵⁄₈in from the cutting line, unless otherwise stated.

Dots or circles may be small or large and indicate where to start or finish seams or gathers, and the position for pleats, pockets and other features.

Grainline This is shown by a solid straight line with arrows at each end and represents the straight grain (direction of weave) of the fabric. It is important to position the arrow accurately, parallel to the selvedges, because the grain affects the 'hang' of a garment. It is usually placed vertically, running from neck to hem, following the strongest threads of woven fabrics, but there are exceptions. In border-prints the horizontal grain runs down the garment while the border, which is the vertical straight grain, runs horizontally round the garment.

Fold bracket This is another grainline marking. The arrows point to the solid outer line which must be placed exactly on the fold of the fabric. It must be left as a fold, so do not cut the fabric when removing the pattern.

Pattern alteration lines These are double lines, placed horizontally across a back, front or sleeve indicating the best position for shortening or lengthening the pattern piece without distorting the shape.

Making fitting adjustments

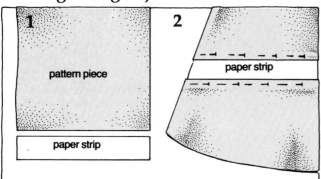
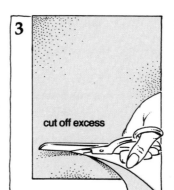
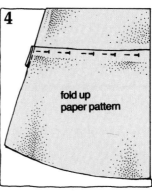

To help you simplify the process of making up, and to see whether any fitting adjustments are necessary, it may help to pin the paper pattern together. If you can see how the pattern works in this way it is easier to put the fabric sections together. Start with any darts, pleats or folds then pin the seams at side and shoulder, handling the tissue very carefully.

Hold it up against you in front of a full-length mirror. You can see where it may be necessary to adjust the length, or where to place a pocket, for example.

Multi-size patterns make it possible to use more than one size in a single garment, and so make easy adjustments for your figure. For example, if you are wide hipped you could combine a larger skirt size with a smaller size top in a dress like the camisole dress on page 199. Here are a few general tips on adjusting patterns – subsequent chapters give more detailed fitting instructions.

Lengthening a pattern
1 Garments with absolutely straight lower edges may be lengthened by adding an appropriately sized strip of paper to the pattern at the hem, or drawing a line across with tailor's chalk for the extra amount before cutting out.
2 Garments with shaped lower edges, or where an alteration is to be made in the body of a garment, are lengthened by cutting across the double alteration line. Insert a strip of paper in the gap to extend the piece by the extra amount required, with enough overlap to secure it to either side of the pattern piece.

Shortening a pattern
3 Where there is an absolutely straight lower edge, simply cut off a strip of pattern to shorten it.
4 If there is shaping at the lower edge, or you wish to make an alteration within the body of a garment, measure up from the alteration line the exact amount by which you wish to shorten the pattern. Draw a line across the pattern at this point and fold across the double alteration marking, taking it up to meet the drawn line. Pin to secure and re-draw any shaped seams.

Adjusting pattern width
Commercial patterns are designed to conform to average body measurements, and include an allowance for ease of movement. Fitting problems can be avoided by checking your own measurements against the pattern before cutting. Allow at least 2cm/¾in on top of your measurements across the front and back for ease of movement. If the pattern proves eventually to be a little large, take in more seam allowance at the side seams. If it is too big all over, you should use a smaller size pattern.

Preparing fabric for cutting out

Most fabrics have a right and a wrong side, apart from reversibles which have two right sides. It is easy to tell the difference on printed fabrics, but plain materials can pose a problem. One guideline is to check the way in which the fabric is sold in the shop. If it is rolled around a tube, the right side is inside. Cotton fabrics sold folded have the right side out, while woollens are wrong side out.

It is easier to judge in natural rather than artificial light, and once you have made a decision, mark each pattern piece that you cut on the wrong side of the fabric with tailor's chalk, to avoid confusion later.

Always check your fabric length for flaws before pinning on the pattern. Look carefully for areas of fraying, pulled threads or small holes. Mark them with chalk and avoid them when cutting out.

Cutting layout

A layout gives vital information on how the pattern should be positioned, according to the style and size of your garment, and the width of your fabric. It shows which pieces should be placed to a fold, which ones are to be cut more than once, and indicates when part of the fabric must be opened out for cutting a wide pattern piece, or one from a single thickness.

Pinning pattern to fabric

Fold the fabric right sides together before pinning on the pattern. This means pattern markings can be transferred directly to the wrong side of the material. However, if cutting a napped fabric, or matching the fabric design, fold with wrong sides together.

Pin the pattern to fabric only when you have enough time to cut out the pattern pieces and transfer the markings as well. Never leave pins in fabric for more than a few days – they attract moisture and begin to rust, leaving marks in the fabric when you eventually remove them.

Positioning pins

Never pin into the body of the fabric as even fine, sharp pins can snag. Insert the pins so that the head and point are both within the seam allowance, parallel to the cutting line. This avoids damaging the shears when cutting out, or pulling threads if the garment is folded with the pins in it.

Pin corners first, to secure the pattern. Use one pin every 15cm/6in along straight seams, but more pins are necessary around curved edges – one about every 5cm/2in. Do not pin across folds – it may mark the fabric. Instead, secure the pattern with weights (any small, heavy object will do). Allow enough room between pattern pieces on the fabric to manoeuvre the shears without damaging the pattern.

How to cut out

Use shears with long blades and angled handles. These allow you to cut out without lifting the fabric and the pattern.

Take long, even strokes on straight edges, using the supporting hand to keep the pattern flat, but take shorter strokes around curves. Cut notches outwards into the spare fabric, not into the pattern as this destroys the seam allowances.

Cutting out checklist

Always make a final check of all the points listed below before starting to cut.

1 Are there any flaws in the material? If so, have you positioned your pattern to avoid them?

2 Are all the pattern pieces required for your chosen style pinned on to the fabric? Tick them off on your layout.

3 Are the pattern pieces aligned to grainlines and placed to folds where necessary?

4 If any pieces are labelled 'cut four' (pockets or cuffs for example) have you allowed enough extra fabric to cut the pattern pieces again?

5 Have any alterations to length or width been made on all corresponding pattern pieces?

Pinning on and cutting out

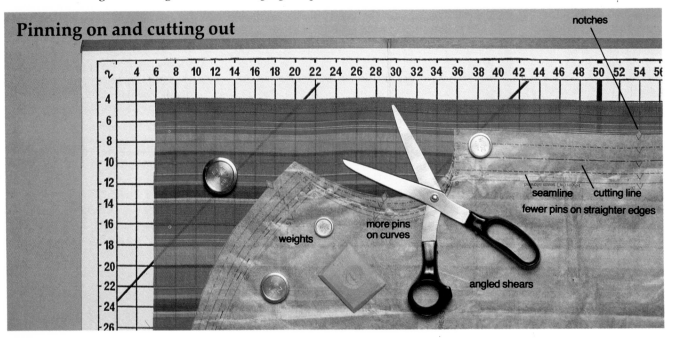

notches

weights

more pins on curves

seamline   cutting line
fewer pins on straighter edges

angled shears

Quick methods of transferring pattern markings

In order to put a garment together accurately, transfer the pattern markings to the garment pieces. This avoids wasting time later in referring back to the pattern.

Markings are usually transferred to the wrong side of the fabric but if you want to interface a piece – a collar for example – mark the interfacing, not the fabric.

When markings are needed on the right side of a garment – buttonholes for example – either choose a marking method that goes through all layers, such as tailor's tacks, or use dressmaker's carbon paper.

If you are using pale-coloured or sheer fabric use only tailor's tacks or pins for marking. Otherwise, you can choose from one of the several methods shown below.

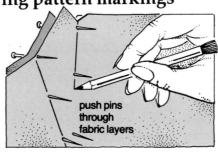

Pins and chalk pencil
Where fabric is folded right sides together, push pins through dots or symbols marking darts, pleats etc, so that they emerge on the other side of fabric. Remove the pattern carefully and make a chalk mark on each wrong side where the pins enter and leave the two layers of fabric.

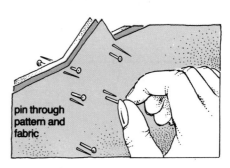

Pins only
This quick method is most suitable for marking darts and pleats. Insert pins as above, but insert a second pin for each mark from opposite side. When the paper pattern is removed a pin will remain at the same point on each garment piece. Deal with the darts or pleats immediately as the pins fall out easily.

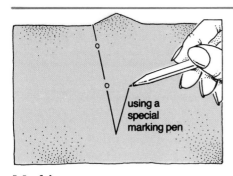

Marking pen
A special marking pen with washable ink can be used on many fabrics. On thin fabrics, the ink shows up on both sides and remains until removed by a drop of water, or by damp pressing.

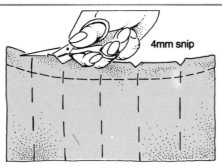
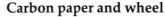

Snipping seam allowances
This is a quick method of indicating pleat and fold positions, gathering points or notches on collar pieces. Use it on seams where the seam allowance will be trimmed down – inside collars for example. Make snips no more than 4mm/⅛in deep.

Carbon paper and wheel
Dressmaker's carbon paper comes in several colours and is used in conjunction with a tracing wheel to transfer whole lines of pattern markings to a garment. Use this method for problem areas – collar edges, for example – where it is difficult to get both sides exactly the same. Choose a colour that is close to your fabric (but still visible). Do not use it on white or sheer fabric where the colour would show through, or on loosely woven fabric, where the marks disappear. Always protect the cutting surface by placing a piece of hardboard or thick cardboard under the work.

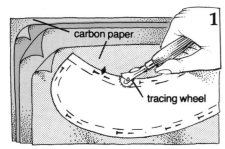

Marking double thickness fabric
1 If fabric is folded right sides together, lay one sheet of carbon paper beneath the double layer and one sheet on top beneath the pattern – coloured side to fabric in both cases. To avoid unpinning the whole pattern, trace off markings required in sections.

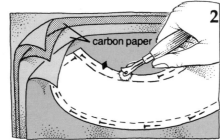

2 If fabric is folded wrong sides together, sandwich two sheets of carbon paper between the two fabric layers, back to back with the colour facing the wrong side of fabric.
Trace as before.

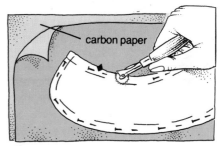

Marking single thickness fabric
When cutting single fabric, pin the pattern to the right side of the fabric and lay the carbon paper under the fabric, coloured side up. Press down firmly on the tracing wheel guiding it along straight edges, using a ruler, and pushing gently round curves.

Basic stitches and seams

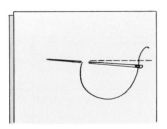

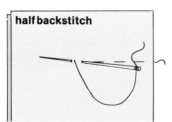
half backstitch

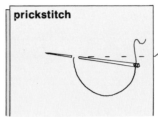
prickstitch

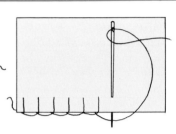

Backstitch
This is a strong hand stitch which has several versions, all useful for different dressmaking purposes. Work from right to left bringing the thread through to the right side. Insert needle to right of first stitch and bring it to right side again, to left of first stitch. Continue in this

way, placing stitches in a continuous line.
Half backstitch is not as strong as backstitch. Work in the same way but space stitches one stitch length apart.
Prickstitch gives a strong but almost invisible stitch which is ideal for inserting zips. The stitch taken on the right side is tiny in proportion to that

on the wrong side. One backstitch is a very good way of securing thread at the beginning and end of any row of hand stitches.

Blanket stitch
Used as a decorative edging over a turned hem or along a raw edge. Work from left to right with the item away from you and the needle pointing towards you. Insert the needle at A and bring it out at B above the loop of thread from the previous stitch.

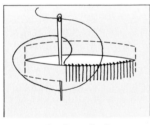

Buttonhole stitch
Work from right to left with the cut edge away from you. Insert the needle into the fabric from the back and, before pulling it through, bring the thread from the needle under the point to form a loop. Draw the needle through the work and pull gently upwards so that a small knot

forms on the cut edge. Work the stitches closely together.

Catchstitch
A loosely worked, flexible stitch (see under Blind hem) used for holding two layers of fabric together. Work from right to left between the layers to be joined. Take a few threads only from each fabric and make one stitch at a time. Make stitches no less than 5mm/¼in in length and do not pull sewing thread tightly or stitching line will show on right side.

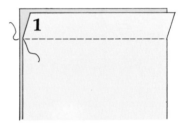

Flat fell seam
This seam encloses seam allowances of both sides of the fabric and is used on garments needing frequent laundering such as shirts, children's and sportswear. It is also ideal for reversible garments.
1 Place the fabric *wrong* sides together and stitch along the seamline.

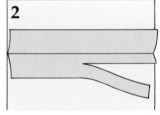

2 Trim seam allowance of the back section, or the bodice in the case of a yoke, to 5mm/¼in. Press seam allowance to one side so that the untrimmed edge covers the trimmed edge.
3 Turn under the edge of the upper seam allowance so that it encloses the trimmed edge. Pin, tack and

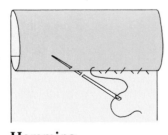

Hemming
This is a closely worked stitch suitable for inner

garment areas which need to be strong and durable, but which cannot be machined. Despite its name, hemming is never used around hemlines. Work from right to left inserting needle into main garment taking up one or two threads. Bring

needle out diagonally 1–2mm/⅛in along, taking a few threads from the fold to be secured.
Hemming is also used to secure folded edges to a line of machining, such as finishing cuffs and collars, waistbands and pockets.

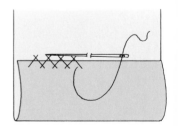

Herringbone stitch
A strong, flexible stitch used for hems and

24

All the instructions for hand sewing given in this book are for right-handed dressmakers. Simply reverse the direction of working if you are left-handed.

Blind hem

This type of hem is so called because the stitches holding the hem turning in place should be invisible from both the right and wrong side of the garment. They are concealed between the hem and the main fabric. A blind hem is particularly suitable for medium to heavyweight fabrics. Tack the neatened hem turning to the wrong side of the garment stitching 1cm/½in from the edge. Several types of stitches can be used for the hem.

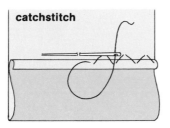
catchstitch

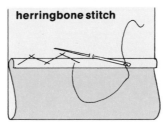
herringbone stitch

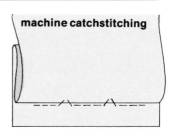
machine catchstitching

Catchstitch (see entry) Fold back ends of hem and, working from right to left, catchstitch hem to garment. Make the stitches between 5mm/ ¼in and 1cm/½in in length. Do not pull thread tight or an impression of the stitches will show on the right side. Where very heavy fabric is used, two rows

of catchstitches may be needed to support the weight. On a 5cm/2in deep hem, place the first row of stitches 2.5cm/1in from the hem edge and the second row 5mm/ ¼in to 1cm/½in from the edge.
Herringbone stitch (see entry) An alternative stitch for blind hems, work as for

catchstitching, above.
Machine catchstitching Blind hems may also be stitched on certain zigzag machines and this is particularly helpful where the hem length is considerable, such as on curtains.

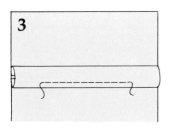
3

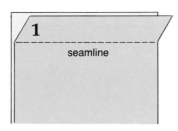
1
seamline

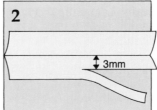
2
3mm

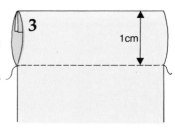
3
1cm

machine stitch, close to the fold.
This seam can also be worked in reverse, placing the *right* sides of fabric together. In this case an additional row of topstitching must be added close to the seamline.

French seam
This is a neat and durable seam which can be made very narrow for comfort on lingerie and nightwear. The finer the fabric, the narrower the finished seam can be made. All raw turnings are enclosed within the seam so there is no chance of fraying.
1 With *wrong* sides

together, machine 5mm/ ³⁄₁₆in from the seamline, within the seam allowance.
2 Press seam open and trim both raw edges to 3mm/⅛in.

3 Fold along machine line with *right* sides together. Tack and machine on seamline. Press seam to one side.

securing interfacing to wrong side of the fabric. Working from left to right but with the needle pointing to the left, take a few threads of the garment. Bring needle diagonally to the right and take next stitch with needle pointing to the left but in the hem

turning. Continue in this way, alternating between garment and layer to be attached. Do not pull the stitches tightly. This is an ideal stitch for knitted fabrics. For concealed herringbone stitch see Blind hems.

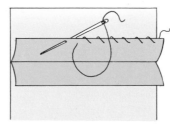

Overcasting
This is used to finish raw edges by hand.

Work from left to right and make evenly-spaced diagonal stitches over the raw edges. Gauge the size and spacing of the stitches to minimize fraying.
Overcasting can also be worked on a zigzag machine using a plain zigzag stitch.

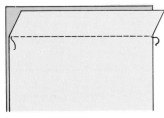

Plain seam
This is the simplest seam which is most often used. Place the fabric right sides together, matching seamlines. Pin and tack along seamline and machine or backstitch by hand. Press seam open and neaten raw edges if necessary.

Prickstitch
An almost invisible stitch ideal for inserting zips by hand (see Backstitch).

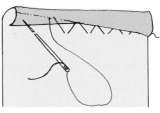

Rolled hem
Used on fine fabrics to give a neat finish when hem is likely to show. Trim hem allowance to 1cm/½in and staystitch 3mm/⅛in from edge with small machine stitches. Trim fabric away to within a few threads of machining. Turn hem to wrong side along hem foldline, rolling raw edge under so that line of machining just shows. Working from right to left, take small loose stitches through machining and garment. Take several stitches before pulling up thread, causing the hem to roll. When pressing do not iron hem, but leave gently rounded.

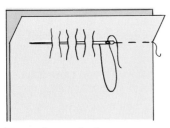

Running stitch
This simple stitch has many dressmaking uses. Work from right to left weaving needle in and out of fabric several times before pulling through.
Gathering Begin with a knot and work small, even stitches.
Tacking Begin with a backstitch and work 1cm/½in stitches 1cm/½in apart.

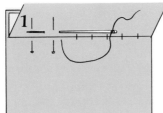

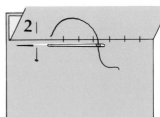

Slip or edge tacking
This is a method of tacking from the right side to ensure accurate matching of designs, checks and stripes at seamlines. It is also used when making fitting adjustments from the right side.
With right sides of garment sections facing upwards, turn under the seam allowance of one piece along the seamline and lap edge over the adjoining seam allowance, matching both seamlines. Pin at right angles to seam.
1 Begin with a backstitch and work from right to left. Insert needle into fold and take a stitch along for 1cm/½in.
2 Pull thread through and insert needle directly above first stitch but through the single layer, close to the fold. Bring it out again 1cm/½in along. Pull thread through, drawing the layers together and matching design exactly. Repeat along length to be tacked, alternating between fold and single fabric. When machined on wrong side, the design will be held firmly in place.

Tacking
See under Running stitch. Other tacking stitches follow.
Diagonal tacking
Provides firmer control over an area than ordinary tacking. Work parallel stitches with the needle pointing right to left, so that diagonal stitches form on the right side. For even firmer control, decrease space between parallel stitches.
Tailor's tacks These are used for marking particular points on a garment. Ideally they are used to transfer all

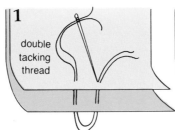

pattern markings to the fabric after cutting out. Use double tacking thread and a fine needle.
1 With paper pattern still in position, take a small stitch where required through all layers, leaving a good tail of thread at the end.
2 Make another stitch at exactly the same position, leaving a loop the size of your fingertip. Remove pattern.
3 Gently ease the fabric apart and snip the threads between the layers. This leaves tufts of thread as very clear markings which are quickly and completely

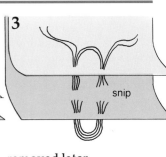

removed later.
Thread tacking Used to mark lines on garment prior to making up. Use single tacking thread and alternate long and short stitches working on the right side of the fabric.

Machines and equipment

Having the right equipment to hand and knowing what your sewing machine and its attachments can do will increase your skills and greatly add to the pleasure of your sewing. This guide describes the variations and capabilities of the various machines.

Most homes today possess a sewing machine of one kind or other, yet few machines, whether simple straight-stitchers or sophisticated electronics, are used to their full potential. Modern machines can do so much more than 'running up the seams'.

Choosing a machine

Choosing a machine, new or second-hand, can be a bewildering experience when there is such a wide choice. The most important factors to consider are the processes you want the machine to perform for you. Use this guide to help you work out which sewing machine will best fulfil your sewing needs.

There are three main types: straight-stitch, automatic and electronic. Within one of these areas you should find a machine to suit your needs and price range.

Straight-stitchers

These are available as 'used models' as they are no longer manufactured. They may be hand, treadle or electrically operated and may only stitch forwards. If attachments are used, the machines can perform many extra functions such as buttonholing, hemming, pleating, binding and free embroidery.

Automatic machines

Swing-needle In addition to straight stitching, these stitch from side to side in a zigzag motion, producing a closed or open satin stitch useful for seam neatening and embroidery, but not suitable for stretch fabrics.
Semi-automatic These incorporate several 'embroidery patterns' on cams or discs which have to be inserted by hand.
Automatic The term 'automatic' refers only to buttonholes, which can be made without turning the garment, but these and embroidery patterns are still controlled by hand.

Fully automatic In addition to all previous features, these machines can produce a greater variety of embroidery patterns. Instead of hand-inserted cams for individual patterns, many models in this range have built-in cams controlled by a knob, making them easier to operate than earlier machines.
Super-automatics These machines incorporate a circular motion stitch. The stretch-stitch, flexi-stitch and overlock stitch (simultaneous stitching and overcasting) incorporate side-to-side, forward and reverse, all within the same pattern, for sewing stretch fabrics. They can also seam knitted garments

Microchip machines

Many mechanical parts have been replaced by micro-circuitry, and levers and dials have been replaced by visual control panels. A touch of the finger engages the stitch selected. Fully-electronic machines are controlled by miniature computers which contain silicon chip memories and a micro-processor. Super-electronic machines have eliminated pattern cams completely, storing the patterns in a silicon chip.

Other considerations

Other factors to consider are the size and weight of the machine (these vary considerably from model to model), and whether you require extra convenience features such as a built-in free arm for stitching sleeves. Whatever your choice, ensure there is an 'after-sales' service. A well-cared for machine rarely needs an engineer's attention, but you still need expert advice if something goes wrong.

Make the best of your machine

If you already own a machine that you are happy with, you may be able to make it perform some extra, useful functions by buying the appropriate 'feet' or attachments which are used in place of the normal presser foot. The photographs on page 30 give an idea of the selection available.

Below: A wisely chosen sewing machine will fulfil your sewing needs and give you pleasure for many years to come.

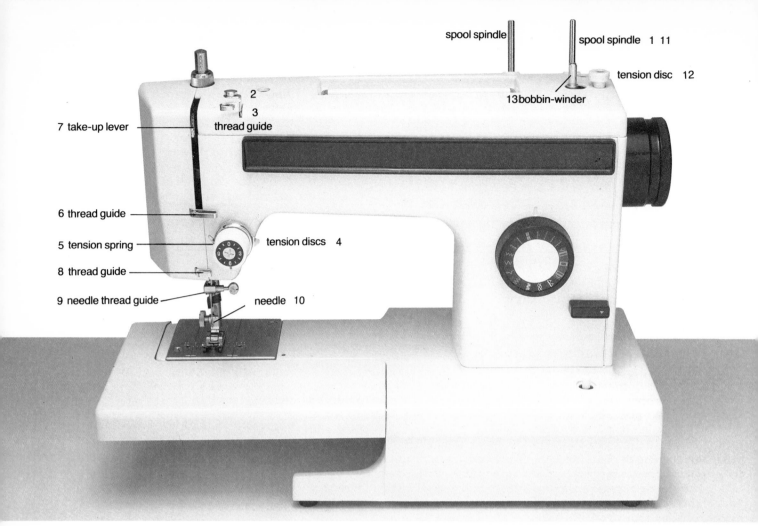

7 take-up lever

6 thread guide

5 tension spring

8 thread guide

9 needle thread guide

tension discs 4

needle 10

2
3
thread guide

spool spindle

spool spindle 1 11

tension disc 12

13 bobbin-winder

Perfect machining

Always check the following areas every time you start to sew: threading, tension, pressures, and correct needle and thread for the fabric. With practice it takes only a few seconds.

Threading

Why is threading so important? Most machines have between eight and ten points through which the thread passes before a stitch can be formed. Some of these points control the thread and stop it tangling. Others are vital to making the stitch. If any are missed the stitch may be affected. Although sewing machines differ in appearance the threading sequences are very similar. Always check with your machine handbook. If you haven't got one, ask the company for a replacement (or photocopy) or advertise for one.

Top threading

Turn the hand (balance) wheel towards you until the thread take-up lever (and therefore the needle) is in its highest position. Place a spool of thread on spindle **1**. Lead thread through points shown: thread

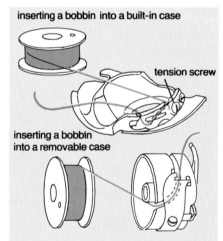

inserting a bobbin into a built-in case

tension screw

inserting a bobbin into a removable case

raising the bobbin thread

guides **2, 3**, tension discs **4**, tension spring **5**, thread guides **6**, take-up lever **7**, thread guide **8**, needle thread guide **9** and through needle **10**, usually from front to back but on older models from left to right or right to left. Leave about 10cm/4in thread free, ready for sewing.

Lower threading

Always start with an empty bobbin as winding over a different thread will distribute the thread unevenly. The thread should be of the same type and size as the upper thread. Do not overfill the bobbin or the thread will

be unable to run out freely. Wind the bobbin according to your machine type. Most machines have an external bobbin-winding system. This takes thread from the spool spindle **11** through a tension disc **12** to the bobbin-winder **13**. If the tension disc is missed, the winding will be uneven.

Insert the full bobbin into the bobbin-case with the thread running in the same direction as the slit in the side of the case, then pull the thread back under or around the tension spring. Where there is no case it has been built into the machine.

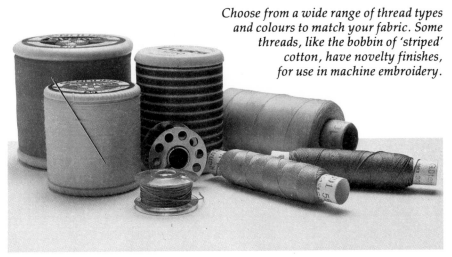

Choose from a wide range of thread types and colours to match your fabric. Some threads, like the bobbin of 'striped' cotton, have novelty finishes, for use in machine embroidery.

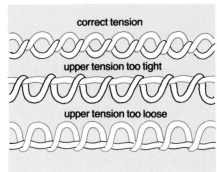

Above: the machine stitches on both sides of your fabric should be identical. If one side is puckered, this may be due to unbalanced tension.

Raising the bobbin thread

The bobbin thread must be drawn up through the hole in the needle plate to meet the upper thread before stitching can take place. Hold the top thread with the left hand, and lower the needle until it draws up the lower thread (by turning the hand wheel). A loop will form. Separate the threads and draw them both to the back of the machine through the slit in the presser foot. You are now ready to sew.

Place the fabric below presser foot. Lower needle into fabric and drop the presser foot. Draw hand wheel towards you before depressing foot control (to avoid going into reverse and snapping thread). This is not necessary on recent machines with variable-speed foot control.

Tension

The tension in the upper and lower threads must be balanced to produce a perfect stitch. Tension discs allow the thread to reach the needle at a controlled rate which ensures an even stitch length. When the presser foot is raised, the discs open and the threads are loose (they can be pulled through the needle by hand). When the foot is lowered, the discs clamp together and stop the thread moving until the machine is started.

It is seldom necessary to adjust the tension from 'normal' for most straight stitching (point 5 on a dial marked 1-10 on most machines) unless different thicknesses of fabric are being sewn or constant changes from straight to zigzag stitching take place. Zigzag stitching needs a lighter tension to prevent the wider stitch drawing up the fabric.

Adjusting the tension

Make a test stitch on a piece of your garment fabric (double thickness). Use the correct size needle and thread for the fabric. (See chart below.) Sew for about 10cm/4in. Remove from machine.

Whenever you stop sewing, make sure the take-up lever and needle are at their highest points, raise the presser foot and draw the threads backwards gently to avoid bending the needle. Cut the threads.

Look at both sides of the stitching. They should be identical. If the top tension is too tight, it will pull the lower stitches up to the surface. Turn the tension control to a lower number (anti-clockwise). If the lower thread is too tight increase the upper tension (by turning the control clockwise). Unlike the tension in the upper thread, the bobbin tension rarely needs changing for normal sewing.

Pressure

The pressure, or force, exerted on a fabric must be heavy enough to keep the fabric layers together while they are machined. Too heavy a pressure affects the stitch length, prevents the fabric moving and spoils the fabric surface. Too light a pressure allows the fabric to slip about and this prevents an even stitch being formed.

To adjust the pressure turn the pressure screw or dial clockwise to increase and anti-clockwise to decrease pressure until the presser foot controls the two layers of fabric and a good stitch is obtained.

Needles and thread

Change needles for *each* new garment. Don't throw them away, they can still be used for odd jobs until they lose their sharp point. Never use blunt or bent needles. Always match needle size to thread and fabric.

Choosing needles and threads

Fabric	Needle	Thread	Stitch-length
lightweight chiffon, organza, crêpe de chine, lawn	regular 70–80 (9–11)	fine mercerised cotton, silk, synthetic, poly/cotton	1–1.5mm
medium weight linen, satin, suiting	90–100 (14–16)	mercerised cotton (50), synthetic, silk	1.5–2mm
heavyweight denim, drill, gaberdine, coating	100–110 (16–18)	mercerised cotton (40), synthetic, poly/cotton	2.5–3mm
leather and vinyl	wedgepoint, size according to thickness	mercerised (50)	2.5–3mm

Special feet for special purposes

There is a 'special foot' or attachment for almost every machine sewing process which cannot be managed with the normal presser foot. Some are included when the machine is bought, others are obtainable as extra options and are surprisingly inexpensive. Sewing by machine is quicker, stronger and more accurate than hand-sewing so it is worthwhile finding out which attachments or guides might prove useful for your style of sewing.

Remember that different feet are not interchangeable between models, so consult your machine handbook.

Most of the feet for modern machines are of the 'snap-on' type. Other types may have to be screwed in to the machine.

Experiment with special feet

Most sewers machine seams, neaten raw edges, insert zips and make buttonholes by machine. Then they resort to hand-sewing techniques to finish the hem, catch down the facings, insert elastic and sew on buttons. Hand-sewing is an enjoyable activity but, if you are short of time or would just like to use your machine more fully, think of your next dress-making project as a completely machine-made garment, using the extra feet that came with your machine and perhaps investing in a few time-saving extras.

Other accessories

There are many other attachments and guides for keeping straight lines when sewing or for stitching in circles. One example is a guide-bar for quilting. This protrudes sideways from the presser foot and has a marker which, when kept along the last row of stitching, ensures even rows of quilting.

Zipper foot
This foot stitches close to the zip teeth, covers a cord, pipes a seam and stitches a blind hem. Some machines have a special blind hem attachment.

Narrow hemmer
A useful foot which puts a fine hem on the edge of neck and sleeve ruffles, on frills for skirts and petticoats. It has a slot for attaching lace to an edge at the same time.

Ruffler
This foot gathers (or pleats), and attaches to a straight edge at the same time. It also has a slot for attaching a trim in the same operation. Use it to gather the frills and ruffles on dresses and skirts.

Even-feed
Also known as a 'walking foot' this seams fabrics which tend to slip or stick. Use it for velvets, silks, quilteds and for matching stripes and checks on two pieces of fabric.

Button foot
Use a button foot for stitching on buttons with surface holes. Put a matchstick between the button and the garment to create a thread shank. Remove the matchstick, draw the top threads through to the inside of the garment and tie off.

Buttonholer
These attachments vary considerably from one machine to another. Some, like the model shown, make every buttonhole the same size if you put a template in the slot provided (no need to measure). Others need several stages and have to be marked. All make strong buttonholes more quickly than by hand methods.

Useful equipment

Apart from a sewing machine, you need some basic equipment.

Tape measure marked in centimetres and made from glass-fibre or other non-stretch material.

Pins Steel dressmaker's pins, and lace pins for fine work.

Needles for hand-sewing Packets of assorted sizes in two types:

Sharps for general sewing. These are round-eyed, medium-length needles.

Betweens for strong but 'invisible' tailor's stitches. These are short and round eyed.

Machine needles Size 70/9 is best for fine fabrics, size 80/11 for light-weight, size 90-100/14-16 for medium weight and size 100-110/16-18 for heavyweight fabrics. Use ball-point needles for stretch/knitted fabrics.

Thimble Use to protect the middle finger of the hand you sew with. Steel is stronger but plastic is better for white and lingerie fabrics as it will neither mark nor pucker the fabric.

Tailor's chalk or chalk pencil For transferring pattern marks to fabrics.

Tracing wheel and dressmaker's carbon paper For tracing pattern outlines quickly on to fabrics.

Scissors For cutting out fabric, use best quality dressmaker's shears with blades at least 12cm/4¾in long. These are designed so as not to lift fabric as you cut. Use small, sharp scissors for general purposes and keep a separate pair for cutting paper.

Knit and sew gauge A handy gadget for marking regular intervals such as buttonholes and for tracing shapes.

Iron Dry irons have a smooth sole-plate and are ideal for smooth-finished fabrics and for pressing small areas with a damp cloth. Steam irons have steam vents in the soleplate; many fabrics develop a shine if touched by the iron so a damp cloth may be necessary, see page 33 and test first.

Ironing board This needs to be firm and designed so that skirts and trousers slip round it easily for pressing. A sleeve board is invaluable for pressing awkward areas as well as sleeves.

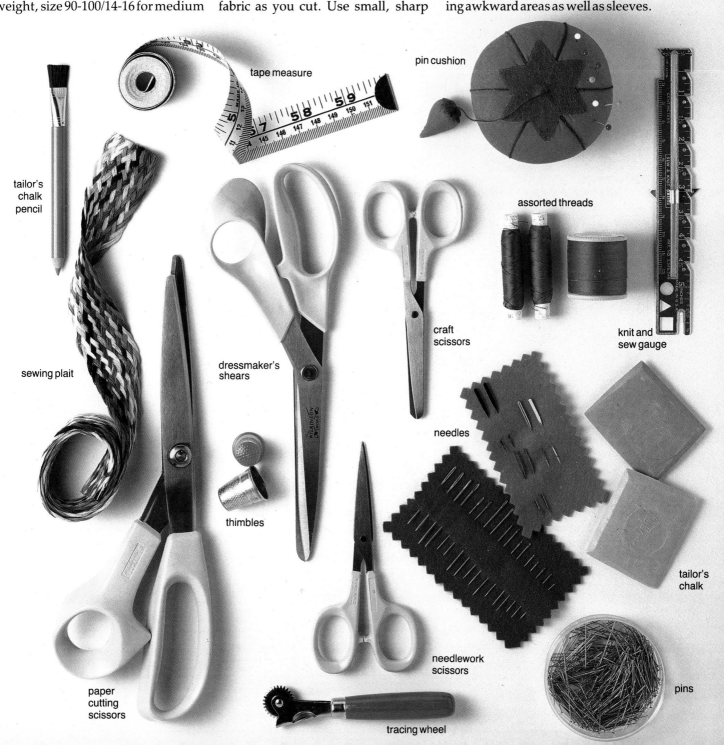

tape measure

pin cushion

tailor's chalk pencil

assorted threads

knit and sew gauge

sewing plait

craft scissors

dressmaker's shears

needles

thimbles

tailor's chalk

paper cutting scissors

needlework scissors

pins

tracing wheel

The art of perfect pressing

Careful pressing at each stage of construction is guaranteed to enhance the appearance of a hand-made garment. Make yourself some basic pressing equipment from the patterns given here, then follow the instructions for a perfect pressed finish.

Pressing and ironing are two different techniques, with different purposes, although some of the same equipment is used. When ironing, you move the iron at random over the fabric to remove creases produced by laundering. When pressing, you concentrate on specific areas, moving the iron by lifting it clear of the fabric and replacing it on the next area, using an up and down movement. You can merely rest the iron on the fabric, holding it so that only the lightest pressure is exerted or you can apply it with pressure.

Pressing equipment

In order to press garments successfully, you need a few basic items of equipment.

The iron A steam iron is the best choice for pressing. The more vents there are in the soleplate the better. Look for an iron with about 20 vents – this ensures good distribution of steam and means that an impression of the vents won't be transferred to the fabric.

When selecting an iron, hold it in your hand and test it for comfort and balance. It should have a toe which is not too pointed and a heel on which it will stand quite steadily. Look for easily accessible control buttons and check if any extra functions are available. A burst of steam is useful when pressing, but irons that spray water are more useful for domestic ironing than pressing. There is a risk of spray leaving a water mark on new fabric so it is safer to use it only for dampening the pressing cloth.

Always use distilled water purchased from a chemist in your steam iron – the sort used for car batteries is not suitable. Do not over-fill – too much water in the iron causes it to bubble and spit, making water marks on the garment.

Serious dressmakers may require a second iron – heavy dry irons are

The three stages of pressing for dressmakers

There are three stages of pressing when dressmaking. First, press the fabric before cutting out so that you can position the pattern pieces accurately. Secondly, press the garment at each stage of construction. Thirdly, give the whole garment a final, careful press.

Before cutting out

Press your fabric before pinning on the pattern pieces.

Woollen fabrics may also need shrinking. Although most are sold pre-shrunk, it is best to damp press a length of wool fabric prior to cutting out. Work on a table protected with blankets and a sheet as previously described. Position one or two chairs, depending on the fabric width, on the far side of the table to support the fabric once it is pressed. Start with the fabric in front of you, folded double and resting in gentle folds on a sheet on the floor so that it does not become dirty.

Lift a length of fabric on to the table, positioning the fold to the left so that you avoid it when pressing, and smoothing the layers together. Spread a damp pressing cloth over the fabric and press, working systematically across from the top left, lifting the iron and replacing it in the next position. Overlap the position of the iron so that every bit of the fabric is covered – the light impression made by the soleplate acts as a guide. Do not move the fabric until the steam has stopped rising and it is cold. Speed up this process in the case of heavy wool fabrics by banging out the steam with a tailor's clapper, the back of a wooden clothes brush or a piece of sanded wood.

As you press each section, fold it lightly on to the supporting chairseats until the entire length is pressed.

If the fabric has an obvious folded edge because it has been rolled on a bale for a long time, open it out to single thickness and press the fold along its entire length.

Pressing during construction

The secret of constructional pressing is never to cross one row of stitching with another until you have pressed the first one. Press on the wrong side wherever possible using a damp cloth and test the iron first on a corner of the fabric.

When in doubt as to the right temperature for pressing your fabric, start on the coolest setting and use a dry cloth. Increase the temperature gradually and introduce moisture until you achieve a satisfactory result. Support as much of the garment as possible when pressing to prevent the fabric weight dragging the warm, damp, newly pressed area out of shape. Do not move the garment until this area is cool and dry again.

Some fabrics take an impression of the seam turnings very easily on the right side, but still require firm pressure, heat and moisture. The answer is to use a pressing roll (see page 34). Lay seam along the top of roll and press from the wrong side. The seam turnings will not create an impression because of the curved roll. Where it is impossible to use a roll, as on a pleated area, insert a strip of brown wrapping paper under each pleat as it is pressed. Leave the pleat to cool before removing the strip and slipping it under the next pleat.

Wool fabrics are often very resilient and therefore require firm handling when pressing. This means using a lot of steam to penetrate the fabric, but avoiding making it too wet. The moisture must rise out while the fabric is still hot if the garment is to be set in the required way. During pressing, bang the hot, damp area repeatedly using a tailor's clapper, smacking the wood smartly up and down at right angles to the fabric, and working systematically over the area to be pressed until the garment is dry and cool.

useful for pressing heavyweight tweeds, suitings and coats. A solid iron with a mirror-finish chromium-plated soleplate is ideal.

The ironing surface As well as an ironing board, a stable, firmly padded, flat surface is useful for pressing. A table covered with several layers of blankets and then a sheet provides an excellent surface on which to work in conjunction with the pressing aids given overleaf.

If the only suitable tables are too low for comfort, just use an ironing board instead. It is worth investing in a new one if yours is rather old, as much research has gone into the latest designs. Choose a board with an adjustable height so that you can position it at the best level for you, and ensure that the mechanism and catch are

Below: Achieve a professional look on a home-sewn garment by careful pressing at all stages of making up.

easy to operate and well made. Check that the cover is removable for washing or renewing. Ideally you should be able to stand the iron on its heel so that it does not produce steam constantly and waste water. A flex holder is also useful.

The board should curve gently to a point for maximum pressing area and a sleeve board is useful for pressing tricky and otherwise inaccessible areas such as sleeve seams.

Pressing cloths Three cloths of differing fabric weights – calico, poplin and muslin are ideal. Make them large enough so that they can be used for a while without continuous re-dampening – 1m × 50cm/40in × 20in is a good size. Neaten the edges by zigzag stitching or turning a single, narrow hem but avoid this area when pressing so that you do not make an impression on your garment fabric. A calico cloth holds more moisture than the other cloths and is best for

pressing medium to heavyweight wools. These need firm pressing because the springiness and close construction of the fabric make it difficult for moisture to penetrate.

Use a lightly dampened muslin cloth on fine fabrics. As the muslin is semi-transparent you can see which areas you are pressing and can therefore avoid overpressing delicate fabrics.

The most useful general purpose pressing cloth is one made from fine poplin or lawn, which is suitable for pressing most fabric weights.

The best way to dampen a cloth is to fold it and immerse it in water. Roll it up, still folded, and squeeze out the excess water. Place it on the ironing board, still folded in seven or eight layers, and apply a dry iron to the cloth to disperse the moisture evenly, turning it over several times as you work. The cloth is now ready to use. Do not allow any area to become dry so moisten as necessary.

Final pressing

When the garment is completed a final, all-over press on the wrong side is necessary before it is ready to wear.

Begin by pressing small areas, such as collars, cuffs, frills and bands. Then press the larger areas such as sleeves, back bodice, front bodice, back skirt and then front skirt.

Avoid pressing over the stitching line of a hem, over fastenings or over raised trimmings as these will either leave an impression on the right side of the garment or be flattened. Run the toe of the iron under seam turnings to remove any trace of the impression of the turnings.

Where it is impossible to avoid pressing on the right side, always use a pressing cloth. Complete the pressing of a lined garment *before* anchoring the lining at the hem edge to avoid crushing the lining.

Techniques for pressing difficult fabrics

Fabrics with surface textures such as embossed and flocked cottons, corduroy, velvet and velour, and embroidered voiles, need pressing with great care to avoid flattening or altering the texture irrevocably.

Cushion the right side of the fabric during pressing to prevent this happening, using the method below which is most suitable for your fabric. Whichever method you choose, do not touch or move fabrics with a pile while they are still damp or hot, or you will mark the surface.

Corduroy, embossed/embroidered cotton Lay a soft, folded, Turkish-type towel over the ironing board when pressing firm fabrics with a surface texture like these. If the towel is sufficiently thick you can press hard on the wrong side of the fabric without damaging the pile.

If you are pressing corduroy and do not have a suitable towel, lay an offcut of the same fabric on the ironing board, pile uppermost. Then lay the main fabric down on to it, wrong side uppermost. The piles of both layers will interlock, enabling you to press the wrong side of the fabric without flattening the pile.

Velvet Use a needleboard to press velvet successfully. This is a sheet of small, slightly bent metal pins, just long enough to support the pile of velvet or corduroy. Simply place the fabric face down on the board and press, using a steam iron.

Velour, flocked and shiny fabrics Use a velour sheet, or a large offcut of firm velour fabric as a pressing surface for the best results. Place the fabric face down on it in the usual way and press from the wrong side.

Man-made fabrics – some of the synthetic crêpe-de-chine type fabrics can present pressing problems. If the iron is too hot, it produces shiny areas and permanent impressions of seams and turnings. To avoid this, start with the iron at the coolest setting and test to find the best temperature on an offcut of the fabric. Press only on the wrong side and use brown paper strips or a pressing roll to prevent seam turnings showing through to the right side.

Three pressing aids to make

As you make up a garment its curves and contours start to appear. These too need pressing, but cannot always be dealt with on an ironing board or sleeve board. A pressing roll, a tailor's ham and a pressing mitt should solve all your pressing problems and are indispensable once used.

A pressing roll is a tube of fabric packed hard with sawdust. It is used to prevent impressions of the seam turnings on the main garment when pressing seams.

A tailor's ham is an oval shape with curved sides, also packed hard with sawdust. It is ideal for using when pressing the head of a sleeve, the seat of trousers or princess seams – all areas which need thorough pressing while maintaining a curve.

A pressing mitt is a thickly padded calico mitten which is worn on the hand and pushed inside smaller curves during pressing. The padding protects the hand from heat and steam.

All these items are available from good haberdashery counters, but you can make them yourself using the patterns and instructions below at a fraction of the cost.

You will need
0.50m/⅝yd of smooth wool fabric
0.50m/⅝yd of calico
Matching thread
Bag of sawdust (from pet shops)
Polyester wadding
Blanket fabric

Cutting out
Enlarge the patterns you require on to dressmaker's graph paper. For the pressing roll and tailor's ham, cut one pattern piece in wool and one in calico.

For the pressing mitt, cut two pocket pattern pieces to the fold, and two pad pattern pieces in calico. Cut two single pad pieces in blanketing and two single pocket pieces in wadding.

pressing mitt

pressing roll

tailor's ham

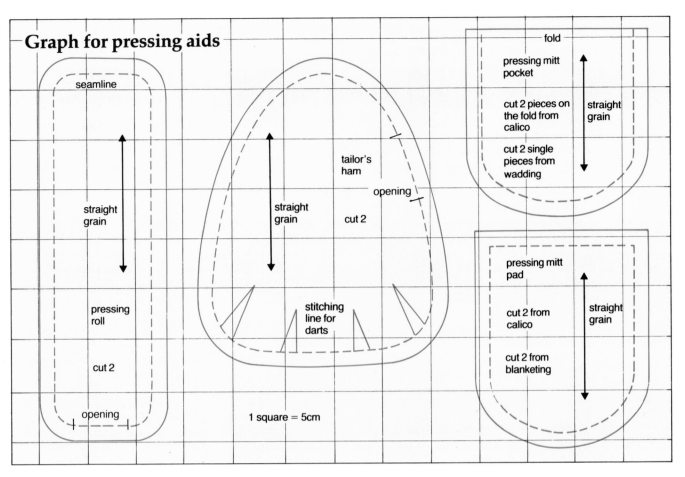

Graph for pressing aids

seamline

straight grain

pressing roll

cut 2

opening

tailor's ham

straight grain

cut 2

stitching line for darts

opening

1 square = 5cm

fold

pressing mitt pocket

cut 2 pieces on the fold from calico

cut 2 single pieces from wadding

straight grain

pressing mitt pad

cut 2 from calico

cut 2 from blanketing

straight grain

Making the tailor's ham

Close the darts on the wrong side of the calico and wool sections with a double row of machining, Begin at the base of the dart, stitch to point, pivot work and stitch back to base. Place the two layers right sides together and stitch starting opposite the marked opening.
Stitch to one marking, pivot the work and stitch all the way round to the other marking. Pivot the work again and stitch back to beginning of the machining. A double row of stitches is essential for strength. Trim seam to 7.5mm/⅜in and turn to right side.
Fill the ham to capacity with sawdust. A cardboard funnel speeds up the process. Hold the opening closed and bang the ham smartly on to a hard floor or table to pack down the sawdust. Continue to fill in this way until it is impossible to get in any more sawdust. As a guide, you should use 600–650g/21–23oz of sawdust. Close the opening by backstitching the layers together tightly using four strands of thread in the needle.

Making the pressing roll

Work as for the tailor's ham, omitting the darts. The pressing roll needs about 250–300g/9–10½oz of sawdust to pack it firmly.

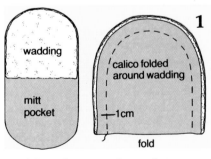

wadding

mitt pocket

calico folded around wadding

1cm

fold

1

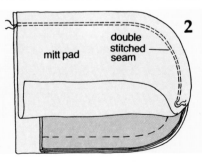

mitt pad

double stitched seam

2

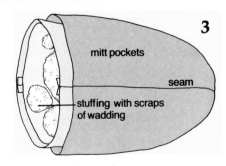

mitt pockets

seam

stuffing with scraps of wadding

3

Making the pressing mitt

1 Lay wadding to the fold on one half of each mitt pocket piece. Fold over the other half and staystitch around outside curve through all three thicknesses, 1cm/½in from cut edge.

2 Place mitt pockets together and add a calico pad section above and below, matching the curve. Machine a double-stitched seam through all layers around the outside curved edge. Trim seam and turn to right side so that wadded pocket pieces sandwich the pad.
3 Lay a double layer of blanketing inside this centre pad pocket and stuff scraps of polyester wadding inside the blanket layers. Oversew the lower edge of the mitt to close, using double thread.

PART 2

A simple skirt

One of the simplest garments to make – and a good introduction to home dressmaking for the beginner – is a gathered skirt, or dirndl as it is also known. Start with a skirt made from a rectangle of fabric, gauging the fullness of the gathers to suit your type of figure. A shaped dirndl is slightly more complex – made from four panels, it is designed to give fullness at the hem while remaining lightly-gathered at the waist. The pattern pieces are given on a multi-size graph pattern and this is an ideal project to learn the technique of enlarging a pattern to full size.

Simple soft pleats are an alternative to gathers, and with these the width and style need to be calculated with care to achieve a balanced effect. All three skirts can be made up in a range of fabrics for either winter or summer.

Various basic techniques are required to give the skirt a professional finish. Learn how to insert a centre back or overlapped zip, how to interface and apply the waistband, how to turn up a hem and, to ring the changes, how to apply bold patch pockets.

The dirndl – a basic skirt

*A gathered skirt, often known as a dirndl, is one of the easiest
skirts to make, needing only a straight length
of fabric and a few measurements. You can make a simple
pattern from a rectangle of paper or
draw the measurements straight on to the fabric.*

A gathered skirt may be as narrow or as full as you wish – the wider the hem of the skirt, the more you gather in at the waist. Whether short, mid-calf or full-length, in its fully gathered form it emphasizes a neat waist.

In its narrower version, a gathered skirt lies smoothly over the hips, is only gently gathered at the waist and falls elegantly in a straight line to the hem. Sizes up to about 102cm/40in hips can wear the narrower version with confidence.

The art of making a gathered skirt look good lies in the way you position the gathers at the waistline. You can either have fewer gathers over the hips or across the stomach depending on which style flatters your figure most.

Choosing fabrics

The traditional dirndl, designed for Alpine peasant dancing, was made from heavy fabric, fully gathered into a strong waistband and the hem was made to stand out further by bands of embroidery. Today's fabrics make the dirndl a much more versatile skirt, suitable for most occasions and very quick to make because the only fitted area is the waistline. The final effect is determined by the weight and texture of the fabric you choose and the amount of extra fabric added to the hip measurement. No darts are required.

To achieve the most flattering line consider using a lightweight fabric such as silk, lawn, crêpe, crêpe-de-chine, challis (the ch is pronounced as in chapter) or pongee (pronounced ponjee), as these will flow in soft fluid lines. Firmer fabrics such as moiré and paper taffeta, crisp cottons, eyelet embroidered fabrics,

Suitable for a variety of occasions, this dirndl in checked Viyella is simple to sew and needs no commercial pattern.

satins and taffetas usually stand out more from their gathers and create a wider silhouette.

If you choose a patterned fabric, take the trouble to work out how to make the most of the design. Check, for example, to see if it looks best centred at the front of the skirt.

How much fabric?

The following amounts are suitable for all sizes up to 102cm/40in hips.

Lightly gathered skirt If you buy 90cm/36in or 115cm/45in width fabric you need twice the finished skirt length plus 20cm/8in for hem and seam allowances, (eg for a skirt 70cm/27½in long, you need 1.60m/1⅝yd.)

If you buy 150cm/60in width fabric you need the finished skirt length plus 30cm/12in for the pockets, waistband, hem and seam allowances, (eg a skirt 70cm/27½in long would need 1m/1⅛yd of fabric).

Full skirt If you buy 115cm/45in fabric you need twice the finished skirt length plus 40cm/16in for the pockets, waistband, hem and seam allowances, (eg a skirt 70cm/27½in long would need 1.80m/2yd of fabric). 90cm/36in fabric is too narrow to make this skirt with only two seams. If you buy 150cm/60in width fabric you need twice the finished skirt length plus 20cm/8in for hem and seam allowances, (eg

a skirt 70cm/27½in long would need 1.60m/1⅝yd of fabric).

Making a pattern

This chapter shows how to make a pattern for a gathered skirt. When making your own patterns you can decide how much seam allowance you need. Most commercial patterns include a seam allowance of 1.5cm/⅝in, but it is easier to insert a zip into a seam of 2.5cm/1in. (The gathered skirt pattern has no seam allowances, position it on the fabric and then allow for seams and hems before cutting out.) When you make your own patterns it is useful to write all the relevant in-

Patterns for the full and lightly gathered skirts

Use tissue, greaseproof or even a spare roll of wallpaper to make your paper pattern or, if you feel confident, miss out the paper pattern stage altogether and mark the pattern measurements straight on to the fabric with tailor's chalk. If you make this short cut, remember that, having marked the pattern measurements on to the fabric, you must mark the seam and hem allowances before cutting out.

Below: This lightly gathered skirt needs less than two metres of fabric.

Lightly gathered skirt

Cut two rectangles of paper exactly the same size, one for the skirt back and one for the skirt front. When they are placed on folded fabric they give two halves of a skirt which are joined together by a seam at each side. The seam and hem allowances are added at the cutting stage.

The longer side of the paper is the exact finished length you want the skirt to be. The shorter side is one and a quarter times your hip measurement divided by four.

Measure the length of another skirt in your wardrobe which is the right length, from just under the waistband to the hemline. Make a note of this measurement, it is the length of the longer side of the paper pattern.

Measure your hips (see page 20), divide this by four and add this figure to the hip measurement. Now divide the total by four and you get the length of the shorter side of the pattern. For example if your hip measurement is 96cm/38in, divide this by four which equals

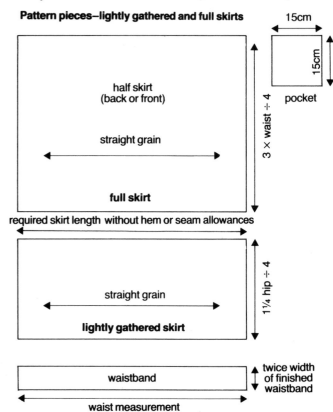

Pattern pieces—lightly gathered and full skirts

half skirt
(back or front)

straight grain

full skirt

$3 \times$ waist $\div 4$

15cm

15cm

pocket

required skirt length without hem or seam allowances

straight grain

lightly gathered skirt

1¼ hip $\div$ 4

waistband

twice width of finished waistband

waist measurement

formation on the pattern pieces. This way if you want to make the pattern up again you can see all the details at a glance. Mark an edge which has to be placed on a fold, a straight grain line (abbreviated as SG), centre fold (CF), centre back (CB), waist (W), hip (H), length (L), side seam (SS), seam allowance (SA), hem allowance (HA) and name the pattern piece (front, back etc.) if there are more than one.

This chapter shows you how to pin the pattern pieces on to the fabric and how to cut it out. Full instructions for completing a range of gathered skirts, including a shaped dirndl are given in the following pages.

24cm/9½in. Add 24cm/9½in to 96cm/38in which equals 120cm/47½in. Divide by four making 30cm/11⅞in. For the waistband cut a strip of paper exactly to your waist measurement and twice the width you want the finished waistband to be. (Most gathered skirts have waistbands between 3-5cm/1¼-2in wide. Unless you are particularly long waisted a 3cm/1¼in waistband looks best.)

For the pocket cut a piece of paper whatever shape and size you want the pocket to be, provided it will fit on the cutting layout. A good finished size is 15cm/6in square.

Full skirt

Cut out two rectangles of paper exactly the same size, one for the skirt back and one for the skirt front. The longer side of the paper is the required finished length of the skirt. The shorter side is three times your *waist* measurement divided by four, (eg if your waist measures 70cm/27½in, multiply by three to give 210cm/82½in and divide by four to give 52.5cm/20½in). For a less full look, use twice your waist measurement divided by four and for a fuller look use three and a half times your waist measurement divided by four. (Note: for waist measurements above 73cm/29in, the maximum finished width around the lower edge of a skirt cut on 115cm/45in fabric is 219cm/86½in.) Cut out a waistband and pocket pattern piece as described above under the lightly gathered skirt.

Positioning the pattern pieces

Choose the appropriate cutting layout for your fabric and the skirt you are making. Position the skirt pattern pieces as below, leaving room for a 1.5cm/⅝in seam allowance at the waist, a 2.5cm/1in seam allowance at the side and a 6.5cm/2½in hem.

Allow 6.5cm/2½in for the top pocket facing and leave a 1.5cm/⅝in seam allowance round the other three edges, and along the two long edges and one short edge of the waistband. Allow 7cm/2¾in at the other short edge for fastening.

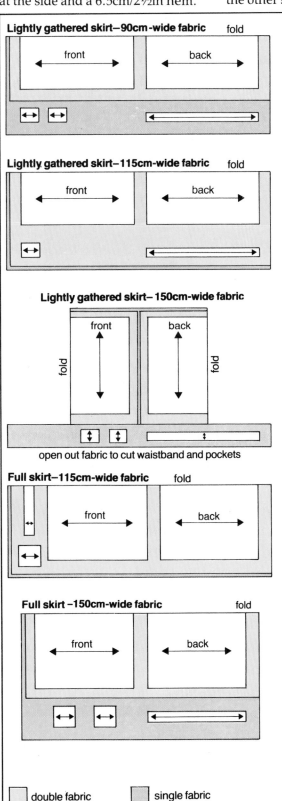

Lightly gathered skirt–90cm-wide fabric fold
front   back

Lightly gathered skirt–115cm-wide fabric fold
front   back

Lightly gathered skirt– 150cm-wide fabric
fold   front   back   fold
open out fabric to cut waistband and pockets

Full skirt–115cm-wide fabric fold
front   back

Full skirt –150cm-wide fabric fold
front   back

☐ double fabric   ☐ single fabric

Lightly gathered skirt

90cm width Fold the fabric as shown with right sides together and selvedges parallel.
Place the two skirt pattern pieces on the folded edge and place the waistband and pocket pattern pieces on the single layer of fabric.
115cm width Fold the fabric in half as shown with right sides together and selvedges level.
Place the skirt pattern pieces on the folded edge and place the pocket pattern piece on the doubled fabric as shown. Place the waistband on a single layer of fabric only.
150cm width Fold the fabric as shown with the selvedges meeting exactly in the centre.
Place the two skirt pattern pieces on the folded edges giving the centre front and centre back. Open out lower part of the fabric and place pockets and waistband as shown.

Full skirt

115cm fabric Fold the fabric as shown with right sides together and selvedges level.
Place the two skirt pattern pieces and the waistband (folded in half) on the folded edge and place the pocket as shown.
150cm fabric Fold the fabric as shown with right sides together and selvedges parallel.
Place the skirt pattern pieces on the folded edge and place the pocket pattern pieces and the waistband piece on a single layer of fabric only.

Pinning, cutting out and marking seamlines

Pin skirt pattern pieces to the fabric as close to the pattern edges as possible. Avoid using pins along the folded edges – the centre front and centre back of the skirt – they may leave marks or tiny holes. Before cutting out, mark the cutting lines on to the fabric using tailor's chalk. The cutting line is the paper pattern piece plus the seam allowance so measure out from the edge of the pattern:

1.5cm/⅝in along waistline edge
2.5cm/1in along side seam
6.5cm/2½in along lower edge
(this represents a 5cm/2in hem with a 1.5cm/½in turning)

Cut out the two skirt pieces. Pin on the waistband pattern piece

as indicated on your chosen cutting layout. Mark a cutting line 1.5cm/⅝in out from the edge of the pattern along long edges and one short edge. Mark a cutting line 7cm/2¾in from edge of pattern at the other short end for the overlap to take a hook or button. Cut out the waistband.

Pin on the pocket pattern piece and mark a cutting line 1.5cm/⅝in from the edge on three sides, and 6.5cm/2½in from the top. Cut out pocket. Because the cutting line is larger than the pattern piece by the exact measurement of the hem and seam allowances, to mark the seamline and hemline simply trace round each pattern piece with tailor's

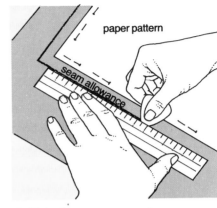

paper pattern

seam allowance

chalk before removing the pattern from the fabric. An alternative method, advisable if using a fine fabric or one with a delicate surface, is to use a row of continuous tailor's tacks.

PROFESSIONAL TOUCH

Tailor's tacks

Single tailor's tack
This is used for marking one particular point such as a button hole or a dart. Use double tacking thread and a fine needle.
1 Make one small stitch.
2 Make another stitch on exactly the same point leaving a loop the size of your fingertip.
3 Gently ease the layers apart.
4 Snip the threads between the layers. This leaves a reference point for making up the garment.

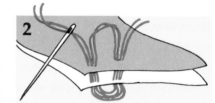

double tacking thread

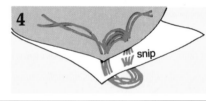

snip

Continuous tailor's tacks
These are used for marking seamlines to give an accurate line for sewing. Use double tacking thread and a fine needle to work a row of single loops.
1 Make one stitch through both layers of fabric, make the next stitch further along the line to be marked, using the fingertip as a guide for spacing.
2 When the tacking has been completed, gently ease the two layers of fabric apart and snip the threads in between the layers.

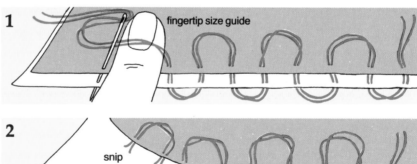

fingertip size guide

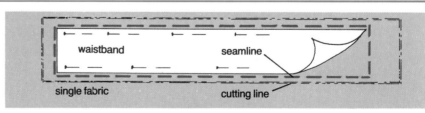

snip

ease fabric layers apart

Marking single layers
For marking a single layer of fabric – for example, the waistband – simply work a row of stitches in single thread around the outside of the pattern.

waistband

seamline

single fabric

cutting line

Shaped dirndl skirt

This skirt has four panels (two at the front and two at the back) and four seams – two side seams and a centre seam at front and back. The panels are flared to give fullness at the hem, and it is lightly gathered at the waist. Sizes are as follows:

Size	Waist	Length
10	64cm/24in	70cm/27½in
12	67cm/26in	72cm/28¼in
14	71cm/28in	74cm/29¼in
16	76cm/30in	74cm/29¼in

Making the pattern

From the grid (far right), copy the pattern pieces in the size you require on to dressmaker's 5cm/2in graph paper. Use a ruler to draw the line for the side of the skirt, and follow the lines on the graph paper for the waistband. The curved lines of the waist edge and hem are easy to draw using a flexicurve, as explained in the section on making graph patterns, page 18.

Fabric requirements

For all sizes, on 90cm/36in or 115cm/45in fabric, you need four times the finished skirt length, plus about 50cm/20in for the waistband, hem and seam allowances (eg a skirt 70cm/27½in long would need 3.30m/3½yd of fabric). If you are using 150cm/60in fabric, you need twice the finished skirt length, plus 30cm/12in for the waistband, hem and seam allowances, (eg a skirt 70cm/27½in long would need 1.70m/1¾yd of fabric). If your fabric has an obvious pattern repeat, allow extra fabric to match the pattern across the skirt seams. On 150cm/60in fabric you can easily see how the pattern matches when you lay down the pattern pieces.

Cutting out

Position and pin your pattern pieces as shown on the appropriate layout. Cut out carefully, with the skirt pattern piece positioned on the fold in every case. Remember to add on seam and hem allowances before starting to cut out.

Right: The shaped dirndl is designed to be flattering to all figures. Insert the zip in the left-hand side seam instead of the back as for the simple dirndl.

Copy your pattern pieces from the multi-size grid (right), making four identical pieces for the skirt. This pattern piece represents half your skirt panel, so always place it on the fold, as shown on the layouts below.

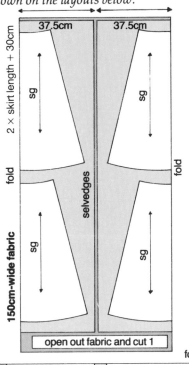

150cm-wide fabric

37.5cm — 37.5cm

2 × skirt length + 30cm

fold — fold

selvedges

open out fabric and cut 1

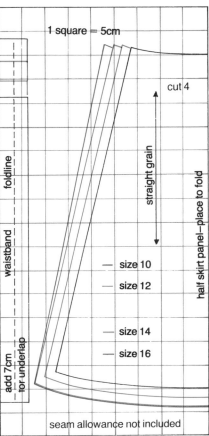

1 square = 5cm

cut 4

foldline

waistband

straight grain

half skirt panel—place to fold

— size 10
— size 12
— size 14
— size 16

add 7cm for underlap

seam allowance not included

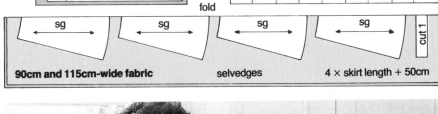

fold

90cm and 115cm-wide fabric   selvedges   4 × skirt length + 50cm

cut 1

Seams in skirts

The position of the seams in a skirt is most important, for they give a definite 'line' or shape to the garment. A simple skirt has two seams, positioned at the sides. Close-fitting straight skirts hang better with a seam added at the centre back, as this strengthens the 'seat' area and keeps the hem edge firm. When only one seam is preferable, as in a skirt made from a border print, you should position it at the centre back.

A plain open seam is the best type for most skirts. The seam allowance is pressed equally to either side of the seam, giving a flat appearance (see page 26). It is easy to insert a zip into this type of seam.

Most seams are 1.5cm/⅝in wide but allow at least 2.5cm/1in on seams with openings. This not only makes it easier to insert a zip, but also allows you to alter the size at a later date if necessary.

Neatening skirt seams The method used to neaten the raw edges of the seam allowances depends on the thickness of the fabric, and how easily it frays. While all woven fabrics fray and knitted fabrics 'run', only felted fabrics do neither.

When neatening the raw edges, sew the plain seam first. Always sew corresponding seams (the side seams, for example) in the same direction. In a skirt this would be from hem to waistband, unless the fabric has a pile running downwards as in corduroy, in which case stitch from waistband to hem.

On the wrong side, press open the seam allowances, then run the iron lightly over the seam on the right side. If pressed carefully at each stage, no 'final pressing' of the garment is necessary. The raw edges can either be turned under and stitched or finished by either of the methods shown right.

When neatening a seam, try to stitch the edges in the same direction as the seamline was stitched, wherever possible.

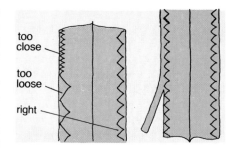

Zigzag overstitching

Before finishing the seam, practise the zigzag stitch on scraps of your garment fabric, experimenting with stitch length and width. The zigzag stitch should be fairly close, so that the fabric does not fray between the stitches, but not as close as satin stitch. If the raw edges curl and form a ridge, try allowing the needle to go just beyond the edge of the fabric on the right-hand stitch. This will keep the edges flat. Alternatively, stitch a line of zigzag just inside the edge of the seam allowance and trim away the excess fabric.

Inserting a skirt zip

Zips come in a bewildering variety of types and forms. Basically, heavyweight metal zips are most suitable for jeans and heavy clothes, and open-ended zips are used in seams that open completely, as in the front of a blouson jacket.

For skirts (and most other garments) use a lightweight metal or synthetic zip, colour matched to your fabric. For fine fabrics, use a nylon zip.

When choosing the size of your zip, remember that the zip opening needs to be long enough for you to get in and out of the garment without putting any strain on the seam or the end of the zip. Generally, an 18cm/7in skirt zip is adequate for small women's sizes, 20cm/8in for medium sizes and 23cm/9in for larger figures. To help you insert the zip into a garment, some zips have a stitching guideline woven into or printed on to the zip tapes. Otherwise, use the weave of the tape fabric as a stitching guide.

There are two main methods of inserting a zip: overlapped insertion and central insertion. The overlapped method is suitable for both side and centre seams, while the central method – used on centre seams only – is shown on page 49.

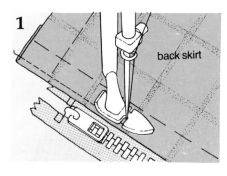

Overlapped zip

1 Prepare and neaten the left-hand side seam, leaving an opening the same length as the zip (measured down from the waist seamline). Press under, or tack, the side seam allowances along seamlines.

Lay back skirt opening edge over front of zip tape, 2mm/⅛in from teeth, with the zip tab 6mm/¼in below waist fitting line. This allows enough space for the zip to open and close when the waistband is attached. Tack, rather than pin, in order to keep flat.

Machine, using zipper foot, from waistline towards lower edge close to fold. The seam should conceal the bottom stop of the zip.

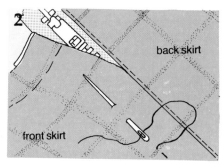

2 Lay front skirt opening edge over entire zip and line up with side seam of back skirt, matching raw edges at waist level.

Tack and machine from waist to zip base. Slide the zip tab down slightly to machine the top of the seam, then slide it back up to the top and machine the rest of the seam with the zip closed. This allows you to stitch the whole seam in a straight line.

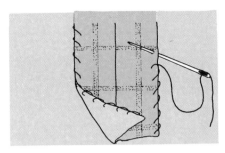

Overcasting by hand

If you do not have a swing-needle device and the fabric is unsuitable for the turned and stitched finish overcast the edges by hand, taking evenly-spaced diagonal stitches over the raw edges. Do not pull the thread too tight or the edge will curl.

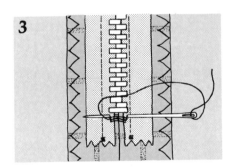

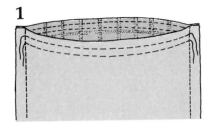

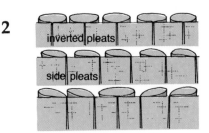

Gathers and soft pleats

1

2

Gathers are small, soft folds formed by drawing the fabric along a row of hand or machine stitches. For small gathers use a small machine stitch (about 8 stitches to 2.5cm/1in) and reduce upper machine tension so that the bobbin thread will pull through easily. Large gathering stitches produce small, flat pleats.
1 Mark the centre front and back of the waist edge of skirt to make it easy to match to the waistband. Work two parallel rows of machine or handstitching on right side of skirt waist, close to each side of fitting line (about 5mm/¼in apart). Leave loose ends of thread at each end to be pulled up.
Where seams create bulk, work in sections taking the stitches right up to the seams, but avoiding the seam allowances.
Prepare for gathering by pulling up threads a little and securing round a pin inserted on wrong side across seamline at each end of gathering section.

Soft pleats or unstitched pleats, are an alternative to gathering on a full skirt. Here are several possible variations (**2**, above), but you can alter the spacing and size of the pleats for the effect that pleases you, or flatters your figure. Just make sure that the finished pleated skirt top fits your waist, and that the pleats are even in size and evenly spaced.
Soft pleats, and indeed any sort of pleats, work best folded on the straight grain, so the design of the dirndl skirt is ideal for pleating. Make the pleats as shown above, using the pattern of your fabric or the straight grain as a guideline, and check the appearance on the right side.
Pin and tack your pleats in the style you have chosen, tacking a little way down the fold so that the fabric is easier to handle while attaching the waistband. When the skirt is finished, remove the tacking and allow the pleats to fall into soft folds.

3 At lower end of opening, pull loose ends of machine threads through to wrong side and secure to zip tape with backstitch.
Stitch across lower zip tape through seam allowance by hand. (Machining across bottom of zip on right side can cause a bulge.)
Add a strip of fabric or petersham ribbon behind the zip to protect lingerie and delicate blouses. Sew by hand to one side of opening and across lower end.

Right: Soft pleats are fun to make, and very easy. Checked or striped fabric is particularly suitable for pleating, as the lines help you to match the pleats and make them even. There are many types of pleats to choose from – this variation has side pleats and a central inverted pleat.

Useful hand-sewn stitches

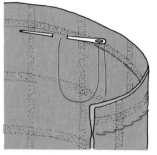 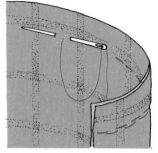 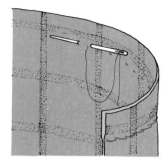 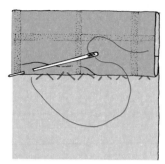

Backstitch
A strong hand stitch, resembling machine stitch on right side.
1 Working from the right side, take a stitch 3mm/⅛in long and bring needle out through fabric 3mm/⅛in ahead on stitching line.
2 Take thread back and insert needle in end of previous stitch, bringing it out one stitch ahead.

Half-backstitch
A neat stitch, evenly spaced on the right side. Work as for backstitch but take needle back only half the length of previous stitch. Continue to bring needle out one stitch length ahead.

Prickstitch
An almost invisible stitch ideal for inserting zips by hand. Work as for backstitch, but take the needle back one or two threads only, so that a tiny stitch forms on the right side.

Catchstitch
A loosely-worked, flexible stitch – not strong, but ideal for hems.
1 Work loosely just inside the hem fold to protect stitches and avoid a ridge on the hem.
2 Catch only a few top threads in the visible part of the garment, but take large stitches in the hem fabric, as shown.

Preparing a straight waistband

The straight waistband is the most common method of finishing the waist edge of a skirt. The waistband is backed with interfacing or, for a stiffer finish, petersham ribbon. The most usual (and most comfortable) finished width for the waistband is 3-5cm/1¼-2in.

Attaching the waistband to the skirt is straightforward since the top edge of the skirt is just gathered up until it fits the straight edge of the waistband.
1 Establish the lengthwise centre of waistband by drawing a line on wrong side or pressing a fold.

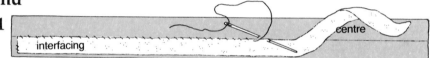

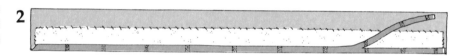

On the wrong side, lay waistband interfacing between one long seam edge and centre. Catch to waistband by hand on all edges, or seal by pressing if interfacing is fusible.
2 Press up seam allowance on non-interfaced long edge. Trim to 6mm/¼in.

3 With right sides together, fold waistband in half along centre line. Machine across ends, trim seams, turn to right side and press.
4 Mark into sections for matching to skirt. With the stiffened side of waistband facing upwards mark off your waist measurement in

Attaching the waistband

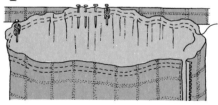 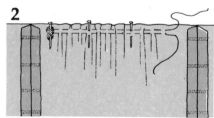 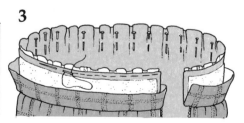

1 With right sides together, lay waistband along waist edge of skirt. Pin across seams at sides and at centres, matching corresponding marks on skirt and waistband. Gently ease the fabric along the gathering thread, holding the loose

ends securely.
2 Gather up each section separately pinning across seams at 2cm/1in intervals, until the skirt is drawn up to fit the waistband. Secure ends of drawn-up thread round a pin, as shown.

3 Tack waistband to skirt along waist fitting line, taking care not to catch in the turned-in free edge of waistband.
Before machining, adjust gathers so that they appear even, taking care that the gathers appear continuous

Instant skirt

You can run up an attractive skirt very quickly from the lengths of ready-shirred fabric that many shops sell. For skirt sizes 10-16 1.5m /1½yd is the recommended amount. Leaving 1.5cm/⅝in seam allowances each side sew fabric in to a tube (from top to bottom to ensure the elastic matches up across the seam). Use a plain seam and neaten the edges by hand or machine overcasting. Fold the bottom selvedge into a narrow hem, fold again to the length required and catchstitch all round on the inside. If you find the shirred section on the waistband too deep, turn half of it to the inside and catchstitch loosely by hand at intervals (to allow 'ease') inside the waistband.

Right: Choose a fabric from the wide range available, complete a seam and a hem and you have an instant skirt.

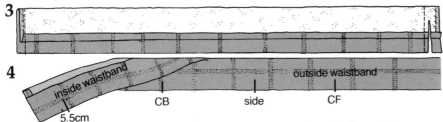

quarters, working from right to left. Leave the 5.5cm/2in underlap for the fasteners on your left.
5 Before pinning waistband to skirt try it round your waist. Waistbands need about 1cm/½in ease to fit comfortably – more if they are wider than 3cm/1¼in.

Pin the waistband where it fits comfortably, allowing the extra 1cm /½in ease. It will tend to tighten up when it is machined.
This fitting is essential – it is very difficult to adjust the waistband after you have machined the gathers.

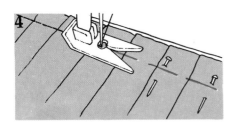

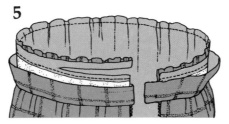

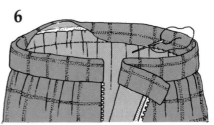

across the seams. With practice, you can omit the tacking and machine slowly and carefully over the pins. This allows you to readjust the gathers while sewing.
4 Machine waistband to skirt along fitting line. This is easier if the

gathers are uppermost, but take care not to catch the free edge of the waistband in the stitching.
5 Remove tackings. Lightly press the seam upwards into the waistband and trim seam allowance to 6mm/¼in.

6 Pull free edge of waistband down inside to cover all raw edges and catchstitch to machine stitches of waistline seam. Catchstitch the lower edges of the waistband together, where it extends to form the underlap.

45

Skirts – the finishing touches

More useful know-how – including simple hemming and how to put in a centre back zip – will help you brush up your dressmaking techniques. Now you have everything you need to know to give a truly professional finish to any type of dirndl skirt that you make.

Hemming a dirndl

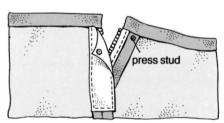

6.5cm hem

You can now make a whole wardrobe of skirts – each one completely different – by following these basic instructions. Lightly gathered, fully gathered, softly pleated or gently shaped skirts, made up in winter weight wool or summery cottons – the choice is yours.

When you are completing your skirt, don't neglect the finishing touches – they will help you to achieve a professional finish. Use hooks and eyes, skirt bars, or Velcro to finish the waistband, and always sew in skirt loops so that you can hang up your skirt.

Pockets are an optional extra, but made in contrasting fabric for a plain skirt, cut on the cross for a checked skirt, or trimmed with lace or binding, they can be used to add that special individual touch.

The easiest type of hem to deal with is one on a straight edge. This is usually finished by just turning up the hem allowance and finishing the raw edge by machine, or with straight seam binding. As the dirndl hem is completely straight, there should be no problems in obtaining an even finish – the side seams should measure the same from waistband to hem, and the centre

Finishing raw edges

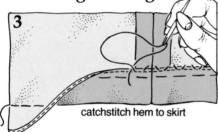

catchstitch hem to skirt

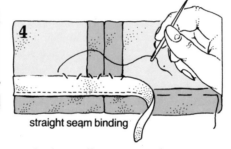

straight seam binding

Two different methods can be used to finish the raw edges of the hem, depending on the fabric's thickness.
3 Light fabrics, for example cottons. Turn 1.5cm/⅝in seam allowance to inside and press. Machine stitch close to this fold if the fabric could fray. Tack hem to skirt, matching seams

on the hem allowance with seams in the body of garment, and catchstitch.
4 Heavier fabrics, for example woollen cloth. Machine straight seam binding to seam allowance, overlapping raw edge of skirt by 1cm/½in. Catchstitch hem to skirt to finish.

Zip protector

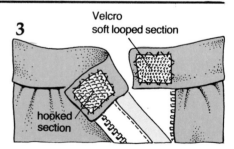

press stud

A protector strip prevents the zip catching your lingerie. Sew the top edge into the waistband when finishing the inside edge. If using petersham ribbon, overcast the top raw edge and press-stud into place.

Skirt fasteners

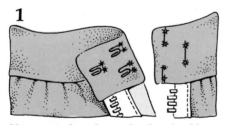

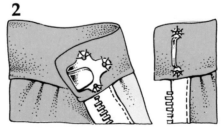

Velcro
soft looped section

hooked section

Skirt waistbands can be finished by a variety of methods. Buttons and buttonholes are dealt with on pages 104, 110, 114 and 146 but other techniques are shown here.
1 Hooks and eyes are, perhaps, the most common finish – use three, positioned as above and sew firmly, securing through interfacing layer.

2 Another alternative is to use a single skirt hook and bar. Sew the base of the hook to inner front edge of overlap, and position the bar above the side seam on the underlap. Sew firmly, making sure the stitches are securely anchored through the layer of stiffening.

3 Velcro can also be used to close the waistband. Cut two pieces the length of the underlap minus 1cm/½in. Trim hooked side by 3mm/⅛in to prevent it catching the skirt. Hem firmly by hand to front inner band. Apply the soft looped section to underlap either by hand or zigzag machine stitching.

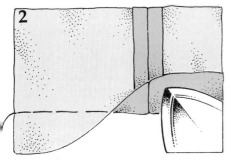

2

front should measure the same from top to bottom as the centre back.

1 Before marking hem, ensure the bottom edge is even all the way round. With a line of chalk or tacking, mark the finished length required all around the hem, at exactly the same distance from the raw edge.

2 Lightly press to inside along this line.

Useful skirt loops

30cm of ribbon, folded in half

inside of skirt

side seam

A shop-bought skirt has loops inside the waistband so that you can hang it in your wardrobe. To make them for your dirndl, cut two pieces of narrow seam binding or ribbon 30cm/12in long. Fold in half and insert at side seams when sewing down free edge of waistband.

Right: A softly pleated skirt made up in fine wool is a versatile addition to your wardrobe. Wear it with a simple, matching jacket and you have a smart but practical outfit that is suitable for any occasion.

Making and attaching patch pockets

Pockets can be many different shapes, with squared or rounded lower edges, made of single fabric or lined. Patch pockets are made up first, then sewn on to the garment like a patch, hence their name. The top edge always needs a facing to prevent it sagging.

It is easier to make up and apply patch pockets in the early stages of the garment, before you have joined the side seams and gathered the top edge. However, you may prefer just to tack them at this stage, adjusting and machining later after you have gathered up the skirt.

1 Cut a rectangle of fabric 18cm× 21.5cm/7in×8½in, or the preferred size for your hand. Cut a piece of lightweight fusible (iron-on) interfacing or ordinary interfacing, measuring 6.5cm×18cm/2½in×7in. Attach this to top of pocket (the facing) by either ironing the fusible interfacing to the wrong side of the fabric, or by catchstitching the ordinary type to the top fold.

2 Neaten edge of facing by hand or machine, trimming seam allowance if necessary.

3 Turn under seam allowances on remaining three sides to wrong side of pocket, folding in bottom seam allowance first. Turn the bottom

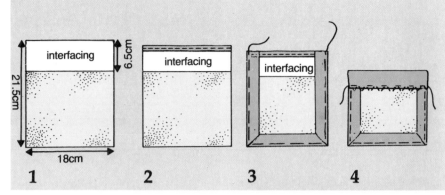

corners of the sides under, to make diagonal folds at the lower corners. Tack and press.

4 Fold top facing over on foldline to inside pocket. Tack, press and catchstitch.

Position pocket on garment with top about 10cm/4in down from waistline and 10cm/4in from centre front. This position will vary, depending on size and fullness of skirt. Tack and machine along sides and lower edges, forming a tiny triangle at the top of each side of the pocket to reinforce the stitching line.

Right: A creative touch for a pocket, making use of the pattern of the fabric to provide a separate, contrasting trim for the pocket top.

Hemming a shaped skirt

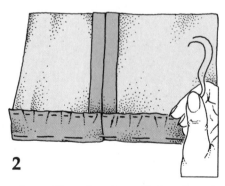

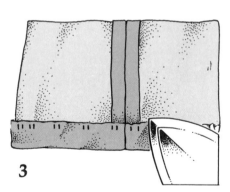

The hem of a skirt that has an A-line design, or is shaped by the flaring of the panels, will have extra fullness round the bottom edge inside the hem. This has to be eased out when completing the hem, to avoid bulkiness.

1 Prepare the hem following instructions for marking a hem on a straight dirndl.
Tack hem to skirt just above the folded bottom edge.

2 Run a line of easing stitches 6mm/¼in from inside raw edge of hem. Distribute fullness evenly along line of easing stitches matching seams on the hem allowance with seams in body of garment.

3 Shrink out excess fullness by pressing hem lightly.
Finish hem by turning raw edge under along line of easing stitches. Tack and catchstitch hem to skirt.

Right: Draw a heart shape on card and use it as a template for cutting a pocket out of fabric or felt. Trim with lace for a soft, feminine finish.

Above: Cut large patch pockets out of plain, toning fabric. Trim with a contrasting piping.

Right: Position your pockets at an angle and flap back to show a contrasting lining. Secure with a button.

Inserting a zip in a centre seam

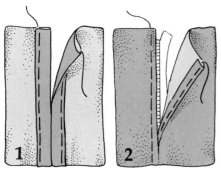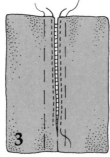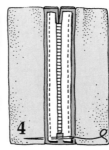

Although a zip can be inserted into a centre seam by the overlapped method, centring it in the opening with an equal allowance on either side gives a neat smooth finish.

1 Stitch the centre back seam, leaving the appropriate opening for the zip. Press under or tack the seam allowances along seamlines.

2 Position seam opening exactly over centre of closed zip, with zip tabs 6mm/¼in below waist seamline.

3 Tack and then machine each side of the zip separately on the right side, using a zipper foot. Work from the waistline to the bottom of zip. The stitching lines should be equal distances from the centre of the zip on both sides of the opening. Slide the zip tab down while stitching top of seam, then close the zip to stitch the rest of the seam.

4 Finish off loose ends on wrong side, and stitch across bottom of zip through lower zip tape and seam allowances by hand.

Making up instructions

Using the techniques given in this chapter, make up your skirt following these step-by-step instructions.

You will need

Cut out skirt sections with paper pattern pieces removed and seam and hem lines marked
Matching thread
Skirt zip
Your choice of skirt fastener
Waistband stiffening or interfacing

Full and lightly gathered skirts only:

Lightweight interfacing for pocket facings
Straight seam binding for hem (where necessary).

Full and lightly gathered skirts

1 If making pockets, make these first and position on front of skirt, either by tacking, or machining if sure of position.
2 Join left-hand seam, leaving opening for zip. Press seam open and neaten edges. Insert zip by overlapped method.
3 Join right-hand seam, press open and neaten edges.
4 Prepare waistband, skirt loops and protector strip if required.
5 Machine a row of gathering stitches on either side of waist seamline. Join waistband to skirt, following instructions for pulling up gathers given on page 44. Insert skirt loops and protector strip before completing inside by hand. Sew on waistband fasteners.
6 Try skirt on, check length and complete hem.

Shaped skirt

1 Join centre front seam and centre back seam, leaving an opening for zip in centre back seam. Press open and neaten edges.
2 Insert zip by centred method. Join side seams, press and neaten
3 Follow steps 4–5 above. Remember waistband closes at centre back, not at side, and mark centre front and sides on waistband accordingly.
4 Try skirt on, check length and complete hem, following instructions for a shaped skirt.

PART 3

A jacket to match

A simple, collarless cardigan jacket with a choice of sleeve lengths is ideal to team with a basic skirt. Start with an unlined version and learn how to set in sleeves and insert shoulder pads using the comprehensive guide to solve any fitting problems.

The basic pattern can be varied in several ways. Design features such as graduated pin tucks at the shoulder or patch pockets will add interest to a plain front. Alternatively, decorative braid and dart shaping will turn it into a Chanel-style jacket.

Interfacing comes in a variety of weights and qualities – learn the facts about interfacing so that you can choose the appropriate type and method of insertion. Full instructions are also given for adding a lining to prolong the jacket's life and give a neat appearance to the inside by concealing all seams and hems.

A wide choice of fabrics can be used for this style which is suitable for both day and evening wear.

Adjusting a jacket pattern

The basic techniques for making a simple jacket are easily mastered, but careful attention to pattern adjustments and fitting are very important. Follow the detailed advice on pattern preparation in this chapter and make yourself a jacket to be proud of.

When you are making a jacket, the most important points to consider are the fit and the finish. A good fabric, crisp front edges, a neat neck-line and professional-looking sleeves provide the finish, but fitting is the key to a perfect garment. It can be the difference between comfort and dis-

Above: Heavier silk, such as this textured silk shantung, is ideal for an unlined cardigan jacket and makes a smart cover-up for a strappy dress.

comfort, as well as influencing the overall appearance.

Making pattern adjustments before cutting out is the first step towards achieving a good fit. Start by pinning the pattern as shown on page 19. Then on the page opposite you can see how to identify the problem areas and make any necessary pattern alterations.

Layouts, fabric suggestions and requirements for the cardigan jacket are given on pages 62–63. Comprehensive fitting instructions are in the next chapter.

Altering the bodice

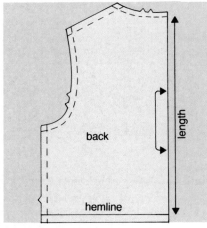

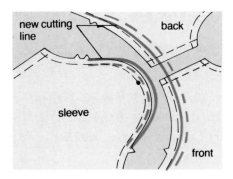

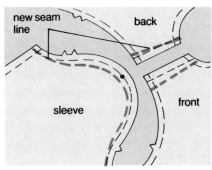

Length
This is usually stated on the envelope of commercial patterns. If not, measure the pattern from centre back neck seamline to the line marked for hem. Compare with your own measurement from nape of neck to proposed length. Shorten or lengthen as necessary (see page 21).

Narrow shoulders
To reduce seam by up to 2cm/¾in, mark the new shoulder point on back and front pattern pieces, measuring from neck point. Re-draw armhole seamline and cutting line on back and front as far as notches. Raise sleeve head if needed to match shoulder position. Do not shorten the shoulder seam too much – instead, slightly extend the shoulder pad into the armhole. If uncertain leave this and following alteration until the fitting stage.

Sloping shoulders
Again, it is better to disguise a pronounced slope with the shoulder pad but if the pattern still requires alteration, re-draw the shoulder seam. Mark a new lower shoulder point on front and back armhole seamlines and connect to neck point.
To remove the surplus from the top of the sleeve, draw a new seamline about 1cm/½in down from centre, curving round top of sleeve to re-join original seamline at notches.

Altering the sleeves

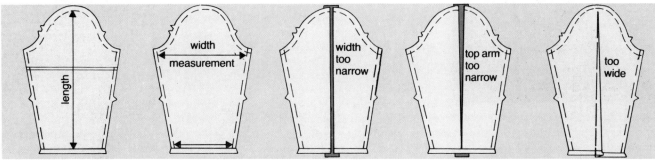

Length
Measure sleeve pattern from top of sleeve to hem fold, excluding top seam allowance. Check your own measurement from shoulder point, over bent elbow to outside wrist, and compare the measurements. Make any adjustments to length on the double alteration line (see page 21), just below the underarm. If alterations are made at the wrist the shape of the sleeve is destroyed.

Width
Jackets are designed to be worn over other garments, so allow plenty of ease. Check your top arm (just below underarm) and wrist measurements and compare with the pattern. Allow enough room to bend your arm comfortably.

Too narrow
If the sleeve is too narrow throughout, draw a line through centre of pattern from top to bottom. Slash open along line and lay the two pieces on to a strip of paper, leaving a gap for the required amount between them. Tape pattern to paper and re-draw seamline.
Trim away excess paper. If the pattern has been enlarged by more than 1.5cm/⅝in let out the bodice shoulder or underarm seams a little to enlarge the armhole for the larger sleeve.

Top arm too narrow
If more room is needed at the top of the sleeve, draw a line through centre of pattern from top to bottom. Slash line from top centre

to within 5mm/¼in of lower edge. Lay pattern piece over paper strip and open pattern at top by required amount. Tape pattern to paper and re-draw seamline. Up to 1.5cm/⅝in extra ease at top of sleeve is acceptable, but let out shoulder or side seams of bodice if necessary.

Too wide
If the sleeve is too wide, draw a line on pattern from centre sleeve at shoulder point to wrist and fold pattern as shown to make a long dart.
If you need to reduce width at under-arm seam of sleeve, make the same reduction on the side seams of the jacket or the sleeve will be too small for the armhole.

Fitting a jacket: the easy way to success

You can give the clothes you make a finish that makes them indistinguishable from expensive shop-bought garments. The secret lies in scrupulous fitting, and the at-a-glance fitting guide given here shows you how to achieve perfect results every time.

Above: Make careful adjustments where necessary during making up, to achieve the good fit characterized by a smooth neckline and shoulderline.

The making up instructions that appear on pages 62–65 should be used in conjunction with the comprehensive fitting chart (below and overleaf). The checklist and diagrams help you to correct any problems that arise during the making up process. Take the time to try on your jacket at the stages indicated and you will be rewarded with a jacket that fits perfectly.

Achieving a perfect fit

Clothes do not necessarily have to fit closely to fit well. They should feel and look good whatever the style, with sufficient ease to allow you to walk, move or sit without straining the seams. When the body is still, they should hang well and keep their shape. Few people would think of buying a garment without first trying it on to see how it looks and fits. The same reasoning should apply to any garment that you make.

For perfect results, try on and adjust at each stage of making up, using the fitting checklist. Do not wait until the end, when alterations might force you to unpick the whole garment. Too many home-made clothes remain unworn because they were not checked for fit during the making up stages, and the prospect of re-making proves too much.

Using a dressmaker's form

Although it is useful to have a dressmaker's form or dummy, the only *true* fitting takes place on the person who is going to wear the garment. Few personal measurements are exactly the same as a dummy – the shoulder slope may be different, for example – and the dummy has to be padded to the correct proportions. However, do use the dummy to work on between personal fittings and to keep the garment in good shape. If you do not have a dummy, keep jackets and coats on padded hangers between sewing sessions, but do not leave heavy fabrics to hang unfinished too long.

When making a personal fitting remember that the garment should always be fitted right side out, the way it will be worn, as the human body is not symmetrical.

Always take into account the clothes you will be wearing under the jacket – a winter version to be worn over jumpers requires more sleeve room than a summer jacket. If possible, ask someone to help you during the fitting process – they will be able to judge the garment's appearance

Jacket fitting problems and how to solve them

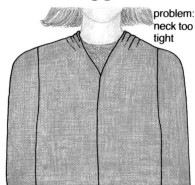

problem: neck too tight

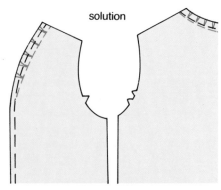

solution

problem: neck too loose

Neck area: too tight
Garment feels too tight and high at neck. Fabric wrinkles at nape of neck, shoulder seams are pulled up and centre front gapes.

Solution Snip entire neck edge from raw edges to staystitching on seamline. If neckline is still tight and is distorting jacket, mark new seamline on both neck edge and facing.

Neck area: too large
Neckline gapes.

Solution Mark a new seamline 5mm/¼in within existing seam allowance to bring it closer to neck,

from every angle more easily than you can, even if you use a second mirror to reflect the back view. The left and right-hand sides should balance and the centre back and front hang vertically.

Fitting checklist

This guide to what makes a 'good fit' applies equally to clothes you have made and shop-bought clothes.

● **Shoulder seam** Straight and slightly sloped, the seam should be towards the back of the shoulder, running from side neck to shoulder point, unless the style dictates otherwise.

● **Neckline** Smooth fit to base of neck with no gaping or pulling across shoulders.

● **Bust** Smooth fit, but enough ease to avoid strained seams, gaping buttonholes or wrinkles at underarm.

● **Back** Enough ease between the shoulder blades for reaching, bending and stretching so that the armhole seam is not strained.

● **Armhole and sleeve** The underarm seam should not be tight in the armpit. Sleeves should be of good appearance both when the arm is straight and when it is bent. Long sleeves should cover the wrist bone when arm is at side.

If problems become apparent in any of these areas during fitting of a garment, use the chart below and overleaf to help you find a solution.

Right: If you have one, work on a dressmaker's form between fittings.

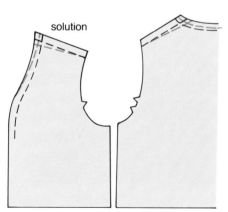

solution

and alter seamline on facing to correspond. If this is insufficient, take a wedge shape out of shoulder seam at neck point, tapering to shoulder point. Alter seamline of facing to correspond.

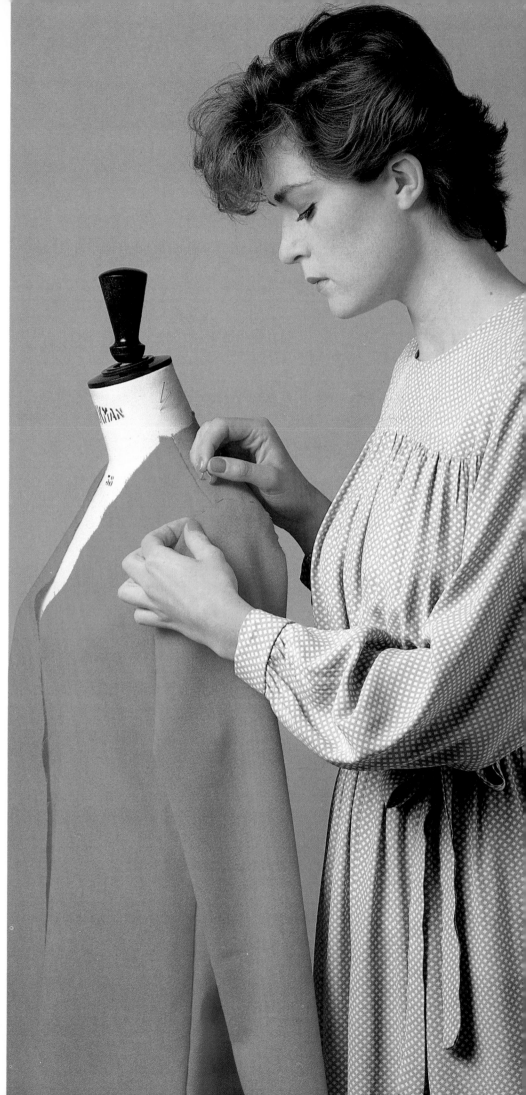

Jacket fitting problems and how to solve them

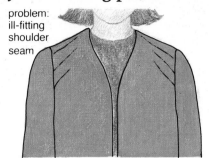

Shoulder area: ill-fitting seam
Folds fall from neck point towards side of armhole, due to sloping shoulders.

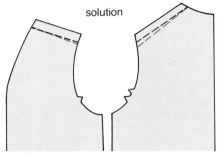

solution

Solution Any drastic alteration will simply emphasize the shoulder slope. Instead, use thicker shoulder pad to level off the shoulder or use a normal thickness pad and take out the excess fabric in a wedge shape with the wide end at the shoulder, tapering towards the neck.

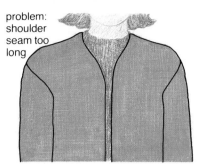

Shoulder area: seam too long
More than the 1.5cm/⅝in seam allowance extends beyond the shoulder point.

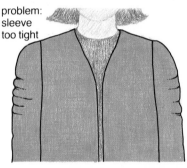

Sleeve: too tight
Upper sleeve too tight, causing fabric to pull into horizontal folds across sleeve head.

Solution Let out top of underarm seam on sleeve, and top of bodice side seams. Take less turning on the sleeve but normal turnings on

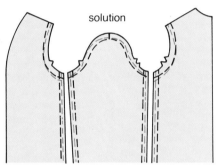

solution

bodice between front and back notches of lower armhole. The extra width gained under the arm and from the sleeve seam should be sufficient, but if not, re-draw entire bodice seamline from shoulder point to underarm on each side of jacket. Make corresponding alterations to sleeve.

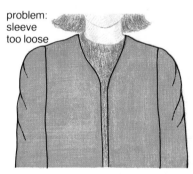

Sleeve: too loose
Long, vertical folds throughout sleeve due to slender arm in too wide a sleeve.

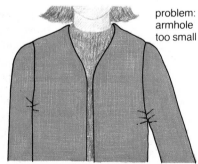

Armhole area: too small
Underarm seam too high and armhole too small. Restricts movement and not enough room allowed for garment underneath.

Solution Clip turnings at underarms to ease curve during fitting. If

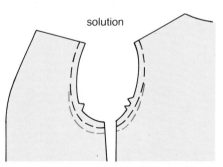

solution

necessary lower armhole at bodice side seam by drawing new lower armhole from underarm, tapering upwards to rejoin notches on front and back. Enlarge the sleeve seam by letting out as much seam allowance as possible.

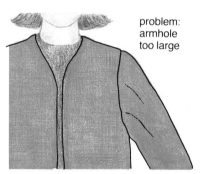

Armhole area: too large
Too much room in armhole.

Solution Take a larger seam allowance at the bodice side seams –in a wedge shape at the armhole, tapering down to join the side seam. If the body of the jacket is the

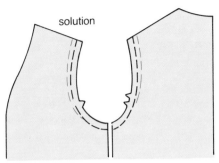

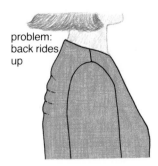

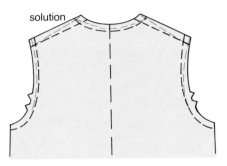

Solution Mark correct shoulder point, then re-draw the armhole seamline on back and front armhole starting from shoulder point and tapering to notches.
If the sleeve does not now fit satisfactorily, take only 1cm/½in turnings at top of the sleeve seam.

Back area: rides up
Garment is stretched across back between armholes and tends to rise up at back neck due to a rounded back. This causes lower hem to stick out and pulls front open.

Solution Let out shoulder seams of back pattern piece only, tapering to the shoulder point. Use a narrower seam allowance at both back neck and back armhole. Take smaller turnings on facings and sleeve to correspond with alterations.

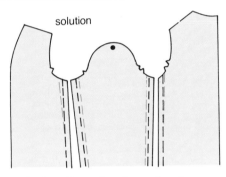

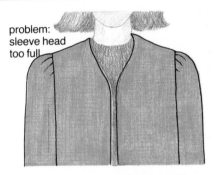

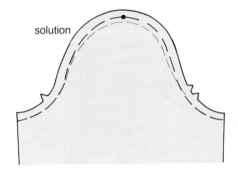

Solution Once the sleeve has been cut, the only solution is to take in the seam by the required amount, either throughout its length, or tapering from underarm to wrist. The bodice side seams must be taken in by the same amount at the top or sleeve will not fit.

Sleeve: head too full
Too much fullness in sleeve head, with pleats instead of gathers, due to too much fabric or incorrect easing.

Solution Measure both sleeve and armhole seamline and compare measurements. The sleeve should

be 2–5cm/¾–2in larger. If it is more, re-draw the sleeve head, lowering the centre point (which matches the shoulder seam of the garment) by up to 1cm/⅜in. Curve the line down to meet the notches and original sleeve seamline. Do not remove all the ease or sleeve will not fit the upper arm.

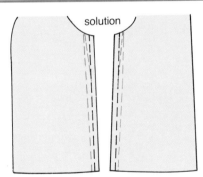

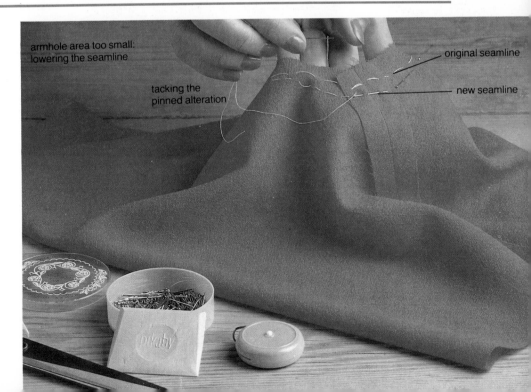

right size make small seam alterations and raise underarm seam slightly. If the jacket is too loose at the hem, take in all down the side seams.
Take in the sleeve seam at underarm so that it will·fit into the smaller armhole.

Sleeves and shoulder pads for simple jackets

A cardigan jacket teams with so many other garments that it is well worth making. This chapter introduces the basic techniques you will need for setting in sleeves – useful both for the jacket shown and for any other garment with plain, set-in sleeves.

Unlined, collarless jackets are ideal for day or evening wear and the neat neckline complements frills, ruffles or any collar detail on shirts, dresses or blouses.

The jacket pattern given on page 74 is of this type – a simple, loosely-structured cardigan style. There is a choice of lengths – to just below waist level or to the hip level – and the sleeves can be full length, elbow length or short.

A cardigan jacket is easy to make but,

Plain set-in sleeves

The one piece, set-in sleeve is most frequently used for jackets and coats. When making a jacket, always bear in mind the style of the garment to be worn beneath it and allow sufficient jacket and sleeve width to avoid crushing full gathered sleeves, ruffles or other trims.

Achieving a good fit

The smooth roll at the top of a plain set-in sleeve is achieved by allowing ease (extra fabric) in the sleeve

Setting in a sleeve

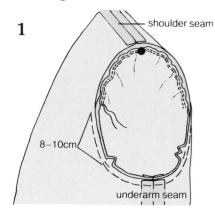

1

— shoulder seam

8–10cm

underarm seam

1 With right sides facing, slip sleeve into armhole. Align underarm seam of garment with sleeve seam, and match front and back notches on armhole and sleeve. Pin and tack underarm section up to notches on each side and run a double row of gathering threads around sleeve top. Working upwards from notches on each side of armhole and matching seamlines, pin, then tack, seam together for a further 8-10cm/ 3¼- 4in towards top of sleeve.

Left: A good shoulderline is achieved by inserting foam or wadding shoulder pads.

as for any jacket – whatever the style – the look of the finished garment very much depends on careful fitting. Having learnt how to make paper pattern adjustments, this chapter is devoted to some of the techniques you need to have at your fingertips when making the jacket. Learn how to set in sleeves perfectly and how to make and fix shoulder pads.

Check the fitting guide on pages 54–57 to achieve a perfect fit at the armhole.

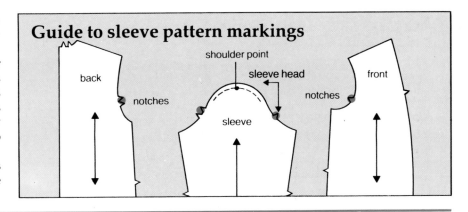

Guide to sleeve pattern markings

back

notches

shoulder point

sleeve head

sleeve

notches

front

head – the top part of the sleeve. The sleeve head is always cut a little larger than the armhole of the jacket so that when the two pieces are joined, the extra fabric allows ease of arm movement where it is most needed – over the top of the sleeve and on the front curve. The back curve of both armhole and sleeve is much less pronounced.

It is important to transfer all armhole and sleeve markings from the pattern to garment sections.

particularly the notches as they are the guides to 'balancing' the sleeve in the armhole so that it hangs perfectly, with the straight grain of the fabric running from shoulder to wrist. The centre top part of the sleeve head (usually marked with a dot or circle on commercial patterns) is a guide to positioning the sleeve correctly at the shoulder. See fitting adjustments on pages 53, 56–57.

Fitting tips

1 Work on both sleeves at the same time, making them up step by step as a pair.
2 Make sure that you cut a left and a right sleeve – it is all too easy to make a mistake and produce two the same.
3 Learn to recognise the shape of sleeves. The front sleeve head has a pronounced curve, whereas the back is fairly straight.
4 Note the difference between front and back notches. The front section of both sleeve and armhole usually has a single notch and the back sections have a double notch.
5 Always join side and shoulder seams and complete all neck and facing details *before* inserting sleeves.
6 Make up sleeves and tack into armhole for an initial fitting. Insert shoulder pads, if used, and check for fit of armhole. Establish sleeve length, allowing an extra few millimetres for tightening up after machining. It is easier to complete sleeve hem before insertion but if you are in doubt about the final length, tack and leave final adjustment until sleeve has been machined in position.
7 If you have never inserted a sleeve before, or are a little unsure about this stage, transfer *all* the markings from the pattern pieces to the garment, including the seamline on both sleeve and jacket, so that you have a very accurate guide to follow.

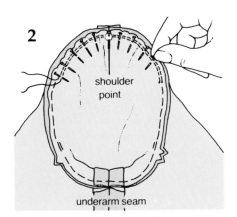

2

shoulder point

underarm seam

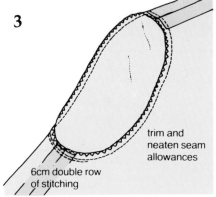

3

trim and neaten seam allowances

6cm double row of stitching

2 Lay the shoulder over one hand and spread the fullness of the sleeve head evenly over it. Pin together the centre shoulder seam and corresponding centre mark on sleeve, then pin round the head of the sleeve at 1cm/½in intervals, inserting the pins at right angles to the raw edges, and matching the seamline exactly. Tack with small stitches, drawing up the gathering to ease sleeve into armhole.

3 Machine sleeve into armhole, with the wrong side of sleeve towards you, starting from the underarm seam. For extra strength, start 3cm/1¼in before the seam and finish 3cm/1¼in after, giving a double row of stitching for 6cm/2½in. Working from the sleeve side makes it easier to avoid creating small pleats in the eased section. Remove tackings and trim seam allowances to 1cm/½in. Neaten both raw edges together, using machine zigzag stitch.

Pressing to finish

The beautifully rounded finish of a sleeve head can be flattened by pressing. If any pressing is necessary, use a tailor's ham, a pad specially designed for the purpose (page 34 shows how to make one), or use a small pad of folded cloth to preserve the roll of the sleeve head. Press only the upper part of the armhole sleeve allowance in towards the sleeve but leave the underarm part upright.

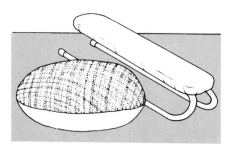

Below: Press the sleeve from the wrong side, using a tailor's ham – its rounded finish maintains the curve of the seam.

Making shoulder pads

Shoulder pads are not just a fashion gimmick, they are an important detail if you want a really good fit on coat or jacket shoulders. They maintain the shoulder line and the shape of the upper sleeve and give support to the rest of the garment, at the same time disguising any tendency to rounded shoulders or uneven shoulder heights.

Ready-made foam or wadding shoulder pads tend to be expensive so it is worth making your own, especially as they can then be layered to the exact size and thickness you require. Foam pads are suitable for dry-cleaning and washing, but are best covered to avoid irritating the skin, or friction with other garments.

Cutting out the pads

Enlarge the pattern for the shoulder pad (right), following the line for the appropriate size. Use this as your pattern piece.

1 Cut two pieces of wadding to make the outside layers of each pad and as many more pieces as necessary to make up the required thickness.

If using foam sheeting, graduate the two shorter edges of all but the two outer pieces for each pad, slicing them at an angle with a razor blade

Inserting shoulder pads

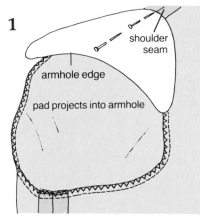

1
shoulder seam
armhole edge
pad projects into armhole

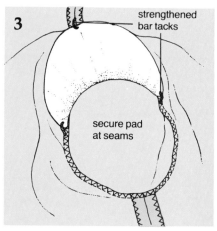

2
position of pad underneath
pin along seam to hold
sleeve cap

3
strengthened bar tacks
secure pad at seams

Insert shoulder pads only when the sleeve has been attached to the garment and all raw edges finished at the armhole. (Although they should be inserted temporarily during fitting.)
1 With the wrong side of the garment towards you and the sleeve hanging inside the garment, position the shoulder pad towards

the back of the shoulder, with the centre point of the armhole edge of pad just to the back of the shoulder seam. The armhole edge of the pad should align with the armhole seam, but project a few millimetres into the sleeve to maintain the fullness. Pin at seams, to hold.
2 Turn garment to right side and insert pins along the shoulder seam

to keep pad in position. Check that it looks smooth.
3 Turn garment back to inside and secure pad to seam allowance on shoulder and armhole seams with 2cm/¾in long bar tacks, strengthened with blanket stitch (see opposite), to allow slight movement, in line with the movement of the body.

or sharp knife. Keep the armhole edge even. Tack diagonally through all layers to secure the pad.

Covering the pads

2 Cut two pieces of lining fabric (such as acetate) for each pad, allowing 2cm/¾in extra fabric all round. Lay pad on wrong side of one lining section, fold the side up over the pad and tack.

3 Position second lining section, wrong side down, on other side of pad. Turn in the edges, taking care not to pull cloth too tight and flatten the pad. Pin and hem to lower section along turned edge with small, neat stitches.

1

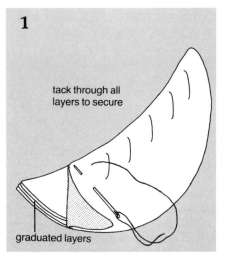

tack through all layers to secure

graduated layers

2

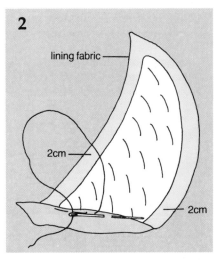

lining fabric

2cm

2cm

3

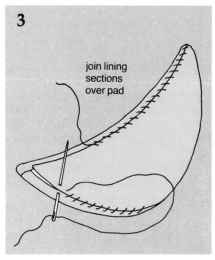

join lining sections over pad

1 square = 1cm

neckline edge

graduate

sizes 10, 12 and 14

graduate

sizes 16 and 18

armhole edge

Enlarge your pattern following the lines for the appropriate size—no need to add seam allowances for the pad, only for the cover.

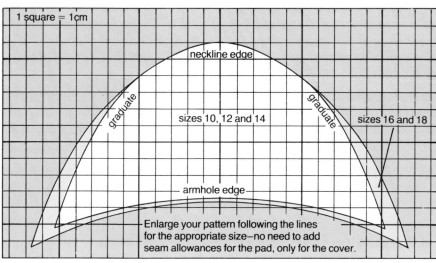

Useful hand stitches

1

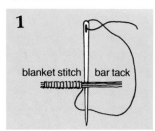

blanket stitch | bar tack

2

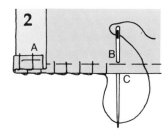

A   B   C

3

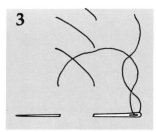

4

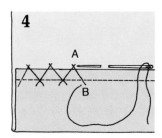

A   B

Bar tack
Used for reinforcement at ends of buttonholes, as thread loop for button or to secure shoulder pads.
Work three or four long stitches closely together to form a loop.
Cover with closely worked blanket stitch (see right).

Blanket stitch
Used as a decorative edging, and in embroidery.
Work from left to right, with fabric edge and needle pointing towards you. Secure thread on wrong side (at **A**) and bring round below edge. Push needle through fabric from right side (at **B**) and bring out (at **C**), within loop of previous stitch.

Diagonal tacking
Provides firmer control over an area than ordinary tacking.
Work parallel stitches with the needle pointing right to left, so that diagonal stitches form on the right side. For even firmer control, decrease space between parallel stitches.

Herringbone stitch
A strong stitch, often used for hems or securing interfacing.
Work from left to right and bring needle through to hem edge. With needle pointing left, catch a few threads of the garment (at **A**). Take another stitch, with needle pointing left, further along the hem (at **B**). Repeat, alternating from garment to hem.

61

The facts about interfacing

The interfacing in a finished garment lies between the facing and the wrong side of the garment. This extra layer of a different fabric gives support, strength and body where necessary. It is usually cut to the shape of the facings, whether these are cut in one with the garment, or separately.

Interfacing is never visible on the completed garment – the only indication of its presence should be the general good finish and crisp edges. It is rare to find a garment requiring no interfacing at all – very soft, floaty designs being one of the few exceptions.

Choose interfacing that is slightly lighter in weight than that of the garment, but firmer to handle. It should be lighter in colour than the garment fabric, and have the same washing or dry cleaning properties. There are two main groups of interfacings – woven ones and non-woven ones that form a fabric with the appearance of lightweight felt. Interfacings are further divided into those that are sewn into place, and those that are bonded on to the fabric, using an iron – hence the name fusible interfacing. Both types are available in a wide variety of weights and widths; the heavier, woven interfacings being the narrowest.

Weights of interfacing If you need a heavyweight interfacing, try using a woven type. This is pliable and will move with the fabric. It may be woven from goat's hair, wool, cotton, or linen – all these work well with coatings and suitings.

Non-woven interfacings are more economical in terms of fabric

required. Because there is no grain line, pattern pieces can be closely interlocked.

The choice of woven interfacings for mediumweight fabrics is wide and varied – lawn, organdie, domette, mull, calico and lightweight canvas are all suitable. For a non-woven interfacing, choose Vilene medium sew-in, or Supershape medium – a fusible type with some 'give' on the bias and width.

Choose from organza (silk or man-made), soft cotton lawn, or net for evening wear if you require a woven interfacing in a lightweight fabric. Suitable non-woven interfacings are Vilene Light iron-on, or Supershape light. It may be best to interface some very fine fabrics with the garment fabric instead.

Attaching interfacings Always test fusible interfacings on a scrap of fabric first to make sure they do not alter the character of the fabric. Put a clean cloth over the ironing board to prevent any adhesive sticking to it and press carefully. Do not move the iron to and fro – this will cause air bubbles between fabric and interfacing.

Sew-in interfacings are normally tacked into position during making up and secured in the seam when the garment is stitched. If a free edge remains, it can be held in place with herringbone stitch or catchstitch.

Availability The range of interfacings on the market is expanding, and many specialist types are now available. Take some of your fabric to the shop and tell the assistant exactly what you require and why. Special interfacings are available for shirts, ties, belts, ball gowns, straps and waistbands.

Cardigan jacket

A jacket is a useful basic garment in any wardrobe – and you can make this one in a variety of fabrics to suit any occasion and to take you right through the seasons. Try a linen-look fabric or raw silk for a smart spring outfit, crisp seersucker for a lovely summery effect and Viyella or light wool for autumn and winter. Later chapters give full instructions for lining the jacket for extra body and warmth.

For an evening look, soft silk is beautiful and luxurious but you could also try velvet, moiré, taffeta or lurex.

You will need
Fabric according to size and style
Matching sewing thread
30cm/12in of 90cm/36in wide
  interfacing
1 pair shoulder pads
Pattern pieces from pages 74 and 75:
1 Jacket back
2 Jacket front
3 Jacket back facing
4 Jacket front facing
5 Jacket sleeve
7 Pocket (optional – see page 72 for instructions)

Opposite: Waist-length versions of the jacket, showing different sleeve lengths.

Fabric quantity chart
Long cardigan jacket

Size	10	12	14	16	18
Bust (cm)	83	87	92	97	102
90cm	2.25	2.30	2.30	2.35	2.35m
115cm*	1.60	1.60	1.60	1.65	1.75m
140cm	1.45	1.45	1.45	1.45	1.50m
150cm*	1.25	1.30	1.30	1.30	1.35m

Short cardigan jacket

Size	10	12	14	16	18
90cm	1.70	1.70	1.75	1.75	1.75m
115cm*	1.20	1.20	1.25	1.30	1.35m
140cm	1.20	1.20	1.25	1.25	1.25m
150cm*	1.00	1.00	1.05	1.05	1.10m

*without nap. All other fabric widths are with or without nap.
Fabric quantities are given in metres and include amounts for optional patch pockets (see layouts).

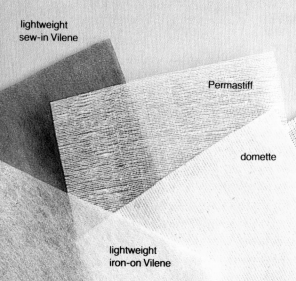

lightweight
sew-in Vilene

Permastiff

tie interfacing

domette

lightweight
iron-on Vilene

linen duck

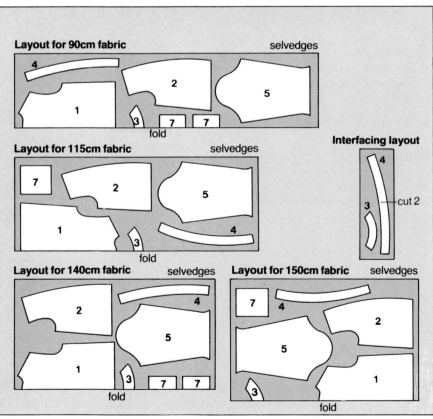

Layout for 90cm fabric — selvedges

4 · 1 · 2 · 5 · 3 · 7 · 7

fold

Layout for 115cm fabric — selvedges

7 · 2 · 5 · 1 · 3 · 4

fold

Layout for 140cm fabric — selvedges

2 · 4 · 5 · 1 · 3 · 7 · 7

fold

Layout for 150cm fabric — selvedges

7 · 4 · 2 · 5 · 1 · 3

fold

Interfacing layout

4 · 3 — cut 2

long jacket
long sleeves

long jacket
short sleeves

short jacket
short sleeves

short jacket
long sleeves

Preparing to cut out

Make any necessary adjustments to sleeve width or garment length remembering that a 4cm/1½in hem allowance is included.

Fold fabric right sides together, as shown on fabric layout for your fabric width. Pin all pattern pieces to fabric, placing back (1) and back neck facing (3) to fold. Cut out carefully. Transfer pattern markings to fabric and remove pattern pieces. Using pattern pieces 3 and 4 again, cut out interfacing for back neck and front edges. Cut one back neck interfacing to a fold, and two front interfacings.

63

Making up the cardigan jacket

Put the jacket together as follows, paying careful attention to each fitting stage. Before you start fitting, consult the charts on pages 54–57. If possible, ask someone you know to help you make any adjustments that are necessary, as it is difficult to mark accurate alterations with pins or tailor's chalk while you are wearing the garment.

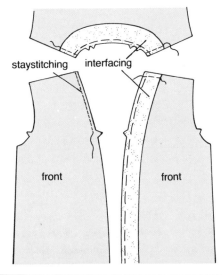

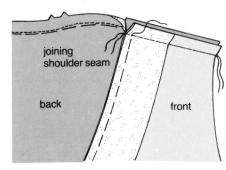

Step 1 Staystitch back and front necklines to prevent fabric stretching. Interface back neck and fronts of jacket, tacking interfacing (or pressing if fusible) to wrong side of fabric.

Step 2 With right sides together, pin and tack side and shoulder seams. Machine shoulder seams only. Remove tacking, press seams open and neaten edges.
Tack one sleeve seam in preparation for first fitting.

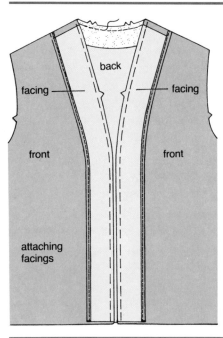

Step 3 Join facings, right sides together, at shoulders. Trim seams to 1cm/⅜in and press open. Neaten outside edge of facing and press. With right sides together, position facings on jacket, matching notches and shoulder seams. Pin, tack and machine all round on seamline. On heavier fabrics reduce seam bulk by layering (see step 4, page 69); for lighter fabrics it is sufficient to snip into neck curve at 1cm/⅜in intervals and trim seam to 5mm/¼in.

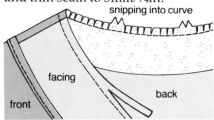

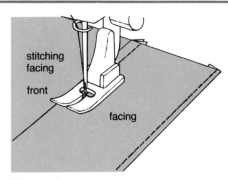

Step 4 On inside, press facing and seam allowances away from bodice. Working on right side, stitch facing to seam allowances as close as possible to seam.
Roll facing back. Tack from wrong side all the way round through facings, catching only a few threads from the front of the garment, 2mm/⅛in in from the edge. Press.

Second fitting
Try on jacket, slipping shoulder pads into position. Check hang of sleeve and width of armhole and mark adjustments if necessary. Remove jacket.

Step 7 Distributing ease evenly, machine sleeves into armholes. Remove tackings and press carefully, using a tailor's ham or roll of cloth (see page 60).
Stitch shoulder pads into jacket as instructed on pages 60–61.
Catchstitch facing to garment at shoulder seam.

Third fitting
Try on jacket, align centre fronts and decide final hem length of both jacket and sleeves. Mark with chalk.

Step 8 Unpick about 10cm/4in of tacking from the centre front edges and open out facing. Neaten lower hem edge.
Cut a strip of interfacing 1cm/½in narrower than the width of the hem allowance and the measurement of the hem edge. Tack (or press if fusible) just above foldline of hem on wrong side.

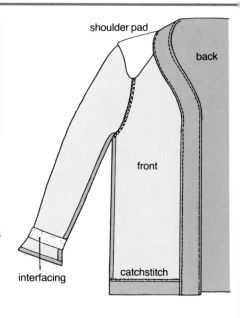

First fitting
Try on jacket bodice and slip
shoulder pad inside shoulder
area. Mark any necessary
alterations at shoulder,
remembering that sewing the
neckline will draw the shoulder
up a little. Check jacket width, and
see how it hangs.
Slip the sleeve over your arm and
pin to shoulder and underarm of
bodice. Check only the sleeve
width at this point. Check the
width of the back between the
shoulders and make sure the
centre fronts meet. Remove the
jacket and unpin sleeve.

Step 5 With right sides together,
matching notches, machine side
seams. Remove tacking, press
seams open and neaten edges.

Step 6 With right sides together,
matching notches, join sleeve
seams following the shape of the
seam at the wrist. This slopes
outwards so it will lie flat at the
tapered wrist when the hem is
turned up.
Remove tackings, press seams open
(using a sleeve arm if you have
one), and neaten.
Pin and tack both sleeves into
armhole (see pages 58 and 59). Do
not try to perfect top ease at this
stage – wait until after the second
fitting so that you will know exactly
how the garment hangs.

Turn up hem over interfacing,
tacking and pressing the hem fold
edge to give a good finish. Pin, tack
and catchstitch neatened hem edge
to garment.
Fold front facings back to inside of
jacket and catchstitch facings to
hem.

Step 9 Finish sleeve hem in the
same way as jacket hem, inserting a
strip of interfacing at wrist for extra
strength.
Remove any tackings left in the
garment and gently press out
tacking marks.

Making a short jacket . . .
Cut out pattern pieces 1, 2 and 4
along the lines marked for the
shorter length. Note that the
pattern pieces interlock more
closely on the cutting layout.
Make up the jacket as above, but to
the shorter length.

. . . with short sleeves
The jacket can also be made up with
elbow length or short sleeves.
Simply measure from shoulder to
elbow, or to length required, and

*Above: The short jacket, made up with
elbow-length sleeves and teamed with a
matching softly pleated skirt, from
page 43.*

transfer this measurement to
pattern piece, measuring down
from shoulder point. Add 4cm/
1½in for hem and re-draw hem
shaping. Cut the pattern piece to
length required and make up as for
long sleeve. (Do not make such a
large alteration in size on the double
alteration lines – it will distort the
shape of the sleeve.)

Lining and trimming a Chanel-style jacket

The Chanel-style jacket is another very easy to make and easy to wear variation of the patterns given on page 74. To make this stylish version, or the short version given on page 51, use the knowhow gained from making the cardigan jacket, adding darts, a braid trim and a simple lining.

The Chanel-style jacket has bust darts, a high, collarless round neck and meets edge to edge at the centre front. It is named after its designer, Gabrielle 'Coco' Chanel (1883-1971), a French fashion designer who played a significant part in the transformation of women's clothing during the twentieth century. Chanel designed casual, yet elegant, easy-to-wear clothes, many of which were inspired originally by men's garments. For example, a polo-necked sweater gave rise to the first jersey dress, and a boy's school blazer was copied and re-cut to make a woman's version. Women appreciated the freedom and comfort afforded by her designs, many of which have proved to have a timeless appeal. The Chanel jacket has re-appeared several times in fashion collections over the years and is as popular now as it ever was. You can turn your jacket into a suit by adding a skirt in a matching or contrasting fabric – an A-line or full dirndl skirt are the most suitable styles to choose. Use a wool mixture for a suit for cooler days, or a slubbed linen for spring or summer. Emphasize the clear cut design lines with parallel rows of braid on the front edges and neckline, and learn how to add a simple lining to make yourself a smart and hard-wearing jacket that will never date.

Adding braid to a jacket

The Chanel jacket is traditionally trimmed with one or two rows of braid, to echo and emphasize the lines of the design and add interest to an otherwise plain finish.

When choosing braid, take a sample of fabric with you and keep the style of the garment in mind. Lay possible trimmings over the fabric and consider points like colour and texture. A heavy braid may be overwhelming, while a dainty trim may be too insignificant.

Scroll braid is most widely associated with the Chanel jacket. It has a textured finish and the best width to choose is 5mm/¼in, particularly if two rows are used. Soutache or Russian braid, ric-rac or any flat, narrow braid are also suitable.

Preparing the braid

If the braid contains a percentage of wool or cotton, it may be subject to shrinkage. It may also have stretched while wound round the card in the shop, so leave it for 24 hours to relax back into shape, then press lightly with a damp cloth. Synthetic trimmings will not require this treatment. The best time to attach the braid is when the hem of the garment is completed. Decide on the best position by laying the braid over the jacket. If you are using a single row of narrow braid, 3cm/1¼in from the front edge looks best. Mark the final position with a line of tailor's chalk or tacking on the right side of the garment. Make sure it is parallel to the front edge, and even around the neckline. If there are two rows of braid, be sure to keep them an equal distance apart.

Applying the braid

Braid can be applied by hand or machine, tacking first. Work from the right side when applying soutache braid, sewing it by machine or by hand using prickstitch. The stitches should be made in the centre groove of the braid, where they will disappear. Thicker, textured braids such as scroll braid are best sewn on by hand, working from the wrong side using fairly loose stitches. If thicker braid is machine-stitched, use a larger stitch with less upper tension than usual, to avoid puckering the garment fabric. Work from the right side, positioning the stitching line where it will be least obvious. Whether stitching by hand or machine, avoid stretching the braid and ease it gently around curves. Take care on sharp, right-angled corners as at the top front neck. Scroll braid and most narrow braids can be bent around right-angled corners and secured with one or two small handstitches. Soutache braid will turn without difficulty.

To prevent fraying or unravelling of ends when cut, bind a piece of sticky tape over the braid, centring it over the point where you wish to cut. Cut through tape and braid – the tape will hold the cut ends in place. Do not remove the tape until you are ready to finish the edges.

Finishing off the braid

If the jacket is to be lined, and the braid is not too thick, the raw edges can be taken round the lower edge and hidden within the hem of the lining. If the jacket is unlined, overcast the raw edges and turn under 5mm/¼in, using tiny slipstitches.

If you are using thick, heavy braid, the raw edges will have to be neatened on the hem fold on the right side. Alternatively, continue the braid round the jacket, parallel to the hem edge.

Right: Flat braid defines the shape of the long version of the Chanel jacket. Inset: A selection of suitable braids.

Mitring a corner on braid

Flat, woven braid in narrow widths (up to 1.5cm/⅝in) is also suitable for trimming the Chanel-style jacket. It is less flexible than other types of braid and therefore a diagonal fold or mitre has to be made where the braid has to turn a sharp corner.

1 Lay braid on the right side of the garment and pin in position as far as the corner. Turn a right-angled corner by folding braid and stitching diagonally on the wrong side of the braid. Pin across the fold, matching the

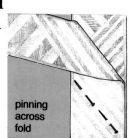
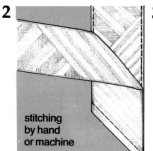
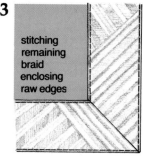

pattern where possible.

2 Sew on the braid and when you come to the corner, machine or hand-sew across the diagonal fold on the wrong side and trim the seam, finger pressing it open.

3 Pin the rest of the braid into place along the next straight edge. Continue sewing around the edges of the braid, enclosing the raw edges.

Making a dart

A dart is a method of disposing of unwanted areas of fullness in a garment, shaping it to fit areas like the shoulders, waist and bust. It takes in a triangular area of fabric which is stitched from the wide end to the point.

Darts vary in width, length and shape. Some are short and straight, others curve slightly, according to the effect required and the area being fitted, but all should be unobtrusive. They are shown on paper patterns by small circles, broken or solid lines. On a multi-size pattern several sizes are given so make sure you transfer the correct size dart.

Transfer the dart pattern markings to the fabric using tailor's chalk, tailor's

tacks or a tracing wheel and dressmaker's carbon paper. For complete accuracy, mark the stitching line of the whole dart. The circles should be treated like pattern notches, and placed together accurately.

Pressing finished darts For the best finish, darts should be pressed over a curved surface, such as a tailor's ham or a pad of clean, smooth cloth placed on the ironing board.

Vertical darts, such as those at shoulder and waist, are pressed towards centre front or centre back. Horizontal darts, such as underarm bust darts or elbow darts, are pressed downwards, towards waist or wrist. Darts on bulky fabric are slashed to within 5mm/¼in of the tip, and pressed open.

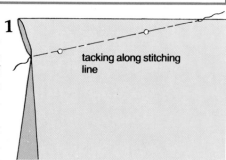

1 Fold dart, right sides together, along centre line matching the pattern markings each side. Pin and tack along stitching line. If you have used tailor's tacks, remove them at this stage.

The Chanel-style jacket

The jacket can be made in two lengths. To make the short version simply cut along the lines indicated on the pattern.

You will need

Fabric according to size and style
Matching sewing thread
0.20m/¼yd of 90cm/36in wide interfacing
2.20m/2⅜yd of 90cm/36in wide lining *or* 1.50m/1⅝yd of 140/54in lining
1 pair of shoulder pads
3.90m/4¼yd of braid (optional)
Pattern pieces, pages 74 and 75:
1 and 3 Jacket back and facing
8 and 9 Jacket front and facing
5 Sleeve

Fabric requirements

Size	10	12	14	16	18
Bust (cm)	83	87	92	97	102cm
(in)	32½	34	36	38	40in

Long version

90cm*	2.20	2.30	2.30	2.35	2.35m
115cm	1.60	1.60	1.60	1.65	1.75m
140cm	1.40	1.40	1.40	1.50	1.50m

Short version

90cm*	1.70	1.70	1.75	1.75	1.75m
115cm	1.20	1.20	1.30	1.30	1.40m
140cm	1.20	1.20	1.20	1.30	1.30m

* without nap

Fabric quantities are given in metres – if your retailer sells fabric in yards, use a conversion chart.

Cutting out

Pin the pattern on the fabric, following the appropriate cutting layout. Cut out carefully and transfer pattern markings using whatever method you prefer. Remove paper pattern pieces and use pieces 9 and 3 to cut out the interfacing for the jacket.

Making up

The jacket is made in the same way as the cardigan jacket (see pages 64 and 65) with the following amendments to the instructions. Complete steps 1, 2 and the first fitting as for the cardigan jacket, stitching the bust darts in the front of the jacket and pressing them down.

Cutting layouts for jacket

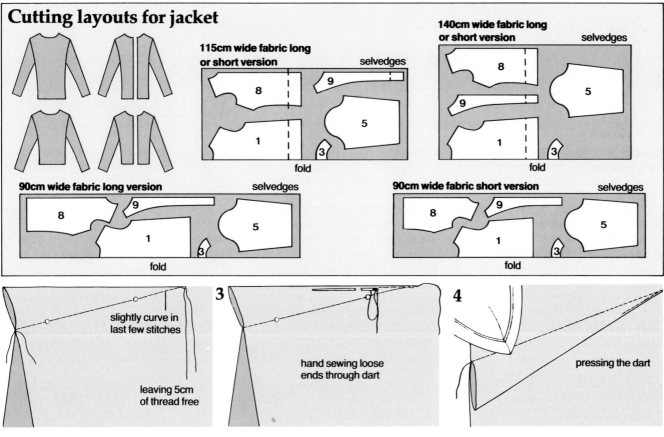

115cm wide fabric long or short version — selvedges

8   9
1   5   3

fold

140cm wide fabric long or short version — selvedges

8
9
1   5   3

fold

90cm wide fabric long version — selvedges

8   9
1   5   3

fold

90cm wide fabric short version — selvedges

8   9
1   5   3

fold

---

3 slightly curve in last few stitches — leaving 5cm of thread free

3 hand sewing loose ends through dart

4 pressing the dart

2 Stitch, following the tacking line exactly, starting at the wide end and tapering to the point. The last few stitches on the fabric should be curved in slightly towards the tip of the dart to prevent a sharp-angled ending which will make the dart noticeable. Allow the machine to run off the end of the fabric. Leave at least 5cm/2in of thread free.

3 Thread needle and stitch back through the dart to prevent unravelling. Do not tie thread ends in a knot as this will wear a hole in fabrics when pressed. Reverse sewing on the machine is not suitable either – it spoils the fine tapered finish.

4 Press the folded edge and stitching as far as the point, not beyond. Then, opening out the garment, press the fabric either side of the dart before gently pressing it in the appropriate direction.
Check the finish on the right side. The stitching line should be flat and the point smooth, with no wrinkles or creases in the fabric.

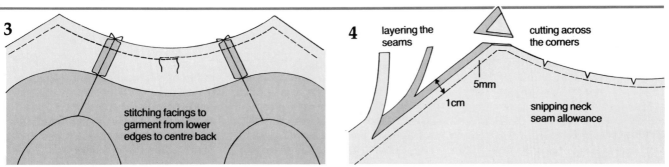

3 stitching facings to garment from lower edges to centre back

4 layering the seams — cutting across the corners — 5mm — 1cm — snipping neck seam allowance

Step 3 With right sides together, join facings at shoulder seams. Trim seams to 1cm/½in and press open. If the jacket is to be left unlined, neaten entire outside edge of facing and press or bind all raw edges with seam binding.
With the right sides together, matching notches and shoulder seams, pin and tack facings to jacket.

Starting at the lower edge, machine along seamline up to neck edge. Leave needle in work at corner, take one stitch across corner and continue stitching carefully round neck curve, to centre back. Break stitching, turn work over and stitch the other side working from hem to centre back of neck in the same way, overlapping the stitching at centre back.

Step 4 Reduce the seam bulk by layering the turnings. Trim the jacket front seam allowance closest to the garment surface to just under 1cm/½in, and the facing seam allowance to 5mm/¼in. Trim and snip the neck seam allowances and cut across the corners.
Complete as for the cardigan jacket, pages 64 and 65, from step 4 onwards.

Inserting a simple jacket lining

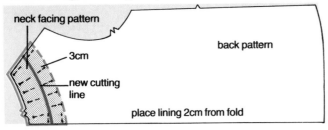

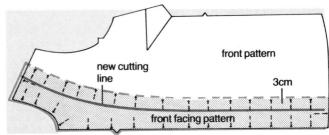

A jacket lining is not difficult to make and the finished result amply repays the little extra time it takes. A lining in a jacket adds warmth and body to the garment and hides seams and darts. Buy lining to suit both the fabric of the jacket and the type of wear it will get. A lightweight, silky lining is preferable for an evening jacket, while a jacket for everyday use requires a heavier satin type of lining.

Making the lining pattern
Lining fabric has very little give and therefore it must be cut with extra ease to allow for body movement. If you plan to use the same pattern frequently, it is worthwhile making a separate lining pattern using greaseproof paper or dressmaker's graph paper and incorporating the following adjustments.

Back Pin back pattern over back neck facing pattern, matching notches at neck edge. Draw a new cutting line around neck, 3cm/1¼in up from lower edge of facing, following the curve.

On the centre back seam, mark an instruction to place the pattern 2cm/¾in from the fold. This gives 4cm/1½in extra allowance in the back which is used to form a 2cm/¾in pleat.

Front Pin front pattern piece over front facing, matching notches. Draw a new cutting line for the lining 3cm/1¼in from the outside curved edge of the facing on the front and neck edges.

No alterations to the sleeve pattern are necessary.

Making the lining

Cut out the lining, observing the alterations made to the pattern pieces and remembering to place the back pattern 2cm/¾in from the fold. Join side, shoulder and sleeve seams of the lining as for the jacket. If the lining is attached all the way round the hem, there is no need to neaten any of the raw edges on either lining or the main garment. If the lining is left free at the hem, neaten the side seams of both jacket and lining.

1 Insert the sleeves into the body of the lining as for the main jacket, easing them to fit the armholes. Make the back pleat by folding 2cm/¾in to one side of the centre, press and tack the layers together at the top. Press a 1.5cm/⅝in turning to the wrong side around the front and neck edge of lining, clipping into the curves where necessary. Trim the armhole turnings to 1cm/½in and press them towards sleeve. Turn the completed main garment inside out and the lining right side out. Apply the wrong side of the lining to the wrong side of the garment. Pin in position along side and shoulder seams, smoothing lining over garment to fit.

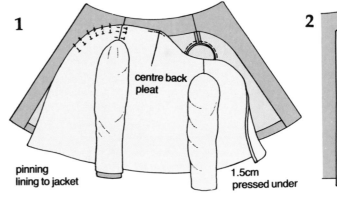

2 Pin lining in position around armholes, inserting pins through all the layers to hold.
Pin pressed edge of lining to jacket all around front and neck edges inserting pins at right angles to seamline. Tack to hold and remove pins. Catchstitch lining to garment, starting 8cm/3¼in above lower hem edge and working up front facing around neck edge and down to 8cm/3¼in above lower edge on the other side.
Trim the lining to 1cm/½in longer than the finished jacket.
If the lining is to be left loose around the hem, press under a turning of 2.5cm/1in and then turn under the raw edge and machine or hand-stitch the hem to finish. The hemmed lining will be 1cm/½in shorter than the jacket. The lining can be secured at the side seams by working a thread chain between the

main garment and the lining. Catchstitch the remaining lower front edges of lining to facings.
If the lining is to be attached at the hem, press under a turning of 2.5cm/1in. Catchstitch the lower, trimmed edge of the lining to the upper edge of the hem turning on the main garment, matching side seams. Take in the excess fabric in a pleat at the lower edge of centre back. When the jacket is worn, the lining will slip down over the stitching, but will not hang below the lower edge. Catchstitch the free lower front edges of the lining to the facings. Remove all pins from side seams. To hem the sleeve, smooth lining towards lower edge and trim to 1cm/½in longer than hemmed sleeve. Catchstitch lower edge of lining to upper edge of hem turning, so that the lining will slip down to hide stitches during wear.

Above: Add graduated pin tucks and patch pockets to the front of a plain jacket.

Pockets and pin-tuck jacket variations

Transform the basic jacket with the addition of pin tucks to the plain front. Learn how to make them, and how to attach patch pockets in a variety of ways, then choose your fabric and make the ideal jacket to complement an evening dress or frilly blouse.

Pockets and pin tucks are both optional features on the cardigan jacket, and this chapter gives you detailed guidance on how to make them. They are valuable and frequently used dressmaking processes – tucks, for example, make an attractive feature on blouses and dresses. Co-ordinate the cardigan jackets with the camisole tops and dresses on pages 192 and 199 – the pin-tucked version is a good choice for fine or evening fabrics.

Patch pockets

Patch pockets are just one of a large variety of pocket types. The easiest to make and apply, they are prepared first and then stitched to the outside of the garment, whereas other types of pocket are inserted into seams or cut into the garment.

Making pockets

Where a pair of pockets is required, as on a jacket front, cut, prepare and make them as a pair to ensure that they are exactly the same shape. Use a pattern piece wherever one is supplied, but for full instructions on how to cut out and make simple patch pockets see page 48.

When tacking or sewing pockets by hand, always work on a flat surface. Support the bulk of the garment on the work surface while machining, so that the pocket edges are not pulled out of line.

Apply the pockets as early as possible during the making up of a garment, preferably before joining the side seams. Follow the pocket placement line on the pattern whenever there is one, or else find a comfortable and attractive position, with the top edge parallel to the garment hem and the sides parallel to the centre front of the garment. (As the side seams are often shaped, they are not a good guide.) If there is no pocket placement line, making it difficult to establish the correct position, wait until the garment hem is completed before applying the pockets.

Pin pocket to garment, checking alignment to centre and lower edges and keeping fabric absolutely smooth. Tack diagonally in rows,

Applying patch pockets

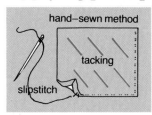 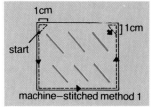 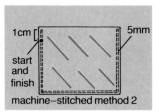 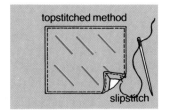

Hand-sewn method Lift pocket edge and slipstitch to garment, keeping stitches very small but not too tight. This method is not suitable for hard wear – to strengthen you can backstitch from inside.

Machine-stitched method (1) A single row of stitches is adequate for most lined pockets. Start about 1cm/½in down from top on side edge. Work diagonally to a point 1cm/½in from top corner, pivot needle, stitch along top edge to top corner, pivot needle and work round outer edges, pivoting needle at each corner until opposite top edge is reached. Complete a triangle to match opposite corner.

Machine-stitched method (2) A double row of stitches is best on unlined pockets to stop seam allowances fraying. Start about 1cm/½in down from top edge and about 5mm/¼in from the side. Work up to top edge, pivot needle and stitch to corner, then pivot needle and work downwards and all around

Tucks – a designer touch

Tucks made on the right side of the fabric add design interest to clothes and may be placed horizontally, across a bodice or yoke for example, or run vertically from neck to waist of a dress or blouse. Some tucks are stitched down their full length, others are only partly stitched and can be used to give shaping to a garment, taking on the function of a dart. These are known as released tucks.

Tucks may be wide or narrow, depending on the fabric and their purpose. Pin tucks are the narrowest, so called because very fine tucks – the width of a pin – were used on the lingerie and fine blouses of the past.

Making released pin tucks

Transfer the pattern markings for pin tucks from the pattern on to the fabric with particular care as they indicate the exact points to join and the stitching lines to follow. Use

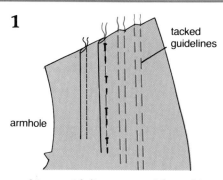

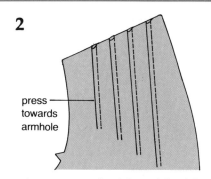

tacking guidelines to avoid marking delicate fabrics.

When sewing, deal with each tuck separately. Do not pin and tack the whole row at once as each perfect stitched tuck is a guide for the next one.

1 With wrong sides together, pin tucks along guidelines, matching marks exactly. Tack, then press before machining to prevent the folded edge from twisting.

Machine from shoulder down to end of stitching line as indicated, using an even-feed foot if the fabric is slippery.

Pull loose threads through to inside of garment. Thread each one separately through a needle and run it back through the stitching for 2.5cm/1in, finishing with a back stitch to secure. Never make a knot on fine fabrics – it may press through and make a hole.

2 Press the stitched part of the tuck only towards the armhole. Do not press the area below as this is meant to fall softly in folds.

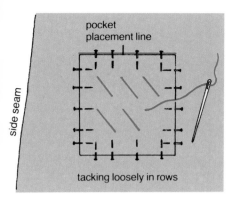

pocket
placement line

side seam

tacking loosely in rows

working from top to bottom and keeping stitches loose to avoid drawing up the pocket.

the pocket. Pivot the needle at each corner. When you reach the opposite top edge stitch along about 5mm/¼in, then pivot needle and stitch down and round pocket, parallel to and inside the row of stitching. Finish where you started.
Topstitched method Sewing a thick pocket directly to a garment tends to draw up the fabric. If your design requires a topstitched finish on such a fabric, topstitch the prepared pocket separately, using a fairly large stitch. Then apply the pocket to the garment by hand, using the invisible hand-sewn method.

Pin-tucked jacket

The pin-tucked version of the jacket is ideal for evening and works well made up in soft fabrics. Choose from silks, crêpe or crêpe de chine for evening or soft cottons or Viyella for day wear. Avoid patterned fabric as the effect of the tucks will be lost.

You will need
Fabric, according to size and style (see chart)
Matching sewing thread
0.20m/¼yd of 90cm/36in-wide interfacing
1 pair of shoulder pads

Making up
Cut out the jacket as instructed on page 63 using the pattern pieces 1, 3, 4, 5, 7 and 6 for the front, instead of piece 2.
Follow the layouts on page 63, noting that the pieces will not

Above: The tucks on this silk evening jacket are all sewn to the same length.

interlock so closely because of the extra fabric required by the pin-tucked front. Follow the instructions, steps 1 to 9 for jacket, on pages 64–65, but pin, tack and machine the tucks on each front during step 1.
Note The pin tucks on the pattern are graduated in length. If you would prefer four tucks the same size, use the shortest tuck as a guide and stitch the others to this length.

Attaching the pockets
Apply the optional patch pockets during step 1, matching the pocket to the jacket front placement line.

Making up a short jacket

To make the short version of the pin-tucked jacket, or a version with short sleeves, follow the making up instuctions on page 65.

Fabric quantity chart

Size	10	12	14	16	18
Bust (cm)	83	87	92	97	102

Long cardigan jacket with pin tucks

	10	12	14	16	18
90cm	2.25	2.30	2.30	2.35	2.35m
115cm*	1.60	1.60	1.60	1.85	1.85m
140cm	1.45	1.45	1.45	1.45	1.50m
150cm*	1.30	1.30	1.30	1.35	1.50m

Short cardigan jacket with pin tucks

	10	12	14	16	18
90cm	1.70	1.70	1.75	1.75	1.75m
115cm*	1.20	1.25	1.25	1.45	1.50m
140cm	1.45	1.45	1.45	1.45	1.50m
150cm*	1.30	1.30	1.30	1.35	1.50m

* fabric without nap. All other fabric widths are with or without nap. Fabric quantities are given in metres and include amounts for optional patch pockets.

Graph for cardigan, tucked and Chanel-style jackets

1.5cm/ 5/8 in seam allowance included

4cm/1½ in hem allowed

1 square = 5cm

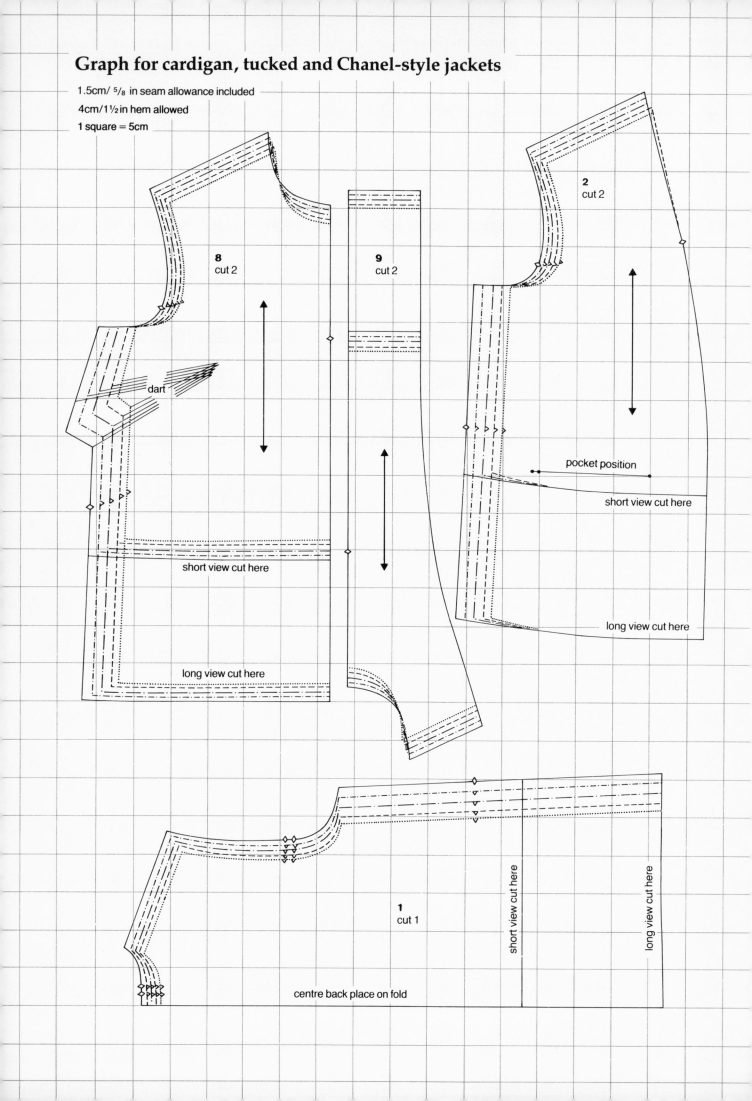

8
cut 2

9
cut 2

2
cut 2

dart

pocket position

short view cut here

short view cut here

long view cut here

long view cut here

long view cut here

short view cut here

long view cut here

1
cut 1

centre back place on fold

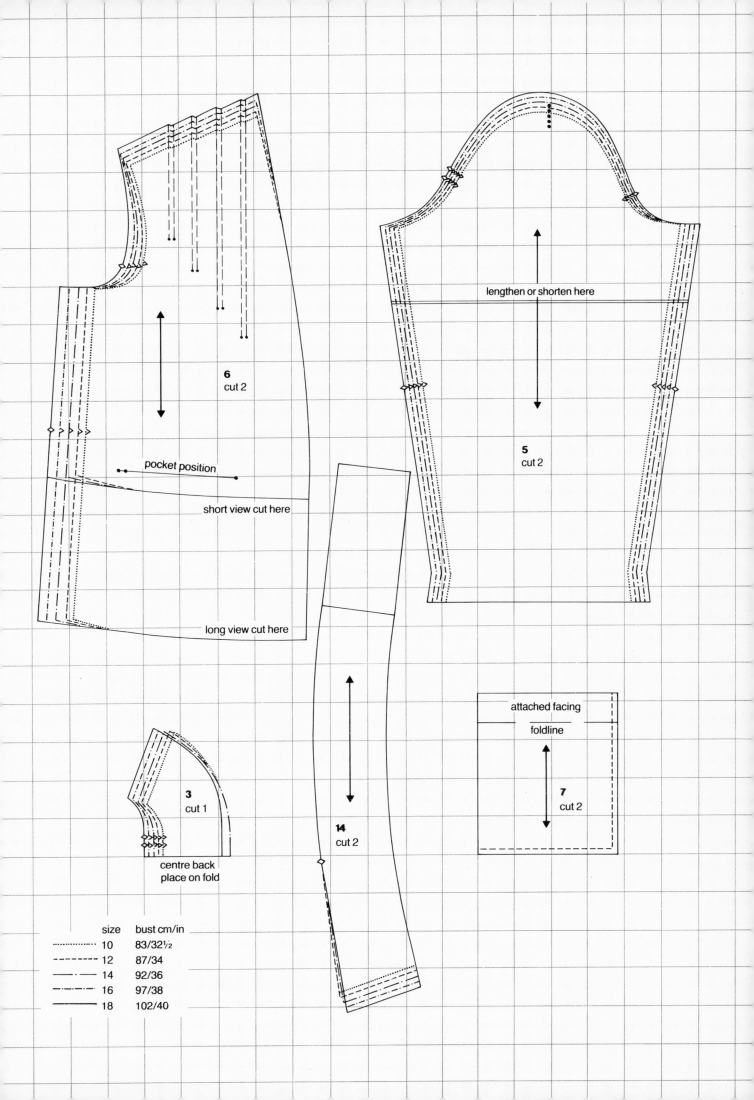

6
cut 2

pocket position

short view cut here

long view cut here

lengthen or shorten here

5
cut 2

attached facing

foldline

7
cut 2

3
cut 1

centre back
place on fold

14
cut 2

size	bust cm/in
10	83/32½
12	87/34
14	92/36
16	97/38
18	102/40

PART 4

More about skirts

Four-gore and straight skirts are classic styles which may vary slightly but never go out of fashion. Details are given in this section for basic pattern adjustments to cater for all figure types, and careful fitting when making up will achieve a made-to-measure finish. A choice of lining styles can be used to help the skirts keep their shape during wear.

Learn how to add a crisp, inverted front pleat with topstitched variations and handstitched arrowhead detail to the four-gore skirt, and choose between a vent or kick pleat at the centre back of the straight skirt.

Details such as covered hooks and eyes, self-fabric belt carriers and hand sewn zips add the finishing touches to a skirt to be proud of.

Correct fitting for a four-gore skirt

Use the information in this chapter to make a simple but flattering four-gore skirt. Use the fitting guide to learn how to correct some common fitting problems, see how to mark a level hem on your own and discover the secret of keeping checks matched across the seams during machining.

Follow the step-by-step instructions to make this four-gore skirt from the pattern on page 88 or use the sewing and fitting guide for any similar design.

This chapter describes all the common skirt fitting problems and describes how to slip-tack alterations. The same technique is also used to keep checks and stripes aligned at the seams during machining.

Skirt fitting problems
Alterations to size and fit that you are already aware of should be made at

Fitting guide

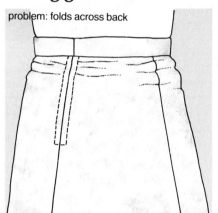

Low waist
Shorter waist to hip measurement than on pattern. Excess fabric forms horizontal folds beneath entire waistline.

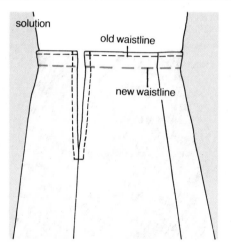

Solution Smooth excess fabric upwards above waist. Re-mark waistline at new level. Lower zip. Take out any excess width from side seams at top of skirt and replace waistband at new level, trimming away extra seam allowance.

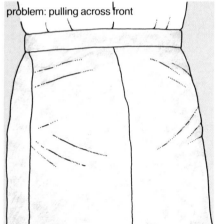

Round stomach
Skirt pulls across front, forming folds below waistline. The side seams slant towards front and front skirt hem rides up.

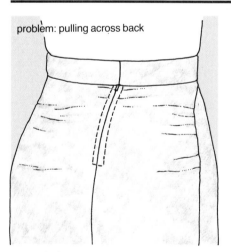

Too tight at rear
Back waistline and hemline ride up, pulling side seams towards back. Pulling also occurs at hip level at back, distorting upper side seams.

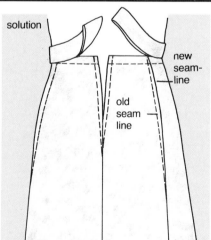

Solution Let out seam at centre back and the back part of side seam allowance, tapering up to original waistline. Re-apply waistband.

Too much fullness at rear
Gives baggy appearance in back skirt, especially near seams.

the cutting out stage. Alterations at fitting stages rely on adjustments within the 1.5cm/⅝in seam allowances, so do check all your measurements and compare them with the pattern before cutting out.

Check the waist, hips and hem level to see if they need adjustment. Problems may occur in more than one area – for example, if the waist is too loose, both waistband and side seams will need altering.

Right: Careful fitting is well worth the effort for this four-gore skirt.

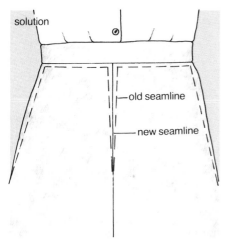

Solution Let out side and centre front seams above hip level, tapering back to original seamline below the hip. Let out some of centre front waistline seam allowance, tapering towards side seams. Re-apply waistband.

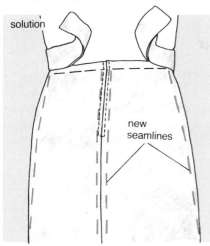

Solution Take in side seams, tapering to original seamline at waist and below the hip. You may need to take in the centre back seam as well, and re-position zip in side seam.

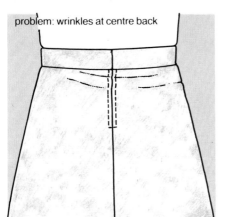

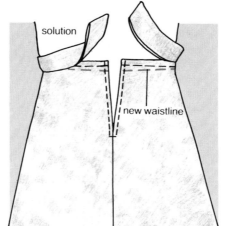

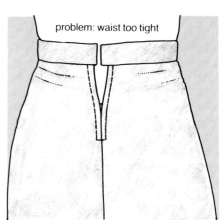

Sway back
A hollow area below back waist causes wrinkles at centre back. Garment fits correctly elsewhere.

Solution Lower waist level at centre back, tapering into original seamline at side waist. Trim away excess seam allowance. If top edge is too wide, take excess fabric out of top side seams on back only. Lower zip. Replace waistband.

Large waist
Zip refuses to close and buttons or hooks strain.

Useful hand stitches

Slip tacking

This stitch, which is also known as edge tacking, ensures accurate matching of checks and stripes at seamlines. It is also used when making fitting adjustments from the right side.
1 Mark seamlines on right side of garment sections. Press one seam allowance to wrong side along its seamline. With right sides of garment sections facing upwards, lap the pressed edge over the

adjoining seam allowance, matching both the seamlines and the design on the fabric. Pin at right angles to seam.
To slip tack, secure thread with a double stitch on wrong side. Bring needle to right side of garment

through folded edge. Insert needle through the single layer close to the fold and bring out again 1cm/⅜in along seam. Pull thread through, matching design carefully. Insert needle into folded edge and bring out 1cm/⅜in further on. Pull thread

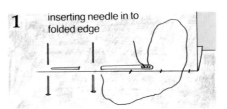

The four-gore skirt

You will need
Fabric according to size and style
Matching sewing thread
18cm/7in skirt zip
0.15m/⅛yd of 80cm/32in wide
  interfacing
Skirt hook and bar
Bias seam binding (if required)

Pattern pieces, page 88:
1 Skirt back
2 Skirt front (four-gore version)
3 Waistband

Cutting out
Pin your pattern pieces to the fabric, choosing the appropriate layout to follow according to the width of the fabric and whether or not it has a nap. Cut out carefully and transfer all pattern markings to fabric before

removing the paper pattern. Use pattern piece 3 to cut the interfacing for the waistband, cutting it to the fold as marked on the pattern.

Stitching curved seams
The side seams of the skirt have a waist to hip curve which requires a little more care when machining to ensure that the fabric is not pulled out of shape. Careful and firm slip tacking is ideal on curved seams. Machine stitch slowly and continuously, working from hem to waist with the weight of the garment supported on a table or working surface. Avoid stitching round the curve in short, sharp bursts as this does not produce a smooth stitching line.

Fabric quantity chart

Size	10	12	14	16	18
Hip (cm)	88	92	97	102	107cm
(in)	34½	36	38	40	42in

Without nap requirements

	10	12	14	16	18
115cm	1.30	1.35	1.45	1.50	1.55m
140cm	0.90	0.95	1.10	1.15	1.25m
150cm	0.90	0.90	0.90	0.90	0.95m

With nap requirements

	10	12	14	16	18
115cm	1.70	1.70	1.70	1.70	1.70m
140cm	1.20	1.25	1.30	1.40	1.50m
150cm	1.00	1.05	1.10	1.15	1.35m

Allow extra fabric for matching checks and stripes at centre seams.

(If your retailer sells fabric in yards use a conversion chart.)

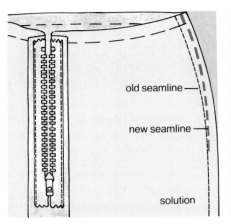

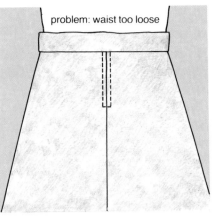

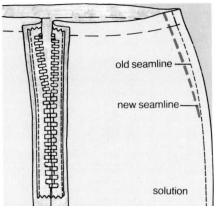

Solution Let out side seam allowance from waist to hip level only. Re-apply waistband.

Small waist
Waistband too loose causing entire skirt to slip down.

Solution Take in side seams, tapering to hip level. Reduce length of waistband and re-apply.

---

through and continue to end.
2 Remove pins. Turn garment to wrong side and open out fold so that fabric is right sides together. Machine down seam through the centre of straight tacking stitches on wrong side, using an even-feed attachment instead of the normal presser foot. (For an extra firm hold it may be preferable to tack along the centre of the tacking stitches before machining the seam, using an even-feed attachment.) Remove all tacking.

Hemming
A closely-worked stitch which is suitable for inner garment areas which need strong sewing but cannot be machined – inside waistbands, for example. Despite its name, hemming is not suitable for use on garment hems – catchstitch or herringbone stitch is preferable.
Secure thread with a backstitch and, working from right to left, insert needle in main part of garment, catching only a few

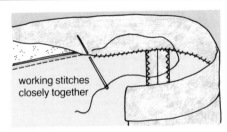

threads of fabric. (On waistbands and binding, work through the line of machine stitching.)
Bring needle out diagonally 1–2mm/ $\frac{1}{16}$in along, picking up a few threads from the fold to be secured.

Cutting layouts for the four-gore skirt

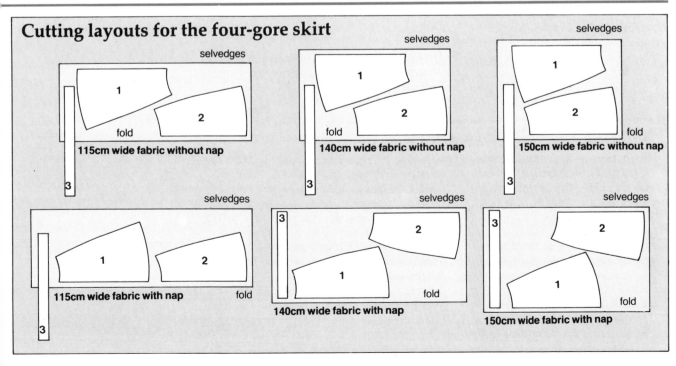

115cm wide fabric without nap

140cm wide fabric without nap

150cm wide fabric without nap

115cm wide fabric with nap

140cm wide fabric with nap

150cm wide fabric with nap

Making up instructions

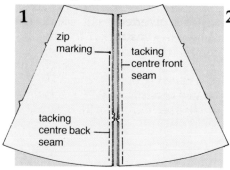

Step 1 With right sides together, matching notches, tack centre back seam from hem up to base of zip marking. Tack centre front and side seams from hem to waist. (Slip tack from right side if using checked or striped fabric. Note that checks will only match at centre seams – not at side seams.)

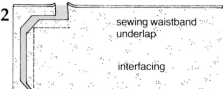

Step 2 Apply interfacing to wrong side of waistband, aligning top edge with fold line of waistband. With right sides together, fold in half lengthwise.
Stitch one short edge and form underlap by stitching other short edge round as far as notch on long edge. Trim end seams and corners and snip to stitching at notch. Turn waistband through and press. Tack waistband to top of skirt.

Step 3 First fitting Try on skirt, checking areas outlined in fitting chart. Mark any alterations.

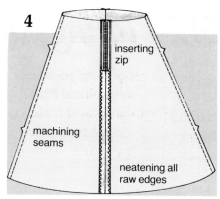

Step 4 Remove waistband and machine centre back seam from lower edge up to circle. Press seam open and neaten edges. Insert zip in top of centre back seam using the central or overlapped method (see pages 42 and 49). Make sure the zip tab is 6mm/¼in below the waist seamline.
Machine the side seams and centre front seam from hem to waist and press open. Neaten raw edges.

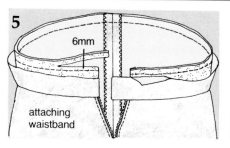

Step 5 With right sides together and underlap to right back, stitch waistband to skirt at interfaced edge. Press the seam upwards into the waistband and trim to 6mm/¼in.

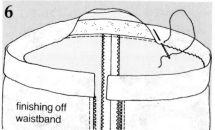

Step 6 Fold free edge of waistband under to cover raw edges and hem to line of machine stitching along waist seamline. Sew on skirt hook and bar.

Step 7 Second fitting. Try on skirt to establish length. Mark the hem level.

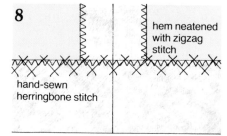

Step 8 Neaten lower edge of skirt by machine zigzag or hand oversewing, or apply bias seam binding to bulky fabric. Complete hem by hand.

PROFESSIONAL TOUCH

Marking a level hem by yourself

The markings and measurements on the pattern are only a guide. Alterations to the length may be necessary after the final fitting. Wear the garment with appropriate shoes and belt if required and measure up from the floor or any level surface. Use a floor-standing hem marker with a bulb of powdered chalk and stand in front of a mirror. Decide on the finished length of the skirt and position the marker accordingly. Stand as still as possible and press the bulb. A line of chalk will mark the hem position. Revolve slowly, leaving the marker stationary, stopping at frequent intervals and allowing the skirt to fall still. Puff a chalk mark each time you stop. After marking, pin up the hem, tack into place and check the length again before completing by hand.

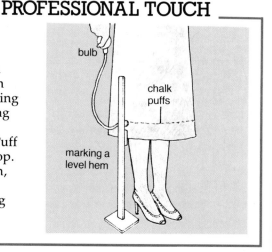

Skirt linings and centre pleats

A crisp front pleat with reinforced topstitching, an arrowhead detail and an integral lining all help to achieve a tailored look. Try out these techniques using the pattern from page 88 to make a skirt which can be both casual and smart.

This skirt is a variation on the four-gore skirt in the previous chapter, with an inverted front pleat. The pleats are constructed by stitching on the wrong side of the garment from waist to about hip level, and then allowing the fabric to fall free. It is usual to reinforce either the whole stitched section or just the base of it in some way.

Topstitching

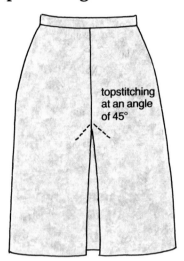

topstitching at an angle of 45°

chevron effect

unobtrusive finish

topstitching close to pleat seam

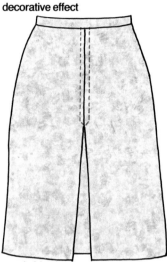

decorative effect

topstitching in a contrasting colour

A simple way of reinforcing the pleat seam is to topstitch it. This anchors the main fabric to the back of the pleat, spreading the strain with a strong, double-stitched seam. Experiment with thread thicknesses and colours and needle size, testing the stitch on three thicknesses of fabric. Use a thicker machine needle – size 100/16 – and adjust the upper tension of your machine if you are using a thicker thread. Always work from the right side of the garment and mark the stitching line with tacking or tailor's chalk.

For a chevron effect stitch down from the end of the pleat seam at an angle of 45° to the fold edge of the back of the pleat on each side.

For an unobtrusive finish edge topstitch just a few millimetres either side of the pleat seam.

For a decorative effect topstitch by hand or machine with a thicker thread, in contrasting or toning colour. Work stitching about 5–10mm/ ¼–⅜in each side of the seam.

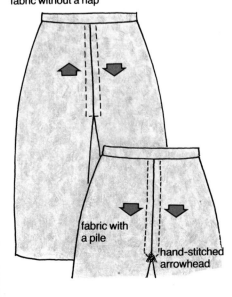

fabric without a nap

fabric with a pile

hand-stitched arrowhead

For fabric without a nap work on the right side and machine a row of stitches parallel to the pleat seam using the presser foot or pattern of the fabric as a guide. Start at the waist edge, one side of the seam and stitch to the lower edge of the pleat. Leave the needle in the fabric and turn the garment, so that you can stitch straight across the seam end at the top of the pleat. Stop the same distance from the pleat seam as the previous row of topstitching, turn the work with the needle in the fabric and machine back up to waist edge. There is no break in the stitching at the point of strain which makes this a particularly strong method of topstitching. An arrowhead can be added (see overleaf) within the stitching for extra strength and decorative effect.

For fabric with a pile work on the right side, machining both rows of stitching in the same direction, following the nap of the fabric. Slope the stitching at the base to join the pleat seam.

As the stitching line is not continuous, extra strength can be added at the top of a pleat by adding an arrowhead by hand as described overleaf.

83

Hand-stitched arrowhead

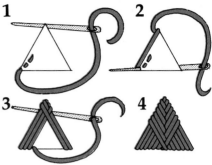

The arrowhead strengthens tops of pleats and sides of pockets, preventing the seam breaking open or the fabric tearing in wear. Work it in buttontwist or thick sewing thread and run the thread through beeswax to prevent tangling during sewing.

Mark a triangle with 1cm/⅜in sides on the right side of the garment, just over the end of the seam for maximum strength, with the point towards the waist edge. Use tailor's chalk or small tacking stitches.

1 Secure thread within triangle on the right side of fabric and bring needle and thread out at lower left-hand corner. At upper point of triangle, take a tiny stitch from right to left and draw needle and thread through.

2 Insert needle at lower right-hand corner and bring out again at lower left-hand side, just to the right of previous stitch.

3 Take a stitch from right to left at the top of the triangle, just below the previous stitch. Repeat step 2, working within previous stitch.

4 Repeat these steps until the triangle is filled. Secure the thread at the back of the work with a backstitch, darning the end in.

Left: Decorative topstitching and an arrowhead add emphasis and strengthen the pleat seam.

How to line a skirt

Most skirts, with the exception of those made for casual, summer wear, benefit from the addition of a lining. It improves the general appearance and hang of the skirt, stops the garment from creasing excessively across the front and helps preserve the shape and minimize 'seating' at the back. A lining also prevents the main fabric from clinging to undergarments, and stops a coarser fabric, such as rough tweed, from irritating the skin.

Lining fabrics

Fabrics suitable for use as lining are grouped together in a fabric department. Man-made linings are the most widely available, but some fabrics may require something a little different. An expensive medium to lightweight wool, for example, is best lined with silk, while cotton and linen garments which may be washed frequently should be lined with cotton lawn or batiste.

When selecting a lining fabric, always take a piece of your main fabric with you for comparison. The lining must be finer and lighter in weight to avoid unnecessary bulk, although it must be strong enough to take the amount of wear it will have.

Rolls of lining are usually marked clearly with fabric content and laundering instructions. These should correspond with your main garment fabric so that both the garment and lining maintain a good appearance during wear.

Cutting out the lining

In most cases, a skirt lining is cut from the main pattern pieces and no special lining pattern is given. If any alterations have been made to the skirt, these must be transferred to the pattern before cutting the lining.

If you are lining a skirt with a pleat the pleat should be omitted from the lining so that the pleat seam continues down to the hem. For ease of movement add vents 20–25cm/8–10in long at the side seams. Apart from this the lining is made in the same way as the skirt. Remember that the raw edges of the lining will face the skirt, away from the body. The lining is usually attached to a skirt before the waistband of the garment is applied.

Lining a skirt with an inverted pleat

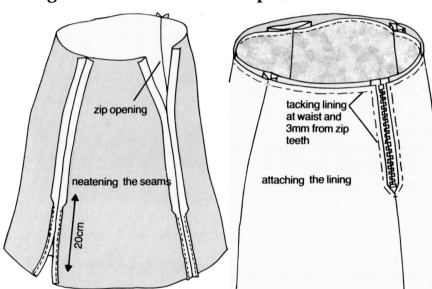

zip opening

neatening the seams

20cm

tacking lining at waist and 3mm from zip teeth

attaching the lining

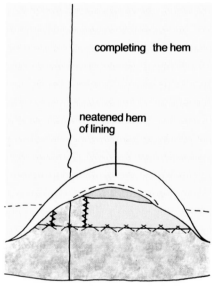

completing the hem

neatened hem of lining

The lining of a skirt with a front inverted pleat should be attached at the waistband and around the zip, but left free at the hem edge.

Cut out and assemble the lining as for the skirt, but omitting the pleat. Either stitch a centre front seam down to the hem or place centre front to fold of fabric. Leave an opening for the zip plus 1cm/½in and at the hem edge leave 20–25cm/8–10in vents in each side seam (see page 96). Do not complete the hem.

Neatening the seams It is best to partially neaten the raw edges of the lining and garment seams. Turn under and machine neaten the lining seam allowances for ɔproximately 20cm/8in from hem edge. Zigzag, bind or oversew the seam allowances of the main garment in the same way. (Neatening the seams all the way to the waist produces unnecessary bulkiness around the hips on a lined skirt.)

Attaching the lining Press the seams open and press under the turnings of the lining around the zip. Place the wrong side of lining to wrong side of skirt, matching seams, and pin raw edges together around waist edge. Tack lining into position around waist and zip, with lining at least 3mm/⅛in from zip teeth. Slipstitch lining to zip tape. (If the garment is to be washed frequently, it is better to leave lining free from zip and machine neaten the edges instead – this will make pressing easier.)

Apply the waistband in the normal way, treating the skirt as if it were made of single fabric and inserting skirt loops at the top of the side seams if required.

Completing the hem During the final fitting, pin the lining up out of the way while finalizing the length of the main garment. Complete the hem, then trim the lining so that it is 5mm/¼in longer than the skirt. Press under a hem allowance of 2.5cm/1in and hem the lining by machine, or machine neaten and finish by hand.

Permanent crisp pleats

On heavier fabrics, where it may
be difficult to keep a crisp lightweight pleat, Vilene Fold-a-band,
which is normally used for waistbands, can be used. Test it first on
a scrap of fabric to make sure it
does not produce too stiff a finish.
After stitching the pleat seam,
measure the length of the pleat
from the lower end of the seam to
the hem fold. Cut two strips of
Vilene Fold-a-band to this length.

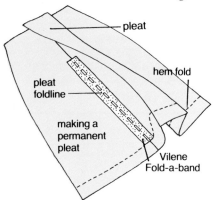

Lay one strip fusible-side-down
on wrong side of skirt front, with
lengthwise centre slots exactly
over front fold line of pleat. Press
to fuse interfacing in position,
using a damp cloth.
Repeat for second pleat edge.
Fold pleat along centre slots of
the Fold-a-band and turn skirt to
right side. Press edge of pleat
using a damp cloth.

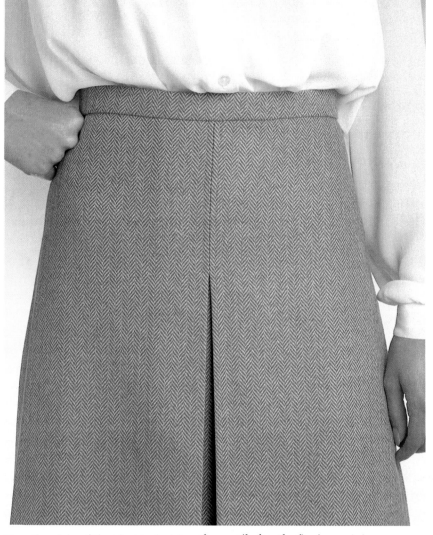

Keep the edges of the pleat tacked together until after the final pressing.

Lining a four-gore or straight skirt

The lining of a four-gore skirt and a
straight skirt may be either a loose
lining, attached at zip and
waistband only, or attached at the
hem as well.
Make any necessary pattern
adjustments before cutting out the
lining. If the centre front seam of
the skirt is on the straight grain,
place to a fold, so omitting seam.
Loose lining Make up the loose
lining following the instructions for
the four-gore skirt on page 82,
steps 1 and 4, remembering that
there is no centre front seam. Press
the seam allowances under where
the lining will be attached around
the zip. Neaten the seams, attach
the lining at the waist and complete
the hem as for the skirt with an
inverted pleat.

Attached lining With a lining
attached at the hem, there is no
need to neaten any of the seams.
Attach the lining around waistband
and zip tape in the normal way, and
establish length of main garment.
Complete hem of skirt and trim lining
to 5mm/¼in longer than the skirt.
Press up 2.5cm/1in hem allowance
to the wrong side of lining. Hang
garment up inside out and working
from the wrong side, pin lining to
fabric 15cm/6in from the hem edge.
Lay the garment on a flat surface,
and push the hem allowance
towards the row of pins. Pull back
the pressed hem fold and
catchstitch lining 1cm/½in from raw
edge to garment hem so that all raw
edges are enclosed. Remove pins
and lining will fall into position.

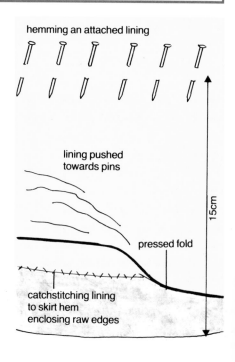

hemming an attached lining

lining pushed
towards pins

pressed fold

15cm

catchstitching lining
to skirt hem
enclosing raw edges

Skirt with inverted front pleat

Follow these simple instructions to make up the skirt with an inverted front pleat (see pattern page 88). The guide on pages 78–81 will help with any fitting problems.

You will need
Fabric according to size and style
Matching sewing thread
18cm/7in skirt zip
0.15m/⅛yd of 80cm/32in wide interfacing
Skirt hook and bar
Pattern pieces, page 88:
1 Skirt back
4 Skirt front
3 Waistband

Cutting out and preparing to sew
Fold fabric length right sides together, following the appropriate layout for your fabric width. Position pattern pieces as shown on the layout with front skirt to fold of fabric. Cut out garment sections carefully, cutting two back sections, one front on double fabric and a single waistband. Transfer the markings from the pattern pieces to the fabric, leaving the front skirt unmarked and with its pattern piece attached.

Making up the skirt

1
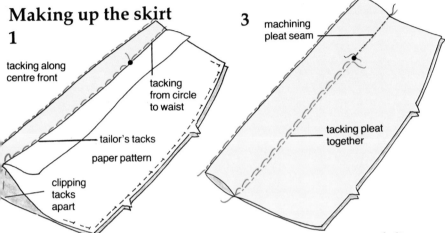
tacking along centre front
tacking from circle to waist
tailor's tacks
paper pattern
clipping tacks apart

3
machining pleat seam
tacking pleat together

4
pleat seam
tacking pleat to skirt front
tacked centre front

Step 1 Before removing paper pattern from front skirt, mark centre front line and pleat seam. Remove pins from centre front waist and hem edges and run a line of tacking stitches along the fold of fabric to establish centre front of skirt. Fold pattern back as far as the inner crease line, and tack fabric layers together, from circle up to waist along this line. With tailor's tacks mark pleat fold (creaseline) from circle on pattern to lower edge. Remove pattern and clip tailor's tacks apart.

Step 2 Preliminary fitting
Before machining the pleat, hold the front section against you to determine whether the pleat seam length is too high or too low for you. Mark any alteration required.
Step 3 Having adjusted length of pleat seam if necessary, tack pleat together down to hem. Machine pleat seam, working from circle to waist, and finish off ends securely.

Step 4 Working on wrong side of front skirt, match tacked centre front markings to pleat seam. Fold pleat along outer crease lines and tack to skirt front across waist edge, just within seamline. (The top of the pleat will be secured within the waistband when this is attached.) Topstitch or reinforce pleat seam by whichever method preferred.
Step 5 Tack centre back seam from hem up to circle, and side seams from hem to waist. Complete skirt as for four-gore variation, steps 2 to 8 (see page 82). Check the back of pleat does not hang below front edges. Press well.

Cutting layouts for skirt with inverted front pleat

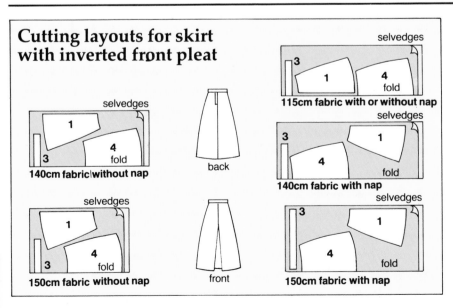

140cm fabric without nap
150cm fabric without nap
back
front
115cm fabric with or without nap
140cm fabric with nap
150cm fabric with nap

Fabric quantity chart

Size	10	12	14	16	18
Hip (cm)	83	92	97	102	107cm
(in)	34½	36	38	40	42in

Fabric without nap

	10	12	14	16	18
115cm	1.70	1.70	1.70	1.70	1.70m
140cm	1.15	1.25	1.30	1.40	1.45m
150cm	0.95	1.00	1.05	1.15	1.20m

Fabric with nap

	10	12	14	16	18
115cm	1.70	1.70	1.70	1.70	1.70m
140cm	1.50	1.50	1.55	1.55	1.65m
150cm	1.30	1.35	1.40	1.45	1.55m

Allow extra fabric for matching checks and stripes.

Graph for 4-gore and inverted pleat skirts

1.5cm/⅝in seam allowance included

4cm/1½in hem allowed

1 square = 5cm

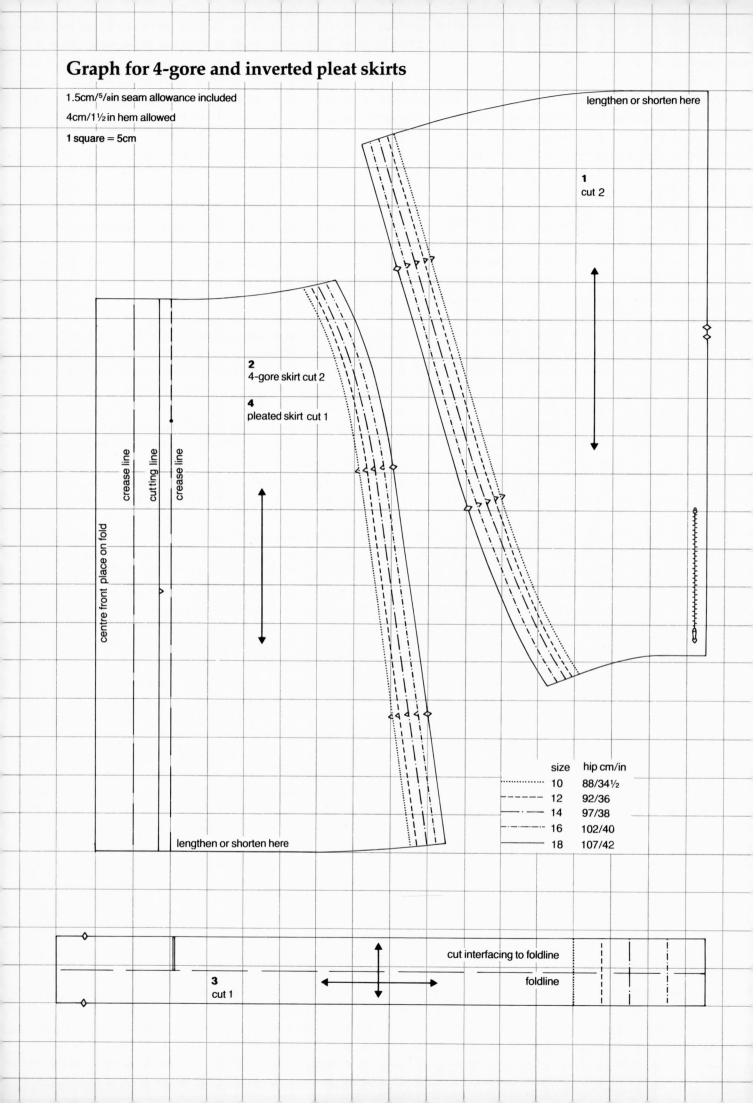

lengthen or shorten here

1
cut 2

2
4-gore skirt cut 2

4
pleated skirt cut 1

centre front place on fold

crease line

cutting line

crease line

lengthen or shorten here

size	hip cm/in
10	88/34½
12	92/36
14	97/38
16	102/40
18	107/42

3
cut 1

cut interfacing to foldline

foldline

A straight skirt with kick pleat or vent

This classic but simple skirt can be made in a variety of fabrics and is suitable for all seasons.
The chapter includes techniques for two new waistband styles and shows you how to add a professional touch with belt carriers and covered hooks and eyes.

Most dressmakers want to make a classic straight skirt at some time or other. They have been fashionable for years and will doubtless endure, with some minor variations, for years to come. There are many well-cut patterns available commercially and, although this section is geared to the graph pattern given on page 98, all the techniques and dressmaking advice are generally applicable. Making up instructions for the skirt are given in the next chapter.

Skirt vents and pleats

Any straight skirt that reaches below the knee needs some provision for movement – usually a vent or pleat let into the centre back seam. This allows the skirt to open when walking and to fall back into line when still.

The extension for the vent or pleat is included in the pattern. The length is usually about 26cm/10¼in long after the hem has been turned up. Any alterations to the length of the skirt and vent must be made *before cutting out*. Both the vent and pleat are assembled in the same way, the difference being the vent is open along its entire length while the pleat is stitched.

Before machining either version mark and tack the centre back seam from the lower end of the zip to the start of the vent or pleat, continuing in a straight line to the lower edge. For a perfect fold edge, leave this tacking in until you are ready to complete the hem.

Left: The straight skirt, made up in lightweight wool. The kick pleat (below) allows ample walking room.

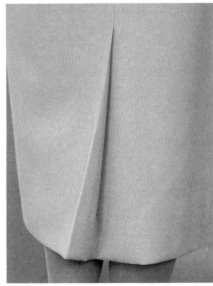

Making a vent

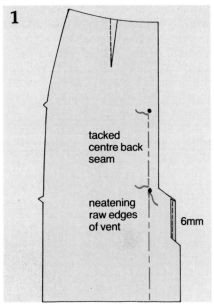

1

tacked
centre back
seam

neatening
raw edges
of vent

6mm

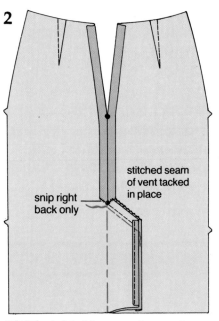

2

snip right
back only

stitched seam
of vent tacked
in place

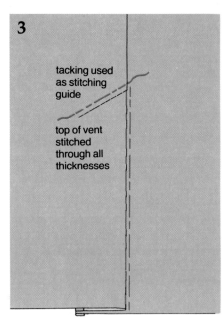

3

tacking used
as stitching
guide

top of vent
stitched
through all
thicknesses

1 If you are using a lightweight fabric, neaten the raw edges of the vent by turning 6mm/¼in to the wrong side and stitch. If you are using a heavyweight fabric, oversew the edge or bind with bias binding to avoid bulkiness.

2 With right sides together and matching circles, join centre back seam from lower zip circle to top of vent, pivot needle at corner and stitch across the top of the vent extension. Snip to seamline at top of vent on *right* back only and neaten the edges. Remove tacking from

centre back seam above vent. Press centre back seam open and press vent towards left back of skirt. Pin and tack into place along seamline across top of vent.

3 On right side of skirt, stitch across top of vent through all thicknesses using tacking as a guide. Take

Making a kick pleat

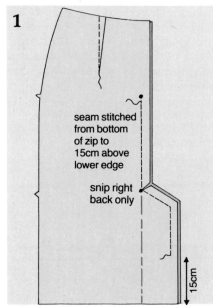

1

seam stitched
from bottom
of zip to
15cm above
lower edge

snip right
back only

15cm

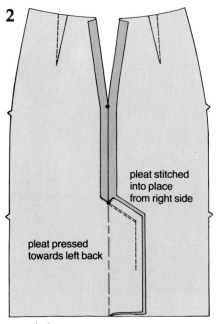

2

pleat stitched
into place
from right side

pleat pressed
towards left back

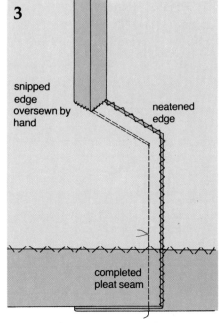

3

snipped
edge
oversewn by
hand

neatened
edge

completed
pleat seam

1 With right sides together, matching circles, machine centre back seam from lower zip circle and across top of pleat pivoting the needle at the pleat corners and ending 15cm/6in above lower edge. Snip to seamline at top of pleat on *right* back only and neaten the edges. Remove all tacking above

top of pleat.

2 Press centre back seam open and lightly press pleat towards left back of skirt. Pin and tack across top of pleat and stitch pleat into place from the right side as for the vent (step 3).

3 Remove the tacking in the pleat and open it out at lower skirt edge.

Turn up the hem and catchstitch or blind hem into place, as for the vent (step 4).

Stitch the remainder of the pleat seam together from the break in the stitching to the hem fold. Finish off ends securely, trim seam to 1cm/ ½in and zigzag or hand oversew seam allowances together to neaten.

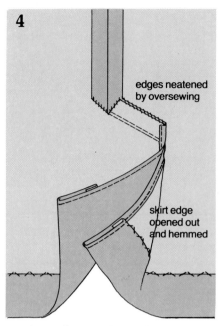

4

edges neatened
by oversewing

skirt edge
opened out
and hemmed

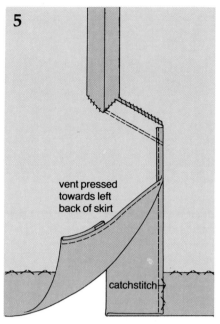

5

vent pressed
towards left
back of skirt

catchstitch

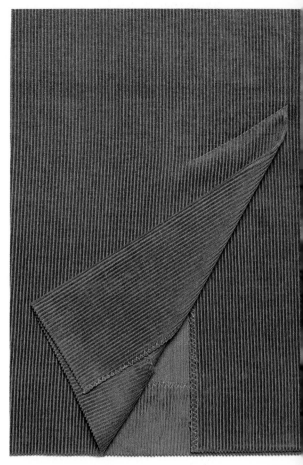

machine threads through to wrong
side and fasten off. Press lightly.
Complete rest of skirt and fit before
turning up the hem.
4 To hem, undo all tacking in the
vent and open it out at lower skirt
edge. Turn up hem and catchstitch
or blind hem. Neaten top of vent.

5 Fold the left-hand side of the vent
extension to the inside along
foldline and catchstitch lightly to
hem. Press.

*Right: The vent is made by neatening
the centre-back seam of the pleat
extension and leaving it open.*

Pattern alterations
Adjusting the length
Shorten or lengthen the pattern on
the double alteration lines (see
page 21).
If your pattern does not have
alteration lines marked, draw a
straight line across both back and
front pattern pieces, at right angles
to centre front and centre back.
Draw the line anywhere between
hip level and the top of the vent.
(The hip level on a pattern is where
the side starts to straighten out.)
If you need to shorten a skirt with
a vent/pleat by more than 5cm/2in
you must alter the length of the
vent/pleat to keep it in proportion
for a shorter figure and to ensure it
does not start too high on the centre
back seam.
Draw a second alteration line,
parallel to the first, halfway down
the vent/pleat on the back skirt
pattern. Draw a corresponding line
at the same level on the front skirt
pattern. Divide the amount by
which the skirt is to be shortened
equally between the first and
second alteration lines on both
pattern pieces. Pin tucks of the

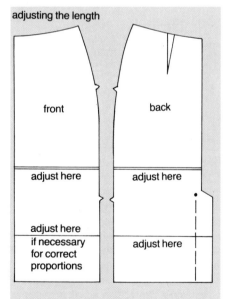

adjusting the length

front

back

adjust here

adjust here

adjust here
if necessary
for correct
proportions

adjust here

required size at each of these points
and try the pattern against you to
check length before cutting out.

Adjusting the waist to hip level
Measure your side waist to hip level
and compare it with the paper
pattern before cutting out. If the
measurement does not correspond
to the average hip level of 23cm/9in

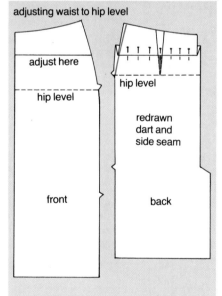

adjusting waist to hip level

adjust here

hip level

front

hip level

redrawn
dart and
side seam

back

below the waist, draw a straight line
across the pattern above hip level at
the same position on back and front
pattern pieces. Lengthen or shorten
the pattern pieces as required.
Re-draw the side seam to make a
smooth curve and re-draw the darts
where necessary. Try the pattern
against you to check the fit before
cutting out.

Ribbon-backed waistband

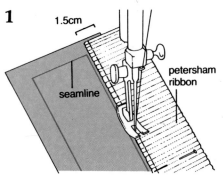

1 1.5cm

seamline

petersham ribbon

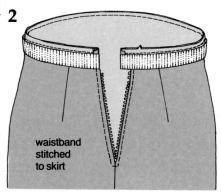

2

waistband stitched to skirt

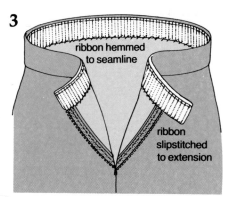

3

ribbon hemmed to seamline

ribbon slipstitched to extension

If you are using thick fabric a double thickness waistband, plus inter-facing and seam allowances, can be rather bulky. An alternative is to use the skirt fabric on the outside of the band only, and face it with a firm petersham ribbon. This does away with bulky turnings and means no other interfacing is needed.
Measure the width of the petersham ribbon. Prepare the waistband pattern by folding it lengthwise to the width of the petersham ribbon plus 3cm/1¼in for seam allowances. This will give you a 1.5cm/⅝in seam allowance along each of the long edges.
Position the adjusted pattern on the right side of a single layer of skirt fabric with the grain running lengthwise and cut out. Cut petersham ribbon to the same length as fabric band.
1 With waistband right sides upwards, lay ribbon over upper raw edge, close to the seamline. Machine along ribbon edge, taking a 1.5cm/⅝in seam on the fabric. Fold waistband along this seam with right side of fabric inside and machine across both ends, taking 1.5cm/⅝in turnings. Trim seam

allowances, turn to right side and press waistband.
2 With right sides together, stitch lower edge of waistband fabric to skirt along seamline. Make sure the waistband extension (marked by a notch) is on right back of skirt.
3 Trim turnings, layering the seam allowances if using thick fabric, and press upwards into the band. On the inside of the skirt, hem ribbon edge to waist on seamline and slipstitch ribbon to fabric waistband along the extension.
Sew on hooks and eyes in the normal way.

Ribbon-faced waistline

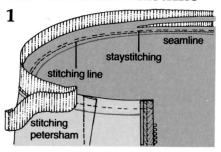

1

seamline

staystitching

stitching line

stitching petersham

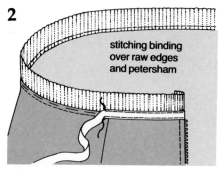

2

stitching binding over raw edges and petersham

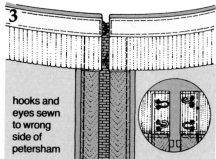

3

hooks and eyes sewn to wrong side of petersham

It is possible to make a skirt without a visible waistband, provided the skirt is straight or fitted, not gathered. Instead of a fabric band, a curved petersham ribbon is stitched to the waistline and tucked inside the skirt top to provide support.
Curved petersham is used because it has one selvedge shorter than the other, giving a curve which moulds round the figure below the waist. The top of the finished skirt then just reaches the waistline without a waistband.
This waistband finish eliminates all bulk at the waistline and is comfort-able to wear. It also gives the impress-ion of a longer midriff, which is flattering to short-waisted figures.
After the ribbon has been attached the waist seamline is taped to prevent

the waistline stretching in wear.
1 Measure the required length of curved petersham by laying it around your waist with the inner curve of the ribbon on the waistline and the outer curve below the waist. Mark the required length with chalk, adding 1cm/½in extra at each end for the turnings. A waistband extension is, of course, unnecessary – the ribbon meets exactly at the zip.
Turn under 1cm/½in at each end of length of petersham. Machine across ends to secure.
Staystitch skirt waistline 5mm/¼in from seamline within seam allowance. Working on the wrong side of skirt, lap inner curved edge of petersham over raw edge, close to staystitching, with the 1cm/½in

turnings towards you. Machine close to edge of petersham. Trim skirt turnings to 5mm/¼in.
2 Cut straight seam binding to waist length, plus 2cm/¾in. Lay binding over raw skirt edges and petersham on the right side of skirt, covering the machine stitches. Turn under 1cm/⅜in at each end of the binding. Machine binding into place along both edges and across ends.
3 Sew hooks and eyes to the wrong side of the petersham. Alternate the fastening so that a hook and eye are above an eye and hook to prevent them slipping undone in wear.
Turn the petersham to the inside, concealing the hooks and eyes and press.

Belt carriers

1

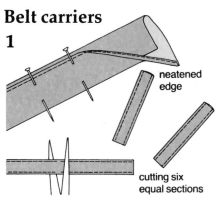

neatened edge

cutting six equal sections

2

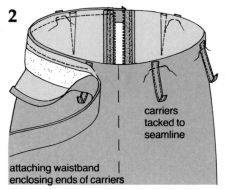

carriers tacked to seamline

attaching waistband enclosing ends of carriers

3

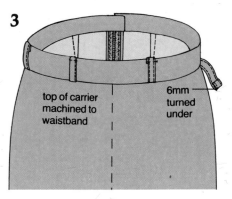

top of carrier machined to waistband

6mm turned under

If you wish to wear a belt with your skirt, you will need belt carriers to keep it in place. Six are best – position one at each side seam and one either side of the centre front and centre back. The carriers should allow the belt to slide through easily – the width of the belt plus 2.5cm/1in to allow for ease and turnings is ideal. The finished width of the carriers is usually just under 1cm/⅜in but varies according to the thickness of the fabric.

Make the carriers from one long strip of fabric and then cut the number required from it, rather than stitching each one individually.

Cut a strip of fabric on the lengthwise straight grain, three times the desired finished width and the total length of all the carriers. Neaten one long raw edge.

1 With right sides outwards, fold the strip in three lengthwise, placing the raw edge inside and the neatened edge on top. Press. With the neatened edge on the underside, machine topstitch 2-3mm/⅛in from the folded edges on both long sides. Mark and cut into six equal sections.

2 With right sides together, taking 6mm/¼in seams on the carriers, tack them into position on the skirt waist seamline. Attach the waistband to the skirt in the normal way, enclosing the lower end of the carrier in the seam.

3 Turn under 6mm/¼in at the top of each carrier and machine it to the front of the waistband close to the foldline. (If the waistband is backed with petersham ribbon, the top end can be enclosed in the upper waistband seam.)

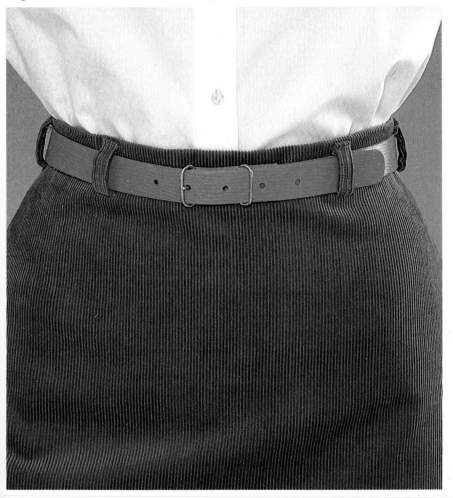

Covered hooks and eyes

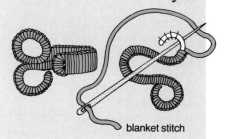

blanket stitch

Covering hooks and eyes or hooks and bars with matching thread gives a highly professional finish to skirt waistbands. Use a double strand of thread for small hooks and eyes, choosing a colour to blend with the fabric. The thread hides the metal fasteners while still allowing the hook to fit snugly into the eye.

Secure the hook and eye or bar with overcasting stitches in the normal way. Then continue working in blanket stitch, from right to left, covering the metal as you go. You can use buttonhole stitch instead if you prefer.

Left: Belt carriers prevent a belt slipping round or off the waistband.

Fitting and lining a straight skirt

Achieve perfect results first time when making a classic straight skirt by fitting frequently and using the professional finishes given here. The fitting checklist and chart will help you know what to look for and how to correct any problems.

This chapter shows you how to cut, fit and complete a straight skirt to perfection. The pattern used comes from the graph pattern on page 98 but the techniques are the same for a commercial straight skirt pattern. Choose either a simple vent or a pleat for ease of movement following the instructions in the previous chapter and making the pattern alterations as described. Alternative waistband styles are given on pages 82 and 92–93 and to give your skirt a really professional finish, insert a lining and a hand-sewn zip.

Follow these techniques and the step-by-step guide to produce a skirt that fits beautifully, wears well and keeps its shape.

Hints for fitting

Make any major alterations to pattern dimensions before cutting out and then fit the skirt frequently between the sewing stages so that you can make minor changes to the shape of your skirt.

General fitting details are given on pages 78–81. The fitting problems which apply specifically to straight

Straight skirt fitting problems and how to solve them

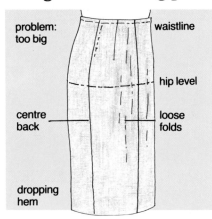

Skirt is too big
Side seam baggy, loose folds and dropping hem.

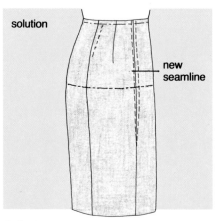

Solution Take in the side seams to fit the curve of the body, following the curve of the original seamline. Reduce the length of the waistband to fit.

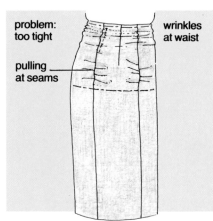

Skirt is too tight
Pulling and wrinkling of fabric across front and at upper side seams.

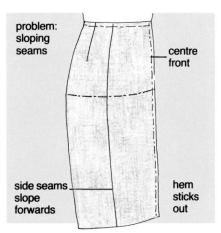

Side seams sloping forward
Hem sticks out, due to high tummy.

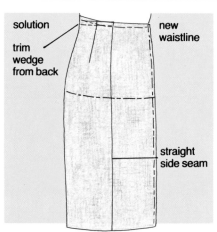

Solution Take a small horizontal wedge from centre back to side seam at waist to lift back skirt and straighten the side seam.

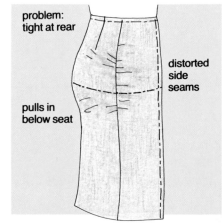

Skirt too tight at rear
Fabric pulls in below seat and side seams distorted.

skirts are dealt with below.

Above all, do not over-fit so that the skirt is skin tight. A reasonably close fit flatters a slimmer figure but a slightly looser fit is kinder to fuller figures.

Special markings for fitting

Fitting is easier if reliable guidelines are established on the skirt as points of reference. They also indicate the grain of the fabric.

After you have cut out the back and front skirt sections and transferred the usual pattern markings, mark the vertical centre front line and the centre back line (if there is no seam) along the fold with a single line of tacking. Run a horizontal line of tacking between the hip notches on front and

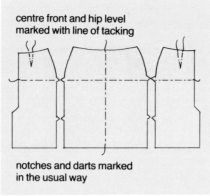

centre front and hip level marked with line of tacking

notches and darts marked in the usual way

back, following the threads of the fabric weave accurately.

Below: The fitting guidelines will help you achieve a smooth fit over the hips – the sign of a well-made skirt.

Fitting checklist

This guide to what makes a good fit applies to any straight skirt pattern and it is also worth bearing in mind when buying ready-to-wear clothes.

General appearance Skirt hangs with centre back and centre front perpendicular to the floor (easy to check using tacked guidelines).

Waistline Close fitting but not tight – there should be 1cm/½in ease.

Hip level Close fit, but with enough ease to sit and walk without straining seams.

Hemline Parallel to the floor.

Darts Tapering to a point, following the curve of the body and stopping 2cm/¾in short of fullest part of hip.

Pleats and vents Firm crisp edges that meet when standing still.

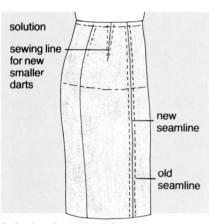

solution

sewing line for new smaller darts

new seamline

old seamline

Solution Let out side seams slightly. This will allow waist to hip area to drop and smooth out. You may also need to make smaller darts. Alter waistband accordingly.

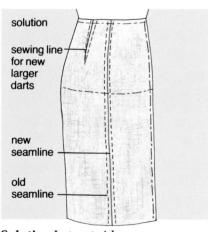

solution

sewing line for new larger darts

new seamline

old seamline

Solution Let out side seams graduating from waist to hem. Any excess fabric can be taken up in back darts. Alter waistband if necessary.

Lining a straight skirt

The straight skirt may be lined in two different ways – with a full lining or with a half lining.

The full lining adds to the comfort of the skirt, preserves its shape, and prevents creasing across the front or back when sitting. It also relieves strain on the vent or pleat and on all the skirt seams. A half lining only covers the back of the skirt and extends down as far as the vent or pleat and helps to prevent seating.

Making a full lining

Cut out lining fabric using back and front skirt pattern pieces. Fold back the vent/pleat extension so that the cutting line extends straight down to the hem. Transfer pattern markings. Close centre back seam from just below marked zip circle to top of vent marking. Press the centre back seam open from waist to hem and neaten. Slipstitch vent turnings back.

Work a bar tack at the top of vent to take the strain, or reinforce with a lining fabric patch (see page 219). Stitch darts and press away from

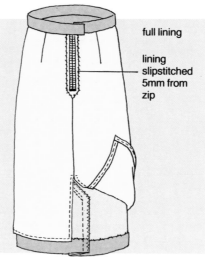

full lining

lining slipstitched 5mm from zip

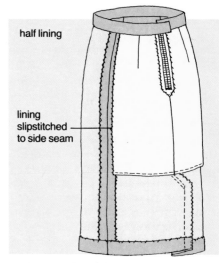

half lining

lining slipstitched to side seam

centre to reduce bulk in waistline. Join side seams and neaten raw edges. With wrong sides together, matching side seams and darts, tack skirt and lining together at waist level (see Making up the skirt, steps 6 and 8 on page opposite). Pin pressed edge of lining around zip tapes, 5mm/¼in from teeth. Slipstitch lining to tapes. Remove pins, complete waistband and skirt hem, then finish hem of lining to 2.5cm/1in above skirt hem.

Making a half lining

Cut the lining from the back skirt pattern, approximately 23cm/9in shorter than skirt. When hemmed this will cover the top of the vent. Complete centre back seam and darts as for full lining. Neaten side seams and hem, then attach to skirt during step 6 tacking along waist seamline to hold in place. Turn under side seam allowances and slipstitch lining to the back seam allowance of each side seam.

Classic skirt

When making a straight skirt, avoid loosely woven fabrics which stretch out of shape easily and tend to seat, or soft fabrics which will cling. There is a wide variety of suitable fabrics – closely woven wools and worsteds such as flannel, suitings, fine tweeds and barathea, cotton drill, linen and linen/synthetic blends, gaberdine, corduroy and polyester mixtures like Trevira. Straight skirts keep their shape better when lined. The best types of linings to choose are acetate, polyester or viscose twill.

You will need

Fabric according to size
Matching thread
18cm/7in zip
Skirt hook and bar
Hooks and eyes
0.15m/⅛yd of 80cm/32in wide interfacing or length of petersham ribbon

Lining requirements

For a full lining, 1.60m/1⅝yd of 90cm/36in wide lining or 0.80m/⅞yd of 140cm/54in wide lining

For a half lining, 0.60m/⅝yd of lining, any width
Pattern pieces, page 98:
1 Skirt back, 2 Skirt front
3 Waistband

Fabric quantity chart

Size	10	12	14	16	18
Hip					
(cm)	88	92	97	102	107
(in)	34½	36	38	40	42
Length					
(cm)	70	70	70	70	70
(in)	27½	27½	27½	27½	27½
90cm	1.70	1.70	1.70	1.70	1.70m
115cm*	1.40	1.50	1.60	1.60	1.70m
150cm	0.90	0.90	0.90	0.90	0.90m

*Without nap. All other quantities are with or without nap.

Cutting out the skirt

Make any necessary adjustments to pattern length, then position as shown on the appropriate layout. Cut out and transfer all pattern markings. Mark centre front line and hip levels to help with fitting.

Making up the skirt

Step 1 Machine staystitch waist seamline on back and front

sections, 1.3cm/½in from raw edge.
Step 2 Tack back darts, right sides together. Matching notches and circles, tack back seam between zip circle and vent top, and both side seams.

Step 3 First fitting Place a strip of fabric or petersham ribbon around natural waistline and pin skirt to it for support during fitting. Try on skirt, positioning waist seamline on natural waistline. Pin zip opening edges together. Allow 1cm/½in ease on the waist at this stage. Check that centre front and centre back are hanging correctly. Check that marked hip level is horizontal. Smooth skirt from centre to sides and check that side seams are vertical.

Step 4 Remove side seam tackings. Machine back darts and press towards centre. Pin, tack and machine the vent or kick pleat (see pages 90–91).
Step 5 Insert the zip fastener in the back seam while it can still be spread out flat. Use the central or

Hand-sewn zip

Inserting a zip fastener by hand is the hallmark of a highly professional dressmaker. It is, in fact, very easy to do and the stitching is just as strong as a machine finish if the stitches are worked fairly close together. The prickstitch used (Basic seams and stitches page 26) leaves a row of tiny indentations on the right side of the fabric. In many skirt fabrics, these are hidden within the weave.

For a perfect finish, use a fine, sharp needle and single thread. Tack the zip into place, positioning it according to whether it is to be stitched in by the central or overlapped method (pages 42 and 49).

Overlapped method Follow the instructions for the overlapped zip in step 1, page 42, inserting the zip into the right-hand side of the centre back seam, rather than the side seam as described earlier.

If you prefer, this first row of

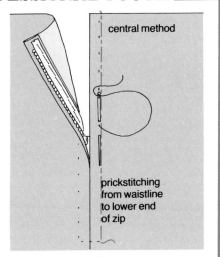

overlapped method

machine or prickstitch concealed stitches

prickstitching left side from waistline to lower end of zip

central method

prickstitching from waistline to lower end of zip

stitches may be machined as the overlap will conceal it. Alternatively, prickstitch the zip into place, working from the waistline to the lower end of zip, with stitches approximately 5mm/¼in apart.

Lay left side of skirt opening over entire zip, just covering the stitching on the right side of the zip. Tack along seamline, then prickstitch from waistline to

lower end of zip. Work a bar tack across the bottom of the zip on the inside of the skirt.

Central method Work exactly as for a machine stitched central zip (see page 49) but replace all machine stitching with prickstitch worked from waistline to lower end of zip. Work a bar tack across the bottom of the zip on the inside of skirt.

overlapped method.

Step 6 With right sides together, matching notches, join side seams. Make up the lining at this stage and place in position. Make hanging loops from lining fabric (see page 47).

Step 7 Second fitting With lining and skirt together, pin skirt to waistband again. Check the line of the seams, the smooth fit of the darts and the flatness of the zip seam. There should still be some ease in the waistline, but the main body of the skirt should now fit well.

Step 8 With wrong sides together, tack skirt and lining together at waistline. Sew lining around zip tapes, 5mm/¼in from teeth. Attach skirt loops to side seams on waistline.

Step 9 Prepare chosen waistband and attach it to skirt (see pages 82 and 92 for alternative methods).

Step 10 Third fitting Check fit of waistband and position for skirt fastenings.

Step 11 Sew hooks and eyes to end of underlap and add skirt hook and bar.

Step 12 Fourth fitting Pin lining up out of the way and mark hem length on skirt. Tack hem up and check appearance.

Step 13 Complete hem of skirt, then finish lining hem (see page 85).

Cutting layouts for skirt

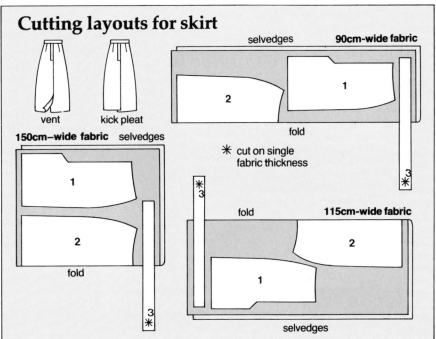

vent / kick pleat / selvedges / 90cm-wide fabric / 150cm-wide fabric / 115cm-wide fabric / fold / cut on single fabric thickness / selvedges

Graph for straight skirt

1.5cm/⅝in seam allowance included

4cm/1½in hem allowed

1 square = 5cm

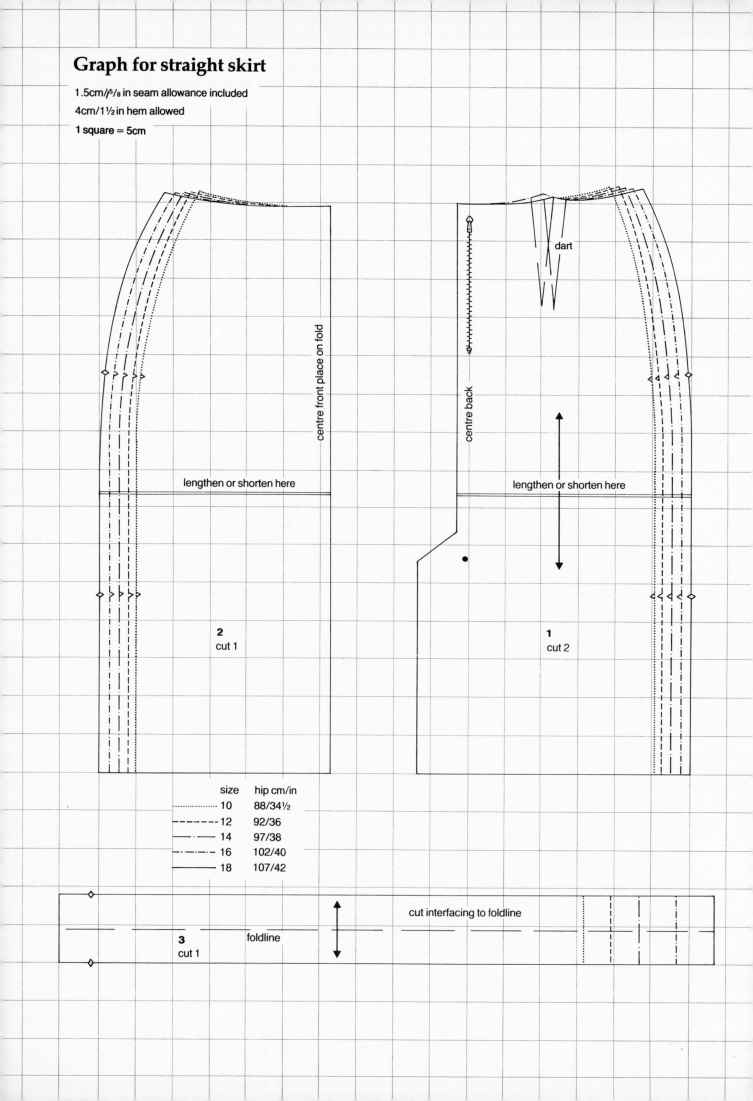

centre front place on fold

lengthen or shorten here

2
cut 1

centre back

dart

lengthen or shorten here

1
cut 2

size	hip cm/in
10	88/34½
12	92/36
14	97/38
16	102/40
18	107/42

cut interfacing to foldline

3
cut 1

foldline

PART 5

Variations on a theme

The classic high-yoked dress in this section is flattering for most figure types and a clever choice of contrast fabrics for cuffs, collar and yoke can vary the look considerably. The simple collar can be worn open at the neck or tied with a ribbon to form a neat closed neckline. Detailed step-by-step instructions are given for applying the collar and buttoned cuffs for perfect results.

Save money by learning how to adapt a basic pattern to make several garments. A dress, a blouse and a wrapover dressing gown can all be made from this simply styled dress pattern – just extend the facings and length of the pattern pieces to make the dressing gown or cut them to the shorter length for the blouse. Vary the trimmings on the dressing gown by inserting lace round the outside edges of the collar or by adding ribbon to the simple patch pockets.

Cuff details are important and useful tips are given here for making covered buttons and successful hand or machine buttonholes, as well as ideas for dispensing with buttonholes completely.

Cuffs, collars, buttonholes and buttons for a perfect finish

This stylish dress from the pattern on page 120 incorporates some new and useful techniques such as making and attaching simple collars and cuffs. There are also alternative ways of sewing on buttons – useful in many other areas of home dressmaking.

This simply styled dress has several classic features, involving basic dressmaking processes that can be used again and again on other shirts and dresses.

The finish on collars and cuffs, for example, can make or mar a garment – this chapter describes how to fit them to perfection.

Following chapters give you fabric requirements, layouts for the pattern pieces and making up instructions. They also show you how to make a blouse from this versatile pattern.

Coping with collars

Collars are usually made from double fabric, cut as two separate pattern pieces known as the upper and under collar. Interfacing between the two layers preserves the shape. Usually, it is applied to the wrong side of the upper collar so that all bulky seams are towards the under collar and therefore concealed. However, some iron-on interfacings are better applied to the under collar – follow the advice on your paper pattern instruction sheet.

The shape of the inner or neck edge of the collar determines how it sits on the garment. If the neck edge is straighter than that of the garment, the collar will stand up, then fall away at the neck. If the neck edge is very curved, the collar will lie flat when attached.

Cutting out It is important to transfer pattern markings accurately so that the collar fits perfectly. If any adjustments made to the body of the garment enlarge or reduce the neckline, you may have to adjust the collar slightly.

Careful marking of the garment at the start will save time later. Transfer all the pattern markings – including seamlines – to the fabric collar, using a tracing wheel and dressmaker's carbon paper.

If the collar is interfaced, transfer the markings to the interfacing instead of the fabric.

Sleeves with cuffs

Long sleeves that are gathered into cuffs usually have a certain amount of fullness to allow ease of movement without constriction at the wrist. The fullness is distributed so that most of it falls to the outside of the arm.

The cuff is made up separately, then attached to the sleeve. To allow the cuff to fit closely at the wrist, but with enough room for the hand to pass through, an opening extends into the sleeve and the cuff fastens with a button.

Techniques for making up a collar

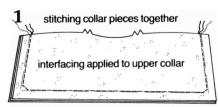

1 stitching collar pieces together
interfacing applied to upper collar

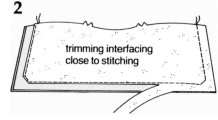

2
trimming interfacing close to stitching

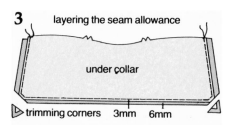

3 layering the seam allowance
under collar
trimming corners   3mm   6mm

Collars are such a noticeable part of a garment, it is essential that they are cut, sewn and turned through precisely. For a perfect finish, you need to know how to layer seams and roll edges.

Layering a seam – which is done before the collar is turned through – helps prevent bulk. This is particularly important on a collar where two seam allowances of fabric plus one of interfacing are sandwiched between the upper and under collar.

Rolling an edge This takes place where an edge consists of a seam – on the edge of a collar or the front edge of a jacket with an attached facing, for example. These have to be finished so that the underside does not roll forwards, exposing the seam.

1 Apply interfacing to wrong side of upper collar. Working with the interfaced side towards you and right sides together, pin under collar to upper collar along the two short edges and long outer edge;

leave the neck edge open. Tack. Machine along seamline on the three tacked edges, using a fairly small stitch. Take one or two stitches diagonally across pointed corners on medium to heavyweight fabric. This produces a better point when the collar is turned through.

2 Layer the seam before turning through the collar by trimming the interfacing on the upper collar close to the stitching.

3 Then trim the under collar seam

Right: The short-sleeved version of the dress, gathered into the yoke and belted for a figure-flattering effect.

Above: The dress neckline can be worn in two different ways – here it is left open with the front facing forming revers.

Above: Make a neat, closed neckline by tying a length of ribbon or a fabric rouleau around the collar.

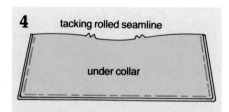

4 tacking rolled seamline

under collar

allowance to 3mm/⅛in and the upper collar seam allowance to 6mm/¼in. Trim corners, clip curves where necessary and turn collar through. Carefully ease out the corners of the collar using a knitting needle or collar-point turner.

4 Roll the outside, seamed edge between the fingers and thumbs until the seam is positioned just to the underside of the collar. Tack close to the outside stitched edges and press on wrong side.

Preparing sleeves for cuffs

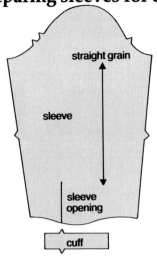

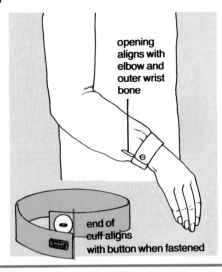

The cuff and the sleeve opening align, and both should be in line with the elbow and outer wrist bones. The opening comes mid-way between the centre sleeve and underarm seam on the sleeve back. The cuff button is stitched to an underlap (an extension of the cuff that laps under the front edge), and the buttonhole is worked so that the end of the cuff lines up with the opening when the button is fastened.

Making the opening
The opening is made before the sleeve seam is joined, as it is easier to manage while the sleeve is flat. The opening is usually marked as a

Binding the sleeve opening

A continuous strip opening – so-called because a single strip of bias fabric is used as a binding – is strong, neat and easy to construct. Use it on fine fabrics, and those that fray easily. From your left over fabric, cut a bias strip 3cm/1¼in wide by twice the length of the opening plus seam allowances. This gives a finished binding width of about 8mm/⅜in.
1 Using a warm iron, crease a seamline 6mm/¼in along one long edge of binding, pressing it towards the wrong side. Repeat on second long side, which will be folded under to form hem.
2 With right sides together, lay sleeve over binding, opening the

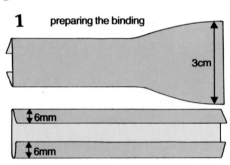

slash out in a straight line. Matching the stitching line on the sleeve opening to the crease line on the bias strip, pin the sleeve opening and strip together along the stitching line, noting that the

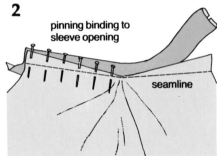

seam allowance on the sleeve opening tapers away to almost nothing in the centre.
3 Working on the sleeve side, machine slowly, keeping just to the left of the original reinforcement

Facing the sleeve opening

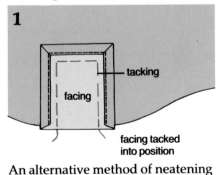

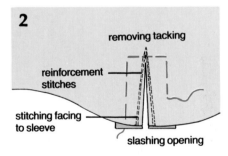

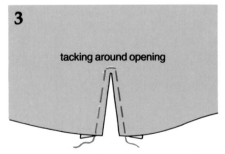

An alternative method of neatening the cut edge of a sleeve opening (best used on medium to heavyweight fabrics), is to use a small facing, instead of a strip of binding. This is applied *before* the opening is slashed through.
1 To make facings, cut two rectangles of fabric 7.5cm×10cm/3in×4in. Press 6mm/¼in to wrong side on two

long sides and one short side and machine stitch to neaten. Reinforce sleeve opening close to stitching line. With right sides together, position facing centrally over cutting line of opening and tack.
2 Working from the sleeve side (where the reinforcement stitches are visible) machine along stitching

line through sleeve and facing, keeping reinforcement stitches within seam allowance. Start at wrist edge, pivot at point, then machine down the second side. Slash through opening along the cutting line as far as point, without cutting the stitches.
3 Turn facing to inside of sleeve, tack around opening and press.

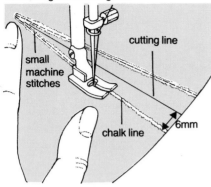

reinforcing the stitching line

small machine stitches

cutting line

chalk line

6mm

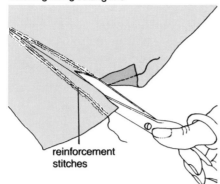

slashing along cutting line

reinforcement stitches

If only the cutting line is marked on the pattern, mark the stitching line on the wrong side of the fabric with tailor's chalk, starting 6mm/¼in either side of the cutting line on the lower edge and tapering to a point at the top.

Reinforce the stitching line by working small machine stitches exactly on this line. Start at the wrist edge, and work up, keeping fabric taut between finger and thumb so that it doesn't pucker. Pivot needle and machine down the second side.
Slash the opening from lower edge to top along the cutting line, taking care not to cut through the stitches. Do not slash for faced opening.

straight line on the pattern. Transfer this marking to the wrong side of the fabric with a marking pen, or mark with a tailor's tack at

the top of the opening and a 5mm/¼in snip into the seam allowance at the lower edge.

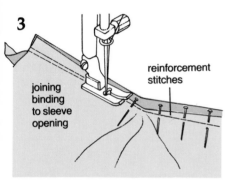

3

joining binding to sleeve opening

reinforcement stitches

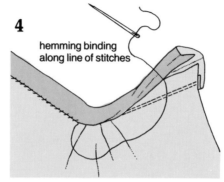

4

hemming binding along line of stitches

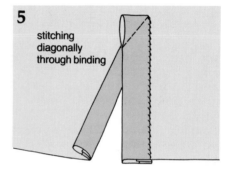

5

stitching diagonally through binding

stitches so that they are concealed by the binding.
At the top of the slashed opening, pause with the needle in the work, raise the presser foot and transfer fullness of sleeve above opening to

behind needle. Lower presser foot and continue machining to end of opening.
4 Bring the folded edge of the binding over to the wrong side of sleeve, lining up the fold with the

line of machining. Hem by hand to the machine stitches. Press.
5 On inside of sleeve, machine or backstitch diagonally through binding at top of opening to keep it tucked inside sleeve during wear.

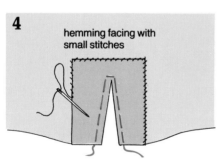

4

hemming facing with small stitches

4 On wrong side, hem facing to garment with small stitches or machine the facing down on to the sleeve. Remove tackings.

Right: The opening of both the cuff and sleeve are aligned. When the arm is bent, the opening lines up with the outer wrist bone and the elbow. The fullness falls to the outer underside of the sleeve.

Making simple cuffs

The simplest type of cuff is made from a single rectangle of fabric, folded lengthwise through the centre. It may be joined to form a circle or, where there is a sleeve opening, cut longer to form an underlap for the button. Like collars, cuffs keep their shape best when interfaced, and some reinforcement is always necessary when buttonholes and buttons are to be added.

The crisp finish of cuffs – again like collars – depends on accurate seam-lines and carefully turned through corners. Where seam allowances are to be trimmed use small machine stitches for strength and cut across corners for a well-defined point.

Before stitching the buttonholes make a sample one first on left over fabric. Cut it and check that the button slides through without strain but not too easily.

If you have an automatic or semi-automatic sewing machine, make the buttonholes following the instructions on page 110. Alternatively, make them by hand (page 114).

Cuffs should be made up as a pair so that the underlap for each button is identical and produced in the right place.

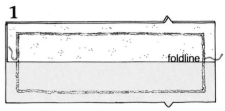

1.5cm seam allowance

Lapped cuff with buttonhole

1 Attach interfacing to cuff, aligning it to foldlines. Transfer all markings from pattern to fabric or interfacing. Where no seam allowances are marked, draw them in 1.5cm/⅝in from raw edges on the wrong side, using a ruler.

Attaching cuffs

Join the sleeve seams before attaching each cuff. If you find it difficult to press an open seam in this area after laundering, use a machine flat fell seam. Alternatively, trim the seam allowance to 3–4mm/⅛–¼in after stitching and machine zigzag or hand overcast together to neaten. Work two parallel rows of large machine or hand gathering stitches on the lower edge of sleeve, placing one row on the seamline and the second row just inside the seam allowance.

1 With right sides together and cuff underlap towards back of sleeve (closest to sleeve seam), pin

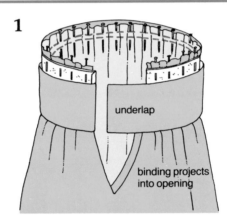

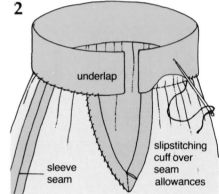

interfaced edge of cuff to sleeve. The binding towards the back of the sleeve (ie below the underlap) projects into the opening, while the

binding towards the front of the sleeve is folded under so it is not visible from the right side.

Pull up gathering threads so that

Sewing on buttons

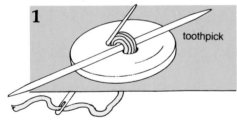

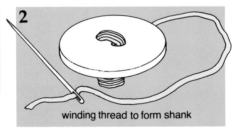

winding thread to form shank

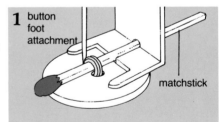

Hand-sewn buttons

Use a double thickness of buttontwist, run through beeswax to prevent the threads parting and tangling. This will also form a firm button shank (the cord of thread that holds the button above the garment and allows room for the buttonhole to slip between button and garment).

1 Start with a backstitch on wrong side of fabric under the button position. Bring needle up through a hole in the button. Centre a

toothpick, matchstick or bodkin over the button, between the holes, to enable you to form the shank. Take several stitches through holes in button, finishing on wrong side of work.

2 Remove toothpick and make sure all extra thread is between garment and button. Take needle through to right side.

Wind thread tightly around strands to form a thread shank. Take thread back to wrong side of work and finish off securely.

Machine-sewn buttons

You can use your sewing machine to attach buttons – a useful method if you have to sew on several. As long as the ends are finished off properly, the buttons will be secure.

1 Thread machine with ordinary sewing thread to match the garment. Replace presser foot with the button foot which grips button and holds it in place.

Set machine to zigzag stitch and adjust stitch width so that the needle enters the centre of both left

2

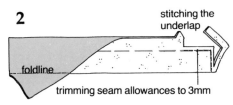

stitching the underlap

foldline

trimming seam allowances to 3mm

3

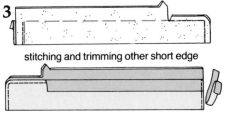

stitching and trimming other short edge

4

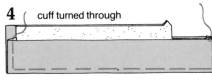

cuff turned through

tacking around cuff

2 With right sides together, fold cuff along centre foldline. Starting at marking on long edge, stitch towards short edge, take one stitch diagonally at the corner, and stitch short edge down to fold. This forms the underlap.
Snip into seam allowance from

marking to seam line and trim seam allowances to 3mm/⅛in, cutting across corner.
3 Fold back seam allowance on lower edge or uninterfaced half of cuff and press. Stitch other short end of cuff. Trim seam allowances to 3mm/⅛in.

4 Turn cuff through, using a knitting needle or collar point turner to form neat corners. Tack lightly around the outer edges and press.

Below: Contrasting cuffs for a crisp finish on the long-sleeved dress.

sleeve fits cuff, and distribute the gathers so that there is more fullness near the sleeve opening in line with the little finger. Too much fullness in line with the thumb is unsightly.
Machine gathered sleeve edge from start of underlap to straight cuff edge, being careful not to catch in folded edge of cuff facing. Trim seam allowances to 5mm/¼in.
2 Tuck seam allowances up into cuff and bring free folded edge of cuff over them. Slipstitch folded edge of cuff to line of machine stitching. Make a buttonhole on the flush edge of the cuff and sew a button to the underlap.

2

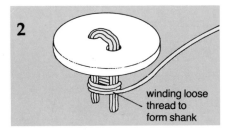

winding loose thread to form shank

and right holes in button.
To create a shank, insert a matchstick or thick bodkin over the button between the holes and take about ten zigzag stitches over it. Adjust stitch width to 0 and take several stitches on the spot to secure the threads.
Raise button foot and remove work.
2 Remove the matchstick and push button to end of threads. Wind loose thread around these to form a shank. Finish off loose ends on the wrong side.

An easy-to-wear classic dress

*The classic lines of this dress are flattering to most figure
types, with gathers falling from a high
yoke, comfortable side pockets and a choice of sleeve lengths.
The style requires little fitting – shape
it at the waist with a sash or elasticated casing.*

Using the collar and cuff techniques covered in the previous chapter, you can now make up either the long or short-sleeved version of the dress pattern on page 120. In the next chapter, you can see how to turn this simple, pull-over-the-head style into a blouse, as well as learning how choice and use of fabric can ring the changes in a pattern.

This dress makes up well in a wide variety of lightweight to medium-weight fabrics. The main criteria are that they should not be too stiff or bulky to gather satisfactorily, or too heavy to make the double yoke. Choose polyester/cotton or cool cotton for summer days, silk or polyester crêpe de chine for special occasions. Brushed cotton, pure wool or wool mixtures are ideal for winter.

You will need
Fabric according to size and style
Matching sewing thread
0.25m/2¾yd of 90cm/36in-wide
  lightweight interfacing
2×13mm/⅝in buttons (long sleeves
  only)
Pattern pieces, page 120:
  1 Back (dress)
  2 Front (dress)
  3 Yoke
  4 Collar
  5 Front neck facing
  6 Pocket
  7 Long sleeve *or* 9 Short sleeve
  8 Cuff
10 Belt
11 and 12 Waist casing (optional)

Fabric quantity chart

Size	10	12	14	16	18
Bust (cm)	83	87	92	97	102
(in)	32	34	36	38	40
Waist (cm)	64	67	71	76	81
(in)	24	26	28	30	32
Hips (cm)	88	92	97	102	107
(in)	34	36	38	40	42
Length* (cm)	114	115	115	118	119
(in)	44¾	45¼	45¼	46½	46¾
Long-sleeved dress					
90cm	4.00	4.05	4.05	4.15	4.20m
115cm	3.40	3.45	3.45	3.55	3.55m
140cm	2.65	2.65	2.70	2.90	2.95m
Short-sleeved dress					
90cm	3.50	3.55	3.55	3.70	3.75m
115cm	3.05	3.10	3.10	3.20	3.20m
140cm	2.50	2.50	2.55	2.55	2.60m

Allow extra fabric for one-way designs
and matching plaids or stripes.
*Length is finished length without belt.

*Left: The optional elasticated casing
holds the dress waistline in position.*

Paper pattern alterations

● **Dress length** Carefully check the finished back length of the dress against your own back length. Remember that the dress is to be belted, or have a waist casing, and allow at least 10cm/4in extra length to take this into account, depending on how much you want the dress to 'blouse' at the waist. If necessary, lengthen or shorten the dress on the double alteration lines and re-position the pockets accordingly.

● **Sleeve length** Alterations to length on a cuffed sleeve must be made on the double alteration lines between the underarm and wrist, not at the shaped lower edge. Remember that the sleeve is full and allow a little extra length so that it is not too short when gathered in to the cuff.

● **Sleeve width** Any extra width in the long sleeve can be gathered in to the cuff. If the short sleeve is too wide, make a vertical dart from the lower edge up to the shoulder point to take it in without altering the size of the armhole seam.

● **Pockets** If you prefer to make the dress without pockets, simply fold back the pocket extensions so that the side seams are even all the way down the dress pattern piece. You will not require pattern piece 6 when cutting out the dress.

Preparing to cut out

Position pattern pieces as shown on the layout for your chosen fabric width. When cutting pieces from double fabric, fold fabric with right sides together. When pattern pieces are shown extending beyond the fold of double fabric, first cut all the double pieces, then open out the remaining fabric and cut all the single pieces, placing pattern to right side of fabric.

Transfer all pattern markings to the fabric, then carefully remove paper. Cut a single piece of interfacing for the collar, using pattern piece 4. Fold pattern piece 8 in half lengthwise and use it to cut two pieces of interfacing for the cuffs.

Cutting layouts for dress

Note: Where pattern pieces are shown white, place paper pattern printed side down to fabric

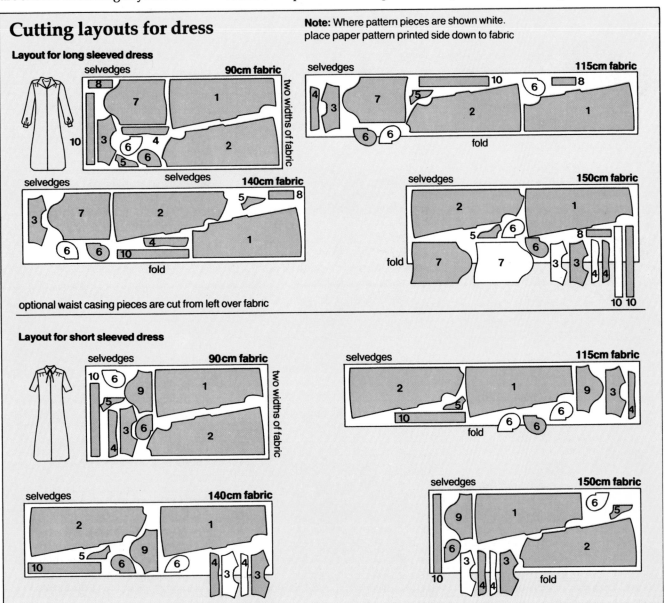

107

Making the long-sleeved dress

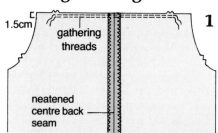

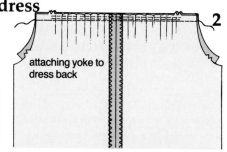

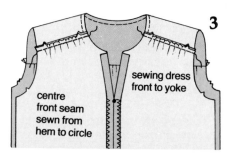

Step 1 With right sides together and matching notches, pin, tack and then machine centre back seam. Press seam open and neaten raw edges.
Staystitch neck curves on both yoke sections and on front facings. Fold yoke sections in half marking centre back on neck edge and lower edge.

Run a double row of hand or machine gathering threads 4mm/³⁄₁₆in apart within seam allowance across upper edge of back dress between notches.
Step 2 Draw the gathers up to fit the lower edge of upper yoke and with right sides together, matching notches and centre back markings,

apply back dress to yoke. Spread the gathers evenly between the notches and pin, tack and machine along the seamline.
Make sure that you do not displace the gathers.
Step 3 With right sides together, join centre front seam from lower hem edge to lower circle. Press

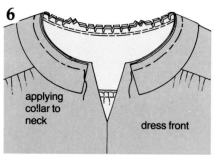

Applying collar to dress

Step 6 Snip seam allowance of dress neckline to staystitching.
Make up collar (see page 100).
Pin and tack collar into position at neckline with upper collar uppermost and under collar next to garment, matching centres and notches.

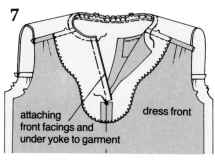

Step 7 Place right side of the under yoke and front facings to the right side of the garment, matching notches and circles. Pin and then tack into position on the seamline around neck.
Work down the centre front from small circles at neckline to base of opening, pinning and tacking

facing to garment. Take care not to catch collar in to this seam.
Before machining, check that the two sides of the collar are identical in length and position, and that no little pleats have formed in the seam around neckline. Snipping into the neckline seam allowance of the garment means the curved seamline can be spread so that the machining is easier.
Machine the seam in two halves, working from base of front opening up to centre back. Pivot the needle exactly on the circle at centre front where the collar joins the neck.
Trim seam allowance to 5mm/¼in, cut across corners and snip turnings if necessary.

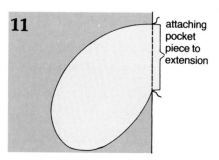

Pockets

Step 11 With right sides together, matching notches, stitch one pocket section to each front and back side seam extension, along seamline as marked. Press turnings towards the pocket and neaten the raw edges separately by machine zigzag or hand overcasting.
Step 12 Join side seams of dress from armhole edge, down to top of

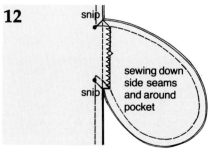

pocket, round pocket to lower edge of sections, then down to hem. Snip to stitching line above and below pocket on back only, press main parts of side seams open and neaten edges. Trim the raw edges of the pocket bag to 6mm/¼in and neaten. Press pocket bags towards front of dress. If you do not require pockets, simply stitch the side seams from armhole edge to hem.

Sleeves

Step 13 Finish the sleeve opening with a facing or strip of binding, join the sleeve seam and make up and attach cuff (see pages 102–105). Insert the sleeve following the method used for the jacket sleeve (pages 58–59).

Step 14: Second fitting
Try on the dress when all neck and sleeve details are complete. Wear the shoes you intend to wear with the dress (heel height makes a difference) and a belt. Arrange the fabric in a bloused effect over the belt and mark the hem length required, getting a friend to help you if possible.

seam open and neaten raw edges from hem to circle.
Run a double row of machine or hand gathering stitches 4mm/³⁄₁₆in apart within seam allowance across two upper front edges of dress between notches.
Draw up gathers on both these edges and with right sides together, matching notches, apply front dress to front edges of yoke. Distribute gathers evenly between notches and pin, tack and machine along seamline. Remove gathering threads and tackings and press all seam allowances on back and front on to yoke, taking care not to flatten gathers.
Trim seams to 6mm/¼in.

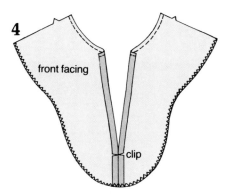

Front facing and under yoke
Step 4 Place front facings right sides together and stitch seam below lower circle. Clip into seam allowance at circle and press seam open. Neaten outer edge of facing.

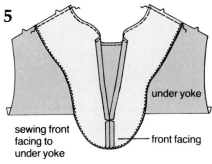

Step 5 With right sides together, pin, tack, and machine under yoke to front facings. Press seam turnings towards under yoke. Press up 1.5cm/⅝in seam allowance to wrong side along back lower edge of under yoke.

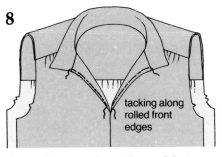

Step 8 Turn under yoke and facings through to wrong side of garment. Tack along centre front edges close to seamline, rolling the facing slightly to the inside of garment. Working on the wrong side with the collar standing upright, smooth the under yoke down to the lower back edge and pin the turned under

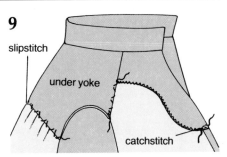

seam allowance to the seamline of dress and upper yoke. Use a dressmaker's dummy if you have one, or slide the dress over the ironing board.
Step 9 Slipstitch pressed edges of under yoke to machine stitching of seamlines. Catchstitch front facing to centre front seam.

Step 10: First fitting
Tack side seams together, leaving pocket opening if pockets are required. Tack underarm seams of sleeves, and tack sleeves into position. Try on dress with a sash or belt and arrange the blouson effect above the waistline.
Check that the centre front and centre back hang vertically, that the shoulder seams are not too long and that the pocket opening is at the right height when the dress is belted. Mark any adjustments with pins and transfer the markings to corresponding sections as soon as the dress is removed.

Hem
Step 15 Neaten lower raw edge and turn hem up, following method used for shaped hem (see page 48), tacking into position.
Try dress on again to check length before finally catchstitching hem into place.

Belt
Step 16 With right sides together, seam two belt pieces together along one narrow end. Press seam open. Fold belt in half lengthwise, right sides together. Seam two short edges and the open long edge, leaving a 10cm/4in opening in the centre of the long edge. Trim seams, clip corners and turn belt through. Stitch up opening by hand, taking small stitches, and press.

Optional waist casing
Join the seams on the waist casing, right sides together, to form one long shaped strip. Press under the seam allowances on both long edges and attach casing to dress, as for an applied waist casing (see page 202).

Making the short-sleeved dress

Make up as for long-sleeved dress as far as step 13. Join sleeve seams, press open and neaten edge. Insert sleeves following the method used for the jacket sleeve (pages 58–59) for a smooth sleeve head.

Press under 5mm/¼in at lower edge of each sleeve and machine stitch to neaten. Try on dress and mark required finished sleeve length. Remove dress and tack up sleeve hems. Try on dress and check that

sleeve lengths are equal.
Catchstitch hems in position.
Complete as for long-sleeved dress, from second fitting to end. If you are making waist casing you can wear the belt on top for a neat finish.

Successful machine-made buttonholes

Successful buttonholes depend on correct positioning, correct marking and correct selection of stitch width and tension. Always make a test buttonhole using the same materials as in the garment.

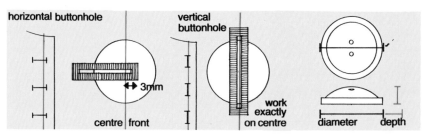

Positioning the buttonhole

In women's and girl's clothes place the buttonholes on the right-hand side, the buttons on the left. Reverse the procedure for men and boys.

The button is always stitched exactly on the centre of a front or back closing. A vertical buttonhole is positioned centrally, but a horizontal one extends 3mm/⅛in beyond the centre to accommodate the button shank and still allow the button to rest exactly on the centre.

Measuring and preparation

Measure the diameter and thickness of the button and add together to work out the length of the cutting line. The finished buttonhole will also have a bar tack worked at each end for additional strength.

Mark a test buttonhole on spare fabric on the same grain as garment, using sharp tailor's chalk or a fabric marking pen, to exact length required. Indicate ends with a short line across top and bottom.

Test zigzag stitch (use slightly less upper tension than for straight stitching). Machines vary, so follow the instructions for your particular model. In general, for the buttonhole sides use a zigzag stitch width *just under* half that of the stitch which forms the bar tack at either end. This ensures a cutting space is left between the two rows.

Machining the buttonhole

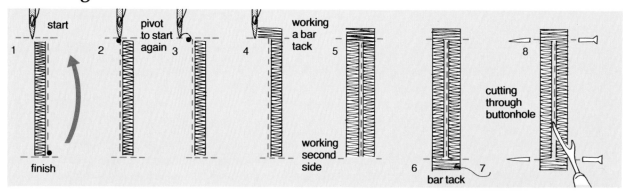

1 Starting at the top left-hand side, work a row of zigzag stitches down the whole length of the marked line, stopping with the needle down in the centre. Raise the presser foot.
2 Carefully pivot the work until the worked row is now on the right-hand side. Lower the presser foot.
3 Using the hand-wheel, take one stitch only to the left, bringing you to a corner.
4 Now change the stitch width to the full width and work four stitches across the entire width of the buttonhole (a bar tack).
5 Return the stitch width to just under half, exactly as for the first row, and work the second row of stitches parallel to it. There should

be only one or two threads of fabric between the rows.
6 Leave the needle down in the lower left-hand corner, change the stitch width to full width and work four stitches to make the second 'bar'.
7 Change the stitch width to zero and work three or four stitches 'on the spot' to prevent stitches coming undone. Raise presser foot. Draw work gently away towards the back of the machine. Cut threads close to buttonhole.
8 Cut through the cutting line, using small sharp scissors or a seam ripper, protecting the 'bar' first by placing pins across each end. Push button through to test for size and adjust length if necessary.

Achieve a professional finish for a shirt with machine-made buttonholes.

Short or long sleeves – a blouse for all seasons

A blouse that can be worn with anything is invaluable, and the simple lines of this one allow you to use fabric as creatively as you please. Useful techniques included in this chapter are hand-sewn buttonholes, covered buttons and quick ideas for cuff fastenings.

The long or short-sleeved blouses from the patterns on page 120 are made up in exactly the same way as the dress on pages 100–109, but you can add some more techniques to your repertoire as you sew.

There are quick ideas for instant cuff fasteners or, for those who prefer the more traditional method, a step-by-step guide to hand-sewn buttonholes.

As the pattern is so simple, why not experiment with colour and pattern to highlight the design features of both garments? For dramatic contrast, you could make up the dress or blouse in dark red, navy or black and add a crisp white collar, front facing and cuffs. For a more subtle effect, cut the main body of the garment in one colour, and the yoke and cuffs in a toning colour as shown below.

Whatever you decide to do, check which pattern pieces are affected, and calculate any extra fabric required accordingly. If you want to cut the yoke or collar on the crosswise grain, for example, you will need to add about half a metre (half a yard) to the fabric requirements – more if you are using stripes that require a one-way layout.

Pattern pieces cut in a different fabric make little difference to the amount of fabric required for most fabric widths. Make a rough layout of the pieces to be cut from the different fabric to help you calculate how much extra fabric to buy.

Below: Back and front views of the blouse, showing different uses of toning fabric.

Fabric ideas for the blouse

The blouse, like the dress, makes up well in a wide range of fabrics, from lightweight cottons to wool mixtures. Try bright seersucker for a casual effect, or use plain white or coloured cotton poplin to make yourself a wardrobe basic. Make a useful long-sleeved shirt in brushed cotton, or a wool mixture, with small checks or a floral design, to be worn belted over trousers.

You will need

Fabric according to size and style
Matching sewing thread
0.30m/⅓yd of 90cm/36in wide
    lightweight interfacing
2×13mm/½in buttons (long sleeves
    only)
Pattern pieces, page 120:
1 Back (blouse)

2 Front (blouse)
3 Yoke
4 Collar
5 Front neck facing
7 Long sleeve *or* 9 Short sleeve
8 Cuff (long sleeves only)

Cutting out and making up

Make any necessary pattern alterations and cut out the blouse following the instructions for the dress, cutting the front and back to the shorter length as indicated on the pattern. Omit the waist casing lines and fold away the pocket extensions.

Make up the blouse following the instructions for the long or short-sleeved dress, steps 1 to 9 and steps 12 to 15, referring to the instructions for a dress without pockets during step 12.

Fabric requirements

Size	10	12	14	16	18
Bust (cm)	83	87	92	97	102
(in)	32	34	36	38	40

Long-sleeved blouse

	10	12	14	16	18
90cm*	2.95	3.00	3.00	3.05	3.05m
115cm	2.20	2.25	2.25	2.30	2.30m
140cm*	1.50	1.50	1.50	1.55	1.55m

Short-sleeved blouse

	10	12	14	16	18
90cm*	2.70	2.75	2.75	2.80	2.80m
115cm	1.85	1.90	1.90	1.95	1.95m
140cm*	1.15	1.15	1.15	1.20	1.20m

*without nap. All other quantities are with or without nap.
Allow extra fabric for one way designs and matching plaids or stripes.

Fabric layouts for long and short-sleeved blouses

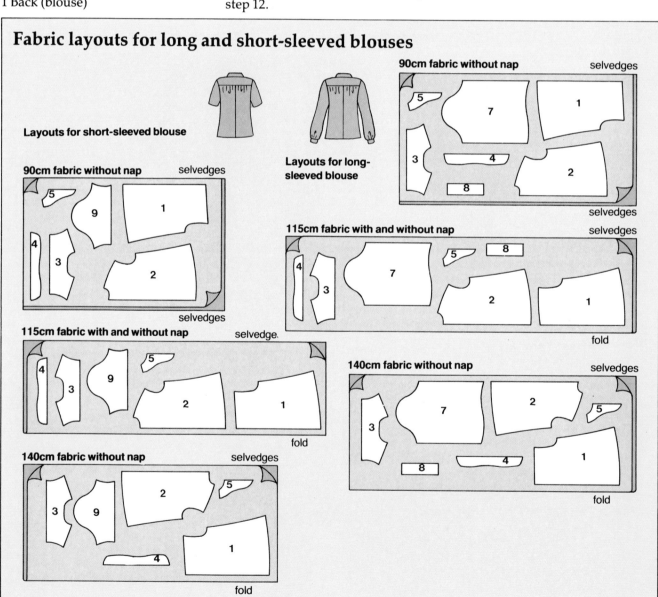

Layouts for short-sleeved blouse

Layouts for long-sleeved blouse

90cm fabric without nap   selvedges

90cm fabric without nap   selvedges

115cm fabric with and without nap   selvedges

115cm fabric with and without nap   selvedge.

140cm fabric without nap   selvedges

140cm fabric without nap   selvedges

Clever ways with stripes

This pattern lends itself well to striped fabrics. As the back and front of this dress or blouse are gathered on to the yoke, only the centre front and centre back seams need the pattern to be matched.

In fact stripes can be used as a design feature in themselves. Cut the yoke and collar (and cuffs, if required) so that the stripes run horizontally (that is, on the cross-wise grain), while the stripes on the main body of the dress run vertically.

Learn to recognise the nature of stripes. They may form an even repeat or a one-way design across the fabric. For example, if a striped pattern consists of a red and white stripe, alternating across the fabric from selvedge to selvedge, and ending with a red stripe, then the pattern is even. This is because the sequence of stripes is the same, viewed from either selvedge of the fabric. An even sequence of stripes is easy to match on straight central seams.

If the pattern is made up of a sequence of say, green, blue, pink and white stripes, interspersed with red, it is a one-way design. This is because the pattern is not the same, viewed from either selvedge of the fabric.

The most important thing to ensure with this dress is that the stripes are well-positioned on the pattern pieces. Before cutting, ensure that the stripes match at centre front and centre back seams. Position the pattern pieces so that when they are joined, the stripes balance across the front and back (they will not match at the side seams, which are shaped).

Follow a one-way layout for fabric with a nap, and be sure to follow the straight grain markings, whether cutting on the straight or crosswise grain.

uneven stripes

stripes to highlight yoke

stripes to highlight pocket

even stripes

113

Making hand-sewn buttonholes

Buttonholes worked by hand are especially suitable for fine and delicate fabrics. They are cut first, then stitched. To prevent fraying of the raw edges while stitching, you can insert a scrap of fusible interfacing between the fabric layers at the buttonhole position (unless interfacing is already present). Tack into position, press and then cut through the interfacing to match the cutting line of the buttonhole.

Use buttonhole twist if extra strength is required. Run the thread through a piece of beeswax for firmness and to prevent twisting.

Buttonhole stitch, which can be confused with blanket stitch as they look similar, is used for hand-sewn buttonholes. Both stitches are used to protect and decorate edges, but buttonhole stitch is worked with the raw edge of the fabric away from you, and the thread is twisted round the needle to form a 'purl' stitch. The rounded end of the buttonhole is made towards the edge of the fabric.

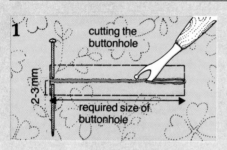
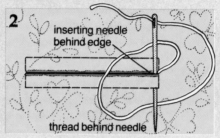
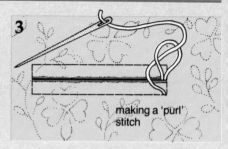

1 Mark centre line of buttonhole on right side of fabric. Machine a rectangle around the marking (or stitch by hand, using small stitches). Begin in the centre of one long side, 2-3mm/⅛in away from marking, and count stitches to ensure opposite sides are the same. Cut buttonhole along marked centre line.

2 Starting at the inner, square edge of the buttonhole, with the fabric edge away from you, secure the thread at the back of the work with a backstitch.

Working from right to left, insert needle behind edge, bringing point out 2-3mm/⅛in down from edge on right side.

With needle in this position take thread behind needle and under needle point from right to left.

Making covered buttons

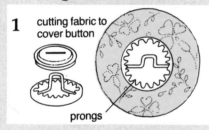
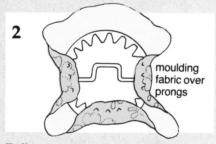
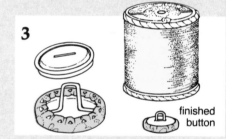

Kits for making covered buttons can be bought from most haberdashery counters. The button is hollow and usually made of metal or plastic, with prongs on the underside to secure the fabric cover. The button back snaps on to the button, hiding the raw edges of fabric. The shank is made of metal, plastic or strong fabric.

Full instructions are usually given with the kits but, in general, buttons are covered as follows:

1 Cut a circle of fabric slightly less than twice the diameter of the button, or use a pattern if supplied. Position any fabric design centrally within the circle.

2 Centre button over wrong side of fabric circle and bring fabric up around button, moulding it over the prongs so that it is held firmly.

3 Ease excess fabric into the hollow of the button and make sure it has a smooth appearance from the front. Place the button back in position and apply pressure until it snaps into place. If this proves difficult, place a cotton reel upright over the shank and rap it firmly with a hammer to force the back into position.

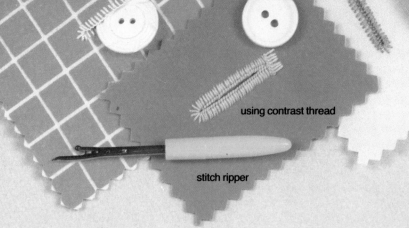

using contrast thread

stitch ripper

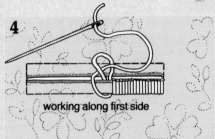

4

working along first side

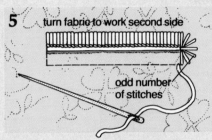

5 turn fabric to work second side

odd number of stitches

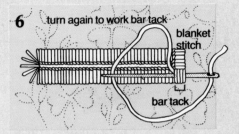

6 turn again to work bar tack

blanket stitch

bar tack

3 Draw needle through work and pull gently upwards so that a 'purl' stitch forms on the raw edge.
4 Repeat along first side of buttonhole, working stitches close together and of the same length.

5 To stitch round the end nearest the open edge, work an odd number of overcasting or buttonhole stitches, fanning out round the end of the buttonhole. The centre stitch should be in line with the opening for the button.

6 Continue with buttonhole stitch along second side and make a bar tack across the end, the full width of the buttonhole. Blanket or buttonhole stitch over bar tack. Take thread through to wrong side and secure with a backstitch.

SHORT CUT

Doing without buttonholes

If you don't want to make buttonholes on cuffed sleeves, here are two quick alternatives to try. They are ideal on children's wear, for small fingers often can't manage buttons, but they should not be used in areas that take a lot of strain.
Press-stud method Sew the socket of the press-stud to the cuff underlap, and the ball part (which locks into the socket) to the wrong side of the overlap. Attach a button to the right side of the cuff, directly above the press-stud, so that the cuff has the appearance of a traditional

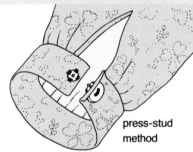

press-stud method

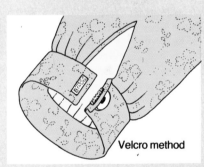

Velcro method

buttoned cuff when fastened. Sew the button flat to the fabric, without making a shank.
Velcro method Apply a small piece of Velcro – about 1.5cm/ ⅝in long – to the cuff underlap,

with a hooked piece on the wrong side of the corresponding overlap. Sew a button flat to the fabric on the right side of the cuff directly above the Velcro, for effect.

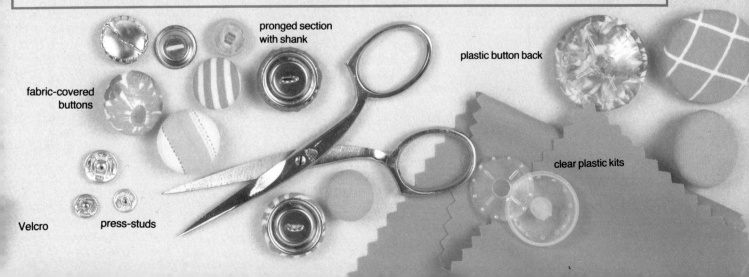

pronged section with shank

plastic button back

fabric-covered buttons

clear plastic kits

Velcro   press-studs

Choose a pretty flower-sprigged cotton for this lightweight wrapover dressing gown, then trim the pockets, belt and front edge with toning ribbon.

A lightweight wrapover dressing gown

Adapt the classic dress pattern from the beginning of this section to make a simple housecoat. The sewing techniques are almost the same, just add facings and lengthen to suit your needs. Patch pockets with ribbon trims and a lacy collar frill add a personal touch.

An existing dress pattern with a front seam, like the classic dress on page 101, can be adapted to turn it into a comfortable, full-length wrapover dressing gown.

Simply lengthen the dress and extend the front facings to full length on each side. The dressing gown makes up well in lightweight cotton or cotton blends. Add a lightweight interfacing to the front edges for a crisper look which will hang better and stay in place when wrapped over.

You can adapt the style by adding patch pockets, with a ribbon trim on pockets, sleeves and hem, or insert a broderie anglaise frill around the collar.

Altering the pattern
The dressing gown is made by simply lengthening dress pattern pieces 1 and 2 and front facing piece 5 to ankle length. You can, of course, make it any length you prefer, mid-calf for example; the method used to extend the pattern is the same.

The amount to be added to the pattern depends on your height, but will probably be between 20–30cm/ 8–12in. Finished lengths for the dressing gown, based on average heights, are given in the fabric chart. If you are taller or shorter than the average of 5ft 6in, work out the amount to be added to the dress pattern by comparing your back neck to ankle measurement (or length preferred), with the finished back length for the dress given on page 106. The difference between the two is the amount to be added. A 4cm/1½in hem allowance is already included in the pattern so do not add any extra.

Fabric suggestions
Choose cotton blends such as polyester cotton and terylene and cotton, which are easy to wash and care for. Poplin, piqué, seersucker, brushed cottons or broderie anglaise are also suitable.

Fabric quantity chart

Size	10	12	14	16	18
Bust (cm)	83	87	92	97	102
(in)	32½	34	36	38	40
Length* (cm)	140	142	145	147	150
(in)	55	56	57	58	59
90cm	5.90	5.90	5.95	5.95	6.00m
115cm	4.30	4.35	4.35	4.40	4.40m
140cm	3.10	3.10	3.10	3.15	3.15m

*length is finished back length from nape to ankle without sash.

Allow extra fabric for one-way designs and matching checks and stripes.

Extending the pattern pieces

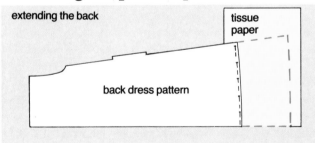

If you are a reasonably experienced dressmaker you can extend the pattern pieces when cutting out. Simply add on the appropriate amount where indicated and mark the new cutting line on the fabric with a ruler and tailor's chalk. If you are less experienced, or wish to make a permanent addition to your pattern, add tissue paper as follows:

Back pattern Pin a sheet of tissue paper to lower edge of pattern, aligning the centre back with the straight edge of the paper. Measure down the amount to be added from the lower edge of pattern at centre back, making marks parallel to the lower edge at 5cm/2in intervals across the width of the pattern. Join the marks, drawing a curve parallel to the lower edge of the pattern. Using a ruler, extend the side seam to the new lower edge, following the cutting line for your size.

Front pattern Lengthen in the same way. The excess tissue is cut away as you cut out.

Front facing pattern Take a strip of tissue paper 20cm × 150cm/ 8in ×60in, joining several small pieces together if necessary. Draw a parallel line 10cm/4in from the straight edge along the full length of the paper. Pin the front facing to the top of the paper, with the centre front to the edge of the paper strip.

Extend the shoulder seam by 2.5cm/ 1in and join this new shoulder point to the line drawn 10cm/4in from the edge of the paper, parallel to the curve of the dress facing.

Trace round the neck curve and shoulder slope of the facing and mark off the length to correspond with centre front edge of extended front pattern. Remove facing pattern from the tissue and cut out the new extended front facing. Mark a straight grain line parallel to the front edge.

Cutting out and making up the dressing gown

You will need
Lightweight fabric – see fabric
  quantity chart on previous page
Matching thread
1.50m/1⅝yd of 90cm/36in-wide
  lightweight iron-on interfacing
Two buttons for cuffs
Pattern pieces, page 120:
1 Back (dress)
2 Front (dress)
3 Yoke
4 Collar
5 Front neck facing
6 Side seam pocket (or Patch pocket
  pattern piece 7, page 74)
7 Long sleeve
8 Cuff
10 Belt

Cutting out
Position pieces as shown on cutting
layouts for your fabric width. For
economic cutting, 90cm/36in and
115cm/45in fabric is folded across
the width; 140cm/54in fabric is
folded lengthwise. Cut out pattern
pieces carefully and transfer pattern
markings to fabric.
Fold interfacing in half to cut two
pieces for the new long front facing
and two pieces for the cuffs, using
pattern piece 8 folded in half
lengthwise. Cut a single layer of
interfacing for the collar.

Cutting layouts for dressing gown

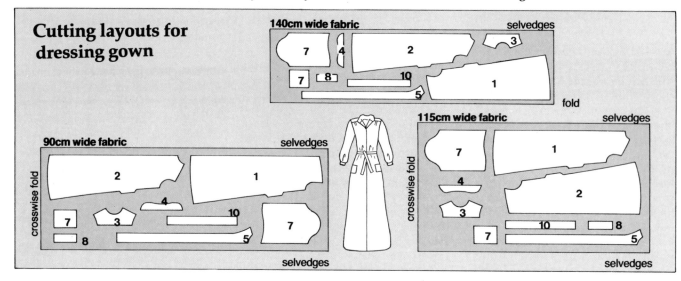

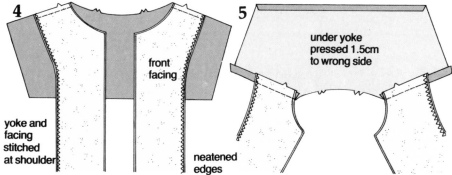

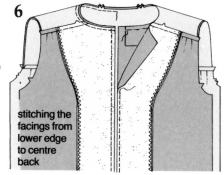

Making up
The dressing gown is made up
following the instructions for the
dress on pages 108–109 with the
following variations:
Steps 1–3 Work as for the dress, but
leave the centre front seam open.
Step 4 Iron fusible interfacing on to
wrong side of extended front
facings and neaten the long curved
edge of the facings. With right sides
together, pin front facings to under
yoke at shoulders. Machine and
press turnings towards under yoke.
Step 5 Press up 1.5cm/⅝in seam
allowance to wrong side on lower
edge of under yoke.
Steps 6–7 Apply collar and facings
as for dress, stitching the facings

from the new lower edge to the
centre back of neck on each side.
Steps 8–14 Complete under yoke,
side seam pockets if required, and
sleeves as for the dress.
Step 15 A narrow machine-stitched
hem (about 1cm/½in) is preferable
for the dressing gown, as there is a
danger of catching heels in a hand-
sewn hem on a full-length garment.
Trim away excess length and press
up hem allowance, easing the fabric
around the hemline curve. Turn
under 5mm/¼in at raw edge and
press, tack and machine hem in
place, keeping line of stitches
parallel to pressed hem fold.
Catchstitch facings into position
over hem.

Step 16 Make the belt as for the
dress.

Adding patch pockets
You may prefer to attach patch
pockets to the dressing gown, using
pattern piece 7 from page 74. Fold
the pocket extensions of pieces 1
and 2 away along the appropriate
seamline when cutting out, and
attach the pockets as instructed on
page 72.
As the dressing gown wraps over at
the centre front, the pockets need to
be nearer the side seams. The exact
position is determined after the
hem has been turned up, and
should be in the most comfortable
position for the hands.

Trimming with ribbon

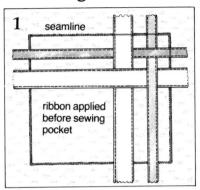

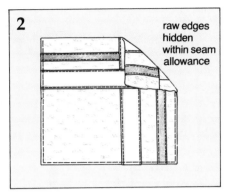

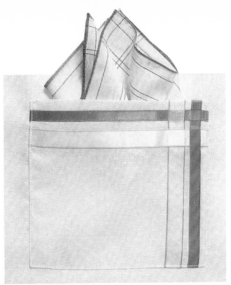

Above: Ribbons can highlight a pocket.

Ribbon is an ideal choice for trimming the dressing gown. You can choose from a wide range of colours and finishes, including satin and velvet. If your dressing gown is to be washed frequently, a polyester ribbon, which will not crease, may be a better choice than nylon, which will have to be ironed.

Ribbons should be attached as invisibly as possible. When machining, try to merge the stitches with the woven edge of the ribbon. Sew each edge in the same direction to avoid diagonal pulling.

1 Ribbon trims look particularly effective on pockets. Apply ribbon to the pocket *before* it is made up.
2 When it is stitched to the garment, the raw edges are hidden within the seamline.
Try combining different widths and colours of ribbon at right angles to one another, overlapping and interweaving the rows where they meet at the top front corner of the pocket. Or, for a simple finish, stitch two parallel rows of 5mm/¼in ribbon across the top of the pocket. Trimmings need not be confined to

the pockets. Add a ribbon band at the edge of the cuff and, instead of using shop-bought buttons, cover your own in a wider, matching ribbon. A hem also benefits from a ribbon trim which can be used to hide the machine stitching and to add weight to a lightweight fabric, so that it hangs well. Small ribbon bows can be tied or sometimes purchased ready-made – use these to add interest at the neckline and on the cuffs.

Trimming with lace

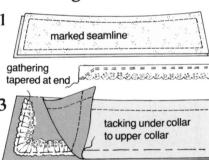

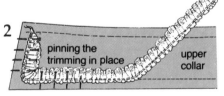

Above: Narrow lace, gathered to make an attractive edging for the collar.

Broderie anglaise and other lacy trimmings can be used very effectively as a dainty, decorative edging for collars. If you buy them ready gathered, you will need about 70cm/¾yd for the collar. Alternatively, you can gather your own using a straight piece of trimming, two to three times the finished length required.

How to apply the trimming
1 Cut out two fabric collar pieces and one piece of interfacing. Mark the seamlines 1.5cm/⅝in from the raw edges all around the collar pieces on the wrong side.
Run two rows of hand or machine gathering stitches 7mm/¼in from the raw edge, along the trimming,

tapering across to the decorative outer edge at each end. Pull up the threads to the required length, distributing the gathers evenly.
2 With right sides and raw edges together, pin the trimming to the interfaced upper collar, matching the gathering line on the trimming to the collar seamline. Start at the front edge of the collar, positioning the tapered end of the trim exactly on the point where the seamlines cross. Pin along one short edge, across the outer edge of collar and back up second short edge to centre front. More gathers are needed at the corners to allow the trimming to spread out evenly when the collar is turned through.

3 Tack the trimming along the seamline, using small stitches. With right sides together, pin and tack upper collar to under collar along seamline, keeping trim well tucked in at corners.
Machine carefully along seamline through all layers. Trim seam allowances to 6mm/¼in and cut across corners.
4 Turn collar through to right side. Tack around outer edges and press. Tack neck edge together, ready to join to garment, and remove all the visible tackings and gathering threads.

Graph for pull-over-the-head dress and blouse

1.5cm/⅝in seam allowance included (except where shown)

4cm/1½in hem allowed   1 square = 5cm

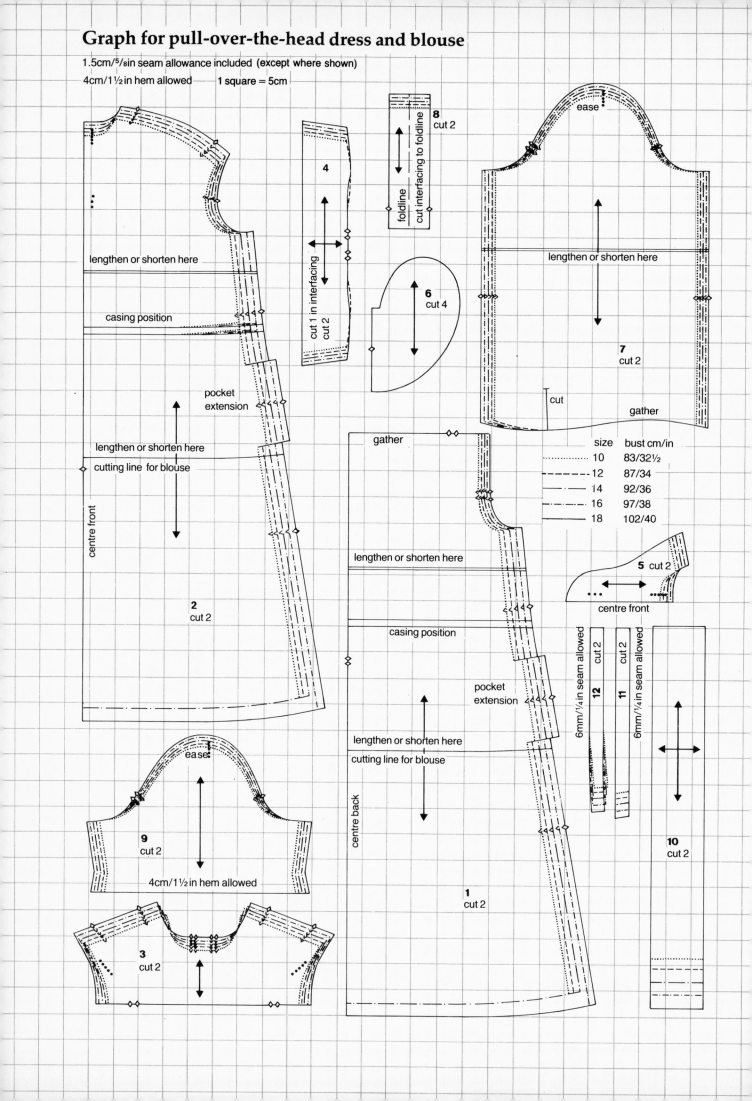

lengthen or shorten here

casing position

cut 1 in interfacing
cut 2

4

8
cut 2

foldline   cut interfacing to foldline

6
cut 4

ease

lengthen or shorten here

7
cut 2

cut

gather

pocket
extension

lengthen or shorten here

cutting line for blouse

centre front

2
cut 2

gather

size	bust cm/in
10	83/32½
12	87/34
14	92/36
16	97/38
18	102/40

lengthen or shorten here

casing position

pocket
extension

lengthen or shorten here

cutting line for blouse

centre back

5 cut 2

centre front

6mm/¼in seam allowed   **12** cut 2

11 cut 2   6mm/¼in seam allowed

ease

9
cut 2

4cm/1½in hem allowed

3
cut 2

1
cut 2

10
cut 2

PART 6

Shirts and shirtwaisters

A classic shirt pattern can form the basis for innumerable variations of style, creating a whole wardrobe of blouses and shirts for day and evening wear for both winter and summer.

The basic pattern has a button band attached to each front and a collar stand with collar. To change the look, replace the pointed collar with a round version or simply use a stand collar on its own. Alternatively, substitute a bias-cut tie for the collar and stand. For a pretty feminine version learn how to make single or double frills to insert into the button band, collar stand or cuffs. In addition simple pattern alterations can turn the long sleeve into a short sleeve, and a short sleeve into a puffed sleeve.

These collar and sleeve variations can also be used on a basic button-through shirt dress. This style, with its fitted bodice and partly-gathered skirt, requires careful cutting out when using patterned fabrics. Learn how to balance the pattern across the front and back, and how to match the design horizontally at the armhole seams and vertically through the bodice and skirt.

Finally, make a feature of buttons on these and other garments and learn how to attach them correctly.

Button bands and collar stands for a basic blouse

Add some new techniques to your sewing skills and some attractive blouses to your wardrobe by making up this ideal basic blouse in a range of fabric weights. It has a simple shirt-style neck, button-through front and long, full cuffed sleeves.

This chapter introduces you to the shirt style blouse with button band and collar stand. All the blouses which follow are made from the same main pattern pieces on pages 149–150, with variations of neckline and long and short versions of the full, gathered sleeves. The bodice of the blouse is softly gathered into a yoke at front and back, and all the blouses have a strip button band with vertical buttonholes.

The basic collar stand can be attached

Making a button band

A button band is a vertical band or strip of fabric which is interfaced and attached to each side of the centre front of a shirt, adding a firm, crisp finish. One button band has buttonholes and laps over the other which carries the buttons.

If you have altered the length of the blouse, remember to adjust the band. Hem the lower edge of the blouse before applying the button band.

1 Interface the wrong side of each button band (on thicker fabrics cut interfacing to half the width of the button band only, that is up to the fold). Fold band in half lengthwise, right sides together, and stitch across the lower edge. Start 1.5cm/⅝in from long edge and take a 1.5cm/⅝in turning. Clip corner, trim seam and press.

Press 1.5cm/⅝in seam allowance to

Positioning buttonholes

Use horizontal buttonholes where there is some strain, for example at the neckline, cuff or across the chest. Use vertical buttonholes where extra ease has been allowed in the pattern so that the buttons are not pulled undone by undue strain.

A fitted shirt or dress bodice should have horizontal buttonholes down the centre front.

The blouse shown left has extra body fullness gathered into a yoke, allowing enough ease for centre-front buttonholes to be positioned vertically. On both styles the horizontal rule still applies to cuffs and collar stands.

Left: Cut the collar, button band and cuffs in crisp, contrasting white and highlight the buttons by covering them in the main fabric. Wear the shirt-style collar open or closed.

on its own for a simple stand collar, or you can add a shirt-style collar or a round collar. For a sophisticated look you can make a tie-necked version. The instructions are presented in such a way that the sewing techniques involved in a particular style can be used for any similar pattern. Add frills to the button band, cuffs and collar stand instead of a collar. Dress up a plain fabric by topstitching the button band, collar stand, yoke and cuffs in contrasting thread.

This chapter concentrates on the classic shirt-style neck line with a pointed collar joined to the collar stand. It may be worn buttoned to the neck, or with the top buttons left open for a casual effect. The sleeves are long and buttoned at the cuff.

The only new techniques to learn are how to make a button band and how to construct and attach a collar stand and collar to a blouse neckline.

A classic shirt collar has two parts made up separately – the stand or

neckband which fits closely to the neck and fastens with a button, and the fall or visible collar which is joined to the top edge of the stand. This method of construction raises the collar above the level of the garment neckline unlike one-piece collars which fall from the neckline without a stand. The finish of the collar and stand is always very noticeable, so mark the seamlines on all pattern pieces, and particularly on the interfacing, for accuracy.

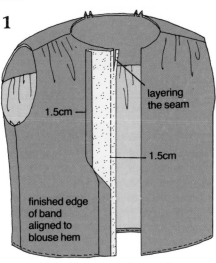

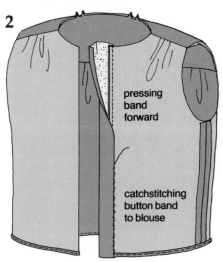

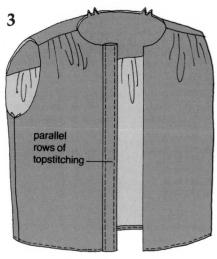

wrong side along one long edge. Turn band through to right side. Lay button band over blouse front edge, aligning seamed lower edge with blouse hem. Tack and machine the long front seam. Layer turnings.

2 Press band forward so that pressed fold of seam allowance just covers line of machine stitching on wrong side. Catchstitch button band in place to line of machine stitching. Press.

3 Topstitch (see page 209) both long edges from right side if required and repeat all steps to attach button band to other front edge.

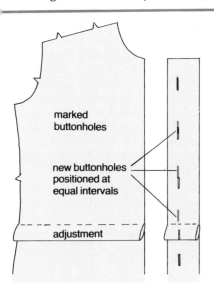

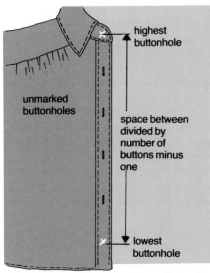

Re-spacing buttonholes
Most commercial paper patterns include markings for the position of both buttons and buttonholes. If you have to adjust the pattern length

these must be re-positioned so that they remain an equal distance apart.
Marked buttonholes Measure the distance between the top and bottom buttonhole and space the

rest of the buttonholes evenly between them. Re-space the button markings to correspond.
Unmarked buttonholes Where buttonholes are not marked on the pattern, as in the graph patterns on page 149, make any adjustment to the length as necessary and make up the blouse.

Mark the position of the highest buttonhole – in the collar stand if there is one – and the lowest, making allowances for the hem. Divide the space in between by the number of buttons to be used, minus one. For example, if there are to be six buttons, divide by five as there will be five spaces between them. This amount gives the distance between the buttons. To mark the position of vertical buttonholes, measure from the top of one to the top of the next.

Making a shirt collar with stand

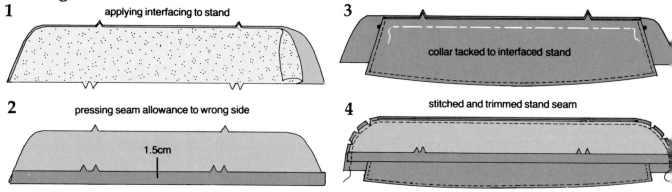

1 applying interfacing to stand

2 pressing seam allowance to wrong side

1.5cm

3 collar tacked to interfaced stand

4 stitched and trimmed stand seam

Make up the collar in exactly the same way as the dress collar on page 100. Tack the layers together along the free edge and topstitch the outer edges if required.

1 Tack the interfacing (or press if fusible) to the wrong side of one of the stand pieces.
2 Press the seam allowance to the wrong side on the long edge of the other stand piece.

3 With right sides together, pin the under collar to the interfaced stand between circles, matching notches. The stand extends beyond the collar ends. Tack along seamline.
4 With right sides together,

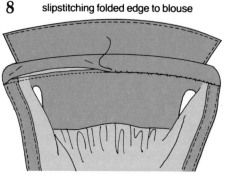

8 slipstitching folded edge to blouse

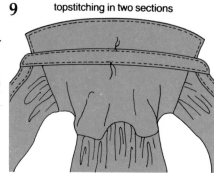

9 topstitching in two sections

8 On wrong side, bring folded edge of stand down to neck seamline and slipstitch to secure.
9 If you want to topstitch the stand, work from the right side and,

starting at the upper centre back, work across and down to the centre back of the neck seamline on both sides of the stand.

Classic blouse

This style of blouse is ideal for everyday wear so choose a fabric which launders well and is easy to care for. Cotton and polyester blends are ideal for frequent washing, and a high proportion of polyester means that the blouse will drip dry and require little ironing. A higher proportion of cotton or an all-cotton fabric is cooler and more comfortable to wear in warm weather, but requires more ironing. Seersucker and crêpe are also suitable for the blouse, but they must be pressed with a cool iron to avoid flattening the textured surface of the fabric.

Shirtings, challis, chambray and madras cotton are also suitable, while lightweight wools, Viyella or brushed cotton make warm and comfortable winter blouses.

Take into consideration the colour and pattern of the fabric as well as its nature. If you want to make a feature of the topstitching on the collar, cuffs and button band, don't obscure the effect by choosing a dominating pattern. Topstitching looks most effective on a plain fabric, or one with a small, regular pattern.

Stripes and checks work well on this blouse – remember to allow a little extra fabric if you want to cut the button band on the cross, and for matching the pattern across the seams.

You will need
Fabric according to size

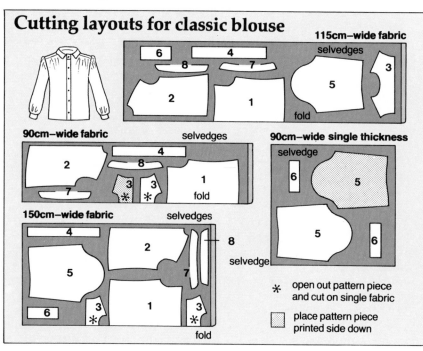

Cutting layouts for classic blouse

115cm–wide fabric

selvedges

fold

90cm–wide fabric   selvedges

fold

150cm–wide fabric   selvedges

fold

90cm–wide single thickness

selvedge

selvedge

* open out pattern piece and cut on single fabric

place pattern piece printed side down

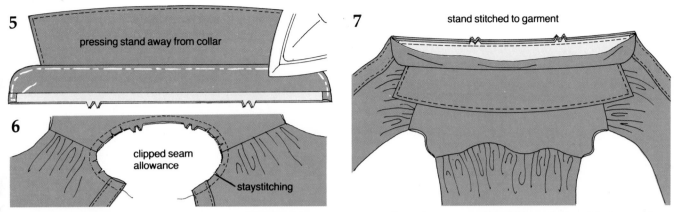

5 pressing stand away from collar

6 clipped seam allowance

staystitching

7 stand stitched to garment

matching notches, pin stand facing over tacked collar and stand. Tack through all thicknesses. Machine stand seam following seamlines carefully. Trim seam, clipping notches at curves to reduce bulk.

5 Turn stand through to right side and press both stand sections away from the collar. Tack close to seamline to keep flat and press.
6 Staystitch neck seamline of blouse. Snip into seam allowance to

staystitching at 2.5cm/1in intervals.
7 With right sides together, matching notches, tack interfaced stand to garment along neck seamline. Machine seam, trim turnings and press towards collar.

Matching thread
0.35m/⅜yd lightweight interfacing
9×1cm/⅜in buttons
Pattern pieces, page 149:
1 Blouse back
2 Blouse front
3 Yoke
4 Button band
5 Long sleeve
6 Cuff
7 Collar stand
8 Shirt collar

Fabric quantity chart

Size	10	12	14	16	18
Bust (cm)	83	87	92	97	102
(in)	32½	34	36	38	40
90cm*	2.30	2.30	2.50	2.60	2.80m
115cm*	2.10	2.10	2.10	2.20	2.20m
150cm*	1.45	1.50	1.50	1.50	1.60m

*without nap.

Allow extra fabric for matching checks or one-way designs.

Preparing to cut out
Position pattern pieces according to the appropriate layout for your fabric width. Cut out carefully and transfer pattern markings to garment sections. Using the same pattern pieces, cut out one collar stand, one collar, two button bands and two cuffs in interfacing.

Right: A back view of the blouse. The gathers in the yoke seam ensure a comfortable fit across the back.

Making the blouse

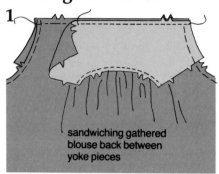

sandwiching gathered blouse back between yoke pieces

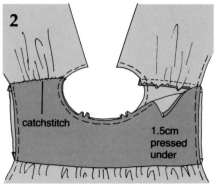

catchstitch

1.5cm pressed under

Step 1 Staystitch neck and armhole edges within seamline on all pieces. Run two rows of gathering threads between notches on back, draw up to match notches on lower edge of yoke. Tack right side of one yoke section to wrong side of blouse back to form the under yoke. With right sides together, matching notches, tack remaining yoke section to back.

Machine along seamline, through all thicknesses. Remove gathering threads and press the yoke and under yoke up.

Step 2 Run two rows of gathering threads along upper edges of each blouse front between notches. Draw up the gathers to fit front yoke edges. With right sides together, matching notches,

machine fronts to top yoke. Press seam allowances towards yoke. Press under turnings on front under yoke and bring it down to meet the seam joining fronts to yoke and catchstitch. Topstitch yoke seams.

Step 3 First fitting Tack side seams together and try on. Pin blouse together at centre front. Check width of blouse across back and front measuring about 10cm/4in below shoulders. The armhole seamline should be in line with the end of the shoulder. Check the body width, remembering that the style should be roomy. Take in any excess at side seams. Make similar adjustments to the sleeve seam if you alter the side seam, or the sleeve fit will be affected.

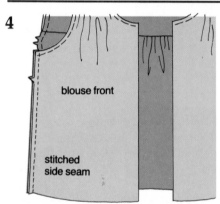

blouse front

stitched side seam

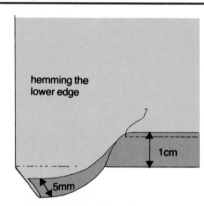

hemming the lower edge

1cm

5mm

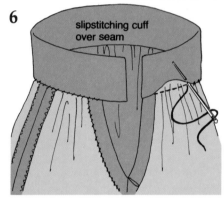

slipstitching cuff over seam

Step 4 Pin, tack and machine the side seams. If you are topstitching the blouse, you may prefer to use a machine flat fell seam instead of an open seam (see Basic seams pages 24–26) to give all the seams a similar appearance.

Step 5 Hem the lower blouse edge by hand or machine, taking a 1.5cm/⅝in turning. Prepare the button bands and join to each front edge as instructed, making sure the lower finished edge of each band lines up with the hem.

Step 6 Face or bind the lower sleeve opening and attach cuff as instructed on pages 102–105. Prepare collar and collar stand and attach to neckline.
Run a row of gathering threads either side of the seamline on the sleeve head and draw up gathers to fit the armhole.

Step 7 Second fitting Tack the sleeve seam, pin and tack into armhole and try on. Pin the blouse together at centre front and check the fit of the sleeve in the armhole. Check that the top sleeve gathers are positioned in a flattering way and that they match each other. Make sure armhole or sleeve are not too tight, remembering that the fit will be looser when the armhole seam is stitched and trimmed.

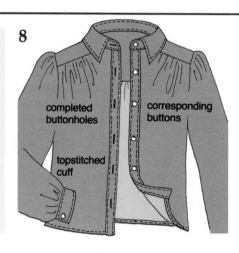

completed buttonholes

corresponding buttons

topstitched cuff

Step 8 Complete sleeve and insert as shown on pages 58–59. Note that this sleeve has a full head and should have a gathered appearance when set in. Topstitch cuff if required.
Make hand or machine buttonholes in button band, collar stand and cuffs. Sew on buttons to correspond.

Making a classic tie-necked blouse

The tie-neck blouse is an elegant variation of the shirt in the previous chapter. Make it up in a silky man-made fabric for everyday wear, using the techniques given here, or dress it up for special occasions by making a glamorous version in pure silk crêpe de chine.

Make this tie-neck blouse in exactly the same way as the blouse in the last chapter, but substitute a bias-cut tie for the collar and stand.

The tie-neck blouse needs a soft fabric that gathers well into the yoke or cuffs, and will not form too stiff a bow when tied. For a soft, silky effect, look for polyester, acetate or viscose, or blends of these fibres. Polyester crêpe de chine, surah, foulard, challis and peau-de-soie all fall into this category. For special occasions treat yourself to a fine silk.

You will need
Fabric as given overleaf
Matching thread
0.2m/¼yd lightweight interfacing
9×1cm/⅜in buttons
1 clear plastic press stud
Pattern pieces, page 149 as for the shirt (see page 125) but substitute the Blouse tie (9) for the Shirt collar and stand (7 and 8)

Making up
Make up the blouse in the same way as the blouse in the previous chapter except for the collar details. Follow the instructions for the button band and tie neck overleaf.

Below: A silky polyester crêpe de chine has been used to make this smart tie-necked version of the classic blouse pattern.

Preparing the button band for a neck tie

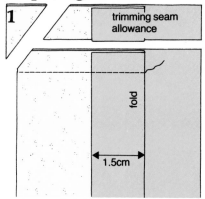

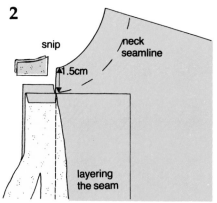

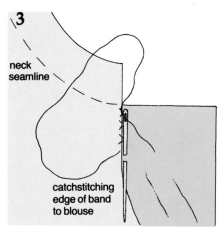

To ensure that a tie sits well at the neck it is attached to the neckline of the shirt only, not to the button band. So the top edge of the button band must be seamed across the top and bottom before it is attached.
1 Tack interfacing to the wrong side of the button band. Press 1.5cm/⅝in seam allowance to wrong side along one long edge.

Fold button band in half, right sides together, and stitch top and bottom edges taking 1.5cm/⅝in turnings. Trim seam allowances, clip corners and press. Turn band through.
2 With right sides together, position button band 1.5cm/⅝in down from raw edge of blouse neckline at front edge, aligning lower seamed edge with hem. Clip to staystitching at

neckline of blouse, 1.5cm/⅝in in from front. Tack and machine the long front seam, leaving the seam allowance on the upper side of the button band free. Layer turnings, clip corner and press.
3 Press button band forwards. On the inside catchstitch the folded-under edge of the band to the line of the machine stitching.

Making and attaching a neck tie

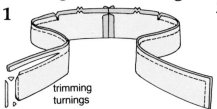

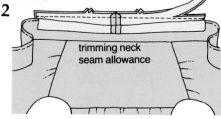

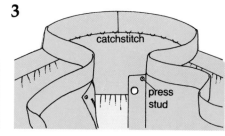

A neck tie is cut on the bias so that it eases to fit the neckline and ties well. It is cut in two sections which are joined at the centre back.
1 With right sides together, stitch the centre back seam and press open. Fold tie in half lengthways, right sides together, and stitch the two tie ends on the seamline as far as the circles, leaving the neckline edge of the tie open. Snip to

stitching at circles and trim turnings only where the seam has been stitched, clipping across corners. Turn right side out and roll seam so that it is positioned to the edge of the tie. Edge tack and press.
2 Working on the right side of the blouse with right sides together and matching notches and circles, pin and tack single layer of neck tie opening to neck edge of shirt on

seamline. Machine seam, ensuring that it aligns with the button band at each side of the front neck. Trim turnings and press up into collar.
3 Fold in seam allowance on free edge of tie opening and catchstitch to neckline seamline. Reinforce junction of tie and button band with a bar tack worked on wrong side. Sew a clear plastic press stud to upper corner of button band.

Fabric quantity chart

Size	10	12	14	16	18
Bust (cm)	83	87	92	97	102
(in)	32½	34	36	38	40
90cm*	2.90	3.00	3.00	3.10	3.30m
115cm*	2.10	2.20	2.20	2.30	2.30m
150cm	1.70	1.70	1.70	1.80	1.80m

*fabric without nap.
Allow extra fabric for matching checks and stripes.

Cutting layouts for tie-necked blouse

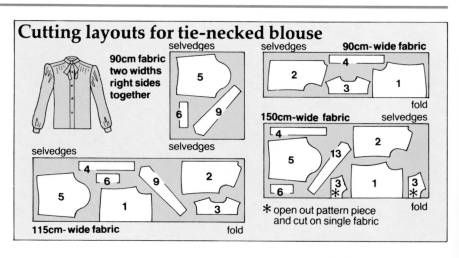

128

A double-thickness frill

Transform the neckline of the casual blouse with the simple stand collar from the graph patterns on page 149. Use a self or contrasting fabric for the stand or add a narrow double frill to the collar and cuffs for a crisp and elegant variation.

A simple stand collar version of the blouse on page 122 (see pattern page 149) is quick to make. Omit the pattern piece for the collar and turn the stand itself into a collar by neatening the top edge. The blouse can be as casual or smart as you please, depending on your fabric choice.

To make a pretty and feminine blouse from the same pattern, just add some frills. Make double frills and insert them in the top edge of the collar stand and around the cuffs as well. The next chapter shows how to insert single frills either side of the button band.

Adding a frill to an ordinary stand collar changes its proportions slightly – both the frill and stand should be narrow or the frill will be uncomfortably high on the neck. A finished frill of a depth of no more than 2cm/¾in with a collar stand of no more than 2.5cm/1in is ideal. If you wish to make the collar stand even narrower, do not make the alteration at the neck edge or it will not fit the neckline. Instead, trace a line parallel to and below the top edge of the stand pattern, to the new height required.

Below: The frilled blouse looks superb made up in crisp white Swiss cotton. Inset: The plain stand collar looks effective made in a crisp white fabric to contrast with the blouse.

Making a double-thickness frill

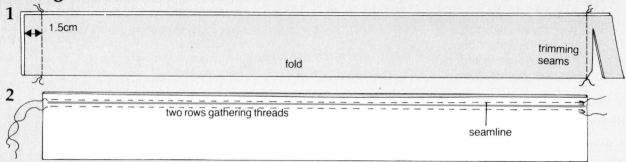

A double frill has a fold along the outer edge with the raw edges inserted into the collar stand or cuff edges.

If you do not have a pattern for a double frill, cut a straight strip of fabric 7cm/2¾in wide (or twice the desired finished width, plus two seam allowances of 1.5cm/⅝in). The length is one-and-a-half to three times the finished length, plus seam allowances, depending on the fullness required. Double frills can be cut on the straight grain or the bias.

1 Fold the strip of fabric in half lengthwise with right sides together and stitch both short ends, taking 1.5cm/⅝in seams. Trim seams, clip corners and turn through.

2 With wrong sides together run two rows of gathering through the double fabric of the frill either side of the seamline.

Making a stand collar without frill

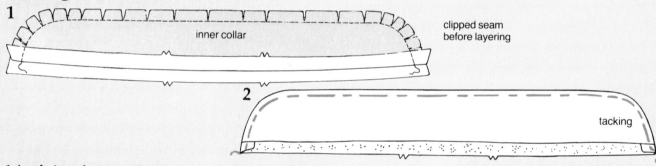

1 Apply interfacing to the wrong side of the outer collar. Press 1.5cm/⅝in seam allowance to wrong side along lower edge of inner collar. With right sides together, lay outer collar over inner collar. Tack around the collar through all layers, leaving the neckline edge open. Machine along seamline and layer the stitched seams. Clip into the seam allowances and cut V-shaped notches at the convex curves.

2 Turn collar to right side, using a blunt knitting needle or a collar-point turner to push out all the seams. Tack close to seamed edges and press.

Apply to blouse neckline as for collar stand (pages 124–125). Topstitch all the way round 2mm/⅛in from the edge for a firm finish.

Making a stand collar with frill

A frill sits best on a collar stand with straight top and front edges.

1 To produce a straight-edge pattern from the rounded one, such as the one on page 149 (pattern piece 7), simply trace the pattern on to tissue paper and continue the line of the top edge of the stand parallel to the lower edge, without curving away.

Left: Close-up of frilled stand collar.

Making frilled cuffs

A frill is inserted at the edge of cuffs in much the same way as in the collar stand. Normally the cuff end which is placed flush to the sleeve opening forms the overlap but in this case take the frill around the short end of the underlap to form a decorative overlap. Adapt the pattern by folding it in half lengthwise. Cut four cuffs to this size, adding 1.5cm/⅝in seam allowance to top edge of each cuff. To make the frill, cut a strip of fabric 7cm/2¾in by length required adding a small amount for extra fullness at the corner. Fold in half lengthways, right sides together, and stitch short edges, taking 1.5cm/⅝in seams. Trim seam allowances, clip corners and turn through.

Run a double row of gathering threads, one each side of the seamline, at the raw edges of the frill, working through both thicknesses of fabric.

1 With right sides together, align the raw edges of the frill with the upper raw edge of the underside of the cuff. Start 1.5cm/⅝in in at the top edge and take the frill down the short side of the cuff nearest the notched lower edge, finishing 1.5cm/⅝in above lower raw edges. Draw up the gathers to fit. Distribute evenly except at the corners where more gathers are required to allow the frill to lie flat when turned through. Pin and tack, then remove pins.

Apply interfacing to wrong side of top cuff. With right sides together,

Above: Detail of frilled cuffs.

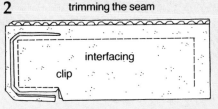

lay the top cuff over frill and under cuff, sandwiching frill.

Tack the two short edges of the cuff and the long upper edge, sandwiching the frill and going round as far as the notch on the lower edge which now forms the overlap.

2 Machine the seams, taking care not to catch in the free fold edge of frill. Trim the seam, clip the corners

and clip to stitching line at notch on lower edge.

3 Turn the cuff through, pulling the frill gently to ensure the cuff turns through fully.

Press the seams, omitting the frill. Finish the cuffs when attached by sewing the button to the straight edge of the cuff and making the buttonhole in the overlap.

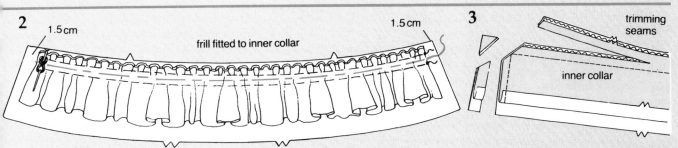

At the front edge of the stand, continue the cutting line up in the same way, until the lines intersect.

2 With raw edges of frill along upper edge of right side of inner collar, pin each end 1.5cm/⅝in from short edges of collar. Draw up gathers to fit, spacing them evenly, pin, tack and remove pins.

3 Apply interfacing to the wrong side of the outer collar. Press 1.5cm/⅝in seam allowance to wrong side along lower edge of inner collar. With right sides together, lay outer collar over inner collar and frill. Tack around the collar through all layers, leaving the neckline seam edge open and being careful not to

catch in the short ends of frill. Machine stitch, cut across corners and trim seams. If the fabric is not too bulky, trim only 5mm/¼in from the upper edge of the seam, as the turnings help keep frill upright. Turn right side out, gently pulling at frill. Tack close to seamed edges and press collar stand only.

Finishing touches for a classic blouse: a rounded collar and centre-front frills

Learn how to make a perfectly rounded collar and attach a frill to the button band of a plain blouse and you have a fashion classic – a smart frilled blouse to dress up a suit or a skirt for special occasions. Trim the frill with ribbon before inserting it for an ultra-feminine look.

A frilled blouse made up in fine cotton gives a crisp, smart appearance to a suit or skirt, while the frills prevent it from looking too severe. This chapter shows how to turn the basic shirt pattern into an attractive frilled-front version with a rounded collar and long sleeves. The frills are made from single fabric, narrowly hemmed then gathered into the seam on each of the button bands. The top short edge of the frill is shaped so that it follows the line of the neck edge below the collar stand. Once you have learnt to make straight frills you can insert them at the neck, cuffs, front or yoke – wherever there is a suitable seam, in fact.

The instructions here are for a single-thickness frill but there is no reason why a double frill should not be used

if your fabric is suitable. The last chapter showed how to make double frills for collars and cuffs.

Making decorative frills

Frills are made by gathering up one side of a strip of fabric along its seamline, to fit a corresponding seamline on a garment.

The instructions given here are for straight frills, cut from rectangular strips of fabric on the straight grain. Cut the frill as one piece, without joins, for the best finish. If this is not possible, cut the pieces on the same grain and join the strips, disguising the seam within the gathers. The frill itself is very simple to make. The raw edges are enclosed in the garment seam and the frill is evenly gathered down the front.

Above: Use pattern pieces 12 and 13 on page 149 to make this frilled round-collared version of the basic blouse.

Making your own pattern

The frill pattern (piece 13, page 149) has a 1.5cm/⅝in seam allowance on one long edge and a narrow hem (6mm/¼in) on the other long edge. If you do not have a pattern for a frill you can make one by cutting a strip of fabric to the required width plus the seam and hem allowances.

The frill is usually cut one-and-a-half times the length of the seam, but for a fuller frill make it up to three times the seam length. Always shape the top edge of the frill by matching it to the curve of the neck on the front pattern pieces so that you can sew it into the seam.

Sewing curved collars

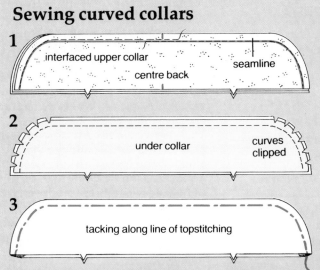

1 interfaced upper collar   seamline
centre back

2 under collar   curves clipped

3 tacking along line of topstitching

Above: Sew curved seams slowly and with care for a neat, even finish.

The secret of producing a good rounded curve on the outside edge of a collar is to stitch the seam slowly and carefully in two halves before layering and notching the seam.
1 Cut and interface the collar sections as normal, applying interfacing to the wrong side of upper collar. Mark the seamlines clearly on the pattern pieces. Place upper and lower collars right sides together and pin and tack along seamline.
Start at the front edge of collar and machine stitch carefully around the curve, using both hands to manoeuvre the fabric so that the stitching follows the curve of the seamline exactly. If

you have an electronic machine, adjust the speed, otherwise use careful foot control. Stitch to 2cm/¾in beyond centre back and stop. Cut thread and remove work from machine.
Turn work over and start again at other front edge, again working carefully around the curve. Overlap stitching at centre back by 2cm/¾in. (If the curve is sharp, take a few stitches, raise the presser foot and pivot the work slightly into the new position. Lower the presser foot and continue repeating the procedure as often as necessary round the curve.)
2 Press the collar on the wrong side. Trim the turnings on the

under collar to 3mm/⅛in and those of the upper collar to 6mm/¼in.
Clip small V-shaped notches from the seam allowances around the curves, cutting right up to, but not into, the line of stitching to reduce bulk.
3 Turn collar through and check turnings are flat. Use a blunt knitting needle or collar point turner to push out collar seamline. Press from underside of collar. If you want to topstitch, tack through all thicknesses the required distance from outer edge of collar before stitching.

Inserting a frill into a seam

1 Neaten the short lower edge and the long outside edge by taking a narrow double hem, stitching it by hand or by machine using a narrow hem attachment if you have one. Work two rows of gathering stitches by hand either side of the seamline – and close to it – on the other long edge to be inserted into the seam.
2 Lay the wrong side of the frill to the right side of the blouse front, with the shaped edge aligned to the neck edge and the lower hemmed edge aligned with the hem of the blouse.
Draw the gathering threads up until the frill is the length required and space the gathers evenly, using the point of a pin. Pin at right angles to the seamline and tack the frill in position, then remove pins.

1 = = = gathering threads = = =

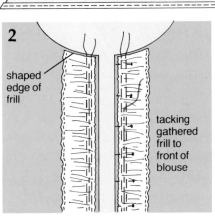

shaped edge of frill — tacking gathered frill to front of blouse

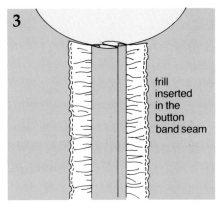

frill inserted in the button band seam

3 With right sides together, join button band to blouse as instructed on page 123. The frill is sandwiched between the first seam on the button band and the front of the blouse. Press the finished frill

and button band lightly along the seam turnings only. Do not press the gathers of the frill flat. Repeat to attach frill to other button band. Tack neckline edge of frill to blouse. The hem edge is left free.

Short-sleeved blouse with pattern variations

To extend your blouse collection here is a short-sleeved version with a round collar. With sleeves in mind, learn how to adapt this and other commercial paper patterns – turning long sleeves into short, and short into puffed sleeves to vary a blouse or dress.

Adding variety to your wardrobe need not involve buying costly patterns for each new garment. You can use favourite patterns again, varying fabrics or trimmings, and you can also make alterations to the basic style. This gives your clothes an individual look, putting a personal stamp on everything you make.

This chapter shows you how you can also make simple sleeve pattern alterations, changing a long sleeve to a short sleeve, or a short sleeve to a puffed sleeve, without buying a new pattern for each one.

Use these sleeve variations on the blouse made up on pages 122–126 or the dress on pages 143–145.

Earlier chapters gave several collar and cuff variations to the basic pattern for a long sleeved blouse. Some of these can also be used on a short sleeved blouse. See how many new looks you can create with a clever choice of colour and trimmings to add an individual look to your own basic pattern.

Short gathered sleeve

This type of sleeve usually has gentle gathers at both armhole and lower edges, with a band rather than a cuff at the lower edge. Cuffs are difficult to fasten at this level, so the band must be roomy enough to slip over the hand and elbows. If the band is pushed up to the fuller part of the upper arm it will keep in place and give the sleeve a puffed effect during wear. (For a basic short sleeve see pieces 10 and 11, page 149.)

If you require a wider or shorter sleeve, you need only make basic pattern alterations, but to make a much fuller, puffed sleeve you must cut through the pattern tissue and spread it apart to form a new pattern.

Puffed sleeve

A puffed sleeve is up to half as wide again as a short, gathered sleeve. The weight of the fabric used, the amount of gathers and the shortness of the underarm seam are responsible for the finished appearance. Fabrics with some body are the best and these may be fine and sheer, or dressweight cottons. For evening

Left: Contrast sleeve bands emphasize the short, full sleeves. Checks cut on the cross look effective on the button band and the covered buttons.

wear, puffed sleeves in moiré taffeta or velvet work beautifully, although these fabrics are slightly more difficult to handle.

Adapting a long sleeve

To change a favourite blouse or dress pattern with long sleeves and a gathered sleeve head into a short sleeved garment, do not simply chop off the pattern to the required length. Where the sleeve is gathered into a band it is important to increase the width at the lower edge on the shortened pattern so that the finished effect is not skimpy and the proportions are correct. A simple pattern adaptation increases the width of the sleeve and a band made to your own arm measurement finishes it off. Allow enough ease on band when cutting out to ensure comfort in wear. (For a basic long sleeve pattern see piece 5, page 149.)

Making a short, gathered sleeve

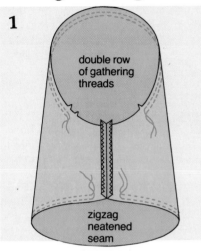

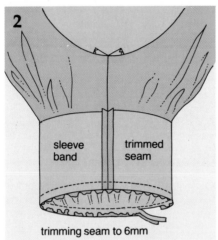

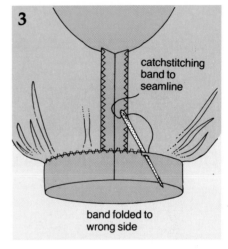

1 With right sides together pin, tack and machine sleeve seam. Press seam open and neaten the edges. Run a double row of gathering threads either side of the seamline at lower edge, and between notches on armhole edge.
2 With right sides together, fold band in half widthways and stitch

seam. Trim turnings and press seam open. Draw up gathering threads on lower edge to fit band. With right sides together, matching seams, pin band to sleeve. Distribute fullness so more falls to the outside of sleeve, away from the underarm seam. Machine band to sleeve, remove gathering threads

and trim seam allowances to 6mm/ ¼in. Press seam turnings towards band.
3 Press 1.5cm/⅝in turning to wrong side on free edge of band. Still working on the wrong side, fold band up to cover previous line of machining and catchstitch in place.

Cutting a puffed sleeve pattern

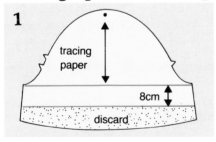

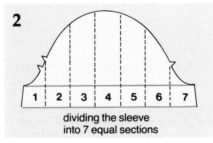

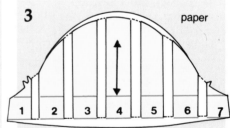

1 Trace your short sleeve pattern on to tracing paper or dressmaker's graph paper, marking notches, circles and grainline.
Draw a line straight across the pattern at underarm level and another line 8cm/3¼in below it. Cut out the pattern.
2 Measure across the lower edge of the pattern and divide the amount by 7. Draw six equally spaced parallel lines this distance apart to divide the pattern into 7 sections.

Number the sections 1–7 and cut the pattern apart along the lines.
3 Mark a straight grainline on a new piece of paper and another line at right angles to it at the base. Position section 4 centrally over the grainline and stick it down. Stick down all the other sections in order, leaving an equal gap in between each section and lining up the lower edges exactly.
Re-draw top and lower sleeve edges, curving out to a maximum of

2.5cm/1in towards the centres and re-joining original cutting line in sections 1 and 7.
Re-mark notches and centres in corresponding positions on new pattern, and cut out. Check the pattern, making up a rough version on an offcut of fabric, before cutting into the proper fabric. Make up as for a short gathered sleeve, distributing the extra fullness evenly.

bold classic colours
suit a variety of
styles and occasions

Turning a long sleeve into a short sleeve pattern

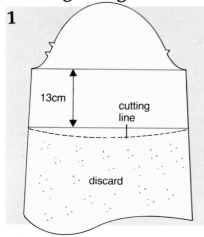

1

13cm

cutting
line

discard

1 Draw a line across the sleeve pattern, 13cm/5in below the underarm seamline. Re-draw the line so that it dips down about 2.5cm/1in at the centre and cut out.

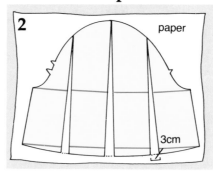

2

paper

3cm

2 Draw three vertical lines on the new short pattern, equally spaced to divide it into quarters. Cut along the vertical lines from the lower edge to within 2mm/⅛in of the sleeve head. Spread the pattern out, increasing the lower edge by a total of 9cm/3½in. Insert paper beneath the pattern and stick it down.

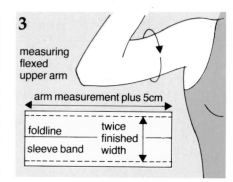

3

measuring
flexed
upper arm

arm measurement plus 5cm

foldline

sleeve band

twice
finished
width

Re-draw the curve of the lower edge and trim away excess paper.
3 Cut a pattern for the sleeve band to the measurement of the flexed upper arm plus 5cm/2in for ease and turnings. The width is twice the finished width required, plus 3cm/1¼in for turnings.

Making pattern alterations

Widening the pattern To give a fuller (but not puffed) effect, draw a line through the centre of the pattern from top to bottom. Cut apart and spread to give the required fullness. Insert paper beneath pattern and stick down. (The distance between the two sleeve halves need not be equal at the top and bottom – you may require more fullness at the lower edge, for example. Maintain the centre of the sleeve on the straight grain as shown.) Complete cutting lines across top and bottom and cut away excess paper.

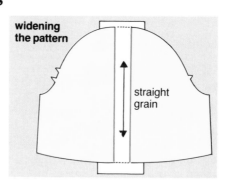

widening
the pattern

straight
grain

Shortening the pattern Make a tuck in the pattern between the underarm and lower edge, half the amount to be shortened. Do not

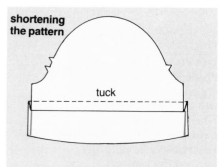

shortening
the pattern

tuck

shorten at the hem – this reduces the sleeve width and spoils the gathered effect.
Re-draw the side seams.

Using patterned fabrics on a fitted dress

This chapter shows you how to make pattern alterations and match fabric designs across the seams on a dress with a fitted bodice. See how to position the bust darts correctly allowing enough room for movement while maintaining a close-fitting shape.

The button-through shirt dress is a style which never seems to date. The pattern from the graphs on page 150 has a fitted bodice, partly gathered skirt, long or short sleeves and several collar variations.

This chapter shows how to make pattern alterations on the fitted bodice to suit your figure type, adjusting the bodice length and position of the darts accordingly. It also shows how to position the pattern pieces on fabric with bold patterns or motifs prior to cutting out so that they match across the centre front and back and balance the garment as a whole, using the fabric design to its best advantage.

Fitted bodices

The fabric of a fitted bodice should lie smoothly over the figure with just enough ease for comfortable movement. To fit the contours of the body, darts are taken to shape the bodice. They can be introduced in several positions on a front bodice – running towards the bust point from the shoulder, side seam, waist seam, etc. The back is also fitted with darts running from the waist towards the fullest part of the shoulder blades.

In this pattern the bodice darts leave the centre of both front and back free to make the most of the fabric design. The bodice can be fitted to a gathered or pleated skirt and the waistline seam is usually covered by a belt or sash. The waist seam allowances are pressed up towards the bodice and should be kept as narrow and as flat as possible.

Hold the belt in position with loops inserted in the side seams at waist level. The bodice and skirt sections are joined before the front facing is turned back (or attached, if separate). The skirt in this pattern is softly gathered midway between the centre and side seams at front and back leaving the centre front flat.

Left: A patterned fabric with a large motif or pattern repeat looks most effective if you take care to match the fabric design where possible on shaped and fitted areas. Balance it each side over the gathered areas and over the garment as a whole.

Making pattern alterations

The width and length adjustments are basically the same for both fitted and looser garments but the former must be precise to ensure a good fit.

Length alteration To establish if this is necessary measure from the nape of the neck to the back waist and compare this measurement with the pattern to establish whether any alteration is necessary. You will know from previous experience if you are unusually long or short-waisted.

An alteration line is often marked on the paper pattern but if not draw a line at right angles to the centre front and back line at a level dividing the waist dart in half.

After the alteration has been made on the pattern, re-shape the dart to give an accurate sewing line.

Width alteration can be made by adding or subtracting up to a maximum of 5cm/2in overall to alter the bodice between the underarm and the waist without changing the garment's proportion. This must be distributed evenly between all the side seams preserving the original dart shaping.

The bust height Check this carefully when making a fitted garment. Young figures tend to be high-busted, more mature figures low-busted. If the underarm dart comes too high or too low the bodice will not fit or flatter your figure.

To find your own bust height, hold a tape measure with one end at the nape of your neck. Allow tape to drape over your shoulder and down to the fullest part of your bust. Read off your bust height on the tape.

Shortening the bodice
Fold front and back bodice pattern pieces on alteration line and pin or tape a tuck of the amount of reduction required.

The dart lines are now distorted so draw new lines from point to waist keeping to original dart width at waist.

Lengthening the bodice
Cut along alteration line on both front and back bodice pattern pieces. Place a piece of paper beneath pattern and spread along alteration line. Pin or tape to hold. Redraw dart lines from point to waist keeping to original dart width at waist.

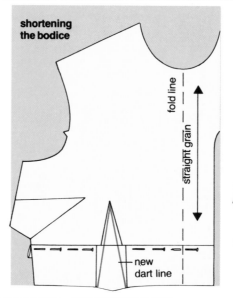
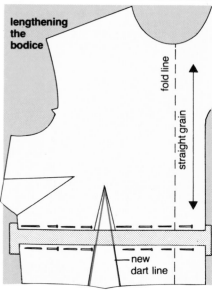

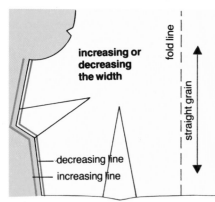
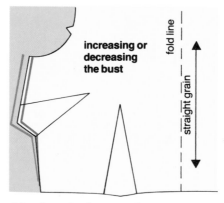
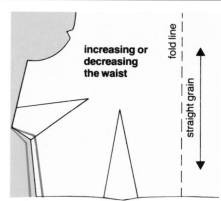

Altering width evenly
Draw a line parallel to the pattern cutting line and the required amount outside or inside. Remember to alter each of the bodice pattern pieces equally.

Altering the bust only
Draw a line parallel to the cutting line from the underarm to the point of the dart. Taper the line from this point to the original waistline.

Altering the waist only
Draw a line parallel to the cutting line from the waist to the dart point. Taper the line from this point to the original underarm seamline.

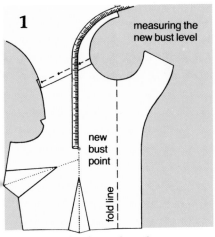

1 measuring the new bust level

new bust point

fold line

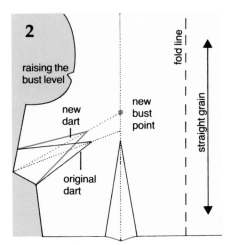

2 raising the bust level

new dart

new bust point

original dart

fold line

straight grain

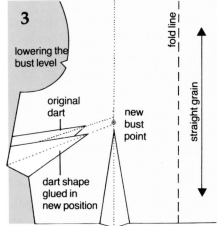

3 lowering the bust level

original dart

new bust point

dart shape glued in new position

fold line

straight grain

Altering the bust level

To determine whether or not the underarm dart will be in the correct position for you, pin up the darts in the front bodice pattern tissue and hold it against your figure, making sure the centre front and the shoulder and side seams are in the right place, and the centre front line vertical. If the dart shaping is in the right place for you, cut out the fabric and tack up the bodice, checking again before machining. If the darts are not correctly positioned establish your own bust

height and alter as necessary.
1 Draw two lines on the bodice pattern straight through the centre of the waist dart and the underarm dart. The bust point is where the two lines cross. Pin bodice back and front together at shoulder and working with tape on its edge so that it will curve, mark your bust height on the centre line of the waistline dart.
2 Re-draw the centre line of underarm dart from new bust point to side seam. Re-draw underarm dart to original size, but on new

line. Re-draw waist dart if necessary. Both darts should finish at least 2.5cm/1in short of the bust point. The angle of the bust dart is also important. On small busted figures the dart can be placed horizontally, larger busted figures are flattered by a dart sloping upwards from the side seam.
3 If the new bust point is lower than the original dart the whole position of the dart must be changed. Trace off the complete dart shape, cut it out and glue it at the correct level and parallel to the original dart.

Matching fabric designs

The design on the fabric must be considered when choosing fabric. Very large motifs work best on garments with few seams and darts but clever positioning can achieve accurate matching of motifs to preserve continuity across a seamed and darted garment. A centre front opening, for example, will interrupt the design but with care the left and right bodice and skirt pieces can be placed on the fabric so that no distortion of the design occurs.

Careful planning is necessary when buying fabric. Remember not only to keep the fabric design in proportion to your size and figure type but also that the style of the dress demands consideration.

Consider the number of seams or darts in the style; every join means adjustments to match fabric motifs and although it is not difficult to

match seams it does take extra thought and care. Use a with nap layout for one-way designs and allow plenty of extra fabric so that the pattern pieces can be moved around as necessary.

Fabric motifs such as leaves, petals or geometric shapes should be matched up as shown overleaf. Bear in mind that the fabric design should balance evenly across the figure and remember to allow extra fabric for one-way and large motifs.

Positioning the pattern pieces

Decide which is the dominant motif, colour bar or feature of the chosen fabric. This will be a guide for cutting out the whole garment.

A feature or motif suitable for the centre front could be repeated down the centre back, the centre of the sleeves and across collar and cuffs. Position large motifs so that they do

not draw attention to particular areas of the figure, such as the bust or hips, in an unflattering way. Hold the fabric up against you to decide which part of the pattern looks best.

Don't be afraid to change the recommended layout for the pattern pieces to achieve the correct match across seams or to position motifs or colour attractively, but always observe the straight grain of the fabric.

Cutting out from double fabric Make sure that the motifs or design match on both layers and pin together if necessary. Plan the large pieces first – do not pin them on, just mark the edge of the fabric with chalk so that you can estimate the fabric you have used. Then see if the rest of the pattern pieces will fit on to the remaining fabric when opened out. Do not cut anything until you are absolutely sure that every piece has been included and on the correct grain.

a selection of large patterned fabrics

Matching the design across seams

Remember that it is the stitching line and not the cutting line that is being matched. Fold back the seam allowance to check on the exact position of the motif against the pattern piece.

Bodice seams The side seams will only match below the underarm darts. Position back and front bodice patterns with the waistlines of both at exactly the same level on the fabric design. It is not always possible to match the design on shoulder seams if there is a back shoulder dart or some ease given in the pattern. If the shoulder seams are of equal length without shaping, place centre back and centre front to same motif and the shoulders will match exactly.

Side skirt seams A flared side seam will cut through design motifs diagonally from waist to hem and complete motifs cannot, therefore, be matched. The design can match up horizontally, however, if the notches are positioned at exactly the same crosswise level. Mark the seamline on the pattern pieces at the point where you wish to position the top of a particular motif or colour.

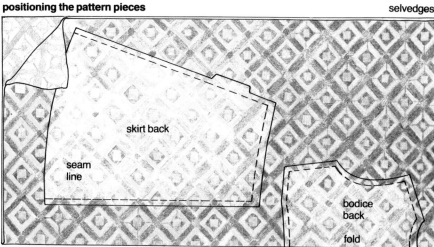

positioning the pattern pieces

selvedges

skirt back

seam line

bodice back

fold

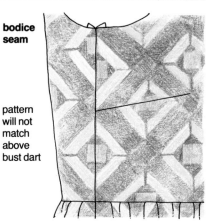

bodice seam

pattern will not match above bust dart

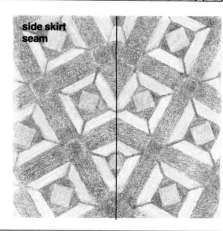

side skirt seam

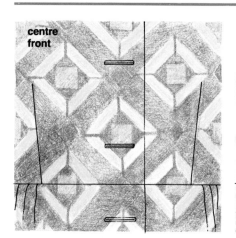

centre front

centre back

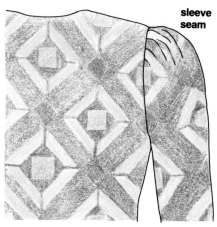

sleeve seam

Centre front seams If the pattern has an extended front facing fold it back temporarily along the centre front line when positioning the pattern pieces to make sure the design matches. If no foldline is marked on the pattern draw a straight line from the circle at the neckline to the waist, parallel to the cutting line.
Make sure the bodice centre front seam matches the skirt centre front seam.

Centre back seams If the centre bodice back is cut on the fold and the skirt has a seam it is not always possible to match the centre back from neck to hem unless the centre back skirt seam is on the straight grain of the fabric. In this case, position the pattern pieces so that the seam matches the same motif or colour as the fold of the bodice. It will then match across the back waistline until the bodice dart and waist gathers interrupt the design.

Sleeve seams It is not possible to match sleeves to both front and back at the armholes if an underarm dart interrupts the design on the front bodice. Instead, try to match the design horizontally across the sleeves and bodice using the pattern notches as a guide.

Opposite: When using a bold patterned fabric for the first time, choose a simple style and concentrate on balancing the pattern on the garment.

140

The shirtwaister – a classic dress

Make yourself this figure-flattering button-through dress using the graph patterns on page 150. The full skirt, gathered into a close-fitting bodice, is ideal for disguising wider hips, while the full and comfortable sleeves guarantee ease of arm movement.

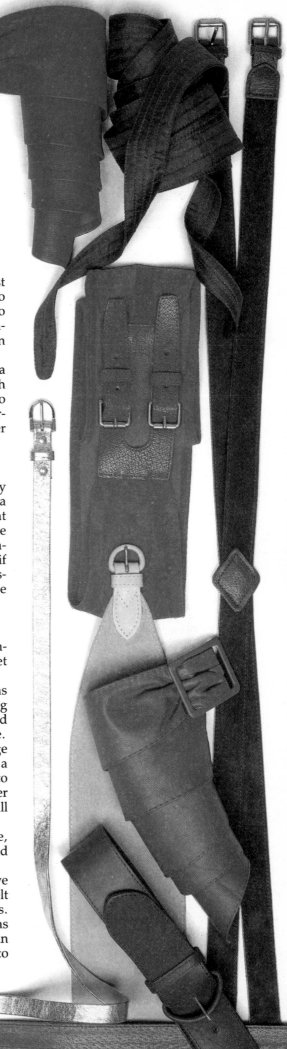

Final fitting and sewing techniques for making up the button-through dress are given in this chapter together with fabric suggestions and making up instructions.

Stitching seams

Great care is needed when using patterned fabric to keep motifs perfectly matched.

Even carefully tacked layers of fabric can move out of alignment during stitching so slip-tack the seams together (see page 80) and leave pins in at right angles while machining. Use an even feed attachment on your machine where possible.

Stitching darts

Bodice waist darts curve slightly inwards following the inner curve from waist to under bust while underarm darts are fairly short and straight – a curve here emphasizes roundness and is not flattering.

You will not be able to match motifs across darts, but it is worth checking where the darts fall before cutting out, to ensure that they will not cut across the design in an ugly way.

Tack darts before stitching and use an even feed attachment on your machine when stitching.

After stitching, press underarm darts down towards the waist, back and front darts towards the centre.

Fitting bodice to waist

The advantage of a waistline seam is that you can adjust the bodice and skirt sections independently but any alterations to the width or length of the bodice will affect the fit of the bodice to the skirt at the waist.

Right: Use different belt widths for the dress (opposite) according to your figure type and the effect you require.

For example, if you take in the waist darts of the bodice you must also draw up the gathers of the skirt to correspond. If the skirt is ungathered, a corresponding alteration should be made to the skirt seams. Check that the waist seam is in a comfortable position. If it is too high it will restrict your movement – too low and the bodice will not fit properly. In both cases the belt will not cover the waist seam.

Pattern matching

Motifs cannot be matched exactly when joining a gathered skirt to a darted bodice except at centre front and back, but it is possible to ensure that the gathers are distributed evenly on the skirt so that the same motif or colour bar occurs at the same position on the right and left sides of the dress.

Choosing belts and buttons

Ready-made belts are easily obtainable but it is not always possible to get just the right colour.

A belt made from the same fabric as the dress or in a toning or contrasting colour adds a distinctive touch and can be made to suit your figure type. A self fabric belt plays down a large waist, a contrast belt emphasizes a slim one. Narrow belts are kinder to short waisted figures whereas wider belts flatter a long back with a small waist.

Whatever type of belt you choose, keep it in place using fabric or thread loops set in the side seams.

If the fabric design has a distinctive motif or colour bar, use it on the belt and repeat it on covered buttons. Make sure that purchased buttons complement the texture on a plain fabric or use shiny buttons and belt to contrast with a matt fabric.

Button-through shirt dress with fitted bodice

Choose the fabric carefully, it must be soft enough for the gathered fullness of the skirt to fall attractively but with sufficient body to give shape to the darted bodice. Choose dress weights in natural or synthetic fabrics or blends of both. Soft wool, wool crêpe, jersey, Viyella and brushed cotton are all suitable for cool days. Crisp cottons and cotton blends and silky synthetics are better for warmer weather.

If you are using a boldly patterned fabric use the information given in this and the last chapter to match motifs and as you make up the dress check constantly that right and left sides are level and the motifs correctly aligned.

The buttons are an obvious feature on this dress so choose them carefully, or use covered buttons. Toning plain buttons look effective on patterned fabrics, contrasting ones on plain fabric.

You will need
Dressweight fabric – see fabric quantity chart
Matching thread
1m/1yd of 80cm/32in wide interfacing
1 press stud
13×1cm/⅜–½in buttons
Optional purchased belt
Pattern pieces, page 150:
   5 Long sleeve
   6 Cuff
   7 Collar stand
   8 Shirt style collar
   15 Dress bodice back
   16 Dress bodice front
   17 Dress skirt back
   18 Dress skirt front
   19 Dress pocket bag

Fabric quantity chart

Size	10	12	14	16	18
Bust (cm)	83	87	92	97	102
(in)	32	34	36	38	40

Long sleeved dress with shirt-style collar

	10	12	14	16	18
90cm**	4.70	4.80	4.90	4.90	5.30m
115cm**	3.20	3.30	3.30	3.40	3.40m
150cm*/**	2.60	2.70	2.80	2.90	2.90m

** without nap.
*/** with or without nap

Cutting out
Make any pattern alterations to bodice (see previous chapter). Position pattern pieces as shown on cutting layouts for your fabric width. Cut out carefully and transfer pattern markings to fabric. Use pattern pieces 7 and 8 to cut a single layer of interfacing for the cuffs. To cut interfacing for the front bodice and front skirt, use the 'attached facing' section of pieces 16 and 18.

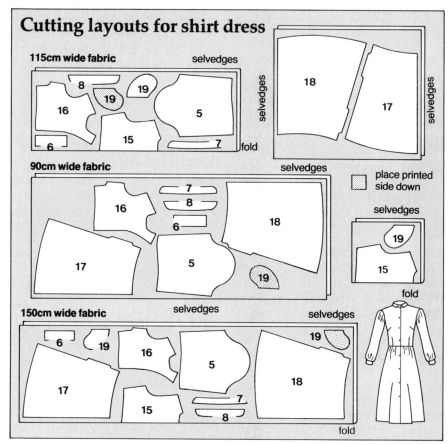

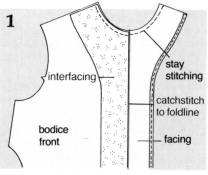

Left: Choose buttons to match one of the fabric colours, or feature the pattern motif on covered buttons.

Making up the dress
As it is easier to stitch and press small sections of a garment, complete as much work as possible on the bodice, then on the skirt, before joining them.

Step 1 Machine neaten the outer edge of the front bodice and front skirt facing. Apply interfacing to the front bodice and skirt, catchstitching it along the foldline of the attached facing which will then fold back to cover it. Interface the collar stand, collar and cuffs, and staystitch the neckline edges.

Fitting the bodice

Tack the bodice together and try on.

Align and pin centre fronts from neck to waist and slip shoulder pads in place if required. Check that:

• the fit is easy but not loose at bust and waist.

• waist seamline is at waist level.

• bust darts give fullness at bust level and point towards the bust, stopping 2.5cm/1in from it.

• waist darts are immediately under widest part of bust stopping 2.5cm/1in from bust point on front and below base of shoulder blades on back.

• side seams run vertically from underarm to waist.

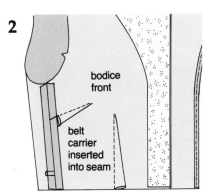

Step 2 Machine back bodice darts and press towards centre back. Machine front waist darts, press towards centre front; and machine underarm darts, pressing towards waist.

Join shoulder and side seams inserting the top of fabric belt carriers (see page 93) 1cm/½in above waistline in each side

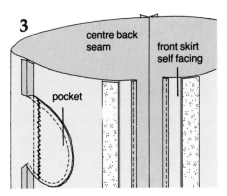

seam if required.
Make up collar and attach to neckline as on pages 124–125.

Skirt

Step 3 Join skirt centre back seam, press open and neaten. Make up pocket bags and attach to side seams (see page 108). Complete side seams.

Joining skirt and bodice

Step 4 Run a double row of gathering threads one either side of the seamline from circle to side seams on front skirt and across full width of back skirt.

With right sides together, matching bodice and skirt side

seams, centres and foldlines, pin skirt to bodice along seamline, drawing up gathers evenly to fit. Include the base of belt carriers if required, at each side seam. Machine. Press seam towards bodice. Trim waist seam allowances to 7mm/⅜in.

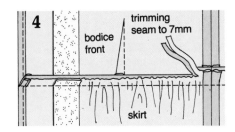

Step 5 Neaten the raw edges by zigzag machining or binding (but not within the area covered by the facing).

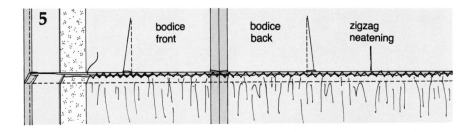

Step 6 Tack fold edge of facing from neck to skirt edge. Press. Catchstitch facing to waist seam. Complete lower edge of facing when the hem is turned up. Make cuffs, attach to sleeves and insert as for blouse (page 126). Complete hem.

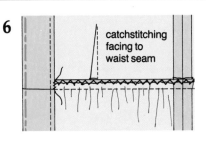

Buttonholes

Step 7 Make ten horizontal buttonholes on right front dress 1.3cm/½in from finished edge. Place the first buttonhole centrally on right collar stand and another 2.5cm/1in above waist seam (to allow for belt). Use

these as markers and space the remainder 9cm/3½in apart – four on the bodice and six on the skirt. Attach buttons on left front to correspond with buttonholes. Secure waist seamline with press stud or hook and eye to prevent it gaping open behind the belt.

Fastenings – buttons, hooks and eyes and press studs

Hooks, press studs, buttons, links, lacings, toggles and frogs – there is a fastening suitable for all fabrics and fashions. Learn the professional way to position and attach buttons and hooks and how to make an invisible press stud fastening.

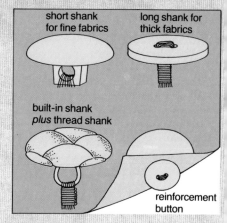

Most garments need an opening to make it possible to dress and undress without putting strain on the seams, and all openings need some type of fastening to hold the garments in place during wear. The design of the garment usually dictates whether the opening is to be obvious and contributing to the look of the garment as a whole, or concealed in some way and as inconspicuous as possible.

Buttons, zips, hooks and press studs are most often used as methods of fastening. There are many and varied ways of applying them to give that touch of individuality to a garment which most home dressmakers hope to achieve.

Besides these popular methods there are numerous others such as laces, eyelets, and frogs, and of course many variations and combinations of these from which to choose.

Buttons

The choice of buttons now available at haberdashery counters has never been wider. Gone are the days when Man sat and fashioned a button from bone, horn, wood or metal though these materials are still being used. Add to these, leather, enamel, glass and a wide range of plastics in vibrant colours and already the range is vast. There are two types of button as far as dressmaking is concerned; those which have a built-in shank with a hole through which the sewing thread is stitched, and those which have holes in the button itself through which the sewing thread is stitched forming a thread shank.

Shank buttons The built-in shank provides depth to accommodate the layer of fabric which will surround the button when buttoned up during wear and prevent it from pulling on the garment. The upper surface of a shank button may be flat or domed and they are available in any of the materials previously mentioned. You can also buy shank buttons in kits to cover yourself.

To attach a shank button stitch the shank firmly in place with at least six or seven stitches and reinforce this stitching on the wrong side by working it into a bar with buttonhole stitch.

Where a shank button is being used on a very thick, bulky fabric, the shank alone may not provide sufficient depth between the underside of the button and the face of the main fabric. In this case, work a thread shank below the button shank as though you were applying a holed button.

Holed buttons Never sew on a button which is to be used as a method of fastening too tightly because the button will not 'sit' properly, instead make a shank from thread (see pages 104–105). The depth of the shank is governed by the thickness of the garment. On a fine lawn blouse the shank can be less than 2mm/⅛in, whereas on a woollen jacket or a coat made in loosely woven fabric the shank will need to be considerably longer. Do not be too generous, however, or the button will hang loosely when done up giving an untidy appearance.

These buttons have two or four holes. Four-holed buttons can be sewn on in a variety of stitching styles, working through the holes in a different order to achieve different patterns. You can also use contrasting colour thread as a design feature. This is especially effective when teamed with topstitching in the same colour.

Positioning buttons

Marking the position of buttons and buttonholes accurately is so important. It can mean the difference between a successful garment and one which *looks* home made. You must always mark positions on the right side of the garment and thread tacking is the most efficient method to use as it is quickly and easily removed.

The ideal position of the button and buttonholes is usually marked on your paper pattern but as a general rule, where a button is to be closed with a buttonhole, neither should be too close to the edge of the garment.

Stitching styles for buttons

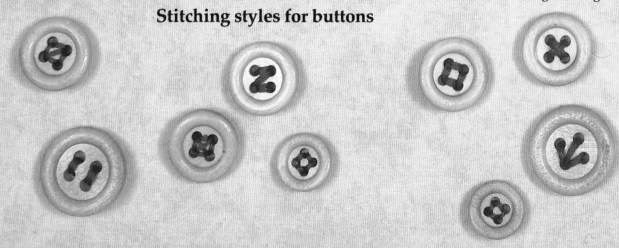

On jackets, coats and blouses which have centre openings, the buttons will be stitched to the centre front. An overlap known as the button band will have been added to the pattern to accommodate the buttons.

The outer edge of the buttonhole and position of the button should both be at least three-quarters of the diameter of the button away from the finished edge of the garment. At the first fitting stage check that the position of the buttons suits your figure and alter both button and buttonhole position accordingly.

See pages 110, 114–115 for machine-made and hand-sewn buttonholes respectively.

Reinforcing the area of stress

Once you have finalized the position of the button and buttonhole you need to ensure that the area will stand up to the amount of wear required. Wherever possible this area of the finished garment should be of double fabric with a layer of interfacing.

Sometimes, because of the nature of the fabric or the type of garment being made, the area around the button itself requires reinforcement. This is usually done in one of two ways; with a clear plastic reinforcing button or with an extra circle of fabric. On loosely woven fabrics which pull easily, a reinforcing button on the reverse of the garment prevents excessive wear.

Buttons with large holes to line up with holes of the bigger button are available specifically for this purpose. Attach them both in one operation making a shank for the top button as usual. The reinforcing button is stitched close to the reverse of the garment.

On leather, suede or cotton-backed pvc, stitch an extra circle of fabric, cut from scraps, to the reverse of the garment – again attaching it in one operation with the button.

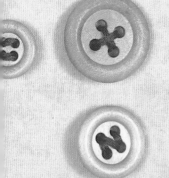

Hooks and press studs

Look carefully along the haberdashery counters and you will find hooks and bars in many sizes, made from various materials and for many purposes. They vary in size from the smallest for children's wear, to those suitable for bras and bikinis, men's and ladies' trousers, and large coloured fur hooks.

As with all fastenings, it is worth taking the trouble to give hooks a really professional finish. Conceal both hook and bar by buttonhole stitching them into place.

The variety of press stud fastenings and snaps continues to grow but few people take sufficient time and care when applying a basic metal press stud. The less obvious a press stud on the finished garment the better, and to achieve this both ball and socket sections must be carefully positioned to line up accurately. This ensures that an opening will lie flat and doesn't pull or bulge between each press stud.

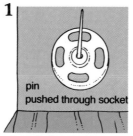

pin
pushed through socket

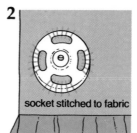

socket stitched to fabric

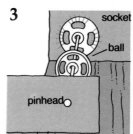

socket
ball
pinhead

Applying a press-stud

When using a press stud to close an opening, the socket part of the stud is sewn to the underneath and the ball part to the overlap or top fabric.

1 Position the socket part of the stud as required and pass a fine pin through the hole in its centre

from the wrong side.
2 Stitch in place, passing the needle through each hole several times, fanning the stitches out neatly to camouflage the edges of the stud.
3 Press the ball part of the stud into the socket and arrange the top layer of fabric as it will be on the finished garment.

Pass the fine pin through the centre hole in both parts of the press stud from the right side of the top layer of fabric and then separate the parts carefully, leaving the ball part on the pin. This way you ensure that the positions of the two parts match perfectly. Stitch the ball part to the fabric as above.

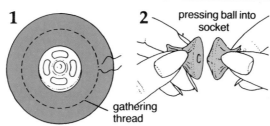

pressing ball into socket

gathering thread

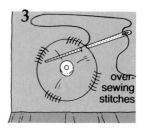

over-sewing stitches

Making an invisible press stud

1 Cut two circles of fabric twice the diameter of the stud and run a gathering thread around the outside edges.
2 Separate the stud and placing the right side of each section

to the wrong side of the fabric, draw up the gathering so that it is smoothly covered. Coax the ball into the socket through the two layers. The ball will pierce the fabric.

Secure the fabric firmly on the wrong side of studs and trim away any excess.
3 Attach studs to garment with small oversewing stitches in the normal way.

Graph for shirts and shirtwaister

1.5cm/⅝in seam allowance included

4cm/1½in hem allowed

1 square = 5cm

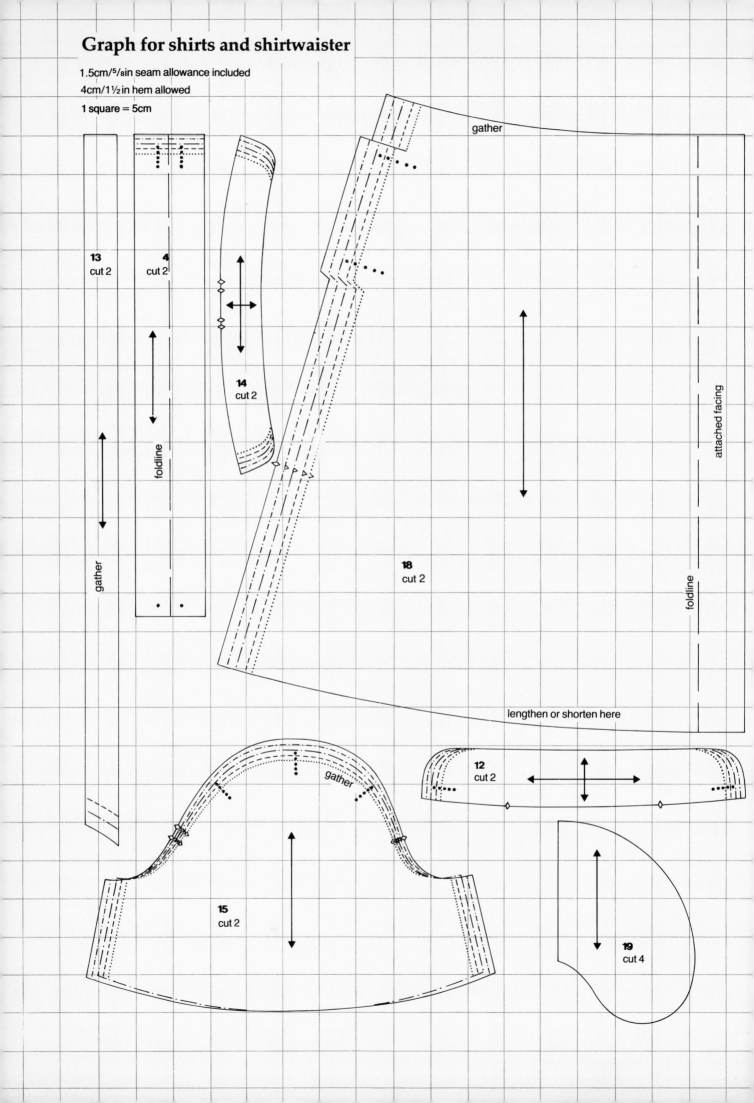

13 cut 2

gather

4 cut 2

foldline

14 cut 2

gather

18 cut 2

attached facing

foldline

lengthen or shorten here

gather

15 cut 2

12 cut 2

19 cut 4

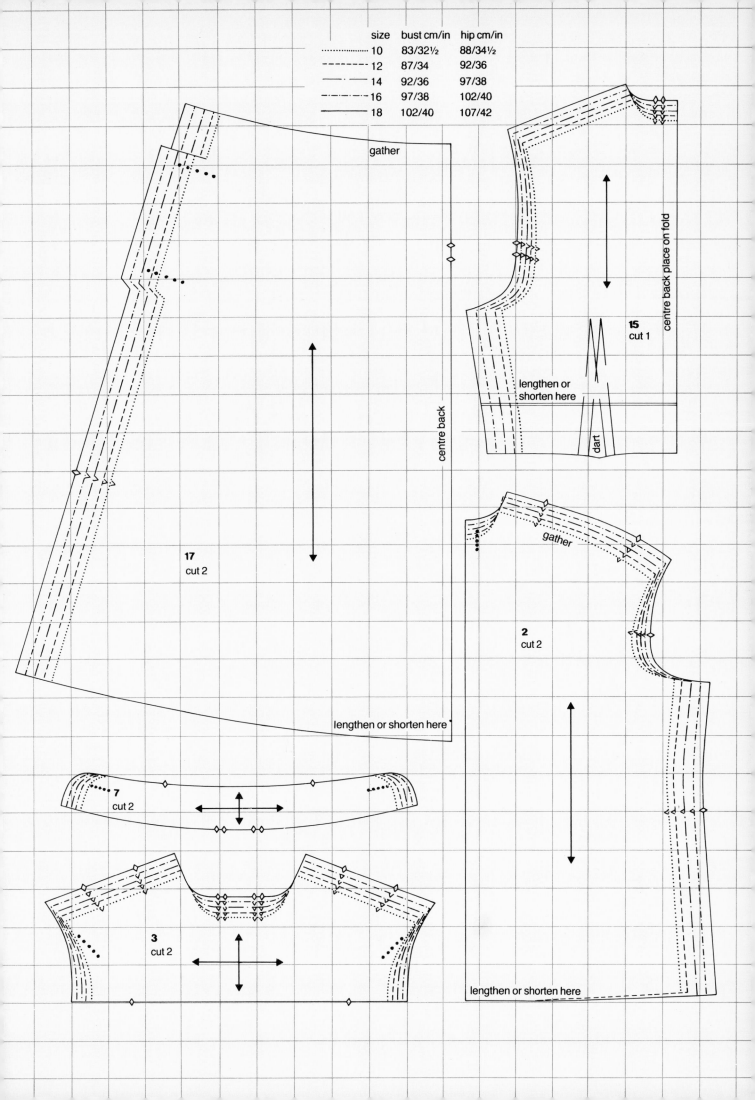

size	bust cm/in	hip cm/in
10	83/32½	88/34½
12	87/34	92/36
14	92/36	97/38
16	97/38	102/40
18	102/40	107/42

gather

centre back place on fold

lengthen or
shorten here

dart

15
cut 1

gather

centre back

17
cut 2

2
cut 2

lengthen or shorten here

7
cut 2

3
cut 2

lengthen or shorten here

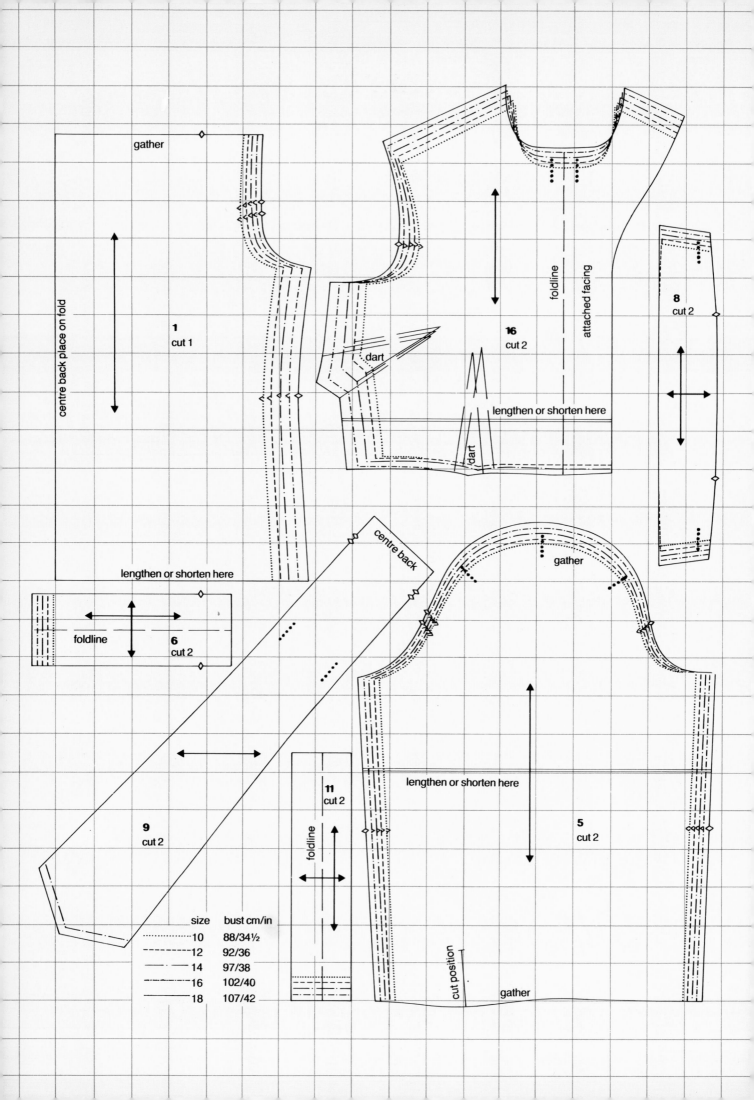

PART 7

Shorts and trousers

Fashions in length may vary but the basic instructions for making simple summer shorts remain the same. Several new techniques are introduced in this chapter – many of which can be used on other garments. The quick and easy method given for inserting a self-faced fly front zip in the shorts can also be used instead of the more traditional technique described when making up the trousers. Mock turn-ups, faced hip pockets, pocket flaps and a decorative half belt provide stylish touches which can be adapted for use on trousers, skirts and jackets where suitable.

Pattern alterations are important for trousers, especially if you need to disguise figure faults or adapt the leg length. Start with careful measuring up, making basic pattern adjustments as necessary, and then check the fitting stages carefully, using the illustrated guide to common fitting problems when making up.

A half-lining made from the same pattern helps close fitting trousers to retain their shape as well as adding warmth and comfort in wear, particularly if the fabric has a rough texture. As a finishing touch, the instructions for making a fabric-covered belt will prove invaluable for trousers and many other garments.

Stylish summer shorts in two lengths

Learn some simple new techniques and make yourself these super summer shorts. The basic design has front tucks, hip pockets and turn-ups and there is a choice of two leg lengths, plus extra design features such as a half-belt or mock back pockets.

You can use the graph pattern on page 155 to make these attractive shorts in two lengths and two sizes; 10–12 (hip 88cm–92cm/34in–36in) or 14–16 (hip 97cm–102cm/38in–40in). The amount of fabric needed is not large so this simple pattern can be used by a beginner as an introduction to trouser making. Many of the techniques are similar to those used in the next three chapters.

Below: Both versions of the shorts.

Fly front zip

This quick and easy method is ideal for casual wear made up in firm fabrics. It gives a smooth, neat finish without the necessity of applying a separate facing or zip shield as given for the true fly front zip described on page 158.

Front hip pockets

The deep, roomy pocket is made using just one pocket pattern piece which is folded into shape.

Mock turn-ups

These are used on the shorter-legged version of the shorts to avoid the bulk of ordinary turn-ups which would interfere with the smooth fit at the top of the leg.

Mock pockets

The 'pockets' consist of decorative flaps which are buttoned-down in position on the back of the shorts. This is another way of avoiding bulk and maintaining a smooth fit.

A decorative half-belt

A half-belt is both decorative and functional, allowing the waistband to be tightened up in wear without altering the garment permanently. The belt consists of two sections which are attached to the back of the shorts and fastened with D-rings. They are positioned so that you can adjust the waistband to fit more snugly by drawing up the half-belt through the D-rings which will prevent it from slipping.

Attaching a front hip pocket

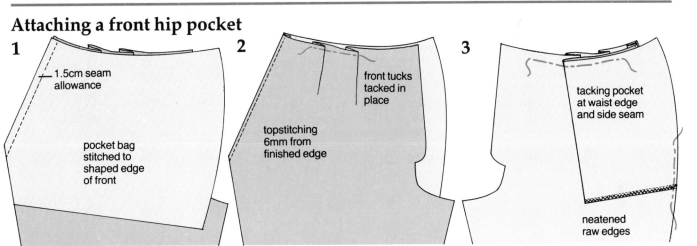

1 With right sides together, matching markings, stitch pocket bags to garment front at side edges.
2 Trim turnings, turn pocket bag to wrong side of garment and press. On right side, topstitch seam 6mm/

¼in from finished edge.
3 On the inside of garment, fold pocket bag, with right sides together along fold line. Stitch across lower edges of pocket bag then zigzag stitch raw edges

together to neaten.
Tack pocket bag at waist edge and down side seams to hold it in position, in preparation for attaching back of garment and waistband.

Fly front zip with self-facing

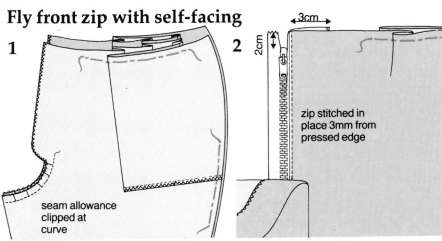
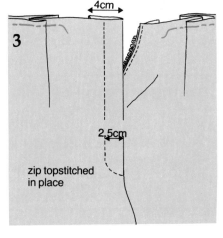

1 With right sides together, stitch centre front seam up to zip marking. Clip into seam allowance at curve and press seam open. Neaten raw edges of seam allowance, continuing the neatening around the curved edge of the fly front facing.

2 On the left front edge, press 3cm/1¼in to wrong side along fly front facing. Place top of zip teeth 2cm/¾in below waist edge and tack through all thicknesses with zip teeth 3mm/⅛in from pressed edge. Using a zipper foot, stitch zip in place.

3 Press 4cm/1½in to wrong side on right fly front facing. Place folded edge so that it just overlaps previous row of stitching and tack through all thicknesses to hold zip in position. From the right side, topstitch 2.5cm/1in from edge, in a smooth curve to base of zip.

Mock pockets

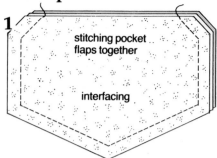

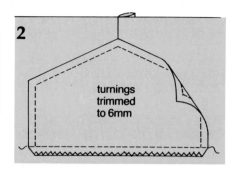

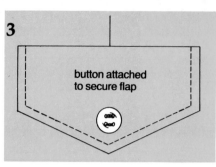

1 Apply interfacing to the wrong side of two pocket flaps. With right sides together, tack an interfaced flap to each of the remaining flaps. Machine stitch around the two short and long shaped edges, following the shaping at the top of the flap. (This gives a neat finish when the flap is stitched in place.)

2 Trim turnings, clip corners and turn right side out and press. Topstitch seamed edges 6mm/¼in from edge. Place right side of flap in position, on right side of garment, with pointed edge towards top of garment. Tack and then stitch raw edge in place, taking a 1.5cm/⅝in turning. Trim turnings to 6mm/¼in and zigzag stitch to neaten edges and secure turnings to shorts.

3 Press flap downwards and attach a button through flap and shorts to hold the flap in position permanently. Reinforce the button position on the wrong side of the shorts with a square of fusible interfacing before stitching.

Mock turn-ups

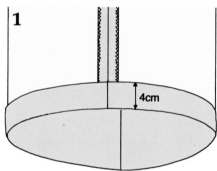

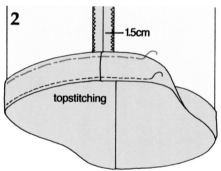

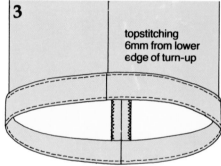

1 Press a 4cm/1½in turning to the wrong side at lower edge.

2 Make another 4cm/1½in turning to the wrong side and tack to hold. Topstitch 6mm/¼in away from outer, folded edge forming a tuck to encase the raw edge.

3 Remove tacking and bring hem down so that tuck turns through to right side. Press tuck upwards and topstitch 6mm/¼in away from lower edge of turn-up.

Making a decorative half-belt

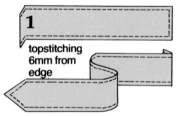

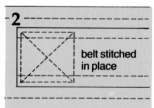

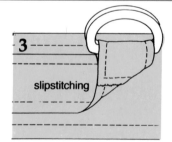

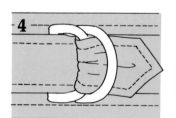

1 With right sides together, fold belt in half lengthwise and stitch around outer edges. Measure 15cm/6in from straight end and cut belt in two. Trim turnings and corners and turn both sections right sides out. Press. Topstitch 6mm/¼in from seamed edge on both sections. Press under 1cm/½in to wrong side on both raw edges of belt.

2 Place belt sections in position on back waistband, with pointed section on right back. Stitch them in place by first stitching a square and then stitching diagonally, corner to corner as shown.

3 Thread square end of shorter belt section through two D-rings and slipstitch securely on wrong side.

4 To fasten, thread other belt section through both D-rings and back through one. Pull up to adjust waistband to size required.

A pair of shorts with a choice of leg lengths

Make up the long version with back pocket flaps and conventional turn-ups, and the short version without back pocket flaps and with mock turn-ups. You can, of course, leave out the back pocket flaps and decorative half-belt in both versions.

Fabric suggestions
Firm cotton, sailcoth, linen, denim and brushed denim, heavy poplin and gaberdine are all ideal for the shorts. Avoid anything too fine and see-through, or too limp, and do not choose thick fabrics, which would make the hip pockets bulky.

You will need
Long version 1.60m/1¾yd of 90cm/36in wide fabric *or.*
1.50m/1⅝yd of 115cm/45in wide fabric
Short version 1.40m/1⅝yd of 90cm/36in wide fabric *or*
1.30m/1½yd of 115cm/45in wide fabric
18cm/7in zip
0.20m/¼yd of 90cm/36in wide interfacing
2×2.5cm/1in D-rings
1×1.5cm/⅝in button (short version)
3×1.5cm/⅝in buttons (long version)
Matching thread

Cutting out
Scale up the pattern from the graph on to dressmaker's graph paper, following the appropriate line for your size. Transfer all notches, pattern markings and cutting instructions. Hem turnings and 1.5cm/⅝in seam allowances are included throughout.
Fold fabric in half lengthwise and position pattern pieces as shown on the appropriate cutting layout. Cut out and transfer pattern markings to fabric.
Cut one waistband and two pocket flaps (if required) in interfacing.

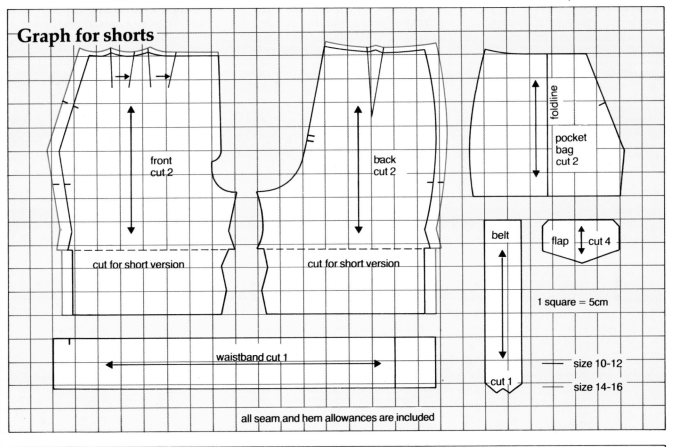

Graph for shorts

front cut 2

cut for short version

back cut 2

cut for short version

foldline

pocket bag cut 2

belt

flap cut 4

1 square = 5cm

waistband cut 1

cut 1

size 10-12
size 14-16

all seam and hem allowances are included

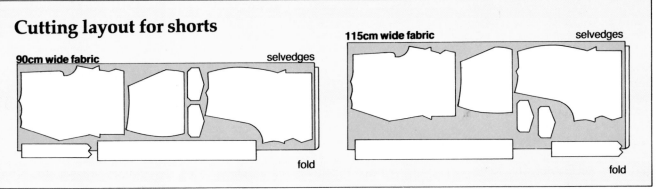

Cutting layout for shorts

90cm wide fabric

selvedges

115cm wide fabric

selvedges

fold

fold

Making the long version of the shorts

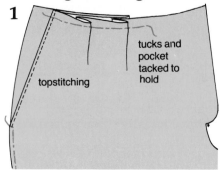

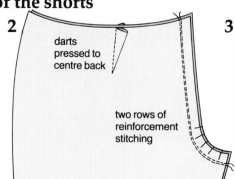

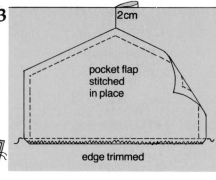

Step 1 Make tucks in each front section and tack them across the top with the tucks towards the side seams.
Make up and attach the front hip pockets, securing them with tacking at waist and side seams.
Step 2 Stitch centre front seam,

leaving 20cm/7¾in open and insert zip following fly front method. Stitch darts in the back of shorts and press towards centre back. With right sides together, matching notches, stitch centre back seam. Work a second row of stitching close to the first, just inside the

seam allowance, to reinforce the seam. Clip into the curves, press seam open and neaten raw edges.
Step 3 Make up and apply mock pocket flaps. Position each flap centrally over back darts, with point of flap 2cm/¾in below upper raw edge; stitch and button into place.

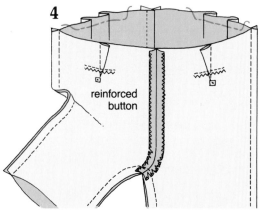

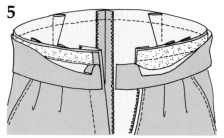

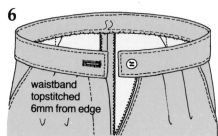

Step 4 With right sides together, stitch front to back at side and inside leg seam. Press seams open and neaten raw edges.
Step 5 Apply interfacing to half of wrong side of waistband. With right

sides together fold waistband in half lengthways. Stitch one short end around to the notch and stitch the other to within 1.5cm/⅝in of raw edges. Trim turnings and corners and snip to stitching at notch. Turn right sides out and press. With right sides together and with extension at left front, stitch waistband to upper edge of shorts.
Step 6 Trim turnings and press

seam towards waistband. Turn under 1.5cm/⅝in on free edge of waistband and slipstitch to previous row of stitching on inside of shorts. Press. Working from the right side, topstitch 6mm/¼in from all edges of waistband starting at centre back. Make a machine or hand-worked buttonhole in centre of right front waistband, 1.5cm/⅝in from finished edge. Sew on button.

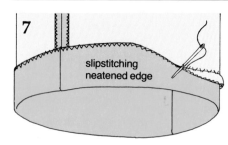

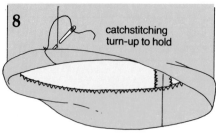

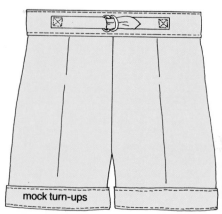

Step 7 Neaten lower edge of shorts and turn 6cm/2½in to the wrong side. Roll back the neatened edge and slipstitch loosely to shorts.
Step 8 Turn shorts right side out and press up 4cm/1½in turn-ups. Working within the fold of the turn-ups, catchstitch them lightly to each side seam or work a bar tack

(see page 61).
Make up the half belt and position each section on the back waistband 2.5cm/1in from the back darts, towards the side seams. Complete the half belt as instructed earlier. Fold shorts with inside leg and outside leg seams matching to press in crease, if desired.

Making the short version
Work as for long shorts, steps 1, 2, 4, 5 and 6. Make the mock turn-ups as instructed earlier.

Basic know-how for making well-fitting trousers

Do you avoid making trousers because you are worried about obtaining a good fit? Follow the advice given here and you will find that the secret lies in taking accurate measurements and making pattern alterations before you even start to cut out the trousers.

These trousers from the graph pattern given on page 171 are designed to flatter most figure types. They have front tucks, side slit pockets with topstitching detail, front zip fastening and slightly tapered legs.

If you have already mastered the basic dressmaking processes covered so far, you should have no problems at all when you make up this pattern.

However, many dressmakers find the most difficult thing about making trousers is the fitting. Yet making all major alterations before cutting out will guarantee a good fit.

Pattern alterations

Always choose your trouser pattern size by your hip measurement – the waist line is easier to alter than the hips if it does not match up to your measurements. Before you begin, it is essential to take a full and accurate set of measurements to compare with the paper pattern so that you can make the necessary adjustments. Ask a friend to help you and wear the undergarments you would normally wear under trousers.

Fly front zips

When making up a pattern with a fly front zip, make sure that you buy the right sort of zip. If it is too weak, you will find yourself having to repair or replace it constantly. Choose one that is labelled specially for trousers. It should be straight, with metal teeth and a strong tab which locks when closed. These zips are usually available in basic colours in lengths from 15cm/6in to 23cm/9in.

When inserting the zip, back it the professional way with a zip guard to prevent the zip teeth catching your skin or underclothes. This will also give extra strength to an area of hard wear.

Fabric choice

Choose your trouser fabric carefully – it needs to be soft enough to form the waist tucks and to be comfortable in wear, yet it must be strong and durable enough to withstand quite a bit of strain in sitting and moving.

Inserting a fly front zip with guard

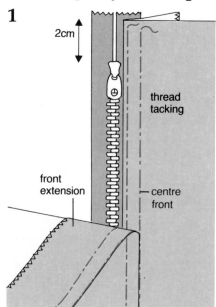

1

2cm

front extension

thread tacking

centre front

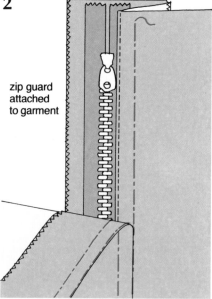

2

zip guard attached to garment

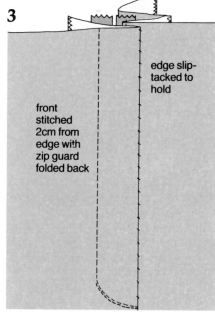

3

edge slip-tacked to hold

front stitched 2cm from edge with zip guard folded back

1 Carefully mark seamlines on all sections and thread tack centre fronts. Neaten the edges of the front extensions with zigzag stitching. Turn under the right front extension along seamline and tack to hold, 1cm/½in from folded edge. Fold under left front extension 1cm/½in within seamline to make a narrower turning, and tack.

With right side of garment and zip uppermost, place left hand folded edge of opening along teeth of zip with the metal stop 2cm/¾in below top edge of fabric. Pin and tack in place.

2 From matching fabric, and using the selvedge as one long edge if possible, cut a zip guard 6cm/2½in wide, by the length of the extension. Shape the rectangle to match the curves of the extensions if preferred, and neaten the raw edges.

Place right side of zip guard to back of zip, aligning it to edge of folded back extension of left front. Pin and tack through left front, zip tape and guard close to folded edge.

Working from the right side of the

Avoid a loose, stretchy weave which may split at the seams and pull out of shape. Instead look for a fabric which does not fray readily, with a firm weave that will not show pin or tacking markings. For the best appearance, it should be virtually uncrushable, yet still take a pressed crease.

A particular problem area with trousers is with friction where the trouser legs rub together; this can cause surface roughness – even bald patches in some pure wool fabrics. Ideally, look for a fabric with a percentage of manmade fibre – this helps give some elasticify and helps to prolong its life. Remember, too, that pure wool fabrics, or those with a high percentage of wool may need to be dry-cleaned, so if you think your trousers will get a good deal of wear look for a fabric which is washable.

Cotton, linen mixtures, gaberdine, lightweight wool blends, wool and cotton mixtures, denim, corduroy and synthetics are all suitable.

Fabric requirements, cutting layouts, full making up and fitting instructions appear in the next two chapters.

fabric and using a zipper foot, machine zip in place close to fold. Leaving centre front marking in place, remove other tacking from left front.

3 Lap right front over the zip, matching centre fronts. Slip-tack (see page 80) folded edge to centre front. On the wrong side, fold zip guard back, away from right front so that it is not caught in the stitching. Working from the right side, tack and machine through right front and zip tape 1.5cm-2cm/⅝in-¾in from folded edge, curving towards base of opening. Fold guard back into position and topstitch through all layers of curved section at base only, to reinforce the stitching and hold guard in position. Remove tacking and slip-tacking and press lightly and carefully from the wrong side.

Right: A pair of classically styled trousers with side hip pockets and figure flattering tucks which form a trim, fitted waistline. The slightly tapered legs give a slimming and elongating effect.

Measuring up

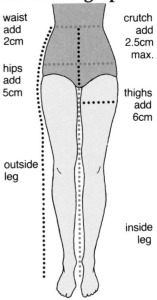

waist add 2cm

crutch add 2.5cm max.

hips add 5cm

thighs add 6cm

outside leg

inside leg

Take all width measurements closely, adding the following allowances for ease, and then check them against the paper pattern but remember that the pattern represents only a *half* garment, and to exclude seams and darts when measuring it.

Amounts for ease
Waist – 2cm/¾in; hips – 5cm/2in; crutch – up to 2.5cm/1in; thigh – 6cm/2½in. Inside and outside leg measurements do not require additional allowances, (except for the hem).
If you are unsure of the exact position of your hipline, take a measurement 20.5cm/8in below the waistline. For more advice on taking measurements, see page 20.
To take an accurate crutch depth measurement, sit on a chair, place a piece of string or tape around the waist as a marker and measure from waist to chair, following the line of the hip.

Left: The basic adjustments apply to most patterns.

Making pattern adjustments

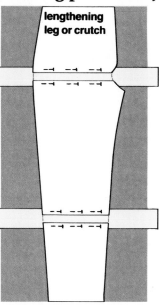

lengthening leg or crutch

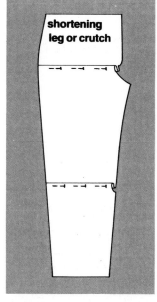

shortening leg or crutch

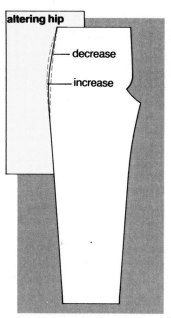

altering hip

decrease

increase

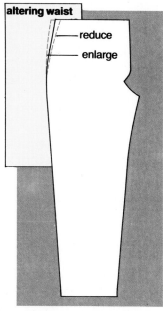

altering waist

reduce

enlarge

Make alterations to length of leg and depth of crutch first, followed by width measurements. Minor adjustments may be made at the first fitting.

Lengthening leg or crutch Cut along the appropriate double alteration lines and spread pattern apart by an amount equal to the extra length required, placing a strip of paper underneath. Ensure that the grain lines are straight and the cut edges parallel and pin or

tape the pattern in place.

Shortening leg or crutch Draw a line above the printed double alteration lines the same depth as the required reduction. Fold the pattern on the alteration line to meet the drawn line and pin or tape in place.

Increasing hip Pin a strip of paper underneath the hip edge of the pattern from waist to crutch level and divide the extra hip width required by four. Draw a new cutting line from the waistline, curving out to the extra

requirement at the hip line and tapering off below the level of the crutch line. Trim away excess paper.

Decreasing hip Use the same principle as for widening the hip but without adding paper, drawing the new cutting line the required distance *within* the original line.

Enlarging the waistline Take slightly smaller tucks or darts. If this alteration is insufficient, make adjustments at the side seams by adding a quarter of the extra

needed on the waist measurement to the waistline, tapering the cutting line down to meet the original line at the hip. Remember to alter the waistband to correspond.

Reducing the waistline Take slightly deeper tucks or darts. If this is insufficient, reduce the waist at the side seams by a quarter of the total reduction required, tapering the new cutting line down to the hipline. Reduce the length of the waistband accordingly.

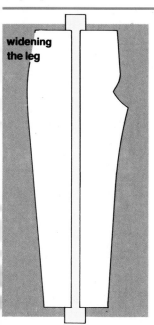

widening the leg

Widening the leg Make minor alterations to the side seams only. If a large alteration is required, affecting the waist and hip as well, leave the side seams as they are and cut the pattern vertically up the centre of the leg from bottom to top. Spread it apart by the required amount, inserting a strip of paper in the gap, and alter the waistband and adjust the tucks accordingly. Do not try and alter the leg part alone as it will distort the finished garment.

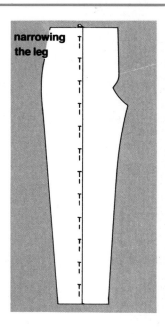

narrowing the leg

Narrowing the leg Take slightly deeper side seams from hip level downwards. If a larger decrease is required, affecting the waist and hips as well, do not try and alter the leg alone as it will distort the finished garment. Make a vertical pleat in the pattern from top to bottom and do not adjust the side seams. Pin or tape it into place. Alter the tucks and waistband to correspond.

Correcting fitting faults on trousers

See how easy it is to correct fitting faults and achieve a smooth look by using the at-a-glance guide to trouser alterations given in this chapter. Use this when making up the trousers from the graph on page 171 or when using any commercial paper pattern.

Fitting a pair of trousers is slightly more difficult than fitting a skirt because trousers are generally close-fitting around the waist, hips and crutch; it is more noticeable therefore if they do not fit well. Even though you learned the basic adjustments for trouser patterns in the last chapter, the chart overleaf is useful for pinpointing any other fitting faults that might appear when the garment is tacked and tried on. It also shows remedies to apply when making up. Use the chart when making up any fitted trousers pattern and you will soon learn to recognise the particular aspects of your figure type that need attention.

The secret is to make all major alterations to the pattern before cutting out, saving only minor adjustments for the making up.

If you have an old pair of well-fitting trousers, you could use these instead of adjusting a paper pattern to cut a new pair. Simply unpick the trousers carefully, press out the pieces and either make a copy pattern, or pin the actual pieces on to your fabric, adding seam allowances as required.

Preparing to make the trousers

Before cutting out trousers from the pattern made from the graph (or from any commercial pattern) make any necessary length and width adjustments to all the relevant pattern pieces following instructions given on page 161.

Cutting out
Position the pattern pieces for the trousers as shown on the appropriate cutting layout below, and cut out. From leftover fabric cut a rectangle 6cm×22cm/2½in×8½in to use as a zip guard. Cut the pocket and pocket bag pattern pieces (4 and 6) from the lining.

Transfer all pattern markings to the fabric and mark centre front line with thread tacking on both front sections. If you are working on plain fabric where right and wrong sides could be confused, then use tailor's chalk to mark each piece on the wrong side.

As an aid to fitting before tacking up the trousers, fold each main leg piece in half vertically with *wrong* sides together and press firmly to give a sharp crease. The back crease is pressed from crutch level to hem and the front from the first tuck to hem. The creases must be on the straight grain of the fabric. They should then hang straight at all

Opposite: To ensure that trousers have a flattering, smooth fit choose your fabric carefully and pay attention to pattern and fitting adjustments.

times, making it easier for you to see where fitting adjustments need to be made. Staystitch all the curves and the slanted edges of the pockets on the front sections before starting to make up the trousers. Full making up instructions appear on page 168.

You will need
Fabric according to size
Matching thread
18cm/7in trouser zip
1×15mm/⅝in button
0.15m/⅛yd of 80cm/32in wide interfacing
0.50m/⅝yd of 90cm/36in wide lining
0.80m/⅞yd of 90cm/36in wide lining for optional half lining
Pattern pieces, page 171:

1 Trouser front
2 Trouser back
3 Waistband
4 Pocket
5 Pocket facing
6 Pocket bag

Fabric quantity chart

Size	10	12	14	16	18
Waist (cm)	64	67	71	76	81
(in)	25	26½	28	30	32
Hip (cm)	88	92	97	102	107
(in)	34½	36	38	40	42
90cm*	2.50	2.55	2.55	2.55	2.60m
115cm*	2.05	2.20	2.30	2.35	2.35m
150cm	1.30	1.30	1.30	1.50	1.70m

*With or without nap. All other widths without nap.
Finished inside leg, all sizes, is 77cm/30½in. Allow extra fabric for longer lengths and matching checks.

Cutting layout for trousers

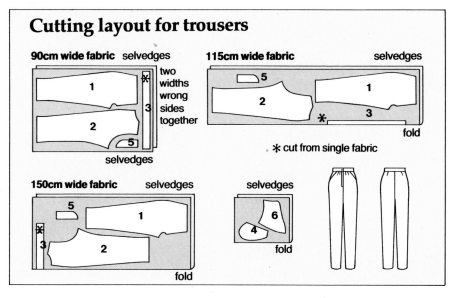

90cm wide fabric selvedges — two widths wrong sides together — 1, 2, 3, 5 — selvedges

115cm wide fabric selvedges — 5, 2, 1, 3 — * cut from single fabric — fold

150cm wide fabric selvedges — 5, 1, 3, 2 — fold

selvedges — 6, 4 — fold

✳ cut from single fabric

Fitting chart for trousers

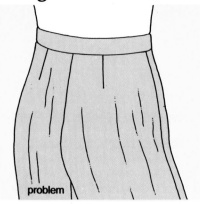

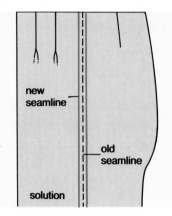

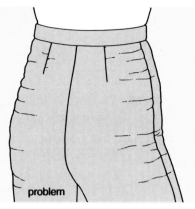

Generally too wide
Fabric hangs in vertical folds throughout.
Solution Take in side seams to give

a smooth but comfortable fit and reduce waistband accordingly. Do not alter inside leg seams.

Generally too narrow
Fabric pulls into horizontal folds at waist, hips and thighs.
Solution Let out both inside and

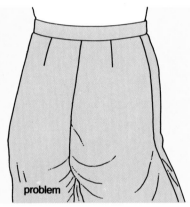

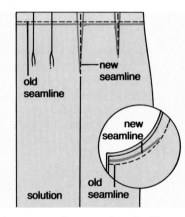

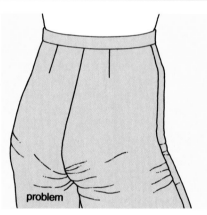

Too long from waist to crutch
Fabric falls in loose wrinkles from crutch down onto upper leg at back and front.
Solution Remove waistband and lift trousers to correct position, then reduce size of waist by taking in at

side seams, darts and tucks if necessary. If this is not sufficient, lift crutch seam by a maximum of 1cm/½in as well. Check fit finally with seam allowances snipped around curve and pressed flat.

Too short from waist to crutch
Fabric pulls into tight folds from crutch towards hips on both back and front.
Solution Remove waistband and lower trousers to correct position, increasing size of waist by letting

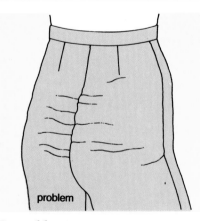

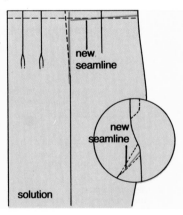

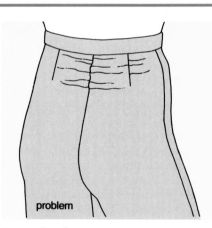

Round bottom
Fabric pulls into horizontal folds across back only. Side seams drag towards back of garment.
Solution Let out upper 10–15cm/

4–6in of inside leg seams. Raise waistline on back only and shorten darts. Let out the *back* side seam allowance only.

Sway back
Horizontal wrinkles form just below waistband.
Solution Lower waist seamline on back only and increase width of

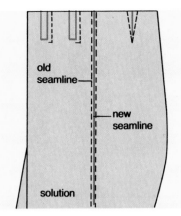

outside leg seams along entire
length to give a smooth fit. Release
waist darts and tucks a little if
necessary and adjust waistband.

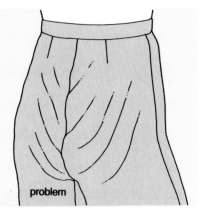

Too wide across back
The fabric hangs in loose, diagonal
folds across the seat.
Solution Lower waistline, lengthen

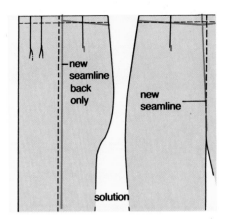

darts and take in *back* side seams
only. If necessary, take in at centre
back seam by a maximum of 1cm/
½in.

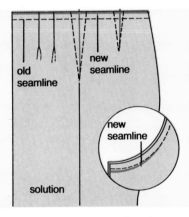

out side seams, darts and tucks.
Re-cut the crutch seam in a lower
position if necessary, but this will
reduce leg length so check whether
there is surplus length before
making the alteration.

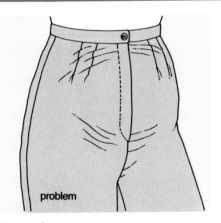

Round tummy
The fabric pulls into horizohtal folds
just below the waistline. Small
wrinkles from crutch towards side
seams show on front only.
Solution Let out darts, tucks and
front side seam allowances and raise

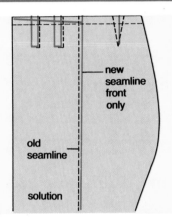

waist seamline to increase width
and depth. Shorten darts if
necessary.

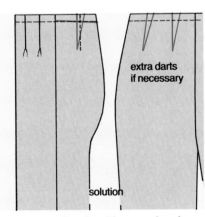

darts accordingly. Alter angle of
darts. If this does not correct
problem, take four darts instead of
two, distributing excess fabric
equally.

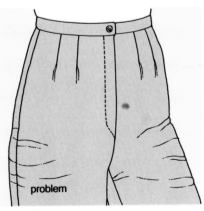

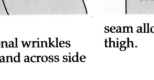

Large thighs
Horizontal and diagonal wrinkles
form below hip level and across side
seams.
Solution Let out back and front side

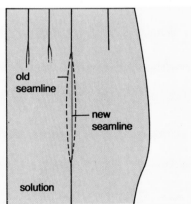

seam allowances from hip to upper
thigh.

Making up and half-lining a pair of trousers

This chapter shows you how to complete the trousers made from the graph on page 171. Use the step-by-step making-up instructions together with the pattern alterations and fitting tips on pages 160–165, and add a half-lining for a comfortable, professional finish.

Make up these trousers with or without a half-lining. Amounts of fabric required, cutting layouts together with advice on fitting are given on pages 163–165.

Learn how to make a fabric-covered belt using matching or contrasting fabric for a really professional finish to trousers or skirts.
If you have never before made a pair

of trousers, it may help you to pin the paper pattern pieces together first, following the order of making up, so that you understand fully how each stage works. The markings printed on the pattern will help you follow any technique you do not immediately understand. This is particularly useful when making the side slit pockets for the first time, so that you see how the three sections of the pocket fit together.

Half-lining a pair of trousers

If you have chosen a fabric which needs support or a rough wool such as tweed which may irritate the skin, you can half-line your trousers in a similar way to a skirt. This helps to retain the shape of the garment.

Cutting out a half-lining

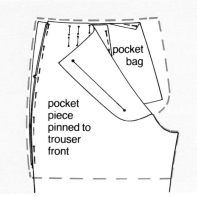

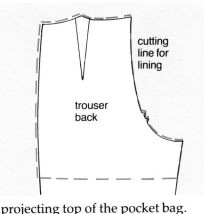

Making the pattern

To obtain the front lining pattern pin together the front, pocket and pocket bag pattern pieces, following the step-by-step instructions for making the trousers but with the tucks released. Turn under the

projecting top of the pocket bag. This gives you the basic shape for half the front lining.
Pin these amalgamated front pattern pieces down on to a smooth sheet of tissue or dressmaker's graph paper. Draw round them

taking the length to just below seat level, or just above the knee. Trace off a shortened pattern for the back in the same way, giving the basic shape for half the back lining. Transfer dart and tuck markings and any pattern alterations to the pattern pieces before cutting out.

Cutting out the lining

Cut two of each new pattern piece in lining fabric, placing the lower edges of the pattern to the selvedge to avoid making a bulky hem which will show on the right side. Transfer all pattern markings to the lining and make up, inserting it into the trousers before applying the waistband, when all other seams are completed and the zip is in place.

Making up and inserting the half-lining

1
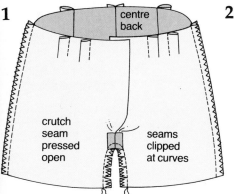

2
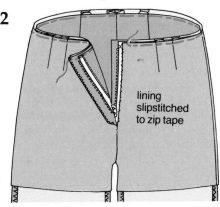

Step 1 Pin, tack and machine darts in back sections and tucks in front

pieces. Press.
Join the side seams and centre back

seams. Neaten the raw edges with pinking shears or zigzag stitch.
Join the crutch seam up to the zip marking and press seam open.
Join the inside leg seam, neaten and press. Clip curves.
Step 2 With wrong side of trousers and right side of lining uppermost, slip legs of trousers through legs of lining. Align the waist edges and tack together all around on seamline.
Trim away the excess fabric in the fly facing, fold in the lining seam allowances and slipstitch to zip stitching.

Making up and fitting the trousers

Step 1 Press creases in place on trouser legs (see page 163). With right sides together, matching circles, pin and tack tucks in place on each front.

Step 2 With right sides together, pin and tack darts in trouser back.

Step 3 With right sides together, and matching notches, stitch pocket to trouser front. Trim seam to 6mm/¼in and press it open. Turn pocket through to wrong side of front and lightly press seamed edge from wrong side.

Step 4 Neaten long curved edge of the pocket facing with close zigzag

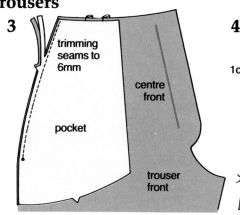

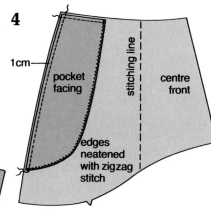

stitching. Place wrong side of pocket facing to right side of pocket

bag, tack and stitch in place taking 1cm/½in turning.

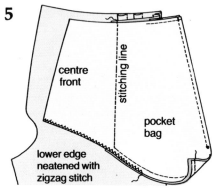

Step 5 With right sides together, matching notches, stitch pocket bag to pocket along lower edge and stitching line parallel to centre front. Trim and neaten lower edge.

Step 6 First fitting Matching centre fronts, tack pocket bag to trousers along centre front, side seam and upper edge.

With right sides together and matching notches, tack left front to left back trouser at side and inside leg seams.

Turn up leg hem and tack. Repeat for other leg. Turn one leg through to right side and drop it inside the other.

Matching raw edges and relevant markings, tack centre back seam and centre front below zip opening. Fasten ends of tacking

securely, especially on centre front to ensure tacking does not give while trying on. Turn garment to right side and try on. Place a piece of petersham around waist and pin waist seam line of trousers on to it.

Make any necessary adjustments to tucks, darts, side seams and width of leg, ensuring that the leg creases hang vertically. Pin carefully, getting someone to help if possible, then take the trousers off and re-tack any alterations. Try on again to check, then remove petersham at waist.

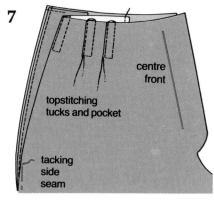

Step 7 Remove tacking at centre back and centre front, and the tacking holding pocket bag in place, in order to expose tucks. With right sides together machine tucks, press them towards centre front and topstitch all round from right side as shown. Re-tack pocket bag and topstitch top of pocket in line with tucks. (If you are careful, and have a free arm on your sewing machine,

all this may be done without removing tacking.)

Step 8 Machine back darts and press towards centre back. Stitch side and inside leg seams and press open. Neaten the raw edges.

Step 9 Second fitting Re-tack centre front and centre back seam as in step 6.

Turn trousers through to right side, re-tack petersham at marked waistline and try on. Lap fly facings and pin into place. At this stage, make any adjustments to crutch seam and waistline, still keeping creases hanging vertically. Alterations to hips can still be made at this stage, but bear in mind that slight creasing around the crutch area will disappear when seam is clipped.

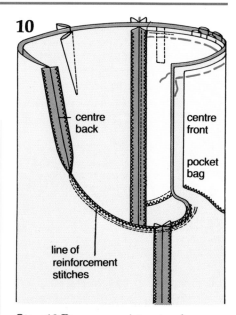

Step 10 Remove waist petersham, re-marking waistline if necessary. Arrange trousers with one leg inside the other as before and

Finishing touches for trousers

Use your knowledge of dressmaking techniques to add some simple finishing touches to the trousers to create an individual look. Mock pocket flaps or a half-belt add interest at the back, while contrast piping used along the pocket edges, or contrast topstitching on the tucks emphasize the lines of the design at the front. You can even add piping to the full length of the side seams, or topstitch them in contrasting thread for effect. Finally, belt carriers in the waistband are a useful addition.

Clockwise: piped seams, turn-ups, half belt, pocket with flap, belt carriers and mock pocket flaps

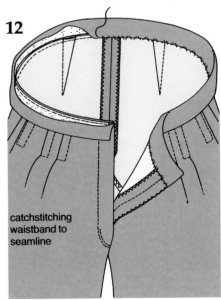

12

catchstitching waistband to seamline

machine crutch seam. Stitch a second row close to the first within the seam allowance, for reinforcement.

Trim curved part of seam close to inner stitching line and zigzag raw edges together to neaten. Press upper part of back seam open and neaten raw edges. Alternatively, clip into the curve up to stitching, neaten, and press seam open. Catchstitch turnings flat at crutch.

Step 11 Insert zip with guard by fly front method (see page 158).

Step 12 Apply interfacing to fold line on wrong side of waistband. Press 1.5cm/⅝in turning to wrong side on long un-interfaced edge. Trim turning to 6mm/¼in, fold band in half lengthwise and stitch 1.5cm/⅝in seams across the two short ends to within 1.5cm/⅝in of raw edges. Trim seams, clip across corners, turn to right side and press. With right sides together stitch interfaced edge of waistband to trousers, aligning one end to the edge of the zip guard and the other to the front folded edge. Layer seam. Bring pressed edge over to inside and catchstitch all round to previous row of machine stitches.

Step 13 Make a 2cm/¾in horizontal buttonhole centrally on the right front of the waistband, 1.3cm/½in in from the finished edge and attach a button to correspond.

Step 14 Final fitting Try on trousers and adjust leg length.

Step 15 Neaten lower edge and loosely catchstitch hems in place. Press whole garment, including leg creases. If these do not hold well, stitch the crease in place by first tacking and then stitching as close to the edge of the crease as possible. Remove tacking.

Fabric covered belts

Belts define the waistline and add interest to a garment, providing a focal point. If you do not wish to draw attention to your waistline, choose a narrow belt, made in self-fabric or a toning colour. For emphasis, choose a wide style in bright, contrasting colours.

Fabric belts are usually sewn, but adhesive can be used on some stiffer fabrics if necessary. The buckles come with or without prongs and buckle moulds are available for covering in fabric rather like covered buttons. Where buckles are used, sew them on or clamp them in place using a special punch tool and metal studs, available from good haberdashery departments. Eyelets for buckle prongs are made by hand or punched in place, using special pliers and metal eyelets. Suitable stiffenings are petersham ribbon, buckram, canvas interfacing, organdie, fusible interfacing, or specially made belting, depending on the weight of fabric used.

The classic belt style shown here is stiffened with belting or other suitable interfacing, formed into a point and fastened with a pronged buckle. The inner measurement of the buckle should be the same width as the belting.

Making an eyelet hole

Puncture a hole in the fabric using a stiletto or a cable needle and use a small pair of fine-pointed scissors to enlarge it if needed. Neaten the edge by hand with buttonhole stitch (see Basic stitches, page 24). Many modern sewing machines also produce very neat, durable eyelet holes. As an alternative to a sewn eyelet use a metal eyelet. These can be applied with a pair of pliers sold specifically for this purpose.

Making a basic belt with buckle

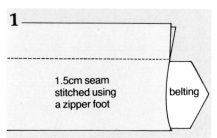
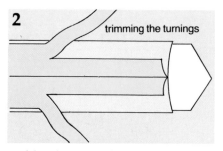
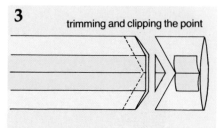

1 Cut a piece of belting 20cm/7¾in longer than waist measurement, by required finished width. With tailor's chalk, draw a point at one end, starting about 2cm/¾in in from the end, and cut to shape.
Cut a piece of fabric on the straight grain, preferably lengthwise, to the same length as the belting, plus 3cm/1¼in turnings; and to twice its width, plus 3cm/1¼in turnings. Do not shape end yet.
Fold fabric over belting so that it meets over the top edge, with right sides inwards. Using a zipper foot and taking a 1.5cm/⅝in seam, machine across the fabric along the top close to the belting. Do not catch it into stitching.

2 Move the fabric around the belting to bring the seam to the centre. Press seam open and trim each seam allowance to 6mm/¼in.
3 Pull fabric over pointed end of belting to overlap by 1.5cm/⅝in. Stitch seam close to pointed end, following its shape. Trim seam to 6mm/¼in and clip across at point.

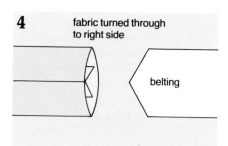
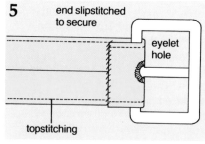
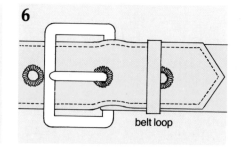

4 Withdraw the belting and turn the fabric tube through to the right side. Press, keeping the seam along the centre in line with the point.
Re-insert belting, pointed end first, into the open end of the fabric tube. Cup the edges of the belting slightly, to help ease it into position.

5 Neaten the straight open end by machine, or tuck in the raw edges and slipstitch over them. Topstitch through all layers if required. Make an eyelet hole 2cm/¾in from the straight end for the belt prong. Insert prong and fold fabric back over bar of buckle to wrong side of belt. Slipstitch end securely on wrong side.

6 Make several eyelets in the pointed end, positioned centrally. Place one to correspond with the waist size and others either side of this at 2cm/¾in intervals. To make a belt loop sew a narrow strip of fabric, twice the width of belt plus turnings, into a circle. Fold in raw edges and slipstitch them together.

Graph for trousers

1.5cm/⁵⁄₈in seam allowance included
4cm/1½in hem allowed
1 square = 5cm

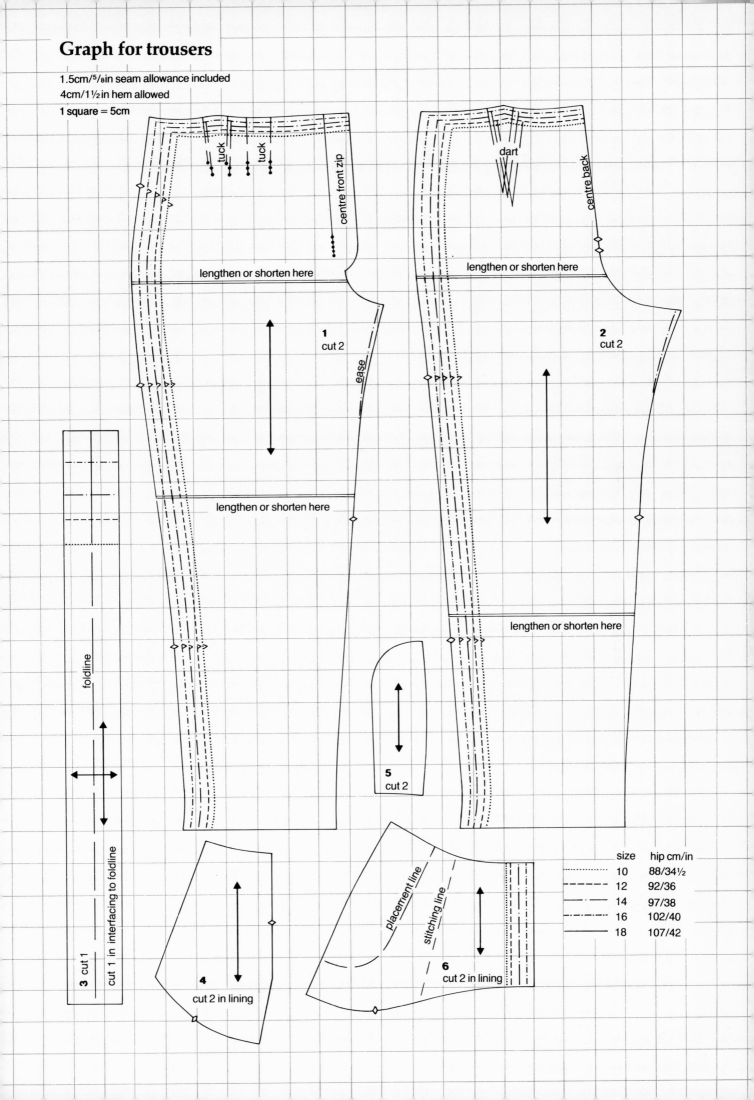

tuck tuck

centre front zip

lengthen or shorten here

1
cut 2

ease

lengthen or shorten here

dart

centre back

lengthen or shorten here

2
cut 2

lengthen or shorten here

foldline

cut 1 in interfacing to foldline

3 cut 1

5
cut 2

4
cut 2 in lining

placement line

stitching line

6
cut 2 in lining

size	hip cm/in
10	88/34½
12	92/36
14	97/38
16	102/40
18	107/42

PART 8

Special techniques for fabrics

Certain fabrics require specific techniques when cutting out, marking, sewing and pressing. Knowing which method to use for a particular fabric makes sewing easier and you will achieve a really professional result.

Ready-quilted fabrics are increasingly available in the shops, some with a reversible finish. Choose an enclosed seam and bind the edges with braid to make a completely reversible garment.

Corduroy, like velvet, is a pile fabric, and so it is essential to lay all the pieces in the same direction when cutting out. Particular pressing techniques must also be used to preserve the surface finish. On fine fabrics, the stitching is particularly visible – learn several new seam and hem finishes or combine them with a decorative stitched edging.

There is a wide range of woollen fabrics and the A-Z guide details the most readily available. These are probably the most versatile and long lasting of fabrics, the more bulky of which need careful layering at seams and darts when making up. Learn how to make bound or piped buttonholes for a smart finish on jackets and coats made from wool.

Finally, stretch fabrics are easy to sew and garments are quick to make up as edges rarely need neatening. Simple pattern styles make up into clothes which are comfortable and easy to wear.

Sewing with quilted fabrics

*Ready-quilted fabrics come in a range of colours and thicknesses
and make up well into crisp garments with
simple lines. Here are some techniques for pinning, cutting out
and working with quilteds, as well as tips
on how to apply braids and bias bindings to the edges.*

Quilted fabrics can be reversible, or with just one right side and a backing layer sandwiching the wadding. Use a plain seam on non-reversible fabrics, and a machine fell seam (which looks equally good on both sides) for reversibles. Here are some sewing tips for quilted fabrics.

Pinning Because ordinary pins with small heads can disappear into the wadding, be careful to use glass-headed ones instead.

Tacking Tacking stitches will not lie flat when you are machining quilted fabrics – they ride up in loops and get caught on the presser foot. The solution is to make smaller tacking stitches than usual, or do without them altogether.

Machining If possible use a special quilting foot or an even feed attachment, designed to stitch thick layers. Test for pressure by seaming two identical scraps of fabric pinned at 3cm/1¼in intervals. The foot should ride over the fabric smoothly without pushing the top layer forwards.

Pressing Do not press fabrics with synthetic fillings because you will flatten them permanently. 'Press' the garment with your fingers as you are making it up.

Below: These two waistcoats have simple lines and are a good choice of pattern for reversible quilting.

Plain seam

This is the simplest and most often used seam. It is suitable for non-reversible quilting.
1 Place two pieces of fabric right-sides together, matching seam lines. Pin across seam line, and machine exactly on the seam line.
2 Because you should not iron quilting, finger press open.

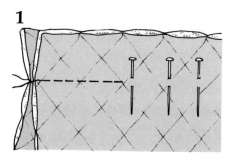

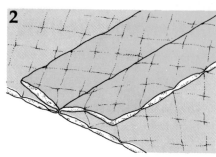

Finishing plain seams

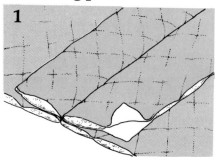

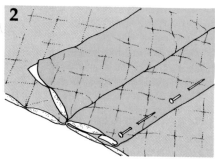

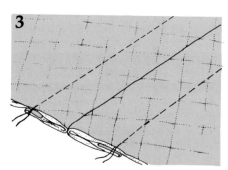

The raw edges of fabric will fray if they are not finished off neatly.

Turned and stitched finish

This is a simple and quick finish which avoids the additional expense

of binding. It can be applied before or after the seam is made.
1 Remove some of the filling near the raw edges of the seam allowance.
2 Turn in the raw edges and pin in position.

3 Machine through all layers of the fabric. If you don't want a stitch line to show on the right side, just machine the raw edges together and hem them to the wrong side of the fabric by hand.

Flat-bound finish

This is a neat finish which is applied after joining the seam.
1 Trim both the seam allowances back to 6mm/¼in.
2 Lay a piece of foldover braid or bias binding centrally over the seam, enclosing the raw edges. Pin to hold, and machine along each edge of binding through the garment. Hem the binding by hand if you don't want the stitch line to show.

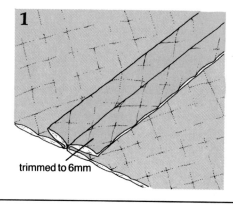

trimmed to 6mm

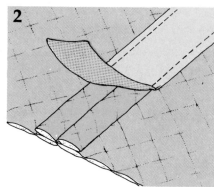

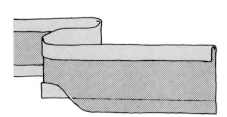

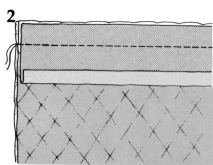

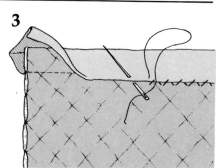

Bound-edge finish

This is a durable finish which has to be applied before joining the seam. Use a bias binding wide enough to enclose quilting (12mm/½in wide is usually adequate). Remove some of

the synthetic filling before applying the binding so as to reduce the bulk.
1 Gently press open one long side of bias binding.
2 Place opened edge of binding along raw edge of garment with right sides

facing. Tack together on opened out fold of binding and machine.
3 Fold the binding over the raw edge of the garment to the wrong side and slip-stitch in position by hand.
Join the seam.

Binding edges

Above: Bias binding and foldover braid.

Binding protects raw edges and also provides a firm decorative finish. It comes in a ready-prepared form in a wide range of colours, widths and textures. Bias binding and foldover braid are the most widely available and, of the two, foldover braid is more suitable for reversible garments as it looks the same on both sides when it has been applied.
Never make a join in the binding at the front edge of a garment.
Before applying any binding, machine along the outermost edge section to be covered. Make sure you have enough binding to go round the edge and add an extra 5cm/2in for join and to allow for fraying.
Apply bias binding as described opposite under the bound-edge seam finish but do not remove any wadding from the quilting to keep a firm edge. (Use 25mm/1in bias binding for decorative edges.)
Foldover braid is even easier to apply as it comes folded and with its edges finished ready for machining. Simply slip the folded braid over the raw edge of the garment and machine through all layers of the fabric. A small zigzag stitch looks best.

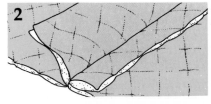

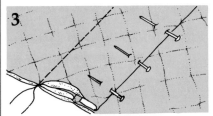

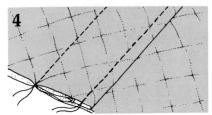

Machine flat fell seam

Choosing the perfect seam is the mark of a professional. The correct seam is the one which will look good and stand up to the wear it is going to receive. A machine flat fell seam encloses all seam allowances on both sides of the fabric and so is ideal for reversible garments. It is also often used in sports wear, children's clothes and shirts.
1 Place two garment pieces wrong sides together then pin and stitch along the seam line.
2 Trim seam allowance of back pattern piece down to 6mm/¼in. With quilting, remove the filling from the outer edge of the other seam allowance and, using your fingers, press all seams flat towards the *back* of the garment.
3 Turn under the remaining seam allowance and pin in place.
4 Machine through all layers.

Unnecessary seam allowances

If you are binding an edge instead of facing or hemming it, you should first cut off the seam allowance if one is included on the pattern.
Transfer the seam line from the pattern using a tailor's chalk pencil. Machine all round the edge to be bound just inside the seam line, to give a firm outer edge to the fabric. Trim off the seam allowance to the line of machining.

Joining bias bindings

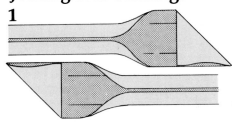

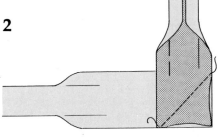

Joins may be made at the pinning stage, before the binding is attached to the garment or as you machine the binding on to the fabric edge.

Joining bias before you apply it

1 Lay the two strips of binding to be joined flat, with wrong sides facing

you. Open out the ends for about 5cm/2in and fold over one corner of each at an angle of 45°. Press a crease along this diagonal with your fingers.
2 Place the two strips at 90° to each other, right sides facing, so that the two diagonals match. Tack along the diagonals and then machine.

Joining bias as you apply it

Pin the bias on to the fabric edge turning under 1cm/½in at the end of the binding to overlap the beginning. Tack and machine in place.
Catch the binding edges together by hand to close up the join.

175

jumbo cord

needlecord

patterned
needlecord

corduroy

Techniques for cutting out and sewing corduroy

Corduroy is an ideal fabric choice for skirts, jackets, trousers and children's clothes. Learn how to work with a pile fabric from the sewing tips given here and you will see how easy it is to make professionally finished, hard-wearing clothes.

The name corduroy is derived from the French *corde du roi*, meaning cloth of kings. A very durable fabric, it is traditionally made from strong cotton yarn and was once used to make working trousers and breeches.

Corduroy, together with velvet, velour, terry towelling and fake fur, is classed as a pile fabric. These fabrics have an extra set of threads which are woven into the fabric at intervals and 'floated' across the spaces in between.

In the case of corduroy, the threads or floats are spaced apart quite widely so that the fibres project in tufts when cut by machine. They form lengthwise ribs – known as wales – on the fabric. The tufts form the pile which is brushed so that it lies in one direction, creating a nap.

It is possible to recognise corduroy entirely by feel as the texture is very obvious. If you brush your hand over the surface of the fabric it will help you decide the direction of the pile, which must be established before the garment is cut out. If the surface feels smooth, you are stroking in the direction of the pile. If it feels rough you are going against the pile.

Characteristics of the fabric

Corduroy is available in two widths – 90cm/36in and 115cm/45in – and a variety of weights. It is usually made from 100% cotton, but sometimes a percentage of man-made fibres is added to improve the quality and durability, and prevent creasing. The fabric is dyed after weaving and lightweight cords are often printed with patterns.

Needlecord is a lightweight cord fabric with about 14–16 wales per 2.5cm/1in.

Corduroy itself has 10–12 wales per 2.5cm/1in.

Elephant or jumbo cord, the heaviest type of corduroy, has fewer wales, and the width of each can vary from 5mm/¼in to as much as 2cm/¾in. As well as varying in width, the wales can also be cut to different levels – low wales alternating with high ones, for example.

Stretch cord is another type of cord that is sometimes available. This has a proportion of elastic fibre such as Lycra added to it and is mainly used for trousers.

Choosing the garment style

Corduroy can be quite a bulky fabric so it is wise to choose a simple style to make up. Needlecord is generally used for dresses, but is prone to creasing, while ordinary corduroy is best for skirts, jackets and trousers. Elephant cord is most suitable for coats and outer wear. If you are using one of the heavier corduroys, avoid bulkiness by replacing pocket and neck facings with a lightweight fabric, such as taffeta, in a matching colour.

The choice of colour when using a fabric with a raised pile is also important. The light reflected by the pile has an effect on the colour. If corduroy is cut with the pile running downwards, more light is reflected, making the fabric appear a shade or two paler. Most dressmakers prefer to cut corduroy with the pile running upwards for greater richness and depth of colour. This also has the advantage of being more flattering to the heavier figure, and prevents marking caused by the pile being rubbed the wrong way around the seat of the garment.

Right: A selection of commercial patterns showing that needlecord, unlike corduroy, is fine enough to be gathered at the waist or cuffs.

The structure of corduroy

floats before cutting

tufts form lengthwise wales

Calculating how much fabric

Most patterns include a with nap or one-way layout and fabric requirements but, if not, you must work out your requirements before buying the fabric. Lay all the pattern pieces in one direction on the floor or a long table and bear in mind the width of the fabric. Because all the pattern pieces must be laid running the same way they cannot interlock as closely as on a without nap layout and there is bound to be some wastage of fabric.

Cutting out

It is possible to cut out the pattern on double fabric with the fabric folded lengthwise. Fold the fabric with the ribbed side outwards. If the pile is on the inside the layers move over each

Below: This skirt appears two-tone because the pattern pieces were not cut with the pile running the same way. Always check before cutting.

other, making it difficult to cut accurately. Do not fold across the width of the fabric as this would reverse the direction of the pile.

It may be easier to cut out each piece separately, on a single layer of fabric. When you require two pieces cut from the same pattern piece remember to turn the pattern piece over, keeping it in the same direction, before you cut the second piece. Otherwise you will end up with two identical pieces, instead of a pair of opposites.

Use fine, sharp pins, placed in the seam allowances of the pattern. Thick pins will mark the fabric. If you prefer, weights may be used instead of pins.

Cut out with sharp shears and transfer any pattern markings using tailor's tacks. Mark an arrow with tailor's chalk on the wrong side of each piece to indicate the direction of the pile.

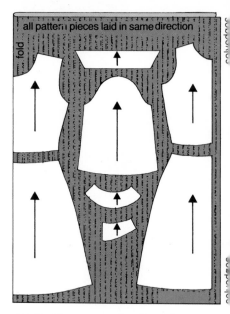

all pattern pieces laid in same direction
fold

Right: To preserve the pile and stop seam turnings showing on the right side, press corduroy on the wrong side with brown paper placed behind seam.

Working with corduroy

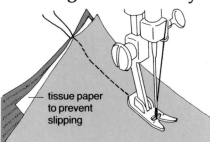

tissue paper to prevent slipping

Tips for sewing

Choose sewing thread to match the fibre content of the fabric – mercerised cotton thread for cotton corduroy and synthetic thread if man-made fibres are included.

Sew fine needlecord with a size 80 or 90 (11 or 14) machine needle, taking 10–15 stitches per 2.5cm/1in. Sew heavy corduroy with a size 90 or 100 (14 or 16) machine needle, taking 10–12 stitches per 2.5cm/1in. Reduce the pressure a little on the presser foot to allow the fabric to move more easily and prevent the pile from being crushed.

Using tissue paper Stitch the seams in the direction of the pile, following the chalked arrows. Place tissue paper between the layers of fabric when stitching the seams to stop them slipping while sewing. Tear paper away after stitching. Try to avoid unpicking seams as corduroy marks easily.

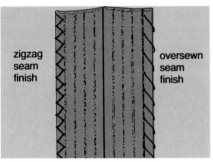

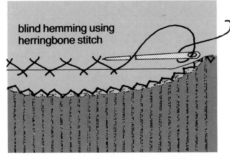

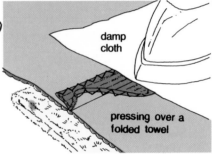

Seam finishes Plain, open seams are usually best as these will avoid a bulky finish, but as corduroy frays easily, neaten the edges with machine zigzag or overlocking. If your machine does not have a swing needle, work a line of straight machine stitching close to the raw edge and then oversew by hand. Alternatively, use a fine crossway binding to bind the edges of the seam allowance.

A flat fell seam may be used for extra strength on trousers and skirts, with topstitching for decorative effect. This must be done with great care, however, as stitching from the right side can flatten the pile and may produce pressure marks. Layer seams at corners and joins to avoid bulk and slash darts to within 5mm/¼in of tip, pressing the dart open.

Hemming corduroy As with seam finishes, it is important to avoid bulk and to neaten the raw edges. Straight hems can be machine neatened or bound with straight seam binding, then blind-hemmed using herringbone stitch. If the hem is curved, the excess fullness can be removed by running a tacking thread close to the raw edge of the hem, pulling it up to fit the curve of the garment and shrinking away the excess fabric in the hem allowance with a steam iron used over a cloth. Keep hems as narrow as possible to reduce fullness.

Techniques for pressing

Press carefully after each stage of making up. Corduroy must always be pressed lightly on the wrong side using a damp cloth or steam iron. To preserve the pile, lay the garment ribbed side down over a needleboard. This is a pad made up of fine wires, pointing upwards, available from good fabric and haberdashery departments. Alternatively, press over a thick, folded terry towel or the right side of an offcut of the fabric, or stand the iron on end with a damp cloth over it and lightly move the wrong side of the fabric across iron. When pressing a seam allowance or a dart, slip a strip of thick paper between it and the main body of the garment, to prevent an impression showing on the right side. Press only the folded edge of hems using the side of the iron lightly. After pressing, leave fabric to cool, then brush pile gently in the correct direction.

Fabric care

Although some corduroys may be machine washed, it is probably safer to dry clean or wash gently by hand. Do not squeeze, wring or rub, or spin dry as creases are then set in the fabric. If the fabric is not colour fast, particularly in the case of dark colours, add vinegar or salt to the rinsing water to prevent the dye loosening and leave the garment to drip dry.

Seam and hem finishes for fine fabrics

Fine fabrics make pretty blouses and lingerie and are not difficult to handle, once you know how.
Follow the advice given here on choice of style and learn how to achieve neat seam and hem finishes to give a professional look to your dressmaking.

Fine fabrics such as voile, lawn and crêpe de chine may be produced from natural or man-made fibres or mixtures of the two. They require careful treatment for the best results, using fine needles, pins and thread and special seam and hem finishes to retain their delicate appearance.

Choosing a style

Fine fabrics look best in soft styles, with gathers and unpressed pleats rather than a close-fitting finish. Try to choose patterns with side and shoulder seams only, avoiding centre seams on front and back, also neck facings as the edges will show through as ridges on the right side of the garment.

Instead, look for styles where the front opening is enclosed in a band, and with collars which do not require back neck facings. Alternatively, use binding instead of a facing to attach the collar, cuffs or frills in a neat, unobtrusive way. Where interfacings are essential, choose the lightest possible weight or use organdie.

Machining fine fabrics

Reduce the number of machined rows to a minimum to prevent the fabric from puckering and, where possible, combine rows of stitching. For example, instead of topstitching a completed seam, incorporate the seaming and topstitching into one operation.

Use a stitch length of about seven stitches per centimetre (15–20 per inch), a size 70/9 needle and fine thread, chosen to suit your fabric type. For working buttonholes and for zigzag neatening, machine embroidery thread, which is finer than ordinary thread, is ideal.

Seam finishes

Neaten turnings using a self-enclosed seam. This encloses the turnings within the finished seam to protect raw edges, or use an over-edge seam with the turnings trimmed to 2–3mm/⅛in and the raw edges finished with a narrow machine zigzag or overcasting by hand.

Self-enclosed seam finishes The French seam and the flat-fell seam

Mock French seam

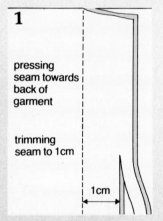

1 — pressing seam towards back of garment — trimming seam to 1cm — 1cm

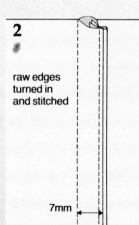

2 — raw edges turned in and stitched — 7mm

Use this where an ordinary French seam is difficult to control – on pronounced curves, for example.
1 With right sides together, machine along seamline. Press both seam allowances towards the back of the garment.

2 Trim seam allowances to 1cm/½in and turn raw edges in 3mm/⅛in to face each other. Finger press, pin together close to folded edges, then machine.

Self-bound seam

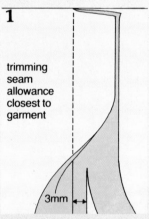

1 — trimming seam allowance closest to garment — 3mm

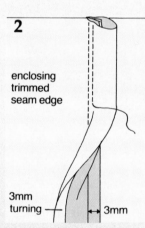

2 — enclosing trimmed seam edge — 3mm turning — 3mm

This is suitable for both straight and curved seams. Trim one seam allowance and use the other as a binding for them both.
With right sides together, machine along seamline. Press seam allowances to one side.
1 Trim seam allowance closest to garment to 2–3mm/⅛in, snipping to stitches if the seam is curved.
2 Turn under 3mm/⅛in of remaining allowance and bring to seamline, enclosing the trimmed edge. Machine stitch or hand finish close to previous machining line.

muslin

silk

(see Basic seams on pages 24–26) are the classic seams of fine fabrics. The French seam is suitable for straight seams on both crisp and soft fabrics but the flat-fell seam is easier to control on crisp fabrics. The finished width of the seam depends on the fabric, but should be no more than 6mm/¼in. Use a fine needle and small stitches to ensure a strong seam.

The narrow French seam is the one most commonly used on fine fabrics, but when dealing with difficult areas such as curves, or finishing the armhole seams after setting in the sleeves, use a mock French seam or self-bound seam.

Overedge seams These are worked on the wrong side of the fabric, trimmed and then zigzagged or overcast by hand. The width of the finished seam should be 6mm/¼in.

Although some sewing machines zigzag stitch perfectly over raw edges, with others the best finish is obtained by zigzagging a little way in from the raw edge and then trimming away the excess fabric.

cotton lawn

Darts and hems

Trim away the fabric of the dart to avoid bulk and neaten the edges by overedging. Hems tend to show up clearly on fine fabrics so you must aim to produce a neat finish.

If a garment needs lengthening at a later date, on children's clothes for example, turn up a conventional hem but make it completely double so that the raw edge runs along the hem edge and does not show through.

Use a normal narrow hem finish for lower hems of blouses which will be worn tucked in. Simply trim the hem allowance to 1.5cm/¾in, press 5mm/¼in to the wrong side, then another 1cm/½in and machine close to the top edge of the fold.

Where a hem in a fine fabric is likely to show, as on a front frill for example, a rolled hem gives a neater finish. Work this in one of two ways either by machine and hand, or entirely by machine using a narrow hemmer.

Some fabrics or garments do not require a turned-up hem at all. In fact, they look better if the raw edge is simply neatened and left, particularly on the edges of frills or sleeve hems. Alternatively, try a decorative machine stitch to make a feature of the hem.

Pressing

Always test the temperature of the iron on a scrap of the same fabric. Press on the wrong side using a cool iron at first and increasing the temperature depending on the fibre content, if necessary. Cover the fabric with a piece of muslin, spraying it lightly with water if the fabric can tolerate it, then press.

Plain overedge seam

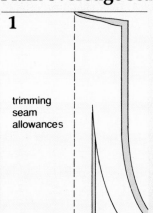

trimming seam allowances

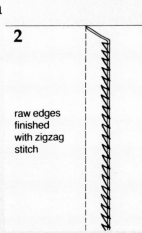

raw edges finished with zigzag stitch

1 With right sides together, machine along the seamline. Press seam allowances to one side. Trim seam allowances to required finished width.

printed silk crêpe de chine

2 Zigzag the raw edges together, using a close, short stitch.

Lingerie seam finish

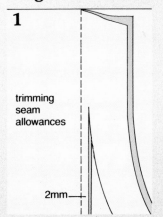

trimming seam allowances

2mm

short and narrow zigzag stitches

This is used for bias cut lingerie where a narrow, flat seam is required, and is a useful method of finishing seams on fine fabric.

You can complete the seam in one motion if your machine has an overlocking stitch. If not work as follows:

1 With right sides together, machine along seamline. Press seam allowances to one side and trim to 2mm/⅛in (or trim after neatening if preferred).

2 Set the machine to sew short stitches and a narrow zigzag, but not quite satin stitch, then zigzag the raw edges together, allowing the left-hand side of the stitches to just enter the straight machine stitches.

spotted voile

Hems for fine fabrics

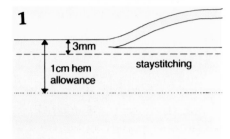

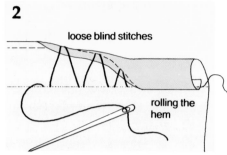

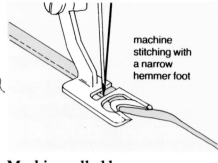

Hand rolled hem

1 Trim hem allowance to 1cm/½in. Staystitch 3mm/⅛in from the raw edge with small machine stitches. Trim fabric away to a few threads from machining.

Alternatively, you may find it easier to staystitch 7mm/⅜in from the hem foldline before trimming the hem allowance. Practise first on a spare scrap of fabric to see which is easier.

2 Turn hem to wrong side along hem foldline and roll raw edge under so that line of stitching just shows. Working from right to left, take small loose blind stitches (like slipstitch) through the machine stitching and garment. Take several stitches before pulling up the thread, causing the fabric to roll. Press gently to remove finger creases, avoiding the rolled edge which should be left gently rounded, not pressed flat.

Machine rolled hem

Trim the hem allowance to 6mm/¼in, then finger press along hem foldline. Turn the raw edge under again to form a double hem and finger press lightly.

Manoeuvre the double hem into place under the narrow hemmer foot (practise first on leftover fabric if you haven't used one before) and stitch, taking care to keep the hem even.

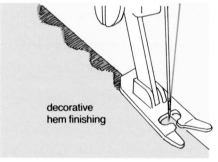

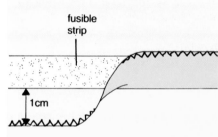

Zigzagged hem

Trim the hem allowance away up to the marked hem foldline.

Use a zigzag stitch, testing it on leftover fabric. Set the zigzag almost to satin stitch width and keep it short so that it does not draw up the fabric. Working with the right side of the garment towards you, and taking care not to stretch the fabric, zigzag over the raw edge all the way round. Fasten off by taking a few stitches on the spot.

Decorative hem

If your sewing machine does decorative stitches, use them in the same way as the zigzag seam finish for an attractive hem edge. Choose a contrasting thread to highlight the stitches.

Below: Machine embroidery stitches look effective when used to finish narrow hems on fine fabric cuffs.

Fused hems

Secure raw edges permanently using narrow *Wundaweb* or other fusible strips. Test first.

Trim the hem allowance to 1cm/½in. Zigzag stitch the raw edge to neaten. Press the hem allowance to the wrong side, lay fusible strip along the foldline of garment and bring hem over to cover it.

Press through all layers, using a warm dry iron over a damp cloth, to fuse the hem in position.

loose weave

close weave

Working with wool – a natural fibre

Warm, comfortable, hardwearing and long-lasting – these are all characteristics of woollen cloth. Consult the A-Z of fabrics when choosing wool and learn how to cut out and sew this versatile natural material so that you obtain a really professional result.

Wool has a long and fascinating history. One of the natural fibres, like cotton and silk, it has been used to make cloth since pre-historic times. The methods of making cloth were refined somewhat when the Romans invaded Britain in 55BC and taught Britons the skills of weaving, later founding the first woollen mill in Winchester in AD80. The cold, damp climate of Britain meant that woollen clothing was very popular because of its warm, damp-resistant properties and by the Middle Ages the prosperity of the country was built on the wool trade.

Gradually, more woollen mills were built – one at the mouth of the River Tweed gave its name to tweed cloth, and another at Worstead, near Norwich, gave the name worsted to the type of closely woven cloth made there.

Nature of the fabric

The properties of wool – its elasticity, crease-resistance and warmth – are due both to the nature of the fibres and the way they are woven.

The Woolmark, sign of pure new wool.

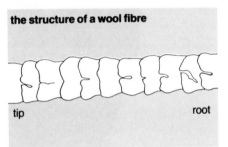

Certification Trade Mark

Most wool is obtained from sheep, although some comes from other animals such as rabbits and goats. Sheep's wool fleeces are washed, carded – a process involving brushing the fibres so that they all lie in the same direction – and spun into yarn. Wool fibres can vary in length from 3.8cm/1½in to 38cm/15in, the longest fibres making the finest quality fabrics.

the structure of a wool fibre

tip   root

Wool fibres consist of a central core covered in an outer skin made up of small, overlapping scales, rather like roof tiles. Air is trapped between these scales, making woollen fabrics bad conductors of heat, and therefore excellent at keeping the body warm.

In addition, the fibres are crimped naturally so that when a fibre is stretched and then released, it always springs back to its original shape. This resilience also means that creases soon drop out of the fabric and it is not easily crushed. Fabrics woven from woollen yarn, therefore, allow plenty of give in wear and yet keep their shape well. If woollen garments get slightly baggy at the elbow, knee or rear after a lot of wear, they can be restored to their original shape by pressing under a damp cloth.

Woollen fibres initially repel water, although moisture is eventually absorbed if you are caught out in a

heavy downpour wearing a woollen coat. However, the woollen fabric remains warm even when wet and the body does not feel chilled – another reason why wool is so often used for jackets, coats and suits.

Handling woollen fabrics

Wool is much weaker when it is wet than when it is dry. It does not wash well naturally, unless it is specially treated, and it is liable to shrink. This shrinking is called felting and is caused by the scales on the fibres being disturbed. The fibres stretch when wet and, on drying, the scales move and lock together, shrinking the fabric.

Although accidental felting is a problem, controlled shrinking is important to the dressmaker and tailor. You can ease out the fullness at the head of a sleeve, in the turning of a hem or in a collar by careful use of moisture, heat and pressure.

Felting is, in fact, one of the oldest methods of producing fabric – early man is thought to have used felted fabrics produced by layers of wet fleeces matting together as they dried and shrank. Today, heavyweight coat fabrics are often felted to make them warmer.

Other types of woollen fabric are produced by treating the wool fibres in a special way, or by using a particular weaving process.

Yarn for weaving is produced by twisting the wool fibres together. If the fibres are combed repeatedly when spinning, the yarn becomes strong and smooth and is used to make worsted. Other woollen fabrics are made from uncombed yarns and therefore have a slightly fluffy surface. It is worth bearing in mind that a rough surface picks up dirt easily and will therefore need cleaning more frequently than woollen fabrics with a smooth surface.

The *Woolmark* (see page 183) is the symbol of the International Wool Secretariat. It is recognized world wide, and guarantees 100% pure new wool of a controlled quality. Look out for it when buying wool fabrics. Wool is often blended with other fibres, which can reduce the cost and alter the properties of the fabric slightly. Wool and polyester mixtures are quite common, and Viyella, a wool/cotton mixture has the advantage of being washable. The A-Z opposite lists some of the most common woollen fabrics, including those made from the wool or hair of animals other than sheep.

Choosing woollen fabrics

A garment made up in wool will not be cheap, but if well made and cleaned regularly, it will give many years of service. Because wool is found in such a variety of weights, take care when choosing fabric for a pattern or vice versa. Take into account whether the fabric drapes easily if you want a bloused or gathered style. A thick fabric, or one which frays easily, needs a pattern with simple, uncomplicated lines.

Closely woven fabrics, such as worsted, are more durable than loose weaves and are generally used for suits, trousers and lightweight coats. Thicker fabrics often do not wear as well and loose weaves lose their shape more quickly. To check the closeness of the weave, hold the fabric up to the light.

Many woollen fabrics are not easy for beginners to handle, but if you have some dressmaking experience you should be able to cope with Viyella or a firm, medium-weight wool like flannel, which does not fray easily.

Confidence in handling different weights and qualities of fabric comes with experience, so if you are planning to use a new dressmaking process for the first time, avoid expensive mistakes by making a trial run. Either make a complete version of the garment in a cheaper fabric, or test the processes on a spare piece of your chosen fabric.

Right: Use the advice on buying and sewing woollen fabric and tackle an advanced sewing project, like a smart woollen coat, with confidence.

184

A-Z of woollen fabrics

Pure wool fabrics are unequalled for warmth, texture, durability and range of colour. Even a relatively inexperienced dressmaker can achieve good results when working with a wool flannel, for example. It is hard to overpress such a fabric and it will not show marks where seams are unpicked. Although the luxury wool fabrics such as alpaca or cashmere are best left to more experienced dressmakers, once you have realised the advantages of working with a wool fabric, you will be unwilling to settle for anything else. Use the chart below to help you recognise different types of wool fabric and their uses.

ALPACA
From a tiny member of the camel family. Smooth and lustrous fabric, used for skirts and dresses.

ANGORA
From the angora rabbit. Blends well with wool, long smooth fibres which tend to rub away. To avoid shedding of fluff when sewing, wrap it in a polythene bag and leave in the freezer for a few hours before use.

BARATHEA
Made from worsted yarns in a twill weave. Smooth surface, springy to handle, used for skirts, suits, jackets. Choose simple styles and use a nap layout to avoid shading.

BOUCLÉ
Woven in knobbly, looped yarns. Warp and weft often woven in different colours. Used for dresses, coats and suits.

CAMEL HAIR
Light and soft, can be bulky. Used for coats. Follow a nap layout.

CASHMERE
From the Kashmir goat. Very soft and fine, often blended with wool. Used for coats, suits and dresses. Follow a nap layout.

CHALLIS
Fine, lightweight, plain weave material. Can be made from worsted yarn. Has a tendency to fray easily. Used for dresses, blouses.

CRÊPE
Made from twisted yarns into different fabric weights – soft with good drape for dresses and blouses, heavier weight for suits. Springy to handle but simple to sew. Frays easily and can shrink if steam pressed.

FLANNEL
Made in wool or worsted. Lightweight, soft, warm and resilient. Does not fray much, easy to sew. Used for skirts and jackets.

GABERDINE
Close twill weave, very springy and difficult to handle. Hard-wearing and lightweight – used for raincoats and suits.

JERSEY
Knitted fabric with plenty of give. Drapes well, comfortable to wear. Used for dresses, suits and skirts.

MELTON
Plain weave medium weight fabric, slightly felted finish. Used for coats.

MOHAIR
From the angora goat. Medium to heavy weight hairy fabric. Used for coats, jackets.

MOUSSELINE
Plain or printed lightweight worsted. Used for dresses.

TWEED
Strong, warm and hard wearing. Rough, natural colours and heavy weave. Used for tailored suits and coats, men's jackets. (Also Harris tweed.)

VIYELLA
Lightweight blend of wool and cotton, plain or printed. Washable, used for blouses, dresses and children's wear.

WORSTED
Smooth surface, hard-wearing, but holds creases and becomes shiny with wear.

Harris tweed

camel hair and wool

worsted wool crêpe

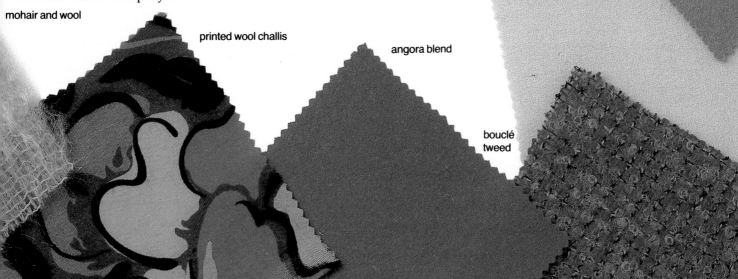

mohair and wool

printed wool challis

angora blend

bouclé tweed

Working with wool

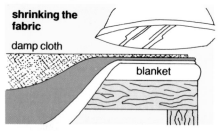

shrinking the fabric
damp cloth
blanket

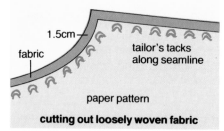

1.5cm
fabric
tailor's tacks along seamline
paper pattern
cutting out loosely woven fabric

Use the following guidelines to help you when making up a garment in a wool fabric.

Shrinking the fabric
The fabric label should tell you whether or not it is pre-shrunk – if not, you will need to shrink it yourself *before* cutting out.
Place the fabric wrong side up on a large surface such as a kitchen table, covered with a blanket and then a sheet to protect its surface. Cover fabric with a piece of damp muslin and hold a hot iron close to the surface above it. The moisture and heat will shrink the fabric. Shrink the whole length in this way and allow it to cool before moving it.

Cutting out
Narrow widths of wool fabric are sold rolled in a single thickness around a cardboard tube, while wider ones are folded and need to be gently pulled into shape, and pressed lightly to remove the fold. Straighten the ends of the fabric by pulling a thread across the grain, and cutting the fabric in line with this. Follow a nap layout if you are using a wool fabric such as gaberdine or crêpe and pin on the pattern using good quality sharp steel pins, placed within the seam allowance.
When cutting out loosely woven tweeds and bouclés, cut wider seam allowances to allow for fraying. Mark seamline with tailor's tacks or chalk so that you do not inadvertently make a larger garment. Cut out jersey knits carefully to avoid pulling them out of shape. Use ballpoint pins and cut out using serrated shears.

Sewing and finishing techniques

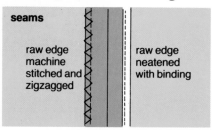

seams
raw edge machine stitched and zigzagged
raw edge neatened with binding

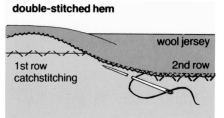

double-stitched hem
wool jersey
1st row catchstitching
2nd row

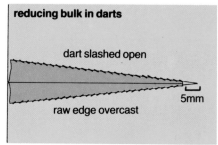

reducing bulk in darts
dart slashed open
raw edge overcast
5mm

Use a mercerised or pure silk sewing thread and sew with a straight stitch, taking 10 to 12 stitches per 2.5cm/1in. Loose weave fabrics may need a larger stitch. A machine needle size 90 or 100 (14 or 16) is suitable for most wool fabrics.
Seams Use open seams on wool fabrics and neaten the raw edges according to the weight and type of fabric chosen. Bind the edges of loosely woven fabric with bias or straight seam binding to prevent fraying. Machine close to the raw edge of seams on closely woven fabric and finish by machine zigzag or overcasting by hand. Neaten finer fabrics such as Viyella by turning the edge under and machine stitching.

Hems Hand-stitch hems on wool fabrics, neatening the raw edges first by machining (if a lightweight fabric) or binding. Reduce any fullness by careful pressing and catchstitch the hem in position by hand, taking care not to leave an impression on the right side.

Hang wool jersey garments for 24 hours before hemming so that the hem can be cut perfectly level. Make a double-stitched hem, catchstitching first halfway up the hem depth and then again just under the raw edge.
Reducing bulk Careful layering of seam turnings is the best way to prevent bulk in collars, sleeves, waistbands or wherever pattern pieces are joined. Slash darts open to 5mm/¼in from the point, overcast the raw edges and press the dart open over a tailor's ham – a shaped pad for pressing curves.
Interfacing Do not use iron-on interfacings for wool, as they do not adhere to the fibres very well. On tailored garments such as jackets, use plain or hair canvas. Non-woven interfacing is suitable for lighter weight garments.
Lining It is best to line woollen garments, particularly skirts. This will prolong the life of the garment and help to prevent seating as well as making the rougher woollen fabrics more comfortable to wear.

Choose the lining weight according to the fabric weight and the amount of wear the garment will have.

Caring for wool
Pressing Always use a damp cloth when pressing wool. A steam iron alone does not always provide sufficient moisture, and direct pressure from the metal soleplate of the iron can damage the wool fibres. Press on the wrong side of the fabric with a moderately hot iron and avoid prolonged contact. After pressing, beat thicker fabric or the bulky edges of a garment with the back of a clothes brush or a pounding block to give the garment a good finish when the steam evaporates.
Laundering Follow laundering instructions on the fabric label and always hand-wash if washable, unless machine-wash is specified. Avoid excessive agitation of the fabric, and too high temperatures. Dry out of direct sunlight. If in any doubt as to whether the fabric is washable, dry clean instead.

Making bound buttonholes

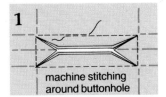

machine stitching
around buttonhole

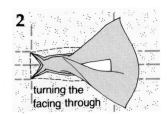

turning the
facing through

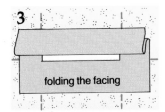

folding the facing

Buttonholes on heavy wool fabrics are usually bound or piped. Mark out buttonhole clearly, marking centre of each*. Cut a facing strip 5cm/2in wide and 4cm/1½in longer than the buttonhole.

1 Lay strip over button-hole position, right sides together. Mark centre and stitching lines. Machine round buttonhole, starting at the centre and counting stitches so that the sides of the buttonhole are perfectly even. Overlap stitching at finish to strengthen. Cut along centre line through facing strip and garment, and cut diagonally into each corner to within a thread of machine stitches.

2 Turn facing through slit facing and pull edges gently to square the corners.

3 Working on wrong side, fold long edges of facing until folds of equal width meet in the centre of the rectangle, enclosing the seam allowances. On right side, tack diagonally to secure folds and press from the wrong side.

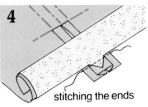

stitching the ends

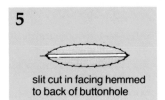

slit cut in facing hemmed
to back of buttonhole

Making piped buttonholes

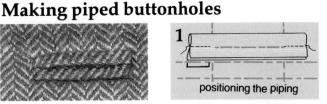

positioning the piping

4 Working on the right side, fold back the garment to reveal the triangular cut ends of the facing and machine across to hold. Oversew folded edges of binding together at either end. To secure buttonhole to facing, prickstitch along seamline of both long sides.

5 To complete the buttonhole, make a corresponding slit in the garment facing. Push pins through the ends of the buttonhole from the right side. Snip the garment facing between pins, remove the pins and carefully snip a further 2mm/⅛in at each end. Fold the raw edges under into an elongated oval, exposing the back of the bound buttonhole, and hem to it. Press.

For piping, cut two strips of fabric twice the depth of the buttonhole* and to the length of the button-hole plus 2cm/1in. Mark centre of buttonhole. Fold strips in half length-wise, wrong sides together. Press lightly. Machine along centre of folded piping. (If fabric frays easily cut piping wider, fold and stitch required distance from fold. Trim.)

1 Place raw edges of first piping strip to marked centre of buttonhole on garment. Centre the piping so it extends 1cm/½in each side of buttonhole. Tack through piping and garment along stitching line.
With right sides together, tack second piping strip to marked stitching line in same way.

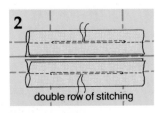

double row of stitching

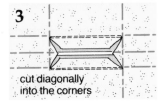

cut diagonally
into the corners

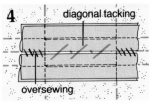

diagonal tacking

oversewing

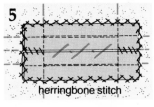

herringbone stitch

2 Double stitch the piping in place to prevent weak ends. Start in the centre of the tacked line, machine to one end, pivot and machine the length of the tacked line, pivot and return to centre. Keep the stitching lines exactly together.

3 On the wrong side, snip through the centre of the buttonhole and cut diagonally out towards end of machining. Do not cut the piping.

4 Push piping and end triangles of garment fabric through to wrong side of garment. Pull ends of piping to straighten.
The folded edges of piping will now come together along the centre of the buttonhole. Tack piping folds together diagonally and press lightly from the wrong side, pressing turnings away from buttonhole. Oversew folded edges of piping turnings together. Working from the right side, fold back garment to expose ends of piping and triangles and machine stitch across.

5 Herringbone stitch around outer raw edges of piping to attach it to interfacing on wrong side. Complete the buttonhole in the garment facing as for the bound buttonhole, step 5.
*Note: The depth of a bound or piped buttonhole is usually about 1cm/⅜in and on finer fabrics 6mm/¼in.

Stretch fabrics

Stretch fabrics are ideal for garments where a lot of give is required. Use them for toddlers' and babies' clothes, and all kinds of sportswear. That built-in stretch factor eliminates the need for darts, pleats or gathers, so learning how to use them won't stretch you at all . . .

Stretch fabrics belong to the wide range of knitted fabrics – though not all knitted fabrics can be classed as stretch. The actual construction of a knitted fabric means it is not as rigid and has more give than a woven one; it handles differently and has a more fluid effect when draped. Stretch fabrics, such as stretch towelling and stretch velour, are not only knitted – they are knitted with an elastomeric thread, so that they 'give' in all directions, yet return to their original size. **Advantages of stretch fabrics** Such

fabrics are very comfortable to wear because of this 'give' factor. They do not restrict the wearer and this makes them ideal for babies' and children's wear, and for sports and leisure wear. Once the techniques for handling stretchy fabrics are understood, they are easy to make up. Darts, pleats or gathers are unnecessary and interfacing to preserve shape is rarely used because the fabric recovers well. Neck and hem edges are usually bound or cuffed and patterns for stretch garments are simply designed.

Recognising stretch fabrics

The most popular stretch fabrics with home dressmakers are stretch towelling and stretch velour. Stretch towelling (also known as terry) is looped on the right side, and has a smooth knit finish on the reverse side. Stretch velour has a cut pile surface, giving a plush, velvety effect.

Both fabrics come in a wide range of colours and patterns – in varying combinations of natural and synthetic fibres, which affects their degree of stretch. Different fibre types and percentages of blended fibres are also combined for specific purposes – bathroom, beach and sportswear, for example, requires fabric with a high degree of absorbency.

Also in the shops are the wholly manmade stretch nylon or Lycra fabrics in matt or shiny finishes, of the type used for leotards, and stretch evening fabrics, which often incorporate metallic threads.

Choosing a suitable fabric for your pattern

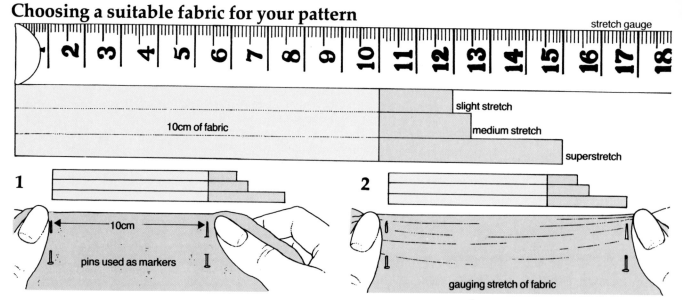

Make sure you choose the right type of stretch fabric for the pattern you intend to use. A pattern marked 'for stretch knits only' is intended for very stretchy fabrics like towelling and velour – it has no extra allowance for ease of movement and is cut smaller than a pattern that states 'for knits only', which does allow some extra ease for body movement.

However, even very stretchy fabrics vary in their degree of stretchiness. Most pattern companies provide a printed gauge on the pattern envelope so that you can test the hori-

zontal stretch capacity of the fabric before buying, to ensure that it is suitable for your pattern. Alternatively, use the gauge given above.
1 Hold the fabric firmly on the left against the start of the gauge.
2 Stretch 10cm/4in of the fabric along the gauge, seeing how far it will stretch without strain.
The degree of stretch in the fabric – slight, medium or super – is indicated on the gauge. After stretching, the fabric should spring back to its original size. If it does not, this indicates that it will lose its shape quickly when

made up.

It is always a good idea to check the list of recommended fabrics on the back of the pattern envelope and ensure that you choose one of these.

It is also a wise precaution to add 5-10cm/2-4in extra to your requirements when buying because stretch fabrics tend to stretch on the roll in the shop. To allow the fabric to relax back to normal size, leave it spread loosely on a table for 24 hours before cutting. If it contains a high percentage of cotton, it should also be preshrunk by washing before cutting.

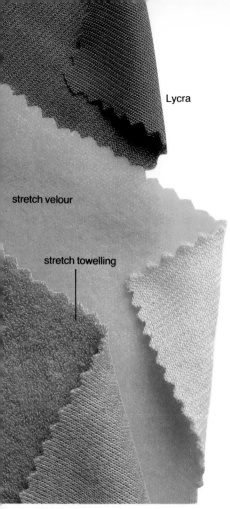

Lycra

stretch velour

stretch towelling

Above: Stretch fabrics come in a good range of attractive colours. Cut out and sew on the smooth, knitted side.

Cutting out stretch fabrics

Stretch fabrics with pile, like towelling and velour, should be cut with all the pattern pieces laid in the same direction, otherwise the garment will have a shaded effect when made up. Always follow the pattern layout – the maximum give is across the width of the fabric, so do not try to economise on fabric.

The straight grain is difficult to follow on stretchy fabrics. To judge correct pattern positioning be guided by the fabric design where possible or straighten one edge by trimming along one row of stitches.

Cutting out checklist

• **Fold fabric** right sides together. This is particularly important when using pile fabrics, as the pile holds the layers firmly together during cutting. It is also easier to work on the smooth, knitted side.

If using striped or checked stretch fabric, make sure the pattern matches on both layers of fabric. Or, if you prefer, open out the fabric and cut pattern pieces singly.

• **Support the fabric** on a table while pinning and cutting out to prevent it stretching out of shape. If there is too much fabric to fit on the cutting area, support the excess in loose folds on a chair.

• **Pin with ball-pointed pins** designed especially for knitted fabrics. They penetrate between the knitted loops, while ordinary pins break the fibres, causing the fabric to run. Use the pins sparingly, as the depth and stretchy nature of the fabric may cause the paper pattern to tear around the pins.

Reinforce the pattern seamlines with sticky tape and weight the pattern with kitchen scale weights to hold it flat.

• **Cut out using long-bladed sharp shears**, with serrated edges. These 'bite' into the fabric as you cut, and stop the layers from slipping. Pin the pattern to double fabric, but cut each layer separately to prevent the lower layer from being smaller than the upper one. Do not lift the fabric away from the table as you cut, as this will stretch it.

• **Mark the fabric** on the wrong side using tailor's chalk or tailor's tacks made with a ball-pointed sewing needle. To mark the start and finish of seamlines make snips about 3mm/ ⅛in deep into the seam allowance.

Sewing stretchy fabrics

Sewing with stretch fabrics involves introducing stretch into all the stitching processes to prevent seams bursting open. It is preferable to use a zigzag or stretch stitch, but simple styles can be attempted with a straight stitch sewing machine.

Seam strength depends on correct stitch tension and pressure, so always make a test seam first on leftover scraps.

Types of seam Stretch fabrics may have plain seams, which are pressed open, or double-stitched seams which are trimmed and pressed to one side of the seamline. When making garments for babies or toddlers, where the seams are subject to stress, it is best to stitch the seam twice. Stitch on the seamline, then stitch again 5mm/¼in within seam allowance. Trim to second stitching line.

Generally, raw edges of inside seams do not require neatening, but they may be hand oversewn or zigzag neatened. Curved seams should be clipped, unless they have been double-stitched and trimmed.

Tack before sewing, using normal tacking if your machine has a stretch stitch, or loose tacking if the seam is to be stretched during sewing.

Stitches to use

Zigzag stitch Use a narrow, shallow zigzag, stretching the fabric as you sew. Check on leftover fabric first, to make sure the fabric returns to its original size after stitching, and that the seam does not break.

Special stretch stitch Modern or more advanced sewing machines may have this facility. The stitch is a straight stitch, but consists of two stitches forward and one back. Some machines may seam and neaten in one operation. Check your manual for the type of stitches available.

Straight stitch Although a zigzag stitch or stretch stitch is preferable, if your machine does not have this facility use a slightly larger straight stitch than usual and stretch the fabric as you sew. Check on leftover fabric first.

If a seam stitched by any of these methods breaks, the stretch is not adequate. Check the points below in conjunction with the table given on page 190.

• Stretch the fabric more while sewing. (If the seam does not return quickly to normal size, however, you have overstretched the fabric.)
• Alter stitch size.
• Use polyester thread.
• Check the tension, and adjust upper tension only.

Finishing raw outer edges

Bindings, welts and cuffs used to finish stretch garments have to be flexible so that they slip over heads, hands and feet easily. Apply elastic or ribbed bands or make simple casings for drawstrings at waistlines and cuffs.

Binding made from self-fabric bias strips or from woven fabric is useful for necklines and armholes. Apply it in the normal manner, stretching as you sew, but to avoid a bulky finish leave the edge that is turned in single, rather than folding it under again. Stitch from right side through all thicknesses to secure binding.

Equipment for sewing stretch fabrics

Polyester thread	Strongest thread, allows maximum stretch
Polyester covered cotton thread	Best for cotton/polyester blends
Ball-pointed machine needle, size 80. (Preferably teflon-coated, anti-static.)	Prevents split threads or runs in knitted fabrics
Ball-pointed hand-sewing needle	Prevents split threads or runs in knitted fabrics
Regular presser foot	Adjust presser control for thicker fabrics
Even-feed foot	Allows layers of fabric to feed through evenly
Roller foot (not available for all machines)	Rides over looped pile fabrics without tangling loops in foot. Fabric layers feed evenly

roller foot

even-feed foot

How to correct sewing problems

Problem	Solution
Seam snaps when stretched after stitching, although tension normal and fabric stretched during stitching.	If *lower* (bobbin) thread snaps, increase top (needle) tension until seam remains firm when stretched. If *top* thread snaps, decrease top tension and test as above. Bobbin tension rarely needs adjustment.
Thick fabric refuses to pass freely under presser foot.	Use an even-feed or roller foot.
Two layers move at different speeds, so that one is longer than the other at end of seam.	Try holding the ends of the seam firmly together while stitching, pulling the lower layer if the top one starts to ripple in front of the needle. Only adjust pressure if other methods fail. Decrease pressure if top layer feeds too fast. Increase pressure if lower layer too fast.

Ribbing Circles of ribbing suitable for cuffs, with the edge to be joined to the garment already neatened, can be purchased from haberdashery counters. Alternatively, buy the ribbing by the metre and join into a circle of the size required.

To apply, mark cuff edge and garment edge into quarters. With right sides together, pin ribbing edge to garment along marked seamline, stretching ribbing to fit within each quarter section, then stitch. The ribbing will relax back to the right size.

Welts Pattern pieces are given in commercial paper patterns wherever a welt for cuffs, ankles or necklines is required. The welt is made of self-fabric, folded and joined then applied to the edge in the same way as ribbing. Stretch it to fit as you sew.

Casing To form a casing for elastic or a drawstring at a waist edge or cuff, fold raw edge over once and stitch. For a casing within the body of a garment, apply a separate casing, stitching as for a stretch seam.

Hems Always allow garment to hang for 24 hours before marking or completing hems.

To make a hem, turn the normal seam allowance (1.5cm/⅝in) to wrong side of garment. Herringbone stitch hem by hand. Alternatively, machine 2mm/⅛in from fold, stretching fabric or using a stretch stitch. Machine a second row of stitching 1cm/½in from fold.

A neckline curve can be turned in and stitched as above, stretching the outer edge of the seam allowance so that it lies flat.

Pressing Stretch fabrics may not require pressing. If they do, press on the wrong side with a steam iron, lifting and lowering the iron very lightly so the fabric is not pulled out of shape. Avoid handling a napped fabric like velour while still damp, as it will fingermark.

Below: From left to right – a welt made from self-casing, a casing for a drawstring, and ready-made ribbing.

PART 9

More things to make

The patterns in this collection are fun to make and each one introduces new techniques, short cuts and decorative design ideas which can be applied to other patterns and styles.

The camisole top can be lengthened to make a sundress or an evening dress with an elasticated waist. Learn how to make rouleaus and use them as straps for the camisole or button loops on the stylish bib-fronted dress or shirt.

The loose-fitting designer top has a roll collar, topstitched seam details and side vents for ease of movement. Extend the pattern to dress length if you prefer. Another garment made from an extended pattern is the fleece jersey lounger. This cosy cover-up features a chunky, front-opening zip and simple band cuffs.

An elegant set of lingerie can be made from a simple graph pattern and given a glamorous treatment by adding a length of purchased lace as a decorative edging. Discover, too, how to use a circle of fabric to make a full swirling skirt or a fluted ruffle. Fullness and frills can also be incorporated into a garment by working shirred bands or panels – techniques which are used to make a simple sundress or nightdress.

Simple camisole tops – sewing with style

This chapter gives you all the know-how you need to make a simple camisole top. It also introduces cutting on the cross and sewing bias seams – the additional techniques that help you make a designer-look evening camisole with an elegant draped neckline.

Camisole tops are quick and easy to make and need very little fitting – the elasticated back or the draped front allows for most in-between sizes.

This chapter gives the making up instructions for two different styles of camisole and features a number of simple techniques. It shows you how to work with fabric cut on the cross, how to make elastic casings and how to stop facings rolling out. The next chapter gives instructions on making plain and corded rouleaus and how to add a professional touch with decorative piping.

A choice of camisole tops for evening. The stylish draped effect of the cowl-necked camisole relies on the cut of the pattern and does not involve any complicated sewing techniques.

The straight-top camisole

This camisole would make up well in crisp lightweight fabrics for summer. A blouse weight challis is also suitable, and slightly warmer. For evenings choose cotton, silk or rayon foulard or a fine faille.

You will need
1.20m/1⅜yd of 90cm/36in wide fabric for all sizes (10–18) *or*
1.00m/1yd of 115cm/45in wide fabric for all sizes (10–18) *or*
0.90m/1yd of 140–150cm/55–60in wide fabric for all sizes (10–18)
Matching sewing thread
25.5cm/10in narrow elastic
0.30m/12in light interfacing

Pattern pieces, page 198:
1 Straight top bodice back
2 Straight top bodice front
3 Straight top straps
4 Straight top back facing
5 Straight top front facing
Extend the lower edge of the bodice back (1) and the bodice front (2) by 17cm/6¾in to give the necessary length for tucking in (see pages 196–197 for how to extend patterns).

Cutting out
Following the appropriate cutting layout, fold the fabric and position the pattern pieces on double fabric as shown. Cut out.

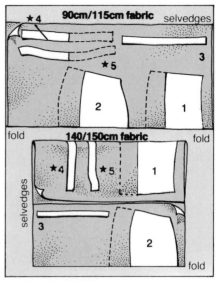

★cut from single fabric

Making shoulder straps

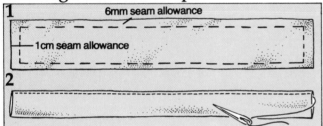

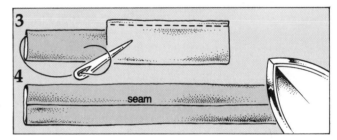

Shoulder straps on dresses and lingerie can be made up in a variety of different widths, from the narrowest rouleaus to wide, dungaree-type straps. Narrow straps can simply be machined on the wrong side and turned through, while wider straps require interfacing for strength.

Simple narrow straps
1 Cut a strip of fabric the length required, plus 1cm/½in at each end for attaching to garment. If you do not have a pattern piece, the strip should be twice the finished width required, plus 6mm/¼in seam allowance on each side. If the strap is to be more than 2cm/¾in finished width it must be interfaced (see below).
2 Fold fabric in half lengthwise, right sides together. Pin 6mm/¼in from raw edge and machine, using width guideline on needleplate of machine for accuracy. Leave about 10cm/4in thread hanging from seam. Thread this through a bodkin, tie a single knot to secure.
3 Insert bodkin into fabric tube and gently push through to opposite end, turning the fabric right side out.
4 Press strap flat, positioning seam centrally on underside of strap.

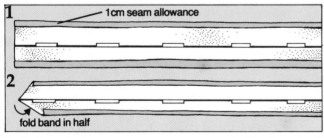

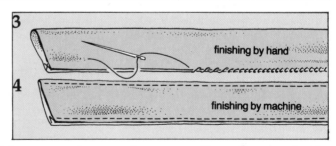

Interfaced straps
Interfacing gives body to a strap, keeps it flat and prevents it stretching in wear. The 'turned through' method (above) is not suitable for interfaced straps as it crumples the interfacing.
1 Cut strip of fabric for strap as above but add 1cm/⅜in seam allowances. For interfacing use a fusible band which has a central marking to aid positioning and cut the same width as fabric strip less 2cm/¾in. Position interfacing to wrong side of strap, leaving 1cm/⅜in seam allowance along both sides. Press, using a damp cloth to seal the adhesive to the fabric. Do not move iron to and fro – this causes air pockets.
2 Press seam allowance on each side to inside of strap. Fold band in half and press.
3 Stitch folded seam allowance edges together by hand, using a very small slipstitch.
4 Alternatively, machine close to edge, topstitching other edge to match.

Attaching facings

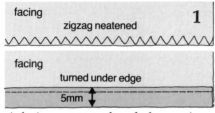

facing
zigzag neatened
1

facing
turned under edge
5mm

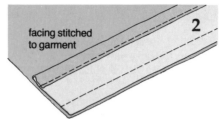

facing stitched
to garment
2

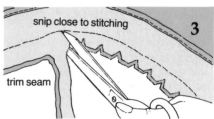

snip close to stitching
3

trim seam

A facing, as you already know, is an extra piece of fabric used to make firm a garment edge. When used to neaten a neckline or armhole the facing should be at least 5cm/2in wide to stay tucked inside the garment in wear.
Interfacing can be inserted as an additional layer between the garment and the facing, to give strength and a better defined edge. For a crisp finish on the straight camisole you may prefer to interface the front neckline with lightweight interfacing.
1 Neaten outer edge of facing by zigzag overstitching, or turn raw edges under 5mm/¼in and edgestitch.
2 Place facing to garment, right sides together. Pin, tack and machine along seamline.*
3 Trim seam allowance to 6mm/¼in. Snip to within 2mm/⅛in of stitching line on curves to allow ease. Press seam allowances towards facing.
4 Before turning the facing to the inside of the garment, machine along the right side of the facing,

Making elasticated casings

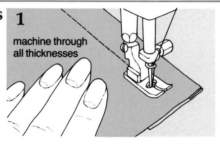

1
machine through
all thicknesses

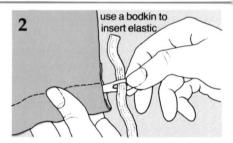

2
use a bodkin to
insert elastic

Casings are tubes in the body of a garment through which elastic, ribbon or ties may be threaded to gather fullness. They are often used to gather a waist, cuff or neckline. A shorter casing can also be used to thread elastic through the back of a waistband or a camisole to gather it to fit.
The simplest type of casing is on a faced edge, such as the top back edge of a camisole.
1 Allowing enough room for the width of the elastic plus at least 6mm/¼in extra, machine a row of stitches below the top edge of the back bodice on the right side, through fabric and facing.*
2 Insert a piece of elastic through the casing using a bodkin.
3 Secure at one end either by hand (lift the facing and stitch end of elastic to seam allowance) or, for a stronger finish, machine from right side through all layers. Adjust elastic to fit before securing the

The cowl-necked camisole

The secret of the appearance of this camisole is that the front is cut 'on the cross', which allows the folds to fall naturally, the two tucks at each side providing any necessary additional fullness. Such a style lends itself readily to an evening occasion, matched with simple crêpe trousers or a stylish skirt, and a wide belt.
A special camisole deserves special fabrics so take time when choosing your material, and always hold it against you to see how it will drape.

Fabric suggestions

Soft, draped finishes need lightweight fabrics, so avoid crisp cottons and concentrate on soft textures, blends of fine wool and polyester, or rayon with polyester which is softer than cotton.
This is an opportunity to use a really striking fabric, such as one with a metallic thread running through it,
or silk. (For tips on sewing with fine fabrics see pages 180–182.)
Remember that the front piece is cut on the cross and take this into account when choosing a heavily patterned fabric or a diagonal print as the front will look very different from the back in these fabrics.

You will need

1.30m/1½yd of 90–115cm/36–45in wide fabric for all sizes (10–18) *or* 1.10m/1¼yd of 140–150cm/54–60in wide fabric for all sizes (10–18)
Matching thread
0.15m/¼yd interfacing

Cutting on the cross

The majority of patterns are cut with most pattern pieces placed on the lengthwise straight grain. There are good reasons for this; in most cases the garment hangs better if all the pieces follow the same direction,
and it is very much easier to sew. However, very few seams follow the exact straight grain. As soon as some shape is introduced, as in a side seam over the hip, the sewing is done on the bias, that is, off the straight grain. Most side seams, armholes, necklines etc. are cut on the bias of necessity because they are curved.
'On the cross' refers to the *true* bias, the most flexible area of the fabric. This is at an angle of 45° to the selvedge. Fabric cut on the cross is easiest to mould: it falls into soft folds, drapes well across bodice or hip and makes bindings and trims and ruffles.
The cowl-necked camisole top is a particularly suitable garment to start with when learning about cutting on the cross. The back bodice is cut on the straight grain and the front is cut on the cross. The side seams are therefore easier to sew than if both

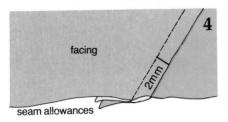

facing

2mm

seam allowances

2mm/⅛in from the seamline, stitching through the seam allowances as well. This prevents the facing creeping up above the seamline in wear. Press facing lightly to inside.
*Note: When making up camisole top, straps are inserted between bodice and facing during step 2.

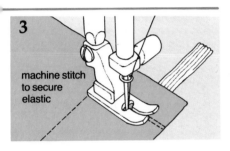

3

machine stitch to secure elastic

other end.
*Note: The casing in the camisole top does not extend along the entire faced edge of the back. Insert between straps as in Making up the camisole, step 7.

Making up the simple camisole

1 With right sides together, pin front to back at side seams, matching notches. Tack, machine and press seams open. Neaten edges.
2 Make the bodice facing by joining front and back facing at side seams, with right sides together. Press seams open and zigzag overstitch to neaten lower edge.
3 Prepare straps by chosen method (see page 193) and pin ends centrally over markings (O) on upper front and back camisole. The straps should be placed to the right side of the garment, with the ends level with the top raw edge. Pin and tack. Try on, and make fitting adjustments to strap length if necessary.
4 With right sides together, matching side seams and Os and enclosing straps, pin facing to camisole top. Stitch all the way round and trim seam allowances.
5 Machine edgestitch 2mm/1/16–⅛in from seam through seam allowances and facings as shown. Turn facings to inside and press.
6 Stitch 1.3cm/½in from upper edge of back bodice between straps to form a casing for elastic.

Measure distance between straps and cut a piece of 6mm/¼in wide elastic to this length minus 3cm/1¼in, to allow for stretch. Insert elastic, sew one end to secure and adjust to fit before securing other end.
7 Catchstitch facing to side seams on inside.
8 Machine a narrow hem (1.5cm/⅝in) along lower edge. Or, turn up hem, neaten edge and catch by hand if preferred. Press.

An elasticated back for a perfect fit.

pieces were cut on the cross. Provided you remember to match the side seams at the notches and keep both upper and lower raw edges absolutely level, you won't have any problems.

How to find the true bias
It is easier to establish the true bias on a new length of fabric than on a scrap left over after cutting.
1 Pull a crosswise (weft) thread to ensure a perfectly straight line across one edge.
Take the corner of the selvedge and lay the selvedge along a crosswise thread so that the two selvedges are at right angles to each other. The diagonal formed by this fold is at an angle of 45° – the true cross.
2 When you are using bias or crossway strips for trimmings you often have to make them from fabric scraps left over after cutting out

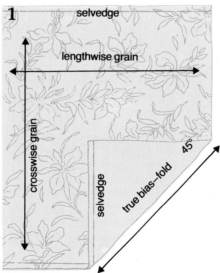

1

selvedge

lengthwise grain

crosswise grain

selvedge

true bias–fold

45°

where no selvedges remain as a guide. Straighten the edges of the scraps by pulling the crosswise thread and trimming to that line. Lengthwise threads (straight grain)

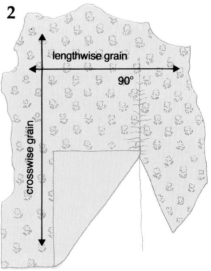

2

lengthwise grain

90°

crosswise grain

will not pull out, so just cut along one of them to make a 90° corner. Then fold in the same way as in step 1 to form a diagonal for the true bias.

195

Layouts for the cowl-necked camisole top

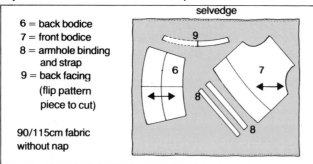

6 = back bodice
7 = front bodice
8 = armhole binding
   and strap
9 = back facing
   (flip pattern
   piece to cut)

90/115cm fabric
without nap

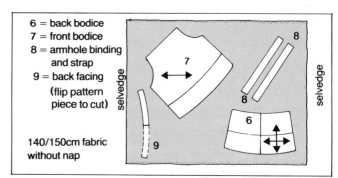

6 = back bodice
7 = front bodice
8 = armhole binding
   and strap
9 = back facing
   (flip pattern
   piece to cut)

140/150cm fabric
without nap

Preparing to cut out

Place pattern piece 7, front bodice, on the fabric, matching grainline markings as shown on the appropriate cutting layout above. It will spread across the fabric at an angle. Allow enough room for extending it to cut the camisole top to the required length (see right),

then pin.
Extend the cutting line at the lower edge of each side seam by 17cm/6¾in with a ruler and tailor's chalk, as shown. Join up these two extended lines across the lower edge with a straight line, which will be on the diagonal.
Place pattern piece 3, the back

bodice, on the fabric as shown on the layout. (It may be easier to trace the half back bodice on to a folded piece of paper. This will open out to give an entire back section which you can use.) Extend the lower edge by 17cm/6¾in in the same way. (This includes a 1.5cm/⅝in hem allowance.) Pin the straps and facing (pattern

---

Working with bias fabric

If you cut both back and front of a garment on the cross, then the seams are sewn where the fabric has most give, and you must take great care not to stretch it out of shape while sewing.

If you are joining a bias edge to a straight edge, the straight edge gives some firmness, making it easier to sew. This type of seam is very common, being used to join a curved waist edge to a waistband, or a straight collar to a curved neck edge, and it is worth learning to do it well. An 'even feed' machine attachment prevents fabric creeping as you sew these seams. If you don't have this attachment, try the methods here.

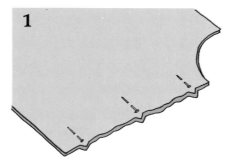

Joining two bias edges

1 With right sides facing, place seam edges together, matching notches and pin at notch position. Match the upper and lower edges and pin at each end of the seamline. The areas between may seem

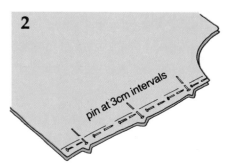

pin at 3cm intervals

flexible, but should match exactly.
2 Pin remaining seam at frequent intervals (about every 3cm/1¼in), then tack. Do not pin from one end and work along, because bias edges tend to stretch and this may result in seams not matching at both

---

Joining a bias and a straight edge

If you are joining one bias and one straight edge, and the straight edge is on top, hold it firmly and allow the more flexible bias edge to feed through the machine. If you are sewing with the bias edge on top, the lower straight edge gives strength to the seam and allows you to ease the bias edge evenly through the machine.

To cut and join crossway strips

Strips cut on the cross are very flexible and are used in a variety of ways as a binding. To stop seams and hems fraying, you can bind them with lining fabric. To trim an edge, you can bind it in shiny satin.

Crossway strips are also used to make narrow shoulder straps or rouleaus.
The strips are easy to cut and make up and it is even possible to buy a gadget known as a binding maker to simplify the process further.
1 Establish the true cross of the fabric as described earlier. Make a crease along it with your fingers or with an iron. This is your starting point for cutting strips for binding or rouleaus. Generally, allow twice the finished width required, plus a narrow seam allowance on both long edges.
2 From the first guideline, measure off widths in parallel lines. Add 5mm/¼in at each end for the seam

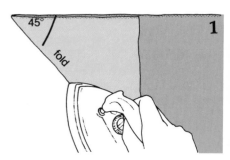

allowance. Cut out the strips.
When you are using short lengths of fabric cut on the cross – to make shoulder straps for example – you can usually avoid joining them. When longer lengths are required for an entire hem, or binding seams, joins will be necessary. Use only very narrow seam allowances

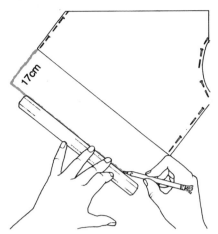

pieces 8,9) on to the surrounding fabric as shown.
Cut carefully round each piece. Mark strap positions and seam allowances.

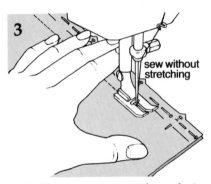

ends. If you cut accurately and pin correctly, it should not be necessary to trim either end of the seam.
3 Sew carefully without stretching the seams, using a thread with some give, such as silk or synthetic.

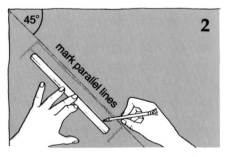

when joining the pieces to avoid a bulky finish. Join on the straight grain, following the instructions given for joining bias binding on page 175. Remember to position joins so that they do not spoil the finished effect of the decorative binding.

Making released tucks

Most types of tuck are made on the straight grain but released tucks, also known as dart-tucks may be off the grain. A released tuck tightens the garment in one area and releases its fullness into a wider area, such as the bust or hips. It may be used instead of gathers, pleats or darts.
1 Bring the two sides of the tuck together, matching the markings from your pattern exactly. Tack into position. If the tuck is not topstitched, leave the tacking in until the garment is completed, then remove. Do not press.

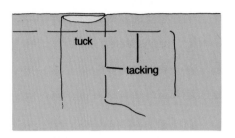

Making up the cowl-necked camisole

1 With right side facing, make tucks on both armholes by bringing lower lines to meet upper lines, following the direction of the arrows.
Tack to keep in place, using a fine needle and soft thread.
2 Neaten raw edge of extended facing on front. Fold facing to wrong side along fold line. Do not press – a firm edge destroys the softness of the folds.
Tack facing at armhole edges to keep in position.
3 Fold straps in half lengthwise, right sides together. Pin, tack and stitch from circle to end along unnotched part of strap, 1cm/½in from raw edges. Leave thread end free to turn strap through. Snip seam allowances to stitches at circle.

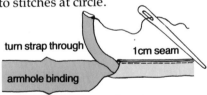

4 Turn straps through using a bodkin. The flat, notched section is for binding the underarm.
5 With right sides together, matching notches on armhole and binding, pin and machine binding to armhole seamline. Turn binding to inside of garment, hem to machine stitches.
6 Stitch front to back at side seams, matching notches and placing bound front armhole edge 1.5cm/⅝in below upper edge of back.
7 Tack ends of straps to back where indicated. Try on and adjust strap length if necessary.

8 Using pattern piece No 9, cut out interfacing for back facing. Tack to wrong side of back facing. Neaten lower, unnotched edge.

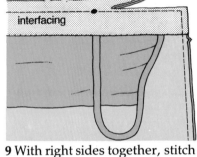

9 With right sides together, stitch back facing to back along top edge and upper parts of side seams, matching notches and circles. Trim upper seams and corners.

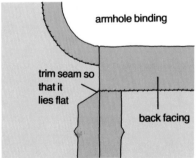

10 Snip into the front side seam allowance to stitching line just below back facing to allow seam to lie flat. Turn facing to inside and press. Press side seams open.
11 Topstitch back bodice 1cm/½in from upper edge. Make a narrow hem (1.5cm/⅝in) on lower edge, machine stitch or hem by hand. Remove tackings and press, avoiding front folds and straps.

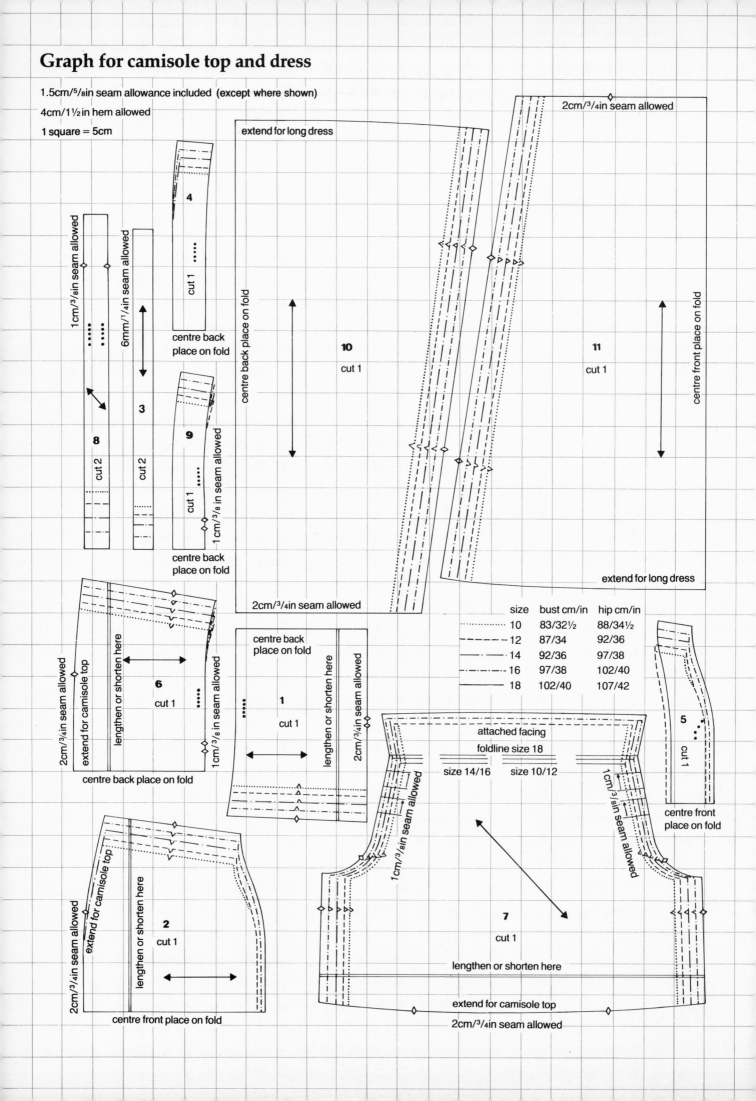

Graph for camisole top and dress

1.5cm/⁵⁄₈in seam allowance included (except where shown)

4cm/1½in hem allowed

1 square = 5cm

extend for long dress

2cm/¾in seam allowed

4 cut 1

centre back place on fold

1cm/³⁄₈in seam allowed

6mm/¹⁄₄in seam allowed

3 cut 2

8 cut 2

9 cut 1

1cm/³⁄₈ in seam allowed

centre back place on fold

centre back place on fold

10 cut 1

centre front place on fold

11 cut 1

extend for long dress

2cm/¾in seam allowed

size	bust cm/in	hip cm/in
10	83/32½	88/34½
12	87/34	92/36
14	92/36	97/38
16	97/38	102/40
18	102/40	107/42

2cm/¾in seam allowed

extend for camisole top

lengthen or shorten here

6 cut 1

centre back place on fold

1cm/³⁄₈ in seam allowed

centre back place on fold

lengthen or shorten here

1 cut 1

lengthen or shorten here

2cm/¾in seam allowed

attached facing

foldline size 18

size 14/16   size 10/12

1cm/³⁄₈ in seam allowed

1cm/³⁄₈ in seam allowed

centre front place on fold

5 cut 1

2cm/¾in seam allowed

extend for camisole top

lengthen or shorten here

2 cut 1

centre front place on fold

7 cut 1

lengthen or shorten here

extend for camisole top

2cm/¾in seam allowed

Dresses for day and evening wear

*The versatile camisole does not stop at a top – it can also be
made up as a sundress, or as an evening
dress in two different styles. Once you know how to add an
elasticated waist to give an attractive blouson
effect you can use this technique to make many dresses fit you better.*

Once you know how to make either
version of the camisole top, you only
need to know how to deal with an
elasticated waist casing to complete
the camisole dress. You can make it
up as a sundress in a knee-length

version with a straight top, or as a
stunning full-length evening dress
with a draped cowl neck. Alternatively, the evening dress can be made
up in the same style as the sundress,
but full length.

Fabric suggestions

The most suitable fabrics for the dresses are the same as those recom-

*Below: The sundress looks equally good
with a straight top or a cowl neck.*

mended for the corresponding style of camisole top. The straight-topped style is best in crisp cottons or cotton/polyester mixes, while the cowl-necked style needs softer fabrics for draping – ideally silk, crêpe de chine or light cotton lawn.

Sundress: You will need
Quantity of fabric as in chart right
Matching thread (silk, if silk fabric)
1.25m/1⅜yd of 6mm/¼in wide elastic

Evening dress: You will need
Quantity of fabric as in chart right
Matching thread (silk, if silk fabric)
0.15m/6in of 80cm/32in wide
 lightweight interfacing
1m/1yd of 6mm/¼in wide elastic

Fabric quantity chart

Size	10	12	14	16	18
Bust (cm)	83	87	92	97	102
(in)	32½	34	36	38	40

Sundress (straight-topped style);
(for long version add 70cm/27½in)

	10	12	14	16	18
90cm	2.30	2.30	*	*	* m
115cm	2.30	2.30	2.30	2.30	2.30m
140/150cm	2.20	2.20	2.30	2.30	2.30m

Evening dress (cowl-necked style);
(for short version 70çm/27½in less)

	10	12	14	16	18
90cm	3.00	3.00	*	*	* m
115cm	3.00	3.00	3.00	3.00	3.00m
140/150cm	3.00	3.00	3.00	3.00	3.00m

* 90cm fabric for small sizes only

All quantities are in metres and are for fabric with or without nap, shading, pile or one-way design.

Making the sundress
There is no need to extend the pattern pieces for the front and back bodice as for the camisole top. However, if you are long or short waisted, lengthen or shorten the pattern pieces on the double alteration lines.
The blouson style only works if there is enough material to give a soft effect above the waistline. Tall women, or those with a full bust, may need to add a little more length to the pattern before cutting out.
Allow for buying extra fabric Whenever you lengthen patterns, For example, if you want to add 10cm/4in to the bodice with fabric 150cm/60in wide you need the specified amount plus 10cm/4in, and with 90cm/36in wide fabric you need the specified amount plus 20cm/8in (i.e. twice the additional amount). Place pattern pieces 1, 2, 3, 4, 5, 10, 11 on the fabric as shown on the appropriate layout and pin carefully. Pieces 4 and 5 are cut from single fabric only.
If the fabric has a nap or one-way design, make sure this runs the same way on all pattern pieces. Cut carefully around each piece and transfer pattern markings.

Making the evening dress
If you are long- or short-waisted, lengthen or shorten the pattern pieces on the double alteration lines. To extend the skirt pattern pieces to make the full-length dress, start by measuring yourself from the back waist to the floor, or to the length you require for the finished dress. Pin pattern piece 10 to the fabric. At the folded edge of the fabric measure the new length down from the waist seamline over the pattern and fabric. Add 4cm/1½in for hem allowance, (full-length dresses do not require deep hems), and mark the cutting point with tailor's chalk. Use a ruler to extend the slope of the pattern at the side seam as shown, and join to the cutting point

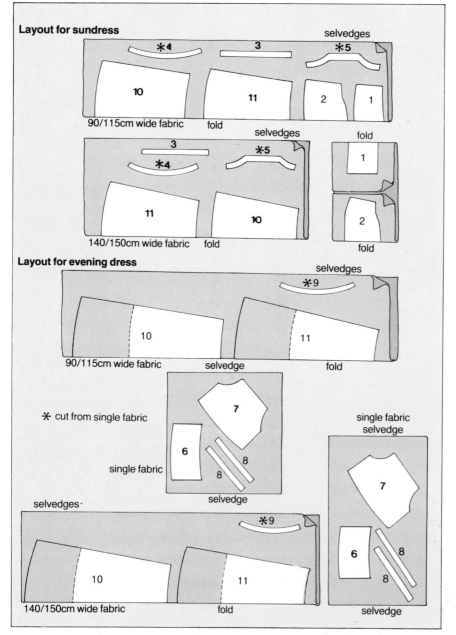

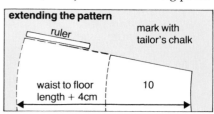

1 With right sides together, join side seams of sundress bodice, matching notches. Neaten edges and press seams open.

2 With right sides together, join skirt side seams from waist to hem, matching notches. Neaten edges and press seams open.

3 With bodice tucked into skirt and right sides together, join waistline seam 2cm/¾in from raw edges, matching notches on bodice to skirt.

4 Press both seam allowances up towards bodice and make a waist casing for the elastic, following the instructions for an extended waist casing (see overleaf). Insert elastic.

5 Make straps, complete upper facing and elasticate between the straps following steps 2 to 7 of the simple camisole top instructions (see page 195).

6 With straps attached securely, try on dress and mark hem position. Following the instructions for a shaped hem (page 48), turn up the hem easing out fullness. Press dress carefully.

Right: The long evening dress looks stunning made up in a silky fabric.

---

at the fold, following the curve of the hem on the pattern piece. Repeat for pattern piece 11. Place pattern piece 9 on single fabric at side of skirt pattern as shown on layout. Open out fabric to pin on pieces 6, 7 and 8, making a full back bodice pattern piece as suggested on page 196 if required. Cut carefully around each piece and transfer pattern markings by your preferred method.

1 Following steps 1 to 11 of making up the cowl-necked camisole top (page 197), make up the dress bodice and straps, remembering that the bodice is waistlength only and does not require hemming.

2 With right sides together, join skirt side seams from waist to hem, matching notches. Neaten edges and press seams open.

3 Complete the dress, joining skirt to bodice, making a waist casing and hemming as in steps 3, 4 and 6 of making the sundress (above). Press carefully when completed, avoiding pressing folds into the neckline.

Elasticated casings

Knowing how to make casings for elastic or ties brings versatility to your dressmaking. They give most garments comfort and style and you can add a casing to an existing garment to give it a fresh look.

Both extended and applied types of casing can be used for the waists of dresses, the lower edges of over-blouses and casual jackets, tops of skirts and trousers, for ankles and cuffs of tracksuits and pyjamas, for lingerie and children's garments.

Dresses with a soft blouson style, like the camisole dress, need some form of control to keep the waistline in position. This usually takes the form of an elasticated casing, or elastic stitched directly to the fabric, or shir-

ring (thread and elastic stitched together, see page 234).

Look at the fabric you are using when considering what to do to the waistline of a blouson-style dress (and this

Above: Elastic anchors the waist of a dress more effectively than a belt.

applies equally to the wrist of a full sleeve, or a peasant-style neckline).

Extended waist casing

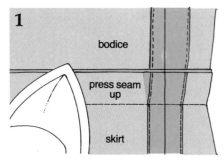

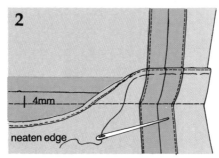

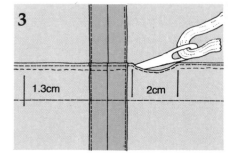

This method is used where the extra seam allowance required for a casing (for example at the waistline) has been included in the pattern. When bodice and skirt have been machined together at the waistline, work as follows:

1 Press both seam allowances up towards the bodice. If fabric is bulky, trim the seam allowance of the bodice to 4mm/⅛in.
2 Turn under 4mm/⅛in on the seam allowance of the skirt and neaten by machine. Tack to bodice.

3 Working on right side of garment, machine 1.3cm/⅝in up from waist seamline, leaving 2cm/¾in open near side seam. Cut a piece of 6mm/¼in wide elastic to waist size and insert into casing with a bodkin. Try on with elastic pinned

Applied waist casing

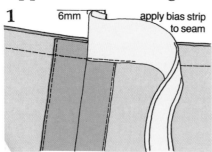

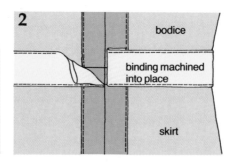

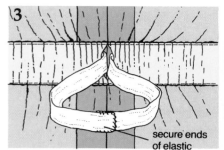

Where the seam allowance is insufficient to form an extended casing for the width of elastic required, use a prepared bias binding to form the casing. Alternatively, make your own using the same fabric as the dress, or a lightweight lining fabric.

Cut the bias strips as described on page 196 and press under both long edges. Apply as for prepared bias binding as follows.
Machine bodice to skirt and tuck the bodice down inside the skirt to give you easy access to the seam allowance.

1 Stitch one folded edge of the binding to the seam allowance of bodice and skirt, starting at a seamline and folding under 6mm/¼in of binding at each end.
2 Bring the bodice out of the skirt and tack the top edge of the binding against the inside of the bodice.

202

The fabric determines the thickness of elastic suitable for the garment, and the method you use to apply it. Ready-prepared bias bindings are suitable for use as casings on light-weight cotton and synthetic fabrics, but are not strong enough for dress-weights of wool or wool blends. For these, use casings made of the same fabric or of toning lining fabrics, or apply wider elastic directly to the in-side of the dress.

Adding a casing may make a fine fabric too bulky, or it may show through and spoil the effect on a sheer fabric. This is the time to use shirring elastic or apply a non-cased elastic especially designed for the purpose.

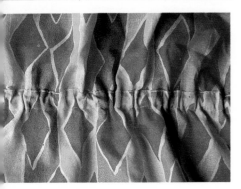

Close-up of an extended waist casing.

or tied, adjust for a comfortable fit and join elastic. Hand stitch the 2cm/³⁄₄in gap to close.

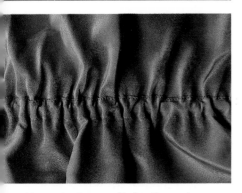

Close-up of an applied waist casing.

Machine top long edge of binding, stitching from the right side.
3 Insert elastic through gap in binding at seam position. Join ends of elastic then close gap by hand.

Elastication without a casing

When sewing fine fabrics or gathering in full sleeves at the wrist, for example, a casing may not be necessary. Apply the elastic directly to the garment by one of the following methods.

Flat or round elastic up to 6mm/¹⁄₄in wide can be encased within a machined zigzag stitch.

Cut the elastic to the correct size first, check around the waist or wrist and join into a circle. Lay elastic on stitching line and machine, using a large zigzag stitch. Stretch it to fit as you go, avoiding catching the needle in the elastic.

The elastic will be free to move within the zigzag, as it would within a casing, but there is no additional bulkiness.

Above: Elastic applied directly to a full sleeve creates an attractive frill.

Applying wide elastic and plush elastic

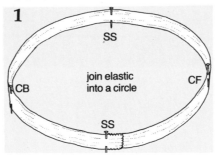

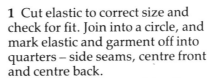

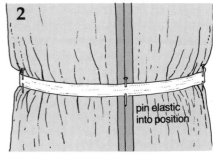

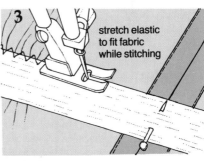

Flat elastic wider than 6mm/¹⁄₄in does not fit within the widest zigzag stitch on most machines. Use the zigzag or straight stitch along both long sides of the elastic to machine to garment.

1 Cut elastic to correct size and check for fit. Join into a circle, and mark elastic and garment off into quarters – side seams, centre front and centre back.
2 Lay elastic along stitching line, pinning only at marked points. The fabric, which is wider, will lie loose between these points.
3 Machine slowly along one edge, keeping the presser foot down and the needle in the work each time you pause. Stretch the elastic to fit each quarter of the garment and ease in the fabric as you go. Complete one full circle.
Stitch second side of elastic in the

same way, removing the pins as you go. If you are using a zigzag stitch, allow the needle to just miss the outer edge of the elastic, to give a less rigid edge.

Plush elastic is soft-backed elastic, originally designed for lingerie but ideal for elasticating a non-cased waist.

Use 1cm/¹⁄₂in width and apply in same way as the flat elastic (above), with the soft side towards the body. Stitch the outer edges only.

Using satin piping

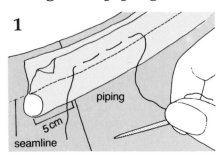

1

5cm

piping

seamline

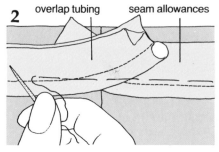

2

overlap tubing   seam allowances

Above: Stripey satin piping brightens the seamed edge of a camisole top. Choose from a wide range of trimmings for an attractive finishing touch.

Piping has long been used as a decorative and very effective finish on clothing, but it is a time consuming and skilled job to prepare it. However, polyester satin piping in a wide range of colours to tone or contrast with your fabric is now widely available at haberdashery counters and it is easy to apply.

The edges of this piping are raw, but they are completely enclosed within the seam allowance of the garment, and neatened with it.

1 Lay the piping on the right side of your garment, with the line of manufacturer's machine stitches behind the cord of the piping corresponding to the seamline. The raw edges of the piping should be towards the raw edge of the fabric. Pin and tack piping into position, leaving 5cm/2in of the trimming free at beginning and end. The piping moulds around any curves in the seamline, so do not try to ease or stretch it.

2 Gently draw out about 2cm/⅝in of piping cord from each end of the satin tubing and trim it off. Overlap the two empty ends of the tubing and curve them away into the seam allowance as shown. Tack over the join.

Stitch the piping to the fabric, using a zipper foot and stitching as close to the cord as possible. Stitch straight across the join where the trimming overlaps. Join the seam in the normal way but use a zipper foot on the machine. Follow the piping cord, which is between the two fabric layers, using it as a stitching guideline.

Piping an edge

Sometimes piping is used at the very edge of the garment, as on the front of a jacket, the edge of a pocket or around a collar. The principle of attaching the piping is much the same as for piping included within an ordinary seam, but you are more likely to have to take the trimming around corners and curves.

Piping moulds well around curves, but needs coaxing around sharp corners. Stretch the turnings on the piping and pucker the cord as sharply as possible for the neatest finish. Tack, then machine into position with a zipper foot.

Cutting and making rouleaus

Rouleaus are long narrow rolls of fabric which are used as decorative fastenings, button loops and pocket trims, and also more functionally as waist ties and shoulder straps. They can be used as an alternative type of shoulder strap on the camisole top or dress.

Because rouleaus are cut from fabric on the cross, they stretch and do not give the same support as if they were cut on the straight grain. Therefore, use them only on lightweight garments, like a camisole top, or where the garment is already supported in another way. A dress supported by

tight shaping in the bodice may have fine rouleau straps which are purely for decoration. To emphasize the roundness of the straps, and to give added body, do not trim off the excess seam allowances when making up but leave them inside the tube to swell out the rouleau.

Making plain rouleaus

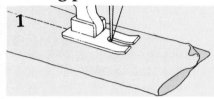
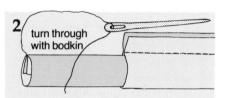
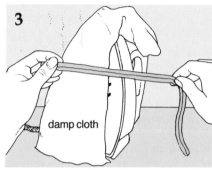

Cut strips of fabric on the cross, twice the finished width plus seam allowances. Join them if necessary to the length required.
With right sides together, fold in half lengthwise but do not press.
1 Machine along seamline, leaving about 10cm/4in of thread at end.
2 Knot thread on to a bodkin (or use

a rouleau turner if you have one) and pull through the rouleau, turning it right side out. Cut thread.
3 Remove any creases by holding the rouleau against an iron stood on its heel with a damp pressing cloth placed over it, but do not press. To finish, turn raw edges in about 1cm/½in but do not stitch – this

will flatten it. If using as a decorative tie make a single knot and push it down to the end of the tie.

Making corded rouleaus

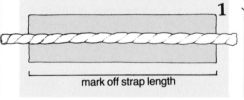

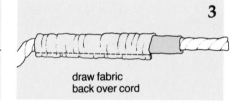

An alternative method of making rouleau straps that really will support a garment is to insert a cord – like soft, narrow piping cord – into the rouleau. This gives it added strength, and prevents it from stretching.
1 Buy twice as much cord as the finished length of rouleau you require for each strap. Wash first to pre-shrink if the cord is cotton. Measure cord off to strap length, plus an extra allowance for attaching to garment. Mark this point, but do not cut it. From this point, with right sides of fabric together, enclose the rest of the cord within the bias strip cut for the rouleau.
2 Machine across both fabric and cord to secure at the inner end of fabric as shown above. Then stitch

along close to cord through the double layer of fabric, using the zipper foot on the sewing machine. Remove from machine. Trim seam.
3 Gently draw the fabric over and along the uncovered cord from the starting point. The tube of fabric will slide over the bare cord, covering it exactly.

To finish, pull the cord out of the open end of the rouleau for about 4cm/1½in and cut off. Slide cord back into rouleau. Turn in ends of fabric. Neaten, or make a knot if making a decorative tie.

Below: A rouleau trim used to make a delicate, decorative neck bow.

Bib-fronted dress with kimono-type sleeves

Simple but effective, this pattern has an inset bib and topstitched detail – a design feature on many garments. There are pockets in the side seams and the skirt is straight – wear it belted and allow the dress to fall into its own natural folds.

This very versatile pattern can be made up in three sizes, covering size 10 to size 16, and in two different lengths. You can also make it as a shirt and give it a variety of looks with the simplest of finishing touches, or by clever choice of fabric.

Cut the bib in contrasting fabric, or try cutting it on the crosswise grain in striped fabric. Make worked buttonholes on the bib, or work loops in thread along the edge of the bib, or use rouleau loops instead. Add decorative buttons and trimmings or topstitching. Make it with or without pockets and wear it with or without a belt – the choice is yours. These are just a few suggestions – you'll probably think up many more.

Even with such potential for variations, the pattern couldn't be easier – the few techniques you need to know are given in these pages. And the following chapter gives you all the information you need to make up both versions.

Right: This attractive dress has very simple lines, but a wealth of detail – a dropped shoulderline, kimono-type sleeves, side seam pockets, a buttoned bib-front and a front pleat.

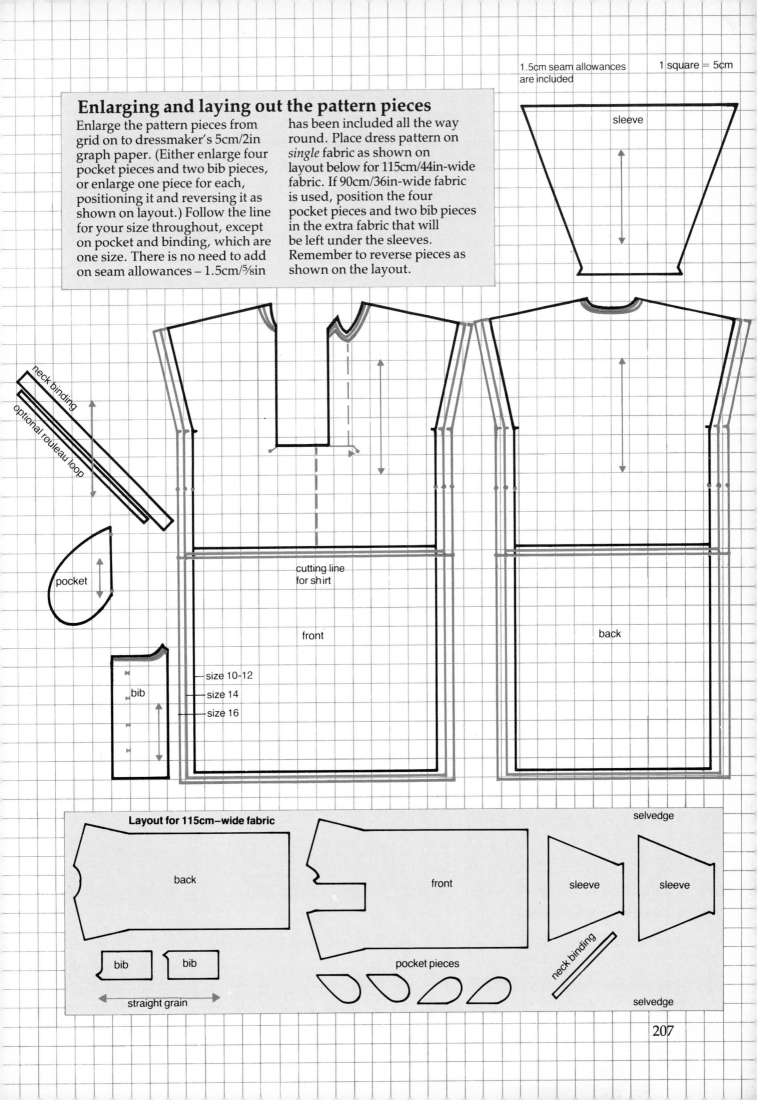

1.5cm seam allowances are included

1 square = 5cm

sleeve

Enlarging and laying out the pattern pieces

Enlarge the pattern pieces from grid on to dressmaker's 5cm/2in graph paper. (Either enlarge four pocket pieces and two bib pieces, or enlarge one piece for each, positioning it and reversing it as shown on layout.) Follow the line for your size throughout, except on pocket and binding, which are one size. There is no need to add on seam allowances – 1.5cm/⅝in

has been included all the way round. Place dress pattern on *single* fabric as shown on layout below for 115cm/44in-wide fabric. If 90cm/36in-wide fabric is used, position the four pocket pieces and two bib pieces in the extra fabric that will be left under the sleeves. Remember to reverse pieces as shown on the layout.

neck binding

optional rouleau loop

pocket

cutting line for shirt

front

back

bib

size 10-12
size 14
size 16

Layout for 115cm—wide fabric

selvedge

back

front

sleeve

sleeve

bib

bib

pocket pieces

neck binding

straight grain

selvedge

Staystitching

Once the fabric pattern pieces have been cut out and the pattern markings transferred, you may have to staystitch. This consists of a row of machine stitching, placed just inside the seamline on certain raw edges to prevent them being pulled out of shape during the making up of the garment. It is used particularly on vulnerable curved or angled edges – necklines or armholes, for example. Staystitching is also valuable for giving additional support where seams have to be clipped or slashed very close to the seamline. Staystitch the edges where necessary as soon as you have removed the paper pattern pieces, before they have the chance to be stretched out of shape. Use the same stitch length as for stitching the rest of the garment, and the appropriate thread, stitching through single fabric only.

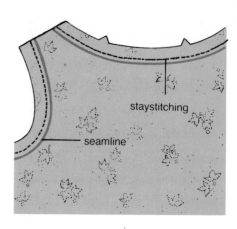

Reinforcing turned through corners

A seamline with a sharp right-angled corner (often found on a shaped yoke or a tab-fronted opening) requires careful handling if it is to look neat and wear well. An inward corner must be clipped or slashed deeply to within two or three threads of the stitching, so that it can be turned through successfully.

1 Reinforce the seam by staystitching just inside the seamline 5cm/2in each side of the corner.

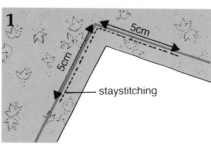

2 Insert a pin diagonally across the corner, just on the stitching line. Clip diagonally through the seam allowance into the corner, stopping

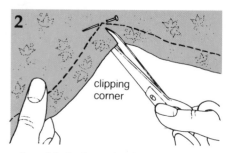

a few fabric threads short of the stitching. (The pin will prevent you clipping too far.)

Pockets in seams

A seam or inside pocket is invisible from the outside of a garment, and consists of an ear-shaped pocket bag which is attached to the seam in any of three ways.

An all-in-one pocket is cut as part of the garment and only requires seaming round its own edge. It is usually small and not terribly strong as the fabric is not always on the straight grain at the pocket opening.

A separate pocket is cut as two pattern pieces which are then attached to the garment in the appropriate seamline. Such a pocket is often inserted into the side seams of dresses or skirts.

An extended pocket is a separate pocket, as above, but it has an extension on both pocket and garment side seam. This means that the pocket can be inserted further into the seamline, so that the seamlines are not all together in one place – thus reducing bulkiness. If a garment made of thick fabric requires a seam pocket, one pocket piece should be cut in strong lining fabric or calico and one piece in the main fabric, so that their combined thickness does not spoil the lines of the garment.

The placement of pockets is usually

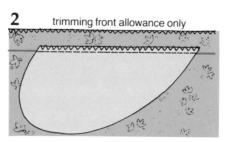

Attaching separate pockets
1 With right sides together, lay one pocket piece in position on seamline with pocket projecting inwards towards centre of garment. Stitch down side seamline to attach pocket to seam. Repeat for second piece.

2 Trim seam allowance on front pocket seam only – not on garment. Neaten seam allowances on these seams, and on untrimmed back pocket and garment seams, separately. Press pocket outwards, away from garment.

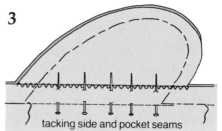

3 Working from wrong side of garment, pin back and front together across pocket openings, matching markings. Pin and tack side seams down to pocket opening, all around pocket seams and from pocket down to hem.

Topstitching

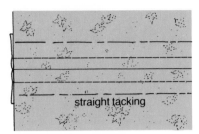

straight tacking

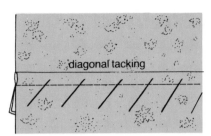

diagonal tacking

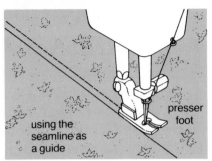

using the seamline as a guide

presser foot

This gives a special finish to a seam on the right side of a garment. It may be functional, holding seam allowances down or together, or purely decorative, emphasizing seam detail and giving a neat finish. It is often worked in contrasting thread on a plain fabric for design detail. **Straight or diagonal tacking** is used to prevent the layers of fabric slipping during topstitching. Where the seam allowances are pressed open, tack firmly in straight lines on each side of the seam. Where the seam allowances are both pressed to one side, use diagonal tacking for strength.

When topstitching, use a longer stitch than usual and adjust the tension accordingly. (Try out the stitch first on a sample of several layers of fabric to ensure that it does not pucker.) An even-feed foot on your sewing machine will give you extra control.
If there is more than one row, care must be taken to keep the rows of stitching straight, and parallel.

The presser foot of your machine (or the even-feed foot) can provide a helpful stitching guideline for narrow topstitching. Keep the side of the foot aligned to the seamline while stitching. Alternatively, the line to be stitched can be marked on the right side of the garment with a contrasting tacking thread so that you have a line to follow while machine stitching. It is not a good idea to use a marking pen, dressmaker's carbon and a tracing wheel or even coloured tailor's chalk, as it may prove impossible to remove the markings from the right side of some fabrics.

marked on the pattern, but will require adjustment if you have made alterations to the length of the garment. If you are in doubt about where to position them, cut practice pockets in paper and experiment until you find a comfortable position.

Reinforcing the seamline
To prevent stretching, reinforce the area of the seam into which the

pocket is to be sewn. To do this, cut a piece of straight tape 10cm/4in longer than the length of the pocket opening. Centre this over opening and tack to the wrong side of the fabric within the seam allowance, with one edge just covering the seamline. Machine stitch close to edge of tape nearest seamline. Repeat for pocket opening on opposite seamline.

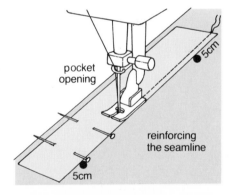

pocket opening

reinforcing the seamline

5cm

5cm

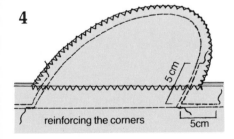

4

reinforcing the corners

5cm

5cm

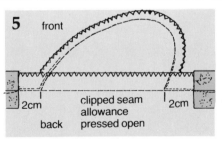

5

front

2cm

clipped seam allowance pressed open

back

2cm

4 Machine stitch down side seams and around pocket, following tacking. Reinforce top and bottom edges of pocket by stitching again 5cm/2in each side of corner, just within seamline. Neaten pocket edges together with zigzag stitch.

5 Clip back garment seam allowance to within a few threads of seamline, 2cm/¾in above and below pocket. Press seam allowances open above and below this point and press pocket towards front of garment.

Above: When side seam pockets are set-in correctly, they are almost invisible.

Making the bib-fronted dress and blouse

See how easily the bib-fronted dress turns into a stylish and versatile shirt. Follow the step-by-step instructions in this chapter to make up either garment, and learn how to use rouleau loops as an alternative to buttonholes on any garment you make.

This chapter gives step-by-step instructions for making up the bib-fronted dress, using the techniques covered on pages 208–209. A simple, drop-shouldered style does not require special fitting – just dress it up with colourful accessories.

The fabric suggestions and requirements are given at the end of the chapter on page 215. Having made up the dress, why not use the know-how to make the shirt, adding rouleau loops for the buttons on the bib front.

Making up the dress

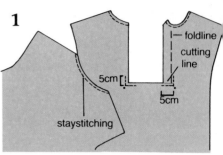

1

Step 1 Make pattern and cut out fabric as instructed on page 207. Transfer all relevant markings to fabric and remove pattern pieces. Staystitch front and back neck edge curves close to seamline (about 1.3cm/⅛in from raw edges). Reinforce lower corners of front opening with staystitching just within seamline, 5cm/2in each side of corner points.

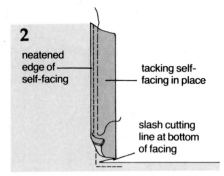

Step 2 Neaten the long raw edge of the self-facing (which is on the right of the neck opening as it faces you) by taking a narrow turning and machine stitching. Fold the self facing to the wrong side along foldline and tack into place. Press the folded edge.

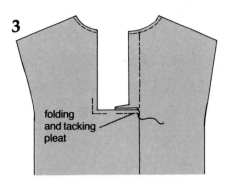

Step 3 Working on the right side, take the fold of the front pleat over until it aligns with the right hand bottom corner of the opening, as marked. Tack pleat along top edge to hold.
With right sides together, stitch shoulder seams, neaten and press open.

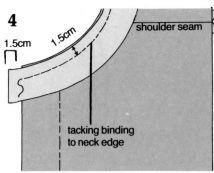

Step 4 Bind neck edge, starting at faced edge of neck and keeping facing folded back. Working on right side, apply crossway binding to neckline, taking 1.5cm/⅝in turnings. Leave 1.5cm/⅝in of binding free, overlapping folded edge, and trim binding at other end, leaving 1.5cm/⅝in extra, overlapping edge. Machine binding into position.

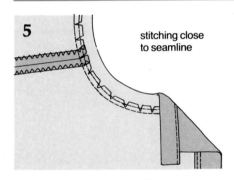

Step 5 Trim turnings, clip curves and press seam towards binding on wrong side of garment. On right side, stitch close to seamline all around binding.

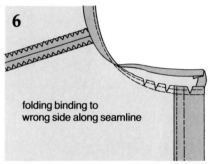

Step 6 Open out binding and press 1cm/½in under on long free edge, folding in the short free edge at the self-faced side of opening. Leave the other short raw edge free – it will be enclosed within the bib.

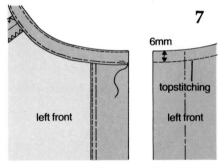

Step 7 Fold binding to inside, tack to garment and press lightly. Topstitch on right side about 6mm/¼in down from neck edge.

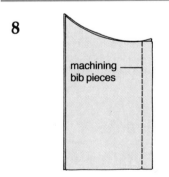

Making the bib
Step 8 With right sides together, stitch down the shorter of the bib's two long edges. Open out flat and press seams.

Left: Stripes used effectively in two colourways. The shirt has extra design details – side vents and rouleau loops.

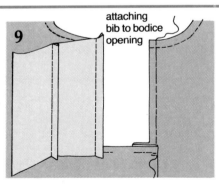

Step 9 With right sides together, stitch long free edge of bib to right-hand side of bodice opening, stopping 1.5cm/⅝in from lower edge of bib and stitching just within staystitching. Remove work from machine and slash through lower corner of bodice opening seam allowance to staystitching.

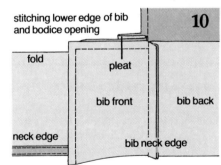

Step 10 With right sides together, pin lower edge of front bib to lower edge of opening. Stitch seam from slashed corner up to the seam joining bib pieces, producing a neat corner. Finish ends securely.

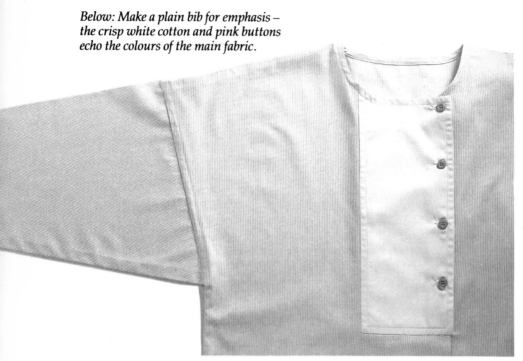

*Below: Make a plain bib for emphasis –
the crisp white cotton and pink buttons
echo the colours of the main fabric.*

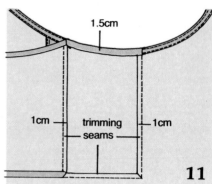

Step 11 Slash the lower corner of
the self-faced edge diagonally to the
staystitching. Open out bib and
trim seams to 1cm/½in. Press in
towards wrong side of front bib.
Press under 1.5cm/⅝in on top edge
of front and back rib, down side and
along lower edge of back bib. On
unslashed corners fold the seam
allowances diagonally and trim
away bulkiness.

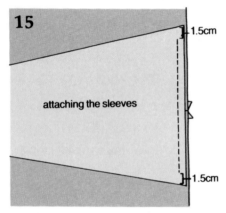

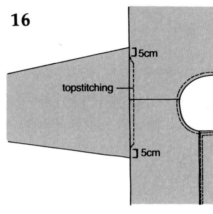

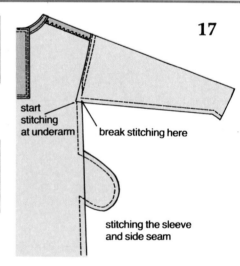

Sleeves and side seams
Step 15 With right sides together,
pin sleeves to armholes, matching
notches. Stitch, starting and
finishing 1.5cm/⅝in from each end
of armhole seam.

Step 16 Press seam allowances
towards bodice and topstitch from
right side, starting and finishing
underarm stitching 5cm/2in above
side seam line in a V-shape going
into armhole seam.

Step 17 With right sides together,
attach a pocket piece to back and
front at each side following steps

Bib-fronted shirt

The shirt is as versatile as the dress
– use your fabric cleverly for
different looks. Make one in narrow
striped shirtings for a subtle effect,
or bold stripes or checks to go with
jeans, or plain colours for any
occasion. To make a design feature
of the bib, cut it in toning or
contrasting fabric or – if the fabric
design is suitable – cut it out on the
crosswise grain.
Why not make the rouleau loops
from contrasting fabric too?

Fabric requirements
The shirt also makes up in three
sizes within the range 10 to 16. The
same amount of fabric is required
for each size.

You will need
2.50m/2¾yd of 90cm/36in-wide
  fabric *or* 115cm/45in-wide fabric
Matching thread
4×1cm/½in buttons
If bib is to be made in a different
fabric you need 0.40m/½yd extra

Cutting out the shirt
Enlarge the pattern from the graph
on page 207, following the shorter
cutting line for the shirt.
With the fabric facing right side
up, pin the pattern pieces on to
single fabric as shown on layout
opposite and cut out. Transfer all
pattern markings by preferred
method.
Don't forget to cut the optional
rouleau loop strip if you want to
make button loops.

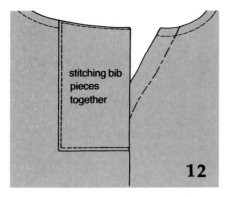

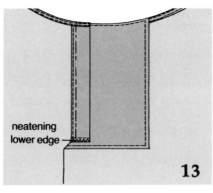

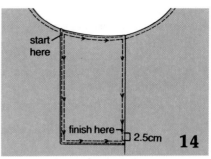

Step 12 With wrong sides together, fold the back bib behind the front bib, enclosing all raw edges. Tack the layers firmly together and stitch carefully from right side on three sides of bib, 2mm/⅛in within seam or, if you prefer, hand stitch on wrong side.

Step 13 Take self facing behind bib and neaten lower raw edge by zigzag stitch or hand overcasting. Tack into place behind bib.

Step 14 Working from the right side of garment, topstitch from top right corner of bib around neck edge to 2.5cm/1in above bottom left corner. Secure threads neatly to inside. Topstitch from top right corner of bib down right side and along bottom, up to the break in stitching, catching in lower 2.5cm/1in of self-facing. Finish ends securely and catchstitch bottom raw edge of self-facing to lower edge of bib on the inside.

1–3 of pocket instructions on page 208.
Place right side of back to right side of front, matching pockets which should lay outwards from each side of side seam. Pin, tack and stitch from wrist of sleeve seam up to underarm. Take care not to catch in underarm seam of sleeve, or it will not turn through neatly. Break stitching and stitch again from underarm down to top of pocket and all around pocket, down to hem. Repeat for other side. Complete pockets, following last part of step 4 and step 5 of pocket instructions on page 209. Finally, topstitch the pockets to front of dress, following the seamline around pocket bag.

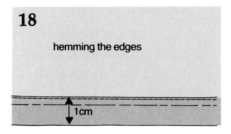

Finishing off
Step 18 To finish hem at wrists and lower edge, neaten by turning under 5mm/¼in and stitching. Press. Turn under another 1cm/½in and tack. Topstitch all around on right side to secure hems.

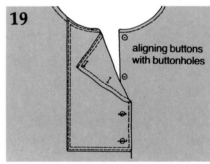

Step 19 Mark buttonholes on the lines indicated on the edge of the bib, taking care not to make them more than 5mm/¼in larger than the chosen button size. Machine stitch them and press. Lay garment out flat and mark position for buttons on right side of self-faced edge. Sew buttons into position.

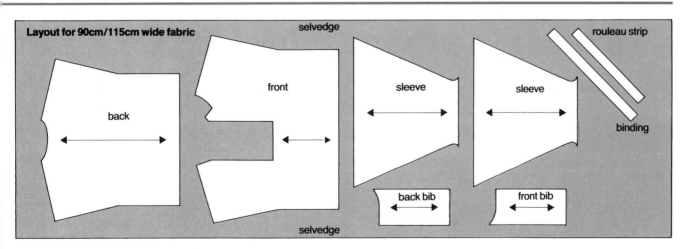

Making up

Make up as for dress, following steps 1-16 inclusive.

With right sides together, pin and tack from wrist to hem along both sleeve and side seams.

Stitch from wrist to underarm and stop.

Stitch side seams from marking for side split to underarm, finishing in line with sleeve seam. Do not catch armhole seam turnings in side seams.

Neaten seams all the way down to top of vent and press open. Turn up front and back hem separately as in step 18 but do not topstitch yet.

To make vents turn under front and back lower edges 5mm/¼in and machine stitch. Press. Turn under another 1cm/½in and tack. Topstitch the hem 1cm/½in from lower edge from side seam to side seam.

Turn back neatened side seams and tack all round vent to hold.

Topstitch from lower edge up to top of vent, making a wide, inverted V across the top before stitching down the other side towards hem. Repeat for second vent.

Complete wrist hems and bib as for dress, steps 18 and 19, and finish the bib with buttonholes, or rouleaus.

Rouleau loops for buttons

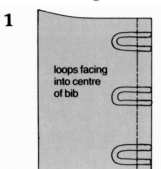

loops facing into centre of bib

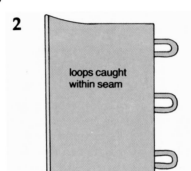

loops caught within seam

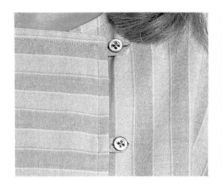

Above: Close-up of rouleau loops.

An effective way of adding an extra touch to the bib front of your shirt – or dress – is to insert rouleau loops at the outside edge of the bib, instead of making buttonholes.

Use the rouleau loop pattern piece to cut a strip of fabric on the cross. Make up a rouleau as shown on page 205.

1 Cut four 6cm/2¼in lengths from rouleau (use longer lengths for larger buttons) and loop them in half.

2 Before stitching the bib together in step 8 of the making up instructions, attach the four rouleau loops corresponding to the markings for the buttonholes on the right side of one bib front. They should face into the centre of the bib, with all raw edges aligning, as shown. Tack to secure, then put bib pieces right side together and make up as normal. When the bib is turned through to the right side, the loops will protrude.

Sew the buttons to the left front of the garment to correspond with the loops.

Thread loops for fine fabrics

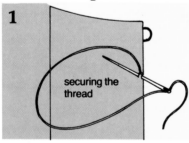

securing the thread

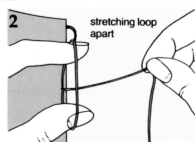

stretching loop apart

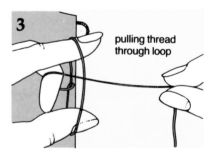

pulling thread through loop

An alternative method is to work thread chains on the edge of the bib, instead of inserting rouleau loops. Thread chains can be made to lie flat against the garment, for belt carriers for example, or looped by starting and finishing the chain in the same spot.

1 Start at the edge of the bib, corresponding to the buttonhole markings. With double thread, take the thread through from the back of bib and bring out between seamed edge. Take two or three small stitches to secure.

2 Draw the thread partly through, keeping a 10cm/4in loop back. Stretch loop apart with thumb and first finger, holding rest of thread in other hand.

3 Using second finger of hand holding loop, pull loose thread through loop. A new loop will form, the old loop forming a chain at the base of the thread. Repeat this process until thread chain reaches required length. Fasten securely by taking several small stitches into the garment before cutting the thread.

Fabric suggestions

The dress is suitable for all seasons and all occasions, and such a simple style lends itself to creative use of fabric. Make it in light or bright printed cottons, seersucker or polyester/cotton for summer, in flower prints, checks or stripes. Choose a warmer brushed cotton, Viyella or soft wool mixture for autumn and winter.

For a more formal occasion, make up the dress in black or navy blue, with a crisp white contrasting bib and two parallel rows (one fake) of black or navy buttons for a double-breasted look. Try large multi-coloured polka dots or stripes on white seersucker for a casual, summery look. Plain colours look equally effective – experiment with a toning or contrasting bib and contrasting topstitching.

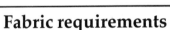

Fabric requirements

The dress makes up in three sizes – 10-12, 12-14, 14-16 – to fit bust sizes 83-97cm/32-38in. Fabric requirements are the same for all sizes – reduce them slightly for a shorter dress.

You will need

4.65m/5⅛yd of 90cm/36in fabric *or* 4.00m/4⅜yd of 115cm/44in fabric
Matching thread
4×1cm/½in buttons
A contrast bib requires 0.40m/½yd of 90cm/36in fabric. If making this, reduce the fabric requirements for the main fabric by 0.40m/½yd for 90cm/36in fabric only. The amount required for 115cm/44in fabric remains the same, due to the cutting layouts.

215

A designer top with a cowl collar

This loose-fitting top is cut and stitched along straight lines for stylish simplicity. Make it in a soft fabric and finish it to whatever length you require – top, tunic, or dress – the cut of the pattern ensures that it will hang beautifully.

This casual top has very simple lines and relies for its effect on its straight, topstitched seams. It has centre front and back seams, a yoke, wide sleeves with turn-back cuffs and a loose roll collar that falls into flattering folds. The side seams are split at the lower edge for ease of movement and reinforced for extra strength.

The top can be made in two sizes and several lengths – hip level, to wear over jeans, trousers or skirts – just above or below the knee to make a dress, or whatever length you prefer. All versions can be worn loose or belted.

The only new technique you need to learn to make this versatile top or dress is how to sew a reversed flat fell seam. This is like a machine flat fell seam, but formed on the wrong side of the fabric. This type of seam has several advantages – it encloses all raw edges, which is a bonus when laundering; it ensures that the seams are extra strong and it also gives an attractive finish to a garment where the seams are a strong design feature.

Fabric suggestions

This versatile pattern can be made up in a variety of fabrics to suit the way you plan to wear it. A soft brushed cotton or Viyella, or lightweight wool is a good choice for both the top and dress. Add woolly tights to the knee-length version for winter warmth.

A fine cotton or silk makes a cool top to be tucked in to a skirt, or belted over it, for warmer days. You could make the top in any length in cotton jersey for a fun look that is easy to pack for a holiday.

Whatever your requirements, remember that the top or dress will hang best in soft fabrics, preferably plain or with a small pattern. However, you could also choose denim to make a hard-wearing and practical top.

Reversed flat fell seam

This type of seam is hardwearing because it is topstitched twice with all the raw edges enclosed. This makes it particularly suitable for sportswear, casual garments which get a lot of wear and trousers or jeans. The seam is similar to a machine flat fell seam (see page 175) but it is formed on the wrong side.

The first line of topstitching runs close to the seamline and the second is parallel to it. The seam acts as a guide to ensure that the stitching is even and straight which is essential when a flat fell seam is prominent, as at the centre front, or curved, as under the arm.

Left: Cool and elegant, this top has simple design lines which makes it flattering to all figure types.

The top makes up successfully using contrast fabrics of similar weight and fibre content.

To make one or more of the pattern pieces in a contrast fabric you will need to calculate the amount of fabric required.

Remember that the pattern pieces usually represent 'half' the made up garment and will probably be cut on double fabric.

Mark two parallel lines, half the width of your fabric apart, on a stout piece of paper. Label one line the selvedge and the other the fold. Arrange all the necessary pieces as economically as possible between the two lines ensuring that straight grain lines are parallel to edges and measure the quantity required. Make a note of the position of the pieces.

217

Making a reversed flat felled seam

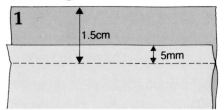

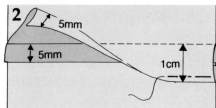

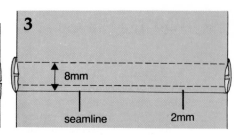

1 With right sides together, stitch seam with 1.5cm/⅝in allowances. Trim one seam to 5mm/¼in. On side or shoulder seams this should be the one to the back of the garment.

2 Open out garment and press untrimmed seam allowance over trimmed seam allowance. Turn under 5mm/¼in and tack flat to garment, enclosing raw edges.

3 Turn garment to right side and topstitch once 2mm/⅛in from seamline and again 8mm/¼in from seamline, taking care to keep stitching lines parallel.

Versatile designer top or dress

The pattern is given in two sizes, to fit 10-12 (bust 83cm to 87cm/32½in to 34in) and 14-16 (bust 92cm to 97cm/ 36in to 38in).

The top has a finished length of 62cm/ 24½in from nape of neck to hem. If you want to make a longer version, simply decide on the finished length you require and subtract 62cm/24½in from this measurement. The amount left over will give you the extra length to add to the pattern.

Add this amount to the lower edge of both front and back pattern pieces, extending the seams down, when cutting out. This means you need to add twice this amount to the fabric quantities given below when calculating your new fabric requirements.

You will need
For sizes 10-12 1.90m/2⅛yd of

115cm/45in wide fabric
For sizes 14-16 2m/2¼yd of 115cm/ 45in wide fabric
Matching thread

Cutting out
Scale up the pattern on page 221 on dressmaker's 5cm/2in graph paper, transferring all notches, pattern markings and cutting instructions. Position the pattern pieces as shown on the layout, with the collar pieces – which are cut on the cross – placed over the fold. Follow the cutting line for the size you require noting that the collar is one size. 1.5cm/⅝in seam allowances have been included throughout except at the hem, where 2cm/¾in has been allowed. Transfer markings for seamlines and side splits, using tailor's tacks or tailor's chalk.

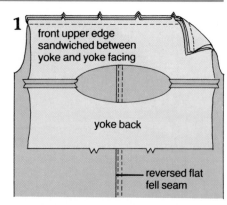

Making up the top
Step 1 Close centre back and centre front seams with a reversed flat fell seam. With right sides together, join back yoke to front yoke at shoulder seams. Press seams open. Repeat for yoke facing.
With right side of yoke front to right side of front, and right side of yoke facing to wrong side of front, matching notches, sandwich

---

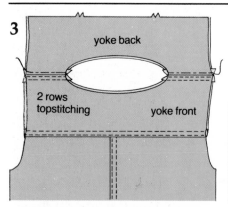

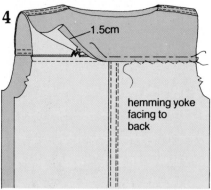

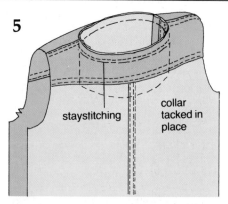

Step 3 With wrong sides together, align shoulder seams of yoke and yoke facing and tack through all thicknesses. Machine two rows of topstitching as above on each of the front yoke shoulder seams.

Step 4 With right sides together, join yoke (not yoke facing) to back. Pin, tack and machine seam. Press up 1.5cm/⅝in to wrong side along lower edge of yoke facing. Smooth facing into position and tack into place. Hem fold of facing along line of machine stitches of

yoke seam. Tack through all thicknesses, then, working on the right side, machine two rows of topstitching as above.
Step 5 With right sides together, pin, tack and machine front collar to back collar at side seams. Press seams open and machine two rows

Reinforcing the top of an opening

When a seam such as a side seam or a centre front seam has a split at the bottom, it is worth reinforcing the base of the seam (that is, the top of the split) with a patch of fabric. This relieves the strain on the base of the seam and prevents the stitching from coming apart.
Apply the patch after the seam has been stitched and neatened.

Applying the patch Cut two squares of fabric to match the garment, each measuring 3.5cm×3.5cm/1⅜in×1⅜in. Press under 5mm/¼in turnings all the way round each square. Apply the squares to wrong side of garment, so that the bottom of the square is level with the top of the opening. Hem into place all round with small stitches.

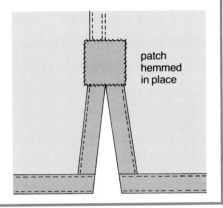

patch hemmed in place

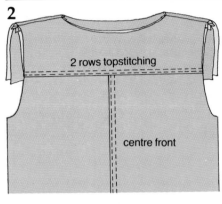

2 rows topstitching

centre front

upper edge of the front between yoke and yoke facing. Pin, tack and machine along seamline.
Step 2 Press yoke and yoke facing up into position and tack through all thicknesses just above seam. From the right side, machine two rows of topstitching 2mm/⅛in and 8mm/¼in above the seam to produce the same effect as a reversed flat fell seam.

of topstitching as above on each of the front collar seams.
Tack the yoke to the yoke facing around the neck edge then staystitch neckline curve of double yoke, stitching through both thicknesses. Working with garment inside out and collar right side out, apply right side of collar to right side of garment. Pin, tack and machine into place. The collar moulds easily around the curve of the neckline because it is cut on the cross.

Right: A fun-to-wear dress for your holidays, made from the pattern extended to knee length. Wear it with a belt at hip level, or leave it loose for a casual look.

6

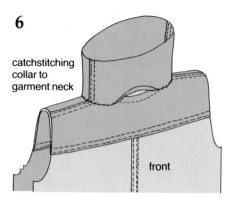

catchstitching
collar to
garment neck

front

Step 6 Take remaining raw edge of collar to wrong side and fold under 1.5cm/⅝in. Pin and catchstitch folded edge to line of machine stitching. Do not press the folded top edge of the collar – allow it to fall into natural folds.

7

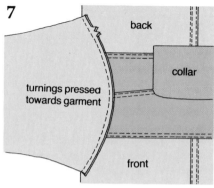

back

collar

turnings pressed towards garment

front

Step 7 With back and front separated and spread out and with right sides together, matching notches, apply sleeve head to flat armhole. Pin, tack and machine into place. Press all turnings towards garment and trim seam allowance of *garment* to 5mm/¼in. Turning under 5mm/¼in at raw edge, lap

8

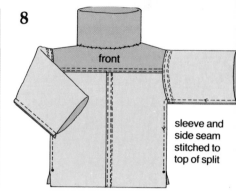

front

sleeve and side seam stitched to top of split

seam allowance of sleeve over this trimmed edge and tack into place. Complete as for reversed flat fell seam.
Step 8 With right sides together, close sleeve seam and side seams with one continuous line of stitching from lower edge of sleeve to marking at top of side split.

9

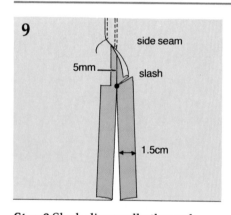

side seam

5mm

slash

1.5cm

Step 9 Slash diagonally through front seam allowance at top of side opening. Trim seam allowance on back seam, above opening, to 5mm/¼in and complete side seams as for reversed flat fell seams.
Press under 5mm/¼in on seam allowance either side of the opening. Topstitch sides of opening 8mm/⅜in from folded edge,

10

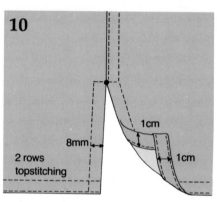

1cm

8mm

1cm

2 rows topstitching

working straight across the top of the split. Reinforce the top of the opening on the wrong side with a patch (see Professional Touch).
Step 10 To make the lower hem, press under 5mm/¼in on each lower edge. Turn under another 1cm/½in and tack. Machine two rows of topstitching on each lower edge to match the seams.

11

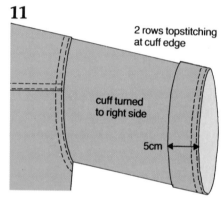

2 rows topstitching at cuff edge

cuff turned to right side

5cm

Step 11 To make sleeve hems, press under 5mm/¼in all round, then turn up 5cm/2in. Working on the wrong side, machine two rows of topstitching at the edge of the hem to match the other seams. Turn the cuff to the right side so that the topstitched edge lies at the lower folded edge, and press.

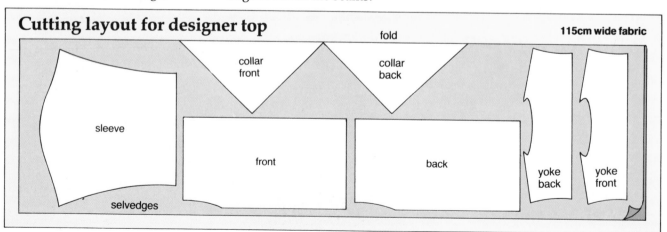

Cutting layout for designer top

fold

115cm wide fabric

collar front

collar back

sleeve

front

back

yoke back

yoke front

selvedges

220

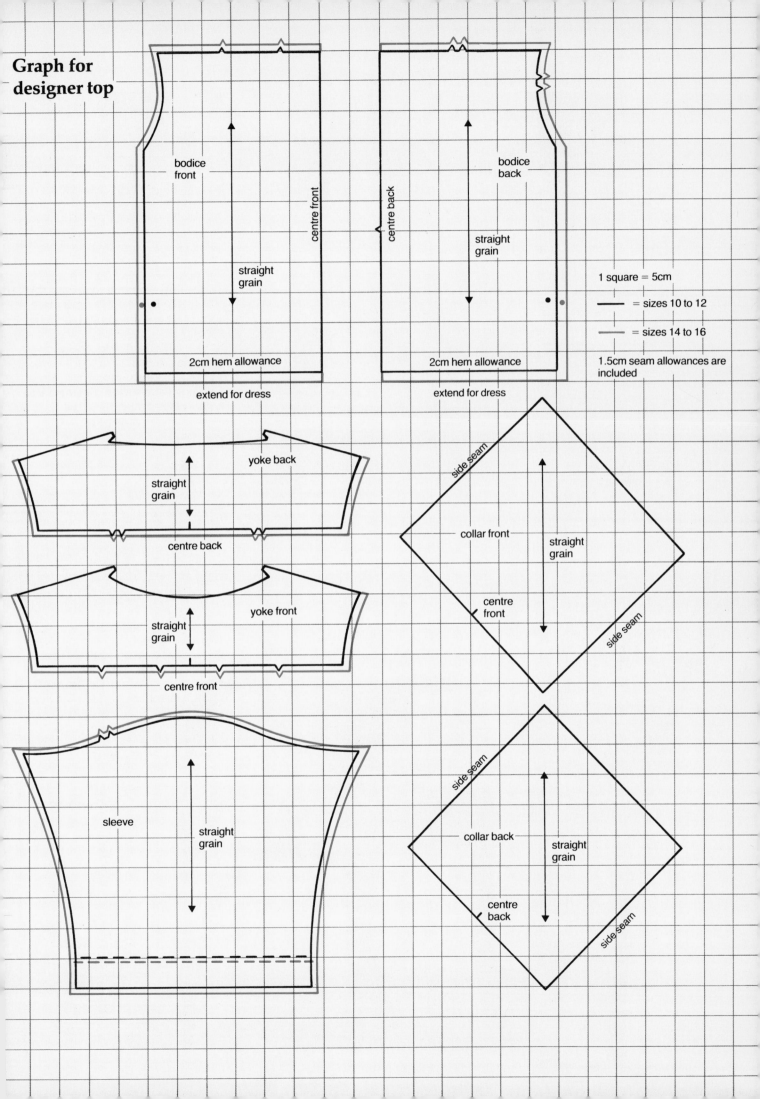

Graph for designer top

bodice front

centre front

straight grain

2cm hem allowance

extend for dress

bodice back

centre back

straight grain

2cm hem allowance

extend for dress

1 square = 5cm

——— = sizes 10 to 12

——— = sizes 14 to 16

1.5cm seam allowances are included

yoke back

straight grain

centre back

yoke front

straight grain

centre front

collar front

straight grain

side seam

side seam

centre front

sleeve

straight grain

collar back

straight grain

side seam

side seam

centre back

Matching pants and slip

This lingerie set includes French knickers, made from one pattern piece, and a half slip, also made from one pattern piece. All the seams are finished with French seams to strengthen the garment and help it withstand constant washing. Both the pants and the slip have waist casings threaded with elastic.

The pattern is to fit three hip sizes: small (87cm/34in), medium (92-97cm/36-38in) and large (102cm/40in). Fabric widths such as 90cm/36in and 115cm/45in are suitable. A 1cm/½in seam allowance is included in the pattern. (1.5cm/⅝in for waist casing.)

You will need
For the knickers
Dressmaker's squared paper 85cm×
   45cm/34in×18in
Pencil, ruler, rubber, flexicurve
   (optional)
1m/1yd polyester/cotton lawn
2m/2yd single lace (or 1m/1yd
   double lace)
Thread to match fabric
3mm/⅛in (4 cord) elastic to fit
   waist plus 2cm/¾in for join
For the slip
Dressmaker's squared paper 85cm×
   70cm/34in×28in
Pencil, rubber, ruler
1.40m/1½yd polyester/cotton lawn
2m/2yd single lace (or 1m/1yd
   double lace)
Thread to match fabric
3mm/⅛in (4 cord) elastic to fit
   waist plus 2cm/¾in for join

Making a French seam

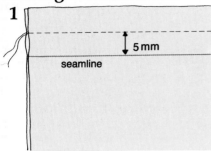

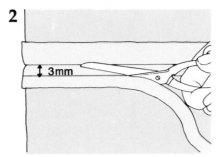

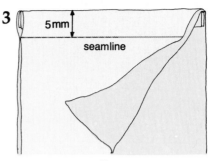

When making lingerie, the ideal seam to use is a French seam. In a French seam all the turnings are enclosed between two lines of machining, the first stitched from the right side, the second from inside the garment. This gives a neat finish,

there is no chance of fraying and the garment can stand up to continual laundering.
Mark the seamlines with a tailor's chalk pencil.
1 With wrong sides together, machine 5mm/¼in from seamline,

within the seam allowance.
2 Press open and trim both raw edges to 3mm/⅛in.
3 Fold the right sides together along seam edge and press flat. Stitch exactly on seamline (5mm/¼in from fold.) Press to one side.

Simple waistband casing

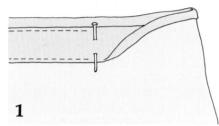

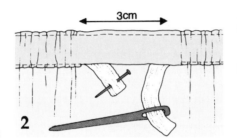

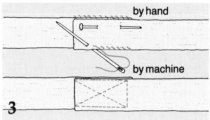

This simple waistband casing is suitable for elasticating half slips, knickers, briefs, shorts for young children and other items which do not need much shaping or reinforcing.
Fold the upper raw edge of the

waistline down 5mm/¼in on the wrong side of the fabric, then fold again a further 1cm/⅜in.
1 Pin and machine along this folded edge, leaving an opening 3cm/1¼in wide at the back for elastic. Machine along top edge of casing.

2 Thread elastic through, using a bodkin or a small safety pin, and adjust to fit the waist comfortably.
3 Handstitch or machine the ends of the elastic together and trim away any surplus. Close the opening by machining along the 3cm/1¼in gap.

Trimming lingerie with lace

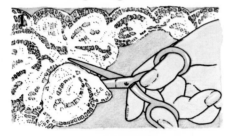

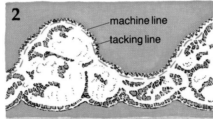

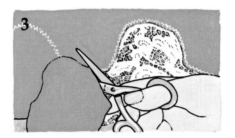

Lace is an ideal edging for lingerie, delicate blouses and handkerchiefs. Nylon or polyester laces are more suitable than cotton because they require no ironing and usually wash well. Look for special lingerie lace, ideally with two decorative edges, one of which may be quite deeply scalloped.
Double lace is also available. This has to be carefully cut in half along the centre.
1 If using double lace, snip through

lace with small sharp scissors, making sure you cut around the flower motifs, not through them.
2 Place the lower edge of the lace (the one with the shallower scallops) along the outer edge of the fabric to be trimmed (often the hemline). Tack the upper edge in position about 2mm/⅛in inside the edge.
Set your machine to sew a small zigzag stitch and carefully zigzag just outside the tacking line. Remove the tacking.

3 Using a pair of small sharp scissors, cut away the fabric underneath the lace, taking care not to cut into the stitching.
After cutting away the excess fabric, make sure that no fabric is visible underneath the length of the lace. Using a small stitch on the lace helps to prevent fine fabrics from fraying and, if you select a lace with a large floral pattern, the curves you machine round will be more gradual and easier to manoeuvre.

223

Making up the knickers

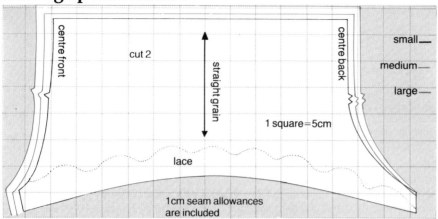

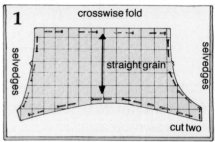

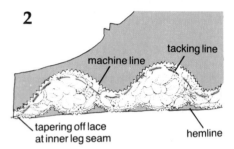

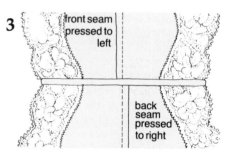

Make a large-scale pattern from the diagram, using squared paper.
1 With right sides together, fold the fabric in half crosswise and pin pattern piece in place as shown on the cutting layout.
Cut out the pattern piece. (As the fabric is folded double you will get two pieces.)
Attach the lace before sewing the pattern pieces together.
2 Place the lower edge of the lace along the hemline and tack the upper edge in position, following the line of the lace and tapering off the lace at the inner leg seam. Machine along the upper edge and then, with sharp scissors, cut away the fabric underneath to the stitching line. Matching the single notches, sew the centre front seam with a French seam.
Matching the double notches, sew the centre back seam with a French seam.
3 Sew the crutch seam with a French seam, turning the front seam to the left and the back one to the right to reduce bulk. Press gently. Elasticate the waist.

Making up the half slip

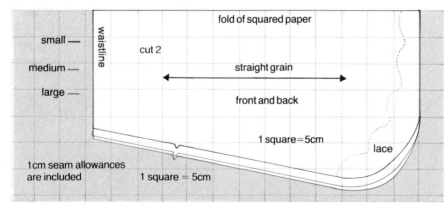

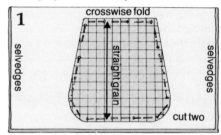

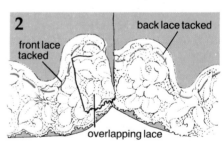

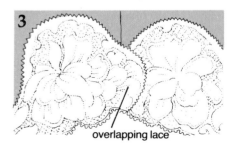

Fold a piece of dressmaker's squared paper 85cm×70cm/34in× 28in in half lengthwise. Transfer pattern outline from the diagram to the squared paper. Open out and repeat pattern outline in reverse.
1 With right sides together fold the fabric crosswise and pin the pattern piece in place as shown on the cutting layout.
Cut out. (As the fabric is folded you will get two pieces.)
Using French seams, sew both side seams and press the garment gently.
2 Place the lower edge of the lace along the hemline of the front piece, curving the lace up at the sides. Tack in position along the upper edge. Position and tack the lace on the back in the same way.
3 Overlap the lace neatly at the side seams and join by hand or using a small zigzag stitch.
Machine the upper edge of lace in position with the same stitch and, with sharp scissors, cut away the fabric underneath the stitching line. Elasticate the waist.

A zip-up lounger in fleece jersey

This casual zip-up lounger is made from warm fleece fabric. Learn how to sew this easy-care fabric, how to insert an exposed zip and add a simple band cuff. The pattern is adapted from the classic dress pattern and is gathered at the yoke in a loose flowing style.

The lounger is a lengthened version of the classic dress pattern given on page 120, simplified for quick and easy making up. Instructions for lengthening the pattern pieces are given on page 117. Insert a decorative long zip in the centre front seam, so you can step into it, and gather the sleeves into a simple welt.

Choosing the fabric

Fluffy dressing gown fabric, technically known as fleece jersey, is a soft and comfortable fabric with some give, which is the ideal choice for the lounger. It makes up quickly as interfacing is unnecessary and the raw edges will not require neatening.

Cutting out

Because of its brushed finish, fleece jersey is a napped fabric, so you must follow a with nap cutting layout. In most cases, place the pieces so that the nap runs from lower edge to the shoulders. The fabric can be folded in half lengthwise, but do not make a crosswise fold. Instead, cut the fabric length in half crosswise, marking an arrow with tailor's chalk to show the direction of the nap on the back of each piece. Turn one piece around and place the two pieces right sides together with the nap following the same direction on each layer. Placing or folding the fabric with right sides together prevents the two layers sliding apart when cutting out.

If the fabric is very thick, cut through the top layer first and then the lower one.

Sewing techniques

Use a narrow zigzag stitch or special stretch stitch where possible, but if your machine is a straight stitch

Right: Lounging in comfort in soft and warm fleece jersey.

model stretch the fabric slightly as you feed it under the presser foot.

A straight stitch must be used when sewing in the zip to prevent distortion of the seam.

Always machine in the same direction as the nap.

Pressing Place garment sections face down on to a terry towel or scrap of the same fabric when pressing from the wrong side to avoid flattening the soft, brushed surface. Always press lightly, using a steam iron if possible.

Inserting an exposed zip

A long, front opening zip can be made a feature on a garment. Choose from the colourful range of heavy-weight metal or chunky plastic zips and insert it so that the teeth are exposed giving a decorative effect. This method of inserting a zip also protects fluffy fabric, such as that of the lounger, from getting caught in the zip teeth.

Reinforcing the seam Insert a strip of fusible Vilene the width of the seam allowance along both seamlines of a long zip opening. Press with a hot iron to bond fabric, this will stabilize the opening and prevent the fleece jersey stretching out of shape when stitched.

Below: A chunky zip, exposed both for decorative effect and to protect the fleecy fabric from snags and pulls.

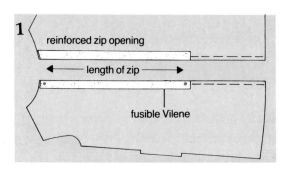

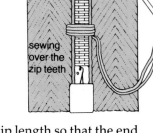

1 Cut two strips of lightweight fusible Vilene 3cm/1¼in wide and long enough to extend 1cm/½in either end of the opening. Align the strips with the raw edges of the seam allowance and fuse them to the wrong side of the garment.
Open-ended zip If you are only able to obtain an open-ended zip you can still insert it as instructed below, and use it as an ordinary zip. Make the opening slightly shorter

than the zip length so that the end is concealed behind the top of the finished seam.
2 Before inserting the zip, stitch on the spot over the zip teeth using double thread at the point where the zip will be concealed by the seam, to prevent the zip slider descending beyond the zip opening.

Simple band cuff

A lapped cuff is only necessary when the fabric will not pass easily over the widest part of the hand. Where the fabric has a slight stretch, you can omit the sleeve opening and gather the lower end of the sleeve into a simple band cuff.
1 Join the sleeve seam and press open. Run two rows of gathering threads along the lower edge, placing one on the seamline and the other 5mm/¼in from it, within the seam allowance.
2 Trim off notches on long edges of cuff sections and with right sides together join cuff into a circle by pinning short sides together, taking

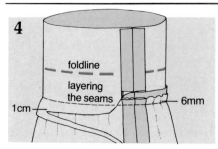

4 Machine cuff to sleeve and press turnings up towards sleeve. Layer turnings by trimming cuff edge to 1cm/½in and gathered sleeve edge to 6mm/¼in.
Fold cuff in half along marked foldline so that it covers gathers and machined seamline. Tack into position along seamline.

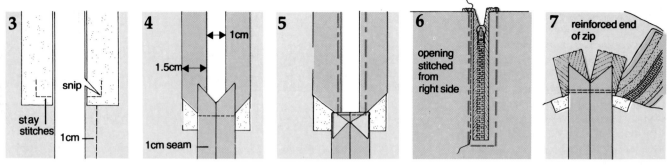

3 Using a small machine stitch, reinforce the end of the zip opening by stitching across the lower edge of the opening and along the seam line for 1.5cm/⅝in on both left and right front. Snip diagonally into the corners. If the zip to be inserted has particularly wide teeth a wider seam allowance will be necessary.

4 To expose the zip teeth the seam allowance below the zip is reduced. Machine the centre seam below the zip opening, taking 1cm/½in turnings. Press seam open.

5 Fold centre front turnings of the zip opening to the inside of the garment along seamlines. Press down the triangle formed by the diagonal cuts at the lower corners. Tack close to the edge and press both the long sides and lower edge of opening.

6 Working from the right side, lay closed zip, right side up under prepared opening. Pin and tack zip in place, positioning teeth centrally. Machine each side in the same direction from the base of the zip to the neck edge which will be with the nap on fleece jersey. Use a zipper foot and stitch close to the fabric edge.

7 Remove tacking on wrong side of garment, reinforce lower end of opening by stitching through zip tapes and fabric triangle.

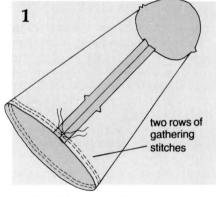

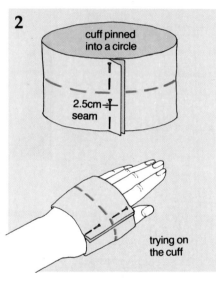

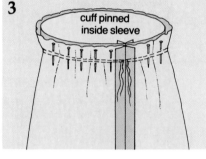

a 2.5cm/1in seam. Try on to make sure it slips easily over widest part of hand and adjust size if necessary. Machine seam, press open and trim turnings to 1cm/½in.

3 Draw up gathers on lower sleeve to fit cuff circle. With right sides together, slip cuff inside sleeve, matching sleeve and cuff seams, then pin gathered edge of sleeve to cuff along seamline. Adjust gathers so that they are evenly distributed.

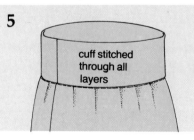

5 Turn sleeve to right side. Machine through all layers on the seamline joining the cuff to the sleeve. Remove all tacking. The turnings all face upwards into the sleeve and no neatening is necessary.

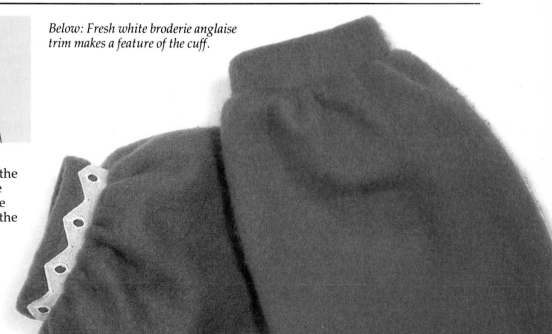

Below: Fresh white broderie anglaise trim makes a feature of the cuff.

Fleece jersey lounger

Fleece jersey is available in bright jewel colours as well as the more traditional darker shades. It is easy to sew following the instructions below and is a good choice for the lounger. If you prefer a different fabric, choose one which is thick enough to hang well and keep you warm. Look for one soft enough to gather into the yoke without too much bulk. To prevent bulkiness in the yoke or pockets, the under yoke and pocket sections can be cut from a lighter weight fabric, such as brushed cotton.

You will need

Fabric according to size and style
Matching thread
Long chunky zip fastener (55cm/ 21¾in or longer)

2 strips Vilene fusible interfacing 3cm×57cm/1¼×22½in each
Pattern pieces, page 120:
1 Back (dress)
2 Front (dress)
3 Yoke
4 Collar
5 Front neck facing
6 Side seam pocket
7 Long sleeve
8 Cuff

Cutting out

Extend the front and back dress pattern (pieces 1 and 2) as instructed on page 117. Position and pin the pattern as shown on the appropriate layout, opening out the fabric to cut a single layer where necessary.

Transfer pattern markings using tailor's chalk before removing paper pattern.

Fabric quantity chart

Size	10	12	14	16	18
Bust					
(cm)	83	87	92	97	102
(in)	32½	34	36	38	40
Length*					
(cm)	135	137	140	142	145
(in)	53	54	55	56	57
90cm	5.80	5.80	5.85	5.85	5.90m
115cm	4.20	4.25	4.25	4.30	4.30m
140cm	3.30	3.30	3.30	3.35	3.35m

*Length is finished back length from nape to ankle.

All layouts are with nap. Allow extra fabric for matching one-way designs, checks and stripes.

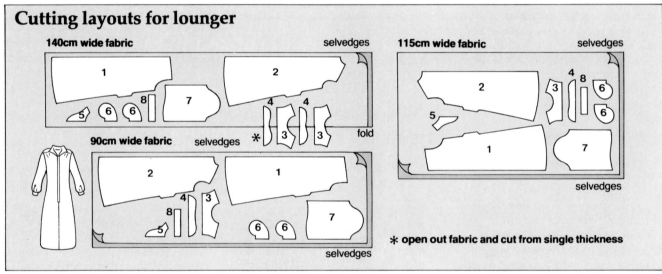

Cutting layouts for lounger

140cm wide fabric — selvedges
90cm wide fabric — selvedges
selvedges
115cm wide fabric — selvedges
selvedges
fold
∗ open out fabric and cut from single thickness

Making up the lounger

To make up the lounger follow the instructions for the dress on pages 108–109, with the following variations:
Steps 1–3 Work as for the dress, but leave the centre front seam open.
Step 4 Insert the zip (see pages 226–227) and close the lower part of the centre front seam.
Steps 5–7 To attach the front facings, under yoke and collar, work as for the dress, leaving the centre front seam of the front facings open and pressing the seam allowances back. Machine the neck seam only during step 7, leaving the front edge of the facings free.
Step 8 Turn under yoke and facings through to wrong side of garment

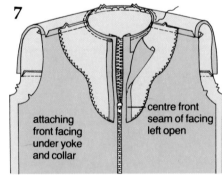

7 attaching front facing under yoke and collar · centre front seam of facing left open

and slipstitch the front edges of the front facings to either side of the zip tape, keeping the fabric well away from the zip teeth.
Smooth the under yoke into position as for the dress.
Steps 9–12 Complete the yoke, pockets and side seams as for the dress.

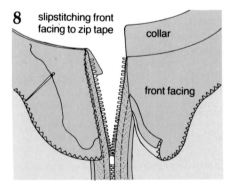

8 slipstitching front facing to zip tape · collar · front facing

Step 13 Make up the sleeve with a simple band cuff instead of the lapped cuff, and insert sleeves as for dress.
Try on the lounger to determine hem length and mark. Turn up a single, narrow hem (about 1cm/ ½in) to avoid a bulky finish. Machine, easing in any fullness.

Sewing with circles – skirts and ruffles

A circle of fabric makes a very simple skirt – it has no darts and may not need any seams – just a zip, waistband and hem. A smaller circle cut from a lightweight fabric can be used to create a delicate, fluted ruffle to apply to a blouse.

Circles of fabric make swirling skirts, and extravagant ruffles which can be applied to both neckline and wrists. You can make a full, floaty skirt from a complete circle of fabric, without any seams, or from two half circles. Ruffles give a softer effect than frills, creating fluid, fluted fullness wherever they are attached.

A ruffle is not gathered – the secret of its frilly appearance is that it is made from a circle of fabric which is cut open and spread out. This forms a strip of fabric with the seamline on the bias, giving a wavy effect to the outer edge.

Fabric suggestions

For a circular skirt choose fabric that is crisp but lightweight – avoid thick, bulky fabric or the skirt will not hang well. Cotton, viscose, taffeta or other synthetic fabrics with some body are all suitable. Closely woven fabric is better than a loose weave, which tends to drop on the bias, making it difficult to obtain an even hemline. A close weave does not fray so much at the hem, or stretch around the waist before the waistband is applied. Felt is expensive in large quantities and is therefore best restricted to a child's version of the

skirt. As felt does not fray it needs no hem and the bright colours look attractive on young children.

Plain colours and small overall patterns are best for the skirt. Larger designs can be used providing you are cutting the skirt as a full circle, without seams. Otherwise, you will have to try to match the pattern at the seams and balance it across the front. Fabric choice is particularly important for a ruffle – too stiff a fabric ruins the lovely fluid effect while too soft a fabric produces a limp look. Silk, crêpe, fine cotton and cotton lawn are all suitable.

Making the pattern

There is usually no need to make a paper pattern for the skirt – you can mark the cutting lines directly on to the fabric before cutting out. If you are likely to want to make more than one skirt in the same size, however, it is worth making a paper pattern, following the instructions below. Use the pattern to make up a test skirt in paper or some spare fabric so that you can check if the waist fits correctly and if the length is right. Transfer any alterations to the basic paper pattern. It is very difficult to make alterations to the skirt once it is cut out, particularly on the seamed version.

A pattern for a circular skirt is simply a large circle with another circle cut out of its centre to fit your waist measurement.

The chart above helps you to do this easily and accurately. Refer to it to find the radius of the inner circle required to produce your waist measurement. Make a rectangle of paper with one side measuring this radius plus the skirt length required, and the other side

Chart for radius of inner circle

Waist measurement	Radius
54cm/21¼in	8.5cm/3⅜in
56cm/22in	8.9cm/3½in
58cm/22¾in	9.2cm/3⅝in
60cm/23½in	9.5cm/3¾in
62cm/24½in	10cm/4in
64cm/25¼in	10.2cm/4in
66cm/26in	10.5cm/4⅛in
68cm/26¾in	10.8cm/4¼in
70cm/27½in	11.1cm/4⅜in
72cm/28¼in	11.5cm/4½in
74cm/29¼in	11.8cm/4⅝in
76cm/30in	12cm/4¾in

measuring twice the radius plus length.

Fold the paper to form a square with the fold on the left-hand side and place it on a firm, flat surface. Insert a drawing pin through the fold at the top left-hand corner. Make a loop in one end of a piece of string and slip it over the drawing pin so that the pin forms a pivot for the string. Measuring down the string from the pin, mark off the amount for radius plus skirt length and make another loop at this point to hold a pencil.

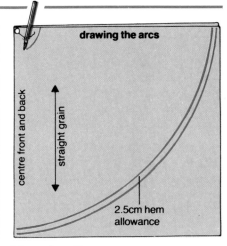

drawing the arcs

centre front and back

straight grain

2.5cm hem allowance

Drawing the arcs

Keeping the string taut, swing an arc from top right-hand corner to bottom left. Remove pencil from loop, make another loop for the waist radius and draw another arc keeping the string taut.

Add 1.5cm/⅝in seam allowance to the waistline and 2.5cm/1in to the lower edge for the hem. Mark foldline as centre front and centre back, and mark a straight grain arrow parallel to it.

Cut out the paper pattern and open it out to make a half circle.

Inserting a zip into a faced opening

1

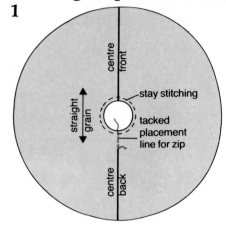

2

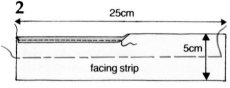

3

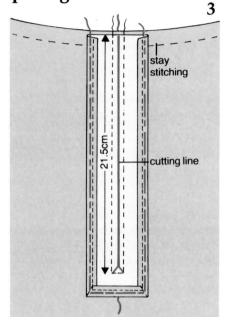

4

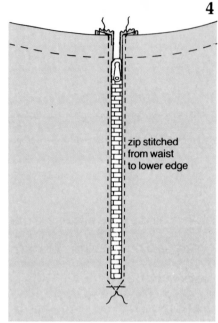

A seamless circular skirt requires a zip opening to enable you to put the skirt on. This is created by making a faced opening in the centre back of the skirt for a 20cm/7¾in zip.
1 Lay the skirt out flat and mark the placement line for the zip with a line of tacking on the straight grain at the centre back marking.
2 Cut a facing strip measuring 25cm×5cm/9¾in×2in on the straight grain of some left-over fabric. Neaten the edges with zigzag stitching or a narrow hem. Mark a line down the vertical centre with tacking.

3 With the right side of the skirt uppermost, and matching the lines of tacking on skirt and facing, place the facing in position. Pin and tack around the edge of the facing. Starting at the waist edge, just to the side of the central tacking line, machine stitch the facing to the skirt. Work down 21.5cm/8½in, pivot and take one or two stitches across, then work a parallel row of stitches back up to the waist edge. The gap between the two rows of stitching should be no more than 3mm/⅛in, centred over the line of tacking.

Cut down the centre line of tacking through both skirt and facing, stopping 5mm/¼in from the lower end of the machining. Make two small snips out at an angle into the corners, but do not cut through the line of stitching. Remove tacking. Turn the facing strip through to the wrong side of the skirt. Tack all around close to the seamed edge. Press.
4 Insert the zip, stitching each side by hand with small, neat stitches. Alternatively, machine stitch using a zipper foot, working from the waist edge to the lower edge of zip.

Hemming a circular skirt

After applying the waistband, leave a skirt cut on the bias to hang for a few days before hemming. The bias parts of the hem will stretch and drop so that after a while the lower edge will appear uneven. It can then be trimmed evenly and hemmed. If you don't leave it to hang in this way, the hem will drop after you have finished and spoil the appearance of the skirt.

Hanging the skirt
The best way to hang the skirt is to use an expanding hanger that keeps the waist of the skirt held taut so the rest of the skirt hangs straight. If you do not have a suitable hanger, sew loops of tape to each side of the skirt and hang it from a padded coat hanger. Pin loops of tape or ribbon

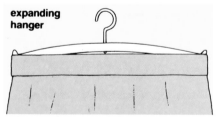

at intervals around the skirt waist, adjusting them to lift the centre of the skirt and keep it hanging with the weight evenly distributed. Leave the skirt hanging about a week before turning up the hem.

Measuring the hem
Try on the skirt with the shoes you will be wearing so that you can judge the length accurately. Ask someone to help you mark the hem, or use a hem marker (see page 82).

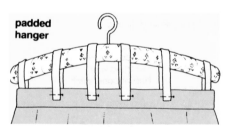

Mark the finished hem level with pins or tailor's chalk.
Take off the skirt and lay it out flat on the floor. Check that the marked hem makes a smooth circle. If not, mark again and try on the skirt, repeating the process until you get it right. When you are satisfied the hem is level, carefully trim away the excess to leave a 1.5cm/⅝in turning.

Choose a fabric with an interesting design and plenty of movement for a striking circular skirt.

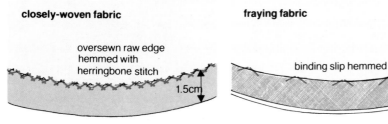

closely-woven fabric

oversewn raw edge
hemmed with
herringbone stitch

1.5cm

fraying fabric

binding slip hemmed

Stitching the hem

There are two alternative ways of turning up the hem and both give a professional finish. If done correctly, there is no hem ridge or stitches visible on the right side when the hem is pressed.

On a closely-woven fabric oversew the raw edge all the way round, then pin up a single hem, taking a 1.5cm/⅝in turning. Where the fabric will not lie flat on the curves, pin at right angles to the hem, spreading the fullness evenly across the hem. Tack and then press with a steam iron to ease out fullness and remove puckers. Sew the hem with herringbone stitch, catching only a thread of the skirt fabric so that the stitches do not show on the right side. Herringbone stitch holds the hem while allowing the excess fabric to move slightly without making a bulky or uneven finish.

Alternatively, if your fabric is suitable, two rows of topstitching all around the hem can be used to keep it in place.

On fraying fabric, trim the hem allowance to just over 5mm/¼in. Sew bias binding all around the lower edge of the skirt, taking a 5mm/¼in turning and joining strips as necessary. Press the binding to the inside, taking care to follow the curve of the hem, and pin and tack. Slip hem the binding to hold and press lightly.

Seamless circular skirt

This skirt requires a square of fabric, so you will need 1.50m/1⅝yd of 150cm/60in fabric plus waistband requirements. This gives a skirt with a maximum waist size of 66cm/26in and finished length of 62cm/24½in. If you have a wider fabric you can make a longer skirt, otherwise you must join fabric to reach the required length. A child's skirt should fit on to 150cm/60in fabric, or even 140cm/54in, depending on the length.

Cutting out

With wrong sides together, fold the material in half and then in half again so that you have four thicknesses of fabric with all the selvedges aligned. Fold the fabric neatly and smoothly so that there are no hidden wrinkles. Fold your paper pattern in half along the centre front/back line so that you have the original quarter circle that you drew to make the pattern. Position this on the fabric with the waist edge nearest the corner of the fabric where all the folds meet. Both straight edges of the quarter circle pattern piece lie along folds of the fabric. Cut out carefully and mark centre front and centre back. Your skirt will open up into a circle with a round hole in the centre.

Completing the skirt

Staystitch the waist 1.3cm/½in from the raw edge to prevent it stretching out of shape.
Make a faced opening and insert zip as shown on page 230.
Attach waistband as described below.

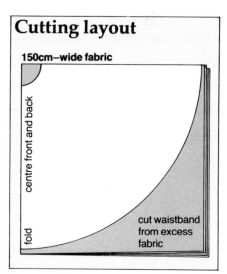

Cutting layout

150cm–wide fabric

centre front and back

fold

cut waistband from excess fabric

Sew skirt fastenings to the waistband.
Hang the skirt for a week and finish hem as shown on pages 230–231.

A seamed circular skirt

Seaming two half circles of fabric together allows you to make the most economical use of 90cm/36in or 115cm/45in fabric. Although you can use 150cm/60in fabric it is rather wasteful for an adult but you could use the extra for a child's skirt.

How much fabric?

The quantity of fabric required depends on the finished length of the skirt and the fabric width. To work out fabric requirements, do a trial layout with your paper pattern on the floor. Mark fabric width and position pattern as shown on the layout, turning the pattern piece over so that the straight edge is placed 1.5cm/⅝in below the selvedge for both pieces. If the waistband does not fit in the left-over area add on an extra 10cm/4in or so of fabric.
For a small child's skirt, use 150cm/60in fabric folded in half lengthwise.

Cutting out

Lay the pattern on single fabric as shown on layout. Place the half-circle pattern piece 1.5cm/⅝in from the selvedge each time, balancing any fabric design across centre front and centre back. Pin on and cut out. Mark centre front and back on the pieces.
Staystitch the waist 1.3cm/½in from raw edge to prevent it stretching out of shape. Place right sides together and pin and tack the two seams. Machine one seam from waist to hem and start stitching the other 23cm/9in down fron waist edge. Press seam open and neaten. Insert zip into open part of seam, using the central or overlapped method (pages 42 and 49).

Making the waistband

To work out the correct length of the waistband, measure your waist and add 9cm/3¾in extra to allow for seam allowances and an underlap. Cut the waistband about 9cm/3¾in wide to give a finished width of 3cm/1¼in, or adjust the width according to your preference. Cut a piece of interfacing the length of the waistband, but half the width. Alternatively, back the waistband with petersham (see page 92). Apply the interfacing to the wrong side of half the waistband. Press 1.5cm/⅝in to the wrong side on the long edge without interfacing. With right sides together stitch the short seamed end and the underlap of the waistband. Trim the seams, clip corners and clip to the stitching at the end of the underlap. Turn waistband through and press. Place the right sides of skirt and waistband together with the underlap at the right-hand side of centre back. Staystitching should prevent the waist seamline from stretching, but ease it slightly if necessary.
Machine waistband to skirt and trim seam allowance. Snip into turnings (but not through the stitching) at intervals of 3-4cm/1¼-1½in. Catchstitch the free folded edge of the waistband to line of machine stitching on inside of skirt. Press. Topstitch waistband from the right side 3mm/⅛in above waist seam and again 3mm/⅛in below top edge.
Sew skirt fastenings to the waistband.
Hang the skirt for a week and finish hem as shown on previous page.

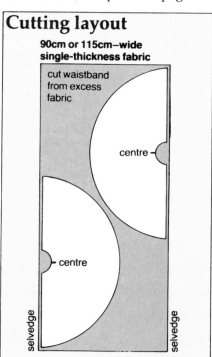

Cutting layout

90cm or 115cm–wide single-thickness fabric

cut waistband from excess fabric

centre

centre

selvedge

selvedge

Decorative ruffles

A pattern is essential when cutting a ruffle and it is easy to make yourself. It consists of two circles, one inside the other and the desired depth of the ruffle apart. The circumference of the smaller, inner circle is the length of the seam to which it is to be attached. For example, if a ruffle is for the wrist of a dress, the inner circle will be the finished wrist measurement.

To draw this circle you need to work out its radius by a simple equation:

$$\frac{\text{circumference}}{44} \times 7 = \text{radius}$$

For example Take a wrist seamline measurement of 17cm/6¾in. Add 1.5cm/⅝in turnings at each end of the ruffle, and work out the size of the inner circle as follows:

$$\frac{17 + 3}{44} \times 7 = \text{radius}$$

$$\frac{20}{44} \times 7 = \text{radius}$$

$$\frac{140}{44} = 3.2\text{cm}/1\tfrac{1}{4}\text{in}$$

Any small discrepancy in size will be absorbed when the ruffle is sewn to the garment, as much of the seam is on the bias of the fabric.

Make the ruffle from a single thickness of fabric, neatening the outside edge with a rolled hem, or join two circles, cutting and turning them through, to make a double thickness ruffle. It is important to make a new paper pattern for each ruffle required – do not try and re-use the same pattern. Alter the ruffle's shape by changing the shape of the outer circle, keeping it symmetrical.

Cutting out the ruffle

Work out the inner circle radius.

1 Draw it with a compass on to a sheet of tissue paper or dressmaker's graph paper. Draw another circle 1.5cm/⅝in within this to form the cutting line. Decide on the width of the ruffle required and add this amount to the radius of the first circle. Keeping the point of the compass in its original position, draw another circle to this larger size. Add another circle 1.5cm/⅝in all the way around the outside edge for the cutting edge. Mark a cutting line between the outer and inner circles along the radius and mark a straight grain line parallel to this. Cut out the paper pattern around the outer circle only.

Pin the circle on to your fabric, observing the straight grain markings. Cut out around the outer circle first, then cut through to the inner circle along the radius cutting line, and cut it out.

2 Staystitch the inner circle close to the seamline, then clip the seam at intervals up to the staystitching so that the seamline can be straightened out, giving a wavy effect to the outside edge. Finish the outside edge with a narrow rolled hem, hand or machine stitched, and insert the ruffle into the seam.

Long ruffles Where a long length of ruffle is required, down the front of a blouse, for example, it is better to cut several ruffles and join them, rather than trying to cut the ruffle as one piece. Join the ruffles with plain seams after staystitching the seamlines and clipping the turnings.

Right: Use a ruffle to emphasize the neckline shaping of a garment.

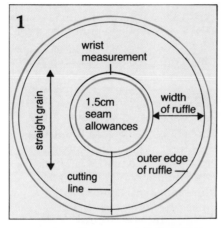

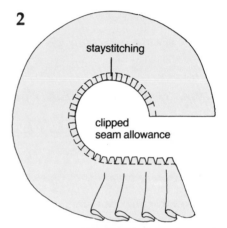

Shirred bands for a sundress or nightdress

Follow the shirring techniques in this chapter to make an attractive sundress or nightdress with side slits. Make them long or short, with or without straps – the shirred back and made-to-measure yoke ensure a good fit and ease of movement.

Shirring consists of a panel or continuous band of parallel rows of gathering. Worked by hand, the stitches are placed accurately below one another to give a neatly shirred area where the gathers form parallel folds. This forms a decorative area in itself, but can also be embroidered.

Shirring has been used as a method of controlling fullness in garments for centuries. As with many old, hand-worked processes it has enjoyed a revival in recent years and is now often worked by machine, incorporating elastic. Shirring elastic is a single cord of covered elastic, widely available in black and white and sometimes in a range of colours. Whether worked by hand or machine the finished appearance depends on accurately worked parallel rows of stitching. With careful choice of colour and variation in the distance between rows of stitching, elasticized shirring imitates smocking and gives a very pretty and practical finish to babies' and children's wear, lingerie, dresses, etc. It also eliminates the need for zip or button openings in garments and so is particularly comfortable for children's clothes. It makes cuffs, ankles, and necklines snug without being restrictive, and shirred garments are easy to pop on to an energetic baby or toddler.

The sundress/nightdress on page 236 has a shirred back panel and a choice of frilled or flat straps.

Setting up the sewing machine

Elasticized shirring by machine is always worked on the right side of the fabric, so that the elastic is on the wrong side of the garment. Wind the elastic on to the bobbin – some machines will wind a bobbin of shirring elastic on automatic, but it is easy to hand wind. Wind the elastic in the same direction used for ordinary cotton. Do not stretch while winding, but do not allow it to become too slack either.

Rotate bobbin between thumb and first finger of the right hand and feed elastic on with the left hand, rather than winding the elastic round repeatedly. Work with the upper side of the bobbin facing you and rotate bobbin clockwise until full, arranging the elastic evenly, layer upon layer. Place the bobbin in position in the normal way.

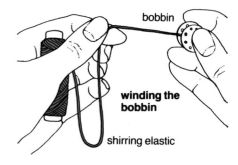

bobbin

winding the bobbin

shirring elastic

Threading the machine

Thread up the machine in the normal way and set it to give the largest straight stitch possible. Most machines will not require any alteration to the upper tension to cope with the shirring, but test the stitch first on a scrap of fabric. If the result is not satisfactory, try loosening the upper tension a little.

To start stitching, hold both upper thread and lower elastic taut and keep a firm hold of the fabric as it goes through the feed. When using a large machine stitch, it is easy for the machine to 'run away' with the fabric if this is not controlled carefully. Unpicking stitches may damage a fine fabric so stitch steadily to ensure that you follow the lines carefully.

Stitching with contrast thread makes a feature of the shirring. Use the thread double for best results. Place a matching reel of thread on each spindle, take a thread from each one and thread the machine in the normal way as if using single thread.

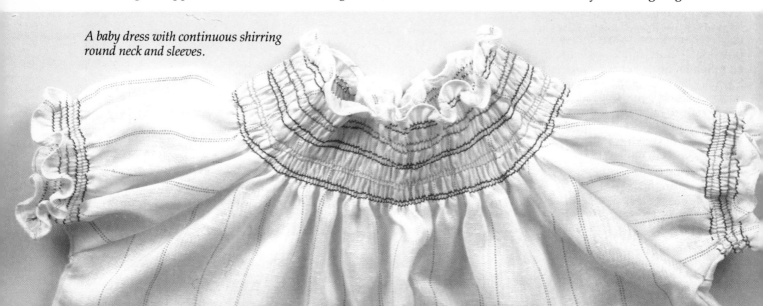

A baby dress with continuous shirring round neck and sleeves.

Working shirring in the round

Continuous bands of shirring are worked around necklines, wrists and waists. It is easy to work near the edge of the garment. Simply use the edge as a guide line for the first row of stitches. If you do not wish to start the shirring close to the edge, mark the stitching lines with tacking or tailor's chalk. A free arm sewing machine is useful, but not essential when stitching small continuous bands, such as cuffs.
If the same colour thread is used for all the shirring, there is no need to break the threads after each round of stitching. Start at a side seam or the centre back, stitch the first round, curving the line of machine

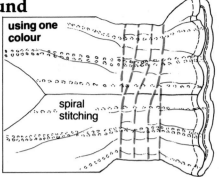

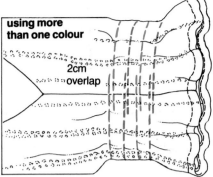

stitches down towards the second row as you approach the starting point. Continue stitching in a spiral fashion until you have completed the required number of rows. Run the rows together to finish.

If more than one colour thread is used, complete each round accurately, returning to the starting point and overlapping by 2cm/¾in. Take the threads to the wrong side for finishing off.

Working shirred panels

A flat block or panel of shirring is usually incorporated into the body of the garment, rather than the neck or sleeves, and the area it is to cover must be marked carefully.
When the stitching lines are close together, it is not necessary to mark every one. Marking the first and last rows is usually a sufficient guide. Use a sharp piece of tailor's chalk on the right side of the fabric, or a line of thread tacking placed 2-3mm/⅛in from the required stitching line. (Do not tack over the stitching line – the

thread is difficult to remove when the fabric is stitched and gathered up over it.) Once you have worked the first row, use it and subsequent rows as guide lines. Provided the stitching lines have a space of between 5mm-1.5cm/¼in-⅝in between them, you can use the edge of the machine foot to guide you. Watch this, and not the needle, as you stitch to keep the rows of machine stitches parallel. If a wider gap is required, mark guides for each stitching line. To

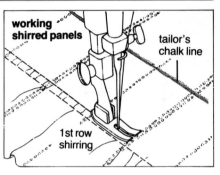

keep the ends even and neat, work every row separately and take the threads to wrong side and secure.

Making frilled straps

Frilled shoulder straps

Shirring flat straps creates a pretty, frilled effect and makes them comfortable and unrestricting for use on nightwear.
Place the shirring along the edge or down the centre of each strap – the technique is the same for both.
Cut two strips of fabric 8cm/3¼in wide by the length required, plus at least one third again. Turn under a narrow hem on each long edge, pressing 2-3mm/⅛in to wrong side and then taking a hem of 5mm/¼in. Stitch by hand or machine (use machine stitches for a garment which will be laundered frequently).
Work rows of shirring along the long, inner edge which will be nearest to the centre front. Start 1cm/½in from the hemmed edge on the right side and work four rows, 3mm/⅛in apart.

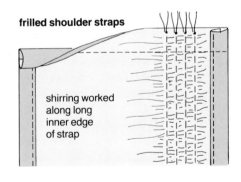

Take the ends of thread to the wrong side and knot them to the shirring elastic. Trim thread/elastic ends to 5mm/¼in. Neaten the short, raw edges carefully. Machine stitch across lines of shirring 5mm/¼in in from knots.
Turn a narrow hem to the wrong side of strap to enclose raw edges and ends of thread and elastic and machine to hold. Attach the straps by hand when the garment is otherwise complete.

Cutting layouts

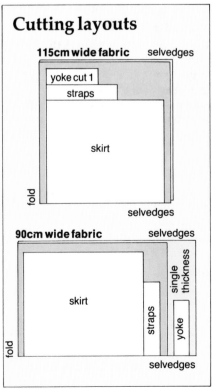

Sundress

This style is most suitable for sizes up to 16. For larger sizes increase the width of the short pattern piece.

Measuring up

The above bust measurement is the most important. It is used for the front yoke, which is cut to suit your figure. Take the measurement against your skin, not over your clothes, passing the tape across the back, high up under the arms and across the front, *above* the bust. Allow a little ease for breathing, but not a great deal – the shirring gives when worn.

The dress length is the measurement from just above the bust to below the knee, or to the ankle if making the nightdress.

Making the pattern

It is possible to mark the pattern rectangles straight on to the fabric with tailor's chalk, but to reduce the possibility of error, make a paper pattern using dressmaker's graph paper, tissue paper or brown paper. This allows you to move your pattern pieces around on the fabric, and also means you can use it again.

For the front yoke, cut a rectangle measuring 13cm/5in × half the above bust measurement, plus 3cm/1¼in turnings. Mark the pattern piece 'Yoke – cut 1' and draw a straight grain arrow along its length, parallel to the edge.

For the skirt, cut a rectangle 84cm/33in wide × the required length, plus 7cm/2¾in turnings (1.5cm/⅝in side seam allowances are included). Mark the top of the vent with a dot on the side seam 27cm/10¾in above the lower edge for the sundress, and 57cm/22½in above the lower edge for the nightdress. Mark the pattern piece 'Skirt – cut 2' and draw a straight grain arrow parallel to the edge.

For flat straps, cut a rectangle measuring 13cm × 60cm/5in × 23½in. Mark this 'Strap – cut 2' and draw a straight grain arrow along the length, parallel to the edge.

For frilled straps, cut a rectangle measuring 8cm × 90cm/3¼in × 36in and mark the pattern in the same way as for flat straps.

Left: Make a sundress with flat straps or (inset) a nightie with frilled straps.

Fabric suggestions

A cool pure cotton fabric is the best choice for the sundress if it is to be comfortable on hot, sticky days, but a percentage of polyester in the fabric content will help to prevent creasing. For the nightdress, choose fine lawn, polyester crêpe de chine or, for a touch of luxury, pure silk.

You will need

90cm/36in fabric Twice the required finished length of the garment, plus 50cm/19¾in extra for turnings, yoke and straps
115cm/45in fabric Twice the required finished length, plus 14cm/5½in for turnings.

Cutting out

Position the pattern pieces as shown on the appropriate layout and cut out according to the instructions marked on each one.

Making the dress and nightdress

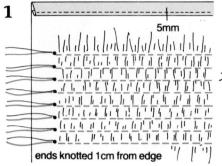

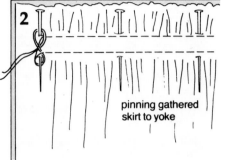

pinning gathered skirt to yoke

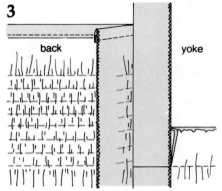

back · yoke

Step 1 Turn 2-3mm/⅛in to the wrong side along the top edge of one skirt piece, and press. Turn under another 5mm/¼in along this edge and machine stitch in place. This piece is now the back.
Work 8 rows of shirring, placing the first row 1.5cm/⅝in from the top edge and the other rows 5mm/¼in apart. Start and finish stitching 1cm/½in from cut edges of side seams, taking ends to wrong side and knotting them.
Step 2 Cut a 5cm/2in strip from the top edge of remaining skirt piece.

The large piece is now the front. Mark the centre of the front and of front yoke with a pin at right angles to the seamline. Run two rows of gathering threads along the top edge of front. Draw up the gathers to fit the yoke, matching centre markings and side seams. Place pins at right angles to the seamline and arrange the gathers evenly, teasing them apart so that they are straight. With right sides together, stitch yoke to front, taking a 1.5cm/⅝in turning and press seam up towards yoke.

Step 3 With right sides together, stitch side seams down to marking for side vents. The lowest row of shirring on the back piece should line up with the yoke seam. Machine neaten edges of seam allowances from top edge to lower edge and press seams open along entire length including side vents.

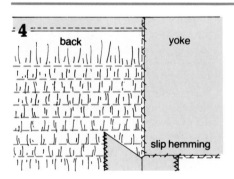

back · yoke · slip hemming

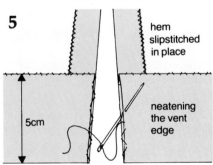

hem slipstitched in place · 5cm · neatening the vent edge

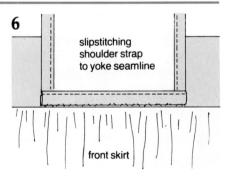

slipstitching shoulder strap to yoke seamline · front skirt

Step 4 Clip back seam allowance up to stitching at level of lowest row of shirring and press turnings towards yoke.
Press 1.5cm/⅝in to wrong side along free raw edges of yoke, then fold yoke in half to wrong side of garment so that pressed-under edges enclose the raw edges of yoke seam and top of side seams. Pin, tack and stitch in place using small, slip hemming stitches.

Step 5 Try on garment and check length, trimming if necessary. Complete hem by pressing 5mm/¼in to the wrong side along raw edge and then taking a 5cm/2in hem.
Slipstitch hem into place, folding turnings of side vents in and catching them within the hem at the bottom, using small stitches to hold.

Step 6 Make flat or shirred straps, according to preference. Try on garment and pin them in place. Slipstitch to yoke seamline on wrong side of garment at front, and to rows of shirring at the back. Stretch the back shirring panel slightly when stitching the straps in place so that the stitching does not 'pop' in wear.

237

Index